The Life and Theology of Alexander Knox

Anglican-Episcopal Theology and History

Edited by

Paul Avis (*Durham University and University of Exeter, UK*)

Editorial Board

VOLUME 6

The titles published in this series are listed at *brill.com/aeth*

The Life and Theology of Alexander Knox

Anglicanism in the Age of Enlightenment and Romanticism

By

David McCready

BRILL

LEIDEN | BOSTON

Cover illustration: 'Alexander Knox' by Henry Adlard, after Sir Francis Leggatt Chantrey. Stipple engraving, published 1834. Printed with kind permission by the National Portrait Gallery.

Library of Congress Cataloging-in-Publication Data

Names: McCready, David, author.
Title: The life and theology of Alexander Knox : Anglicanism in
    the Age of Enlightenment and Romanticism / by David McCready.
Description: Leiden ; Boston : Brill, 2020. | Series: Anglican-Episcopal
    theology and history, 2405-7576 ; 6 | Includes bibliographical
    references and index.
Identifiers: LCCN 2020011348 | ISBN 9789004355224 (paperback) | ISBN
    9789004426986 (ebook)
Subjects: LCSH: Knox, Alexander, 1757-1831. | Church of
    England—Doctrines—History. | Church of England—Biography. | Anglican
    Communion—Doctrines—History. | Anglican Communion—England—Biography.
    | England—Church history.
Classification: LCC BX5199.K548 M33 2020 | DDC 230/.3—dc23
LC record available at https://lccn.loc.gov/2020011348

Typeface for the Latin, Greek, and Cyrillic scripts: "Brill". See and download: brill.com/brill-typeface.

ISSN 2405-7576
ISBN 978-90-04-35522-4 (paperback)
ISBN 978-90-04-42698-6 (e-book)

Printed by Printforce, the Netherlands

Contents

Acknowledgments

In a comment preserved by Bossuet, Pascal reprobates those who dare to speak of "My Book, my commentary, my history, and so forth" (*Ils feraient mieux de dire: Notre livre, notre commentaire, notre histoire*). In the present case, certainly, there could be no truer words. This book began life as a Ph.D. thesis, undertaken at the Irish School of Ecumenics, Trinity College, Dublin, and the first person I want to thank is my supervisor there, Professor Andrew Pierce. I hope that he will understand the profound depth of my gratitude to him, for his wisdom, friendship, and guidance. He it was who introduced me to the Reverend Professor Paul Avis, General Editor of this series; and to him also I owe a tremendous debt, as I do, likewise to my contacts at Brill, Mirjam Elbers and Ingrid Heijckers-Velt. The latter, especially, has been an unfailing source of help and encouragement. I must thank, too, Professor James Lindsay of Colorado State University for reading various chapters, and for his insightful comments. Last, but by no means least, I want to acknowledge my wife, Andrea, for her love, patience, and support, as well as for her much needed technical help and advice. To her I dedicate this book; truly, γυνὴ ἀνδρεία στέφανος τῷ ἀνδρὶ αὐτῆς.

Abbreviations

A. D. V.	Association for Discountenancing Vice
B. C. P.	Book of Common Prayer
B. L.	British Library
D. S.	Denzinger-Schönmetzer, *Enchiridion Symbolorum*
L. &. D.	*Letters and Diaries of John Henry Newman*
N. L. I.	National Library of Ireland
O. C. M. C. H.	Oxford Centre for Methodist and Church History
O. D. C. C.	*Oxford Dictionary of the Christian Church*
O. D. N. B.	*Oxford Dictionary of National Biography*
P. G.	*Patrologia Graeca*
P. L.	*Patrologia Latina*
P. R. O. N. I.	Public Record Office of Northern Ireland
R. I. A.	Royal Irish Academy
T. C. D.	Trinity College Dublin

Introduction

1 The Importance of Alexander Knox

This book examines the thought and influence of Alexander Knox (1757–1831), the remarkable Irish Anglican lay-theologian. Knox was a friend and disciple of John Wesley, as well as being a precursor of the Tractarians. Standing at the cusp of the Enlightenment and Romanticism, Knox invites comparison with Friedrich Schleiermacher in Germany and Samuel Taylor Coleridge in England. At the same time, he serves as a reminder of the Platonic tradition within Anglicanism. Claude Welch has written that, if we look at the British theological scene at the beginning of the nineteenth century, we find that "the Church of England was marked by an absence of ... vitality or excitement."[1] Knox shines out amidst this encircling gloom: he is, in William Lecky's words, "one of the most earnest and profound religious writers of his time."[2] This time was one of considerable ferment on both the intellectual and the spiritual plane, and Knox is of note because of the ways in which his ideas relate to the age in which he lived, not least with regard to the phenomenon of heart religion, a religion which, in Knox's case, appeared in the form of Christian Platonism. One of the first writers to use "spirituality" in the current sense of that which pertains to the believer's relationship with God, Knox was concerned above all with *praxis*, which is perhaps why the designation which best describes his theology is that which he himself provides, "the science of true piety."[3] This piety, Knox derived from John Wesley, his intimacy with whom means that the examination of Knox's life and writings can contribute to our understanding of Wesley, not least in regard to what Henry D. Rack calls the "perennially arguable question" of Wesley's relationship to the Church of England.[4] Knox is important, too, as an exemplar of the often-neglected High Church tradition within the Church of Ireland, but, more than this, he is of considerable significance for Anglicanism generally. As with "spirituality," Knox was one of

---

1 Welch, *Protestant Thought in the Nineteenth Century*, p. 109. For the use of the designation "Church of *England*," with reference to Knox, see below, p. 37.

2 Lecky, *History of Ireland in the Eighteenth Century*, Vol. 3, p. 359, note. For similar appreciations, see: Gunstone, "Alexander Knox," p. 474; Nockles, "Knox" p. 5; Brilioth, *Anglican Revival*, p. 47; Maclagan, "Preface" to *The Grace of Sacraments*, pp. v–xxxv, at ix; Storr, *Development of English Theology*, p. 90.

3 *Remains*, Vol. 1, p. 251.

4 Rack, *Reasonable Enthusiast*, p. 558. The title of Rack's book is inspired by a remark of Knox's, which Rack quotes as an epigraph (p. viii).

the first writers to use the term "Anglican" on a regular basis. He also made a substantial contribution to the definition of what Anglicanism means, and what distinguishes it from other forms of Christianity. An avowedly confessional theologian (albeit with qualifications), Knox is a prime example of what is often seen as *the* Anglican theological method, the three-fold appeal to Scripture, tradition, and reason. In particular, he instantiates the classical Anglican appeal to the Fathers, while at the same time developing that appeal in a new direction.[5] It was this, above all, which made him, in the words of Peter Nockles, "a seminal religious thinker," a man of widespread influence on subsequent theologians, not least those of the Oxford Movement, of which he was, to quote Vernon Storr, "the direct precursor and prophet." He has, as Geoffrey Rowell expresses it, "a special significance in the pre-history of Tractarianism" and the investigation of his thought helps contribute to our understanding of its origins.[6] Perhaps more importantly still, Knox has something practical to offer Anglicans today, namely a model for comprehension and tolerance. Knox, however, is not only significant for Anglicans; as a proto-ecumenist, one who looked forward to the eventual reunification of all Christians, his writings provide a contribution to the realization of that goal.

2   Previous Examinations of Knox

Although no in-depth study of Alexander Knox has ever been published, he has by no means gone unnoticed. Whenever the background to the Oxford Movement is discussed, he receives a mention; and the same is true with regard to surveys of late eighteenth- and early nineteenth-century Anglicanism and Methodism. The first substantial examination of his ideas appears in the introductions to his *Remains*, penned by Knox's editor, J. J. Hornby.[7] The *Remains* came out in two instalments of two volumes each, the first in 1834, the second in 1837, with a second edition of the first two volumes appearing

---

5   On the Anglican appeal to the Fathers see, Quantin, *The Church of England and Christian Antiquity*.

6   Nockles, "Knox," p. 5; Storr, *Development of English Theology*, p. 85; Rowell, "Theological Forerunners," p. 38.

7   James John Hornby (1777–1855) was, from 1812 until his death, Rector of Winwick in Lancashire, a living with which his family had close connections. See Farrer and Brownbill, eds, *Victoria History of the County of Lancaster*, Vol. 4, p. 129. Although Hornby never met Knox personally, he had corresponded with him. More importantly, Hornby's wife, Catherine Boyle (c. 1780–1859), had "enjoyed the rare privilege of having been brought up at the feet of Alexander Knox," being the foster-daughter of Peter and Elizabeth La Touche, to whose house in Delgany Knox was a frequent visitor (Teignmouth, *Reminiscences*, Vol. 1, p. 182). For the La Touches, and their Delgany home, see below, p. 27.

in 1836. Hornby provided introductions as follows: "Editor's Preface" (to the first two volumes); "Editor's Preface to the Second Edition;" and "Editor's Preface to the Third and Fourth Volumes."[8] The *Remains* also received in-depth analysis from reviewers, as did the other main source of Knox's thinking, his *Correspondence* with Bishop John Jebb, which appeared at the beginning of 1834.[9] These reviewers came from both the High Church and Evangelical camps within the Church of England.[10] The most important of the High Church reviews were those furnished by the *British Critic* and the *British Magazine*. The comments of the long-established *British Critic*, which furnished notices on the *Correspondence* and on the first and second editions of the *Remains*, were generally positive, although, significantly, the reviewer found fault with Knox's view of justification, as well as with his teaching on the providential nature of Non-Conformity.[11] The *British Magazine*, founded in 1832 by Hugh James Rose to combat what he saw as the dangers facing the contemporary Church of England, gave the *Correspondence* a brief but very favourable notice when it first appeared. The subsequent publication of the first two volumes of the *Remains* was mentioned, but they were not reviewed, since Rose did not get around to reading them until June 1835, and then only in part. The volumes nonetheless provoked a lively exchange of letters in the pages of the *Magazine*, and, thus, when the second two volumes came out, they were given much fuller scrutiny, albeit far less significant than that accorded to them elsewhere.[12] The main Evangelical reviews of Knox's thought appeared in the *Christian Examiner* and the *Christian Observer*. The *Christian Examiner and Church of Ireland Magazine*, to give it its full title, was founded in 1825 by Caesar Otway and Joseph Singer, with the stated aim of defending the Church of Ireland, by which was meant the stern denunciation of Roman Catholicism, and anything seen as approaching it.[13] Given this perspective, it is no surprise to find the *Examiner's* two-part review of the *Correspondence* highly critical

---

8   *Remains*, Vol. 1, pp. vii–xxii, xxiii–xxxii; Vol. 3, pp. vii–cxviii.

9   For John Jebb, see below, pp. 29–30.

10   Throughout this book, Evangelical, with an upper-case E, is used to denote membership of the Evangelical party within Anglicanism.

11   For the *British Critic*, see: Houghton and Altholz, "The *British Critic*, 1824–1843;" Skinner, "Newman, the Tractarians and the *British Critic*." For its reviews of Knox, see: 17. 33 (January 1835), pp. 157–82; 17. 34 (April 1835), pp. 257–95; 23. 45 (January 1838), pp. 1–23. For its criticisms of Knox's views, see below, pp. 173, 177–78, 217–18.

12   *British Magazine* 6 (July 1834), p. 68; 7 (January 1835), p. 111; (June 1835), pp. 670; 668–70; 8 (July 1835), pp. 68–70; (August 1835), pp. 173–76; (September 1835), pp. 309–12; (November 1835), pp. 536–41; (December 1835), pp. 687–90; 12 (August 1837), pp. 180–84.

13   For Caesar Otway (1780–1842), see *Dublin University Magazine* 14. 82 (October 1839), pp. 396–97. For Joseph Henderson Singer (1786–1866), see *O. D. N. B.* For the *Christian Examiner*, see Welch, ed., *The Oxford Companion to Irish Literature*, p. 97.

of the Knox and Jebb's understanding of justification, a criticism repeated thirty years later in a review of the second edition of James Thomas O'Brien's sermons on the topic, which included several sections on Knox's views.[14] *The Christian Observer*, which ran from 1802 until 1874, was closely associated with the "Clapham Sect," the small but highly-influential group of Evangelicals, mainly based in Clapham, London, around the rector of the church there, John Venn.[15] It carried an extended review of the *Correspondence*, covering two issues, which was highly critical of Knox's theology, especially, like the *Examiner*, of his understanding of justification. "The radical vice of the whole system is the omission of the 'articulus stantis vel cadentis ecclesiae' [the doctrine on which the church stands or falls], *Justification by faith in Christ crucified*," the reviewer opined.[16] The journal which carried the most sustained analyses of Knox's thought was, however, the Non-Conformist *Eclectic Review*, founded in 1805. It subjected the *Correspondence* to a long dissection of what it saw as the deficiencies of Knox's thought, particularly, once again, with regard to justification. The *Remains* received similar treatment at the *Eclectic's* hands, the author of both pieces being, perhaps, the journal's editor from 1814 to 1837, the Congregationalist Josiah Conder.[17] As well as these reviews, two other Evangelical criticisms of Knox's theology to note are those of James Thomas O'Brien, already mentioned, and George Stanley Faber. O'Brien's 1833 sermons on justification, preached in the chapel of Trinity College, Dublin, had become a standard Evangelical work on the subject, and it was in large part to combat what he saw as Knox's errors that he republished them in 1862, with two extended notes directed specifically against Knox's teaching.[18] G. S. Faber was an Evangelical writer whose treatment of the doctrine of election had so pleased Hornby, Knox's editor, that he somewhat imprudently invited Faber to

14   *Christian Examiner*, new series, 3. 35 (September 1834), pp. 623–42; 36 (October 1834), pp. 687–720; new series, 47, (November 1862), pp. 282–85. The author of the initial review, who betrays a personal acquaintance with Knox, was possibly Robert Daly, for whom see below, p. 239. For James Thomas O'Brien and his work, see immediately below, and also p. 169.
15   See Hennell, *John Venn and the Clapham Sect*; also, below, pp. 46, 47.
16   *Christian Observer* 34. 11 (November 1834), p. 699 (emphasis in the original). For the *Observer's* reviews of Knox, see: 34. 11 (November 1834), pp. 691–702; 34. 12 (December 1834), pp. 765–72.
17   For the reviews of the *Correspondence* and *Remains* see: *Eclectic Review*, third series, 12 (November 1834), pp. 376–405; 13 (February 1835), pp. 61–88; (April 1835), pp. 287–304; new series, 2 (December 1837), pp. 559–79. For the journal in general, see Hiller, "The *Eclectic Review*, 1805–1868;" for Josiah Conder (1789–1855), see O. D. N. B.
18   For James Thomas O'Brien (1792–1874), see O. D. N. B. For his criticisms of Knox, see *Justification*, third edition, "Note X," pp. 436–64, and "Note Z," pp. 469–96.

deal with the topic of justification, believing that the result would be a vindi-cation of Knox's views.[19] When it appeared in 1837, however, Faber's *Primitive Doctrine of Justification* proved highly antagonistic to Knox's position.

A quarter-of-a century after the initial controversy over Knox's teaching had died down, a new and different debate erupted in 1887, with the publication of an article by the then Professor of Ecclesiastical History at Trinity College, Dublin, G. T. Stokes. Entitled "Alexander Knox and the Oxford Movement," the article argued that Knox was "the mediator or channel connecting John Wesley and the Wesleyan movement … with the Tractarian movement," and that of this latter movement Knox was, in fact, "the secret, the unacknowledged, but, none the less the real fount and origin."[20] The article met with a sharp rejoin-der from the historian of the Oxford Movement, R. W. Church. Church declared that there was no evidence to support Stokes's view; what evidence there was, showed, he contended, that the Tractarians entertained "a distrust of [Knox's] manner of speculation, even when they were in general agreement with his conclusions." Church furthermore pointed out that Knox could not have influ-enced the Oxford Movement, because his writings were only published after it had begun. Stokes replied that Knox had, in fact, published several works dur-ing his lifetime, and that, even apart from this, his views had been widely dis-seminated, both by himself and by others, including such influential figures as Hannah More, Lord Castlereagh and, above all, Bishop Jebb. Stokes further im-plied that, in the particular case of John Henry Newman, knowledge of Knox's theology had been mediated to him by Newman's brother, Francis, who had met with Knox while visiting Ireland in 1827 and had engaged in several con-versations with him on topics of theological interest. Despite the defence he gave of his position, under Church's assault Stokes backtracked considerably from his original claims: rather than being the "idol" of the Tractarians, and the true author of their teaching, he now depicted Knox simply as someone who had helped create an "atmosphere" which the Tractarians had "imbibed."[21]

---

19   Hornby, "Editor's Preface to the Third and Fourth Volumes," p. cxii. For the controversy over justification ignited by Knox, see below, pp. 172–73.

20   Stokes, "Alexander Knox and the Oxford Movement," p. 185.

21   For the controversy, see the *Guardian*, 7 September 1887, pp. 1337–38; 14 September 1887, pp. 1381–82; 28 September 1887, p. 1449. For George Thomas Stokes (1843–1898), and Richard William Church (1815–90), see *O. D. N. B*. For Hannah More, see below, pp. 49–54. For Lord Castlereagh, see below, p. 18. For John Henry Newman (1801–90), there is a vast bibliography; see, for a good guide, Ker and Merrigan, eds, *The Cambridge Companion to John Henry Newman*. See, also, below, pp. 38, 39, 43, 55, 247-53. For Francis Newman (1805–97), see *O. D. N. B*. In connection to Stokes's claim about Francis Newman, one may note the latter's remark: "Puseyism did not *begin* with my brother, but with old Alexander Knox, a pious admirer of Wesley, who condescended to give me several private talks in

Even so, Stokes's contention that Knox formed a link between Wesley and the Tractarians was subsequently upheld by G. W. Taylor in his essay *John Wesley and the Anglo-Catholic Revival* (1905), as well as by Dieter Voll in his 1960 *Hochkirchlicher Pietismus*, translated into English three years later under the title *Catholic Evangelicalism*.[22]

John Hunt gave some space to Knox in his *Religious Thought in England in the Nineteenth Century* (1896), while in 1913 Vernon F. Storr's *Development of English Theology in the Nineteenth Century* also devoted several pages to him.[23] The most important treatment of Knox in the earlier part of the twentieth century came, however, in Yngve Brilioth's *Anglican Revival* (1925). Believing that Knox had "scarcely anywhere been estimated at his true value in the history of Anglican Theology," Brilioth accorded Knox, together with Jebb, a whole chapter and a short appendix.[24] In 1933, J. R. H. Moorman's essay on the "Forerunners of the Oxford Movement" appeared, although its treatment of Knox was somewhat cursory.[25] More substantial was the Edinburgh Ph.D. thesis produced by George Wynne Hughes in 1937, "The Life and Work of Alexander Knox, 1757–1831," which has, however, remained unpublished. Despite its many merits, this thesis suffers from two major drawbacks. The first is that it relies almost exclusively on printed materials. There is no reference to any unpublished primary sources, bar the single mention of a manuscript letter in Marsh's Library, Dublin. Second, although Hughes underlines the link between Knox and Wesley, he explores neither the arrière-fond of their thought in the Platonic tradition, nor does he contextualize Knox in his historical setting, that of the post-Enlightenment period.

In 1956 J. Baird Ewens brought out a small volume under the title *Three Hermits: Short Studies in Christian Antiquity, Methodism and Tractarianism*. Ewens sought to amplify Stokes's contention that Wesley influenced Knox and Jebb, the first two hermits of the title; and that they in their turn influenced the leaders of the Oxford Movement, especially Newman, the third hermit. The first part of the book provides a useful introductory biography of Knox;

Ireland" (*Contributions Chiefly to the Early History of the Late Cardinal Newman*, p. 42, emphasis in the original).

22   The Tractarians' genealogy from Wesley via Knox is Taylor's central contention, and the theme runs throughout his tract. For Voll's treatment of Knox, see *Catholic Evangelicalism*, pp. 34–35.

23   Hunt, *Religious Thought in England in the Nineteenth Century*, pp. 44–46; 160–61; 379; Storr, *Development of English Theology*, pp. 80; 85–91; 353.

24   Brilioth, *Anglican Revival*, Chapter 4, "The Forerunners of Neo-Anglicanism," pp. 45–55; Appendix 1, "Note on the Question of the Dependence of the Oxford Movement on Knox and Jebb," pp. 331–33. For Brilioth's remark on the failure to esteem Knox at his true value, see p. 47.

25   For Moorman's treatment of Knox, see "Forerunners of the Oxford Movement," pp. 10–14.

the second part, however, which aims to confirm Stokes's thesis, contains little of substance. Nor is there any analysis of Knox's theology. Much more useful is John Gunstone's "Alexander Knox, 1757–1831," also published in 1956. Based on an M.A. dissertation undertaken at Durham, it provides an excellent introduction to its subject, but, by its own admission, it leaves much more to be investigated. Also useful, but even briefer, is the treatment accorded to Knox by Bernard Reardon in his survey of nineteenth- and early twentieth-century British theology, *From Coleridge to Gore: A Century of Religious Thought in Britain* (1971), subsequently re-published in 1980 as *Religious Thought in the Victorian Age*.[26] In 1994, under the direction of Sheridan Gilley, Michael Thompson produced an M.A. dissertation on "The High Church Tradition in Ireland, 1800–1870, with particular reference to John Jebb and Alexander Knox." Although never published, this is one of the most substantial pieces of research previously carried out on Knox; nonetheless, it does not fully develop the subject. In 1996 Geoffrey Rowell published an article entitled "'Church Principles' and 'Protestant Kempism', Some theological forerunners of the Tractarians," which included an examination of Knox and Jebb.[27] In 2000, Peter Barrett made a brief study of Knox's Eucharistic theology in his essay "Alexander Knox: Lay Theologian of the Church of Ireland." Barrett was also the author of a Trinity College, Dublin, M.Phil. dissertation on "The Ecclesiology of Bishop John Jebb," which involves throughout a discussion of Knox, on whom Jebb was dependent for his theology. Among the most important work carried out on Knox has been that of Peter Nockles. In 2004 Nockles provided the entry on Knox for the *Oxford Dictionary of National Biography*, which he followed in 2012 with an article on reactions to Southey's *Life of Wesley* (1820), which included a discussion of Knox.[28] Useful material can also be found in the 1998 article by Nockles, "Church or Protestant Sect," which explores the relationship between the Church of Ireland and the Oxford Movement, as well as in his ground-breaking *Oxford Movement in Context* (1994). None of these, however, provides an in-depth examination of Knox.

3   The Present Study

From the above, it will be clear that what Gunstone wrote more than half a century ago remains true today: "[N]o one has ever given [Knox] the individual,

---

26 For Reardon's treatment of Knox, see *From Coleridge to Gore*, pp. 37–41.
27 For the discussion of Knox, see Rowell, "Theological Forerunners," pp. 38–50.
28 See below, pp. 58–62.

detailed study which he undoubtedly deserves."[29] It is the object of the present work to fill this lacuna, by providing an historical account of Knox's teaching. The book is not a theological dialogue with Knox; it is concerned not with critique, but with exposition. It has thus been constructed using an historical methodology. There is a strong focus on the study of the primary sources. The sources are presented, which is why there is such an emphasis on quotation, then analyse in as objective a manner as possible, through an examination of the context in which they are situated, both diachronic and synchronic.

Following the dictum of Michel Foucault, "The work is more than the work; the subject who writes is part of the work," the book begins with an examination of Knox's life.[30] After a brief introduction to the later Hanoverian age, depicting the political and ecclesiastical background to the period 1757–1831, this chapter explores Knox's early years, and his association with John Wesley; his short time of public service, as assistant to Lord Castlereagh; his subsequent religious retirement; his relationship with John Jebb; his attitudes towards Roman Catholicism; and his death, and the controversy which surrounded it. Since much of Knox's life was devoted to religion, and especially to the Church of which he was a member, the second chapter explores his Anglicanism. Beginning with his theory of what it means to be Anglican, it examines the appeal which he made to antiquity; his use of the Prayer Book, and the other "standards;" his High Churchmanship; and his relationship with Evangelicals, especially Hannah More. Since it is one of the contentions of this book that Knox initially derived his High Church Anglicanism from John Wesley, the third chapter considers the theological relationship between the two men. From an examination of Knox's early defences of Wesley, the chapter goes on to look at his important *Remarks on the Life and Character of John Wesley*. It investigates Wesley's influence on Knox; and the areas in which the two both diverged and agreed theologically. The chapter concludes with the topic of Knox's opposition to those whom he termed "Separating Methodists." Since Knox depicts Wesley as belonging to the Christian Platonic tradition, chapter four examines this tradition. After a brief historical introduction to the tradition, the chapter looks at those whom Knox regarded as its chief representatives in the patristic period: Clement of Alexandria, Pseudo-Macarius and John Chrysostom. After them, Knox held, the tradition degenerated into mysticism, and so his understanding of this phenomenon is also explored, before continuing with those in whom Knox believed the Platonic tradition to have been revived: the Anglican moderates of the seventeenth century and Wesley himself, considered here as

29   Gunstone, "Alexander Knox, 1757–1831," p. 463.
30   Foucault, *Dits et Écrits*, Vol. 4, p. 607 (my translation).

a Christian Platonist. The chapter closes with an appreciation of Knox's own place in the tradition. Having thus situated Knox diachronically, chapter five sets him in the context of his times, looking at his relationship to heart religion, to the Enlightenment and to Romanticism, including a comparison between him and two men often hailed as exemplars of Romantic theology, Samuel Taylor Coleridge and Friedrich Schleiermacher.

Chapter six turns to Knox's own theology, looking at its general characteristics: it was consistent, practical, consensual, eclectic and "philosophic." Chapter seven then examines Knox's theological method. Showing how he approaches theology as a science, in the Enlightenment understanding of the term, it looks at his understanding of the Bible, his appeals to what he terms the *consensus omnium* and the *consensus patrum*, and at the role which he gives to experience and intuition. The succeeding chapters offer a detailed analysis of Knox's theological teaching on various specific topics: God and human beings; Christology and pneumatology; justification and perfection; the sacraments; the church; providence and predestination. In exploring these topics, I hope to have realized the plan projected by Hornby but never put into effect: the exposition of the "entire system of Mr. Knox's published sentiments, and profession of doctrinal belief."[31] At the same time, I will argue that Knox's thought reflects both the concerns of the post-Enlightenment era in which he lived and the Christian Platonic tradition to which he belonged, echoing the teaching of Wesley and the Anglican moderates, as well as being rooted firmly in the patristic period. I will argue, too, that it was his conscious desire to present himself always as an Anglican, one who was in unfailing accord with what he termed the "real doctrines and genius of our Church."[32]

4   Sources

The main source for this study is Knox's own *oeuvre*. To quote Jebb: "[T]he most faithful portrait of his mind, will undoubtedly be found, in the writings which he has left behind him."[33] Of these, the most important are the already-mentioned *Correspondence* and *Remains*. The *Correspondence*, edited by Jebb's chaplain and companion, Charles Forster, was typical of the time in which its authors lived, a period which produced, in the words of Peter Gay, "untold millions of letters and diaries." Estimations of its value vary. Some may agree

---

31   Hornby, "Editor's Preface to the Third and Fourth Volumes," p. cxvii.
32   *Remains*, Vol. 3, p. 190.
33   Jebb, "Introduction" to Burnet's *Lives*, p. xxx.

that it constitutes a "treasure of christian [*sic*]wisdom;" others would regard it with the *Christian Examiner* as "the hypochondriac complaints of two sickly valetudinarians."[34] As an editor, Forster's principles of omission are clear. He excludes what is mundane and repetitious, as well as anything that might place the two correspondents in a bad light. Thus, while the published letters still contain much information on Knox and Jebb's ill-heath, Forster excluded anything that was too graphic in detail, such as Knox's account of "a disagreeable attack of Piles," or his description of the "inflammation of the bowels" suffered by his housekeeper, Miss Ferguson. Forster likewise passes over anything that seems unduly harsh: for instance, the accusation that the Rector of Killeshandra, William Hales, was guilty of countenancing Arianism, or the dismissal of Hannah More's *Coelebs* (1808) as "in every way, a poor business." He omits, too, anything that is unflattering to his protagonists, such as Knox's uncharacteristically peevish outburst: "Have you deliberately ... renounced me? I wrote two letters, with an interval of two weeks between, ... in answer to which I have not yet been favoured with a single line." Omissions such as these are entirely comprehensible, but, at the same time, there are others which are difficult to understand. For no apparent reason, some valuable material has been left out of the published *Correspondence*, which is one of the reasons that the originals, housed in the British Library, need to be consulted. Also, Forster fails on several occasions to transcribe the correct date of the letters, sometimes, one suspects, because of a problem of eyesight, for example, reading "5" instead of "8," which appear similar in Knox's rather difficult hand.[35] The *Correspondence* helps clarify much of what is contained in the *Remains*. The first three volumes of these comprise forty-one pieces by Knox, mostly essays, several in letter-form, written between 1802 and 1828. They are arranged

---

34   Gay, *The Naked Heart*, p. 311; Forster, *Life of Jebb*, Vol. 1, p. 61; *Christian Examiner*, 3. 35 (September 1834), p. 624. For Charles Forster (1789–1871), see Boase, *Modern English Biography*, Vol. 1, col. 1084.

35   The Knox-Jebb correspondence consists of four pieces: Add. Ms 41163, Correspondence between Alexander Knox and John Jebb (1799–1811); Add. Ms 41164, Correspondence between Alexander Knox and John Jebb (1812–30); Add. Ms 41165, Correspondence between John Jebb and Alexander Knox (1800–12); Add. Ms 41166, Correspondence between John Jebb and Alexander Knox (1813–31). For the passages cited in the preceding paragraph, see: B. L., Add. Ms 41164, Correspondence between Alexander Knox and John Jebb (1812–30), fol. 3, Knox to John Jebb, letter, July 20, 1812; fol. 44., Knox to John Jebb, letter, May 20, 1814; fol. 4, Knox to John Jebb, letter, July 20, 1812; Add. Ms 41163, Correspondence between Alexander Knox and John Jebb (1799–1811), fol. 197, Knox to John Jebb, letter, March 17, 1809; Add. Ms 41164, Correspondence between Alexander Knox and John Jebb (1812–30), fol. 39, Knox to John Jebb, letter, March 19, 1814; fol. 60, Knox to John Jebb, letter, June 8, 1815 (dated June 5, 1815, in the published *Correspondence*, Vol. 2, p. 226). For Miss Ferguson, see below, p. 24. For William Hales (1747–1831), see *O. D. N. B.*

seemingly without order, and with virtually no editorial comment. Volume four contains mostly letters from Knox, dating from 1795 to 1831, arranged chronologically. The first twenty-one letters, however, are addressed to Knox, and come from John Wesley's correspondence with him.

Knox's writings are more extensive than the *Correspondence* and the *Remains*, although their number has not always been appreciated. Stanley Kunitz and Howard Haycraft, for example, in their *British Authors of the Nineteenth Century* (1936), attribute to Knox only three principal works: the *Remains*, the *Correspondence* and the *Essays on the Political Circumstances of Ireland* (1798). The reason for this is that Knox often wrote anonymously or pseudonymously, having "*chosen*," as he explained to Joseph Cooper Walker, "retirement in preference to publicity."[36] Despite this, one can discover a fuller list of Knox's publications from a careful scrutiny of the *Remains* and the *Correspondence*. This list appears in the bibliography, which also includes an inventory of Knox's unpublished papers.

Most of those who have written about Knox have been concerned with his teaching, rather than with the details of his life. Before concluding this survey of sources, therefore, mention must be made of four pieces germane to Knox's biography. One is the "Introduction" to Jebb's edition of Burnet's *Lives* (1833), a large part of which is taken up with a description of Knox. The second comes from the September 1834 issue of *The Dublin University Magazine*, which contains what is ostensibly a review of the *Correspondence*, although its author admits that his main object is "to present ... as full a portraiture of Mr. Knox as [he] could."[37] Although unsigned, the article was the work of Samuel O'Sullivan, in whose *Remains* (1853) it was subsequently reprinted. The third is Knox's obituary by his friend Charles Dickinson, which appeared in the July 1831 issue of the *Christian Examiner*. Lastly, there are the *Reminiscences* of Lord Teignmouth, who met Knox frequently at Bellevue, the home of the La Touche family.[38]

36   T. C. D., Ms 1461, Volume 5, Correspondence of Joseph Cooper Walker (1761–1810), fol. 117, Knox to Joseph Cooper Walker, letter, June 8, 1803 (emphasis in the original). For Joseph Cooper Walker, Irish antiquarian, resident at Bray, see *O. D. N. B.*

37   *Dublin University Magazine*, 4. 21 (September 1834), p. 250.

38   Jebb, "Introduction" to Burnet's *Lives*, pp. xxix–xli; *Dublin University Magazine*, 4. 21 (September 1834), pp. 241–61; O'Sullivan, *Remains*, Vol. 3, p. 278; *Christian Examiner*, 11. 73 (July 1831), pp. 562–64; Teignmouth, *Reminiscences*, pp. 183–200. For Samuel O'Sullivan (1790–1851), Chaplain to the Royal Hibernian Military School in Dublin, see Leslie, *Clergy of Dublin and Glendalough*, p. 945. For Charles Dickinson (1792–1842) and his relationship with Knox, see below, pp. 241–42. For Lord Teignmouth, Charles John Shore (1796–1885), see his *Reminiscences*.

CHAPTER 1

The Life of Alexander Knox

"[T]o write a biography of Knox would be impossible," comments J. R. H. Moorman, "because nothing ever happened to him." Even Knox's much-admiring editor, J. J. Hornby declared: "His life had very little of any interest."[1] Such statements are a sure stimulus to research, and in fact Knox's life does merit attention, not least as an introduction to his theology. The present chapter begins by setting Knox in context, with a brief over-view of the political and ecclesiastical background of the period in which he lived. It then moves on to examine his early life, and especially his association with John Wesley, his brief career as a public servant and his long years of religious retirement. It looks at his friendship with John Jebb and at his support for Roman Catholic Emancipation, as well as his views on Catholicism more generally. The chapter ends with his death and the controversy surrounding it.

1 Background, 1757–1831

When Knox was born in 1757 Britain was in the second year of the conflict which was to become the Seven Years War (1756–63). This war ended with Britain confirmed as the dominant imperial power, and although after six years of further conflict (1775–83) the American colonies were lost, the Empire continued to expand, fuelled by and fuelling the Industrial Revolution at home. In 1789 came the seismic shock of the French Revolution, in the wake of which Britain entered into a twenty-three-year period of almost unbroken conflict with France: the French Revolutionary and the Napoleonic Wars (1792–1815). During this time of turbulence, the British government was only too well aware of the potential danger to which it was exposed on its western flank, especially after the Rebellion of the United Irishmen in 1798 which was carried out with the help of the enemy French. The government's solution was the Act of Union of 1800 by which Great Britain and Ireland were joined together as a single kingdom. This, at the time, was generally seen by the majority of Irish Protestants as a blow to their aspirations: throughout the 1770s their main

---

1 Moorman, "Forerunners of the Oxford Movement," p. 10; Hornby, "Editor's Preface to the Third and Fourth Volumes," p. x.

© KONINKLIJKE BRILL NV, LEIDEN, 2020 | DOI:10.1163/9789004426986_003

political concern had been for greater legislative independence, which had culminated in 1782 with "Grattan's Parliament."[2]

When England and Ireland became a united kingdom, their churches likewise became one. Sean Connolly has described the Church of Ireland at the beginning of the nineteenth century as "a weak and ineffective organisation."[3] Nonetheless, the period was also marked by a concerted effort to achieve what Donald Akenson has termed "graceful reform," an effort led by the triumvirate of Archbishops William Stuart, Charles Agar, and Charles Brodrick.[4] At the same time, reform of a different kind was coming from the Evangelical movement. The rise of Evangelicalism in Ireland, as in Britain, reflected a growth in religious fervour that was observable throughout much of Western Europe during the early- and mid-nineteenth century, partly in response to the insecurity caused by the Napoleonic Wars and partly as a reaction to the rationalism of the Enlightenment.[5] Destined to dominate the Church of Ireland from the mid-nineteenth century onwards, Evangelicalism was already a force to be reckoned with at the start of the 1800s, having grown significantly in strength through the two preceding decades. Thus, for instance, one finds Knox himself complaining in 1819 of the extent to which "Calvinism," as he called it, was spreading through the Irish Church.[6] This growth provoked a certain degree of tension within the Church of Ireland, since the opening decades of the nineteenth century also witnessed a High Church revival, something which Knox exemplifies.[7] This internal tension was matched by an increasing strain in relations with the Roman Catholic Church, to which the vast majority of

---

2   For Irish politics at this period, see, e.g., Beckett, *Making of Modern Ireland*, chapters 12–15; pp. 227–305.

3   Connolly, *Religion and Society in Nineteenth-Century Ireland*, p. 7.

4   For the Church of Ireland at this period, see especially, Yates, *Religious Condition of Ireland*. See too, Akenson, *Church of Ireland*. The phrase "gracious reform" is taken from the title of the second chapter of his book, which covers the period 1800–30. For William Stuart (1755–1822), and Charles Agar (1736–1809), see *O. D. N. B.*; for Charles Brodrick (1761–1822), see McGuire and Quinn, eds, *Dictionary of Irish Biography*, Vol. 1, pp. 856–57. Knox and Brodrick were close friends, who kept up a long and intimate correspondence, which is now housed in the National Library of Ireland: Ms 8868, Brodrick Papers. On this collection, see Jenkins, "The Correspondence of Charles Brodrick."

5   On the religious situation in Europe at the time, see McLeod, *Religion and the People of Western Europe*.

6   N. L. I., Ms 8868, Brodrick Papers (folder 8), Knox to Charles Brodrick, letter, December 24, 1819; Hempton and Hill, *Evangelical Protestantism*, p. 14. For the topic of Evangelicalism in the Church of Ireland during the eighteenth and nineteenth centuries, see, besides Hempton and Hill, Acheson, "Evangelicals in the Church of Ireland;" and Liechty, "Irish Evangelicalism."

7   The classic study of Irish High Churchmanship is Bolton, *Caroline Tradition of the Church of Ireland*. See also, Nockles, "Church or Protestant Sect." For the state of High Churchmanship

Irish people belonged. From about 1770 to 1784, a relative détente had existed, but thereafter sectarian hostility became the norm, especially after the 1798 Rebellion. Fear and insecurity gripped not only members of the Church of Ireland, but those also from other Reformed denominations, and led to the creation of a "Pan-Protestant" identity, in which differences of doctrine and polity were minimized. In the forging of this identity, Evangelicalism also had its part to play, regarding as it did everything else as secondary to what it saw as the core doctrines of the Gospel. These doctrines were: the depravity of fallen humankind; substitutionary atonement; justification by faith alone; and adherence to them was viewed as uniting all genuine believers, no matter what their church affiliation might be. Protestant fear was matched by increasing Roman Catholic confidence. Following the Roman Catholic Relief Act of 1829, Roman Catholics began agitating against the privileged status of the Church of Ireland, not least in relation to the issue of tithes. In so doing, they joined a wave of discontent then sweeping through England, where an alliance of Whigs, Radicals and Non-Conformists was seeking to undermine the ecclesiastical status quo. As Knox lamented in 1826: "The Church never more needed the protection of providence ... God only can frustrate the united attack of its false friends and rancorous enemies."[8] This "united attack" made the Irish Church its primary target, as the most vulnerable part of the Establishment and the most open to criticism.

2   Knox's Early Life and the Influence of Wesley

Alexander Knox was born on March 17, 1757, in Londonderry, in the north of Ireland, the eldest of four siblings. After him came George, Sarah (Sally), and a second sister, whose name is not recorded.[9] His father, also called

---

specifically at the start of the nineteenth century, see Acheson, *History of the Church of Ireland*, p. 153.

8   B. L., Add. Ms 41164, Correspondence between Alexander Knox and John Jebb (1812–30), fols. 202–203, Knox to John Jebb, letter, October 6, 1826. For a summary of the situation see: Gilley, "Introduction" to Keble's *Christian Year*, and for a fuller treatment, Brown, *National Churches*. For a contemporary view from the Church of Ireland, see Forster, *Life of Jebb*, Vol. 1, pp. 249–51.

9   For Knox's birth-date, see *Remains*, Vol. 4, p. 417; *Correspondence*, Vol. 1, p. 541, note; Vol. 2, p. 56; Hughes, "Life and Work," p. 1. For his siblings, see O. C. M. C. H., B/Wes/J, letter 19, John Wesley to Knox, August 16, 1778; B/Wes/J, letter 33, John Wesley to Knox, December 2, 1782; B/Wes/J, letter 44, John Wesley to Knox, June 8, 1785; B/Wes/J, letter 51, John Wesley to Knox, July 26, 1790. See also *Remains*, Vol. 3, pp. 478–79, as well as Colby, *Ordnance Survey*, p. 96. Colby states that Knox was his parents' second child, but in this he is mistaken, as he is in giving Knox's birth-year as 1761.

Alexander, was a man of independent means and a leading member of the city Corporation.[10] Both deeply pious, he and his wife had an important impact on the spiritual formation of their eldest son, not least by their support for the Derry Methodist "society," which Knox attended with them. As he later wrote to Jebb, in an unpublished portion of their correspondence, "What would have been my career thro life if I had not known the Methodists? ... God was pleased to teach me thro them the nature of inward religion."[11]

It was not simply Methodism, however, that made an impression on Knox. There was also the towering figure of John Wesley himself.[12] "Never man possessed greater personal influence over the people connected with him," Thomas Haweis declared,[13] and this influence appears to have been particularly strong on Knox, occurring as it did during his formative years, spanning the time that, as he put it, he "passed from childhood to youth, and from youth to manhood."[14] "Mr. Wesley seems to be your own idol," John Walker later jeered;[15] and, despite the unpleasant tone of the remark, it is evident that, as well as being impacted by Wesley theologically, as we will see in subsequent chapters, Knox retained a strong personal affection for the man whom he dubbed "my-never-to-be-forgotten old friend."[16] Wesley's, he told Jebb, was 'a great mind, if any mind can be made great, by disinterested benevolence, spotless purity, and simple devotedness to that one supreme Good, in whom, with the united αἴσθησις [aisthēsis]of the philosopher and the saint, he saw, and loved, and adored, all that was infinitely amiable, true, sublime, and beatific.'[17]

---

10   Nockles, "Knox," p. 1. The Corporation was the body which had governed the city's affairs since the seventeenth century; see Hume, *Derry Beyond the Walls*, p. 41. The city is known both as Londonderry and as Derry.

11   B. L., Add. Ms 44163, Correspondence between Alexander Knox and John Jebb (1799–1811), fol. 91, Knox to John Jebb, letter, November 7, 1805. For the early influence of Methodism on Knox, and for the influence of his parents, see *Remains*, Vol. 1, p. 78; Vol. 4, pp. 107, 142–43, 417–18; Crookshank, *History of Methodism*, Vol. 1, pp. 234–35. See, too, for Knox's parents, Hughes, "Life and Work," pp. 2–9.

12   Knox almost never mentions Charles Wesley (1707–88). "Wesley" in this book thus always denotes John (1703–91). He is the subject of an immense bibliography; see Maddox and Vickers, eds, *The Cambridge Companion to John Wesley*.

13   Haweis, *Impartial and Succinct History*, Vol. 3, p. 275.

14   *Wesley*, p. 416.

15   Walker, second letter to Alexander Knox (1802), in *An Expostulatory Address*, pp. pp. 91–120, at p. 99. For John Walker (1769–1833), see Carter, *Anglican Evangelicals*, pp. 77–96. For the controversy between Walker and Knox, see below, p. 58.

16   *Remains*, Vol. 1, p. 278.

17   *Correspondence*, Vol. 2, p. 460. (For the meaning of *aisthēsis*, see below, pp. 138–41.) For similar plaudits, see *Remarks*, p. 10; Knox's letter to the *Dublin Chronicle*, June 27–30, 1789, pp. 206–7; *Remains*, Vol. 3, p. 467.

Knox's acquaintance with Wesley began in 1765 when Knox was eight and Wesley came to stay with his family during a preaching-trip to Derry.[18] It was the first of ten such visits to the city, during which time Wesley developed a deep fondness for the boy he termed "my dear Alleck." The appellation appears in the fifty letters which he addressed to Knox over a fifteen-year period, beginning June 6, 1775, the year after the sudden death of Knox's father, and continuing until July 26, 1790, the year before Wesley's own demise. Though brief, these letters show a real solicitude for Knox, and it is little wonder that he later spoke of Wesley as "my tender and constant comforter, writing the wisest and gentlest letters to me." "Singularly tender" is the description given to the letters by John Telford in his edition of Wesley's correspondence; the care they show for Knox is beautiful, Telford comments.[19]

3   Public Life

Knox was a sickly child, afflicted by epilepsy and depression.[20] He was thus unable to attend school or university; nonetheless, he evidently spent his invalidity studying, for as his writings testify, he had a wide and deep knowledge not only of theology but also of ancient and modern literature. As Hannah More remarked: "From the conversation of so highly gifted a man as Mr. Knox much may be learned, as he is overflowing with information as well as such an original genius."[21] In 1795 Knox was elected a member of the Royal Irish Academy (R. I. A.) and served three terms on its "Polite Literature Committee," 1796–97, 1799–1800, and 1805–6. For the term 1805–6, he also held the office of Vice-President.[22]

In his personal papers, Knox confessed that his early religiosity was related to his ill-health, and that, as his physical constitution improved, his spiritual life declined:

---

18   Wesley recounts his first meeting with Knox senior in his *Journal* entry for Saturday May 11, 1765. See *Journal*, Vol. 5, pp. 114–15. For Wesley's visits to Derry, see Rogal, *Wesley in Ireland*, Vol. 2, pp. 765–72, with the caveat that Rogal needs to be read with caution.
19   *Remarks*, p. 237; Telford, *Letters*, Vol. 7, p. 160; Vol. 6, p. 64.
20   *Correspondence*, Vol. 2, p. 25, note; *Dublin University Magazine*, 4.21 (September 1834), p. 241.
21   Bodleian, Ms. Eng. lett. d. 124, "Letters to C. A. Ogilvie, K-Z," fols. 101–103, Hannah More to C. A. Ogilvie, letter, July 19 [1815], fol. 102. For Hannah More, see, below, pp. 49–51. For Ogilvie, see, below, p. 257.
22   I am grateful for this information to the present Librarian of the Royal Irish Academy, Siobhan Fitzpatrick, sent in a letter to me, March 26, 2007. See, also, the *Treble Almanack* (1805), p. 135. There is no record of Knox having made any learned contribution to the Academy's proceedings. For the Academy, see O'Raifeartaigh, ed., *The Royal Irish Academy*.

> I was once strongly impregnated with evangelic religion, but it was from mere pressure of affliction; and, as that grew lighter, the other lessened apace ... Temptation after temptation drew me, by degrees, from my fear of God, and my early practice of private prayer: my taste for religion decreased; I began to love company – to love talking on worldly subjects, until I launched out into the world ... and became a politician.[23]

This new trajectory was one which Knox pursued with enthusiasm. As Thomas Colby records, "[T]here was no event, civil or political, involving the interests of his native city, in which Mr. Knox did not take a zealous and efficient part."[24] Much light is shed on this stage of his life by the *Essays on the Political Circumstances of Ireland* which he composed between 1795 and 1797 and published in a single volume in 1798. These essays show that, *pace* Gunstone, Knox was never a member of the United Irishmen. He admitted to "a temporary intercourse with the convention-politicians," but asserted that he "always had a just abhorrence of [their] principles and views," regarding them, from the beginning, or so he claimed, as nothing but "systematic traitors." For his own part, he confessed to starting out as "a sincere and zealous advocate for a limited parliamentary reform," but he soon became convinced, not least by the behavior of the United Irishmen, that any "popular reform would infallibly lead ... to complete democracy," something which he equated with the excesses of the French Revolution.[25] Accordingly, he felt it his duty "to abandon a pursuit which appeared to him as dangerous as it was visionary, and to become, to the utmost of his power, an unqualified supporter of the existing constitution."[26]

Unyielding defence of the status quo animates the *Essays*. Not only, however, are they striking by their reactionary nature, but also by their limpid style. "[L]ively, readable, and occasionally witty," is the accolade afforded to them by J. C. Beckett, while the contemporary *British Critic* described them as "able and energetic," no other author having, in its opinion, more clearly explained or better combatted what it called "the traitors and Jacobins in

---

23   *Remains*, Vol. 4, pp. 56–57. See, also, pp. 74–77. For the term "evangelic" here, see *Remains*, Vol. 4, p. 138, where Knox argues that "to be truly evangelical, is to feel that the Gospel is the power of God unto salvation."

24   Colby, *Ordnance Survey*, p. 96.

25   Knox also had a theological objection to democracy. "[P]olitical power," he held, "emanates not from the will of man, but from the will of God" (*Brief Confutation*, p. 6).

26   *Essays*, pp. viii, vii, xi, vii, 34, vii. The term "convention-politician" comes from the United Irishmen's intention of holding mass rallies to press for political reform. In the event, only one such convention took place, in 1793, in Dungannon. For the movement, see Curtin, *United Irishmen*. For Gunstone's comment, see "Alexander Knox," p. 464. He is followed by Barrett, "Knox," p. 43.

Ireland."[27] More importantly, the *Essays* brought Knox to the attention of the
authorities, and in 1798 Lord Castlereagh, the newly-appointed Chief Secretary
for Ireland, invited Knox to enter his employ.[28] Knox once referred to himself
as "one of [Castlereagh's] secretaries." In fact, he was, as he wrote elsewhere,
Castlereagh's private secretary.[29] Knox was hesitant about taking up the position. Despite going into politics, he had never wholly lost his religious sensibili-
ties, and, following a prolonged bout of psychological distress, he underwent
what he described in terms of a spiritual experience.[30] What exactly happened
is difficult to discern. Knox gave two different versions: one in the fragments of
a diary he kept in 1800; the other in a letter he addressed to his friend, George
Schoales, in 1803. To Schoales, he wrote:

> Six years ago, in the house of your brother Adam, I underwent a revolu-
> tion, that emancipated me from the slavery of this world. To that wonder-
> ful time, therefore, I trace back every thoroughly good habit. I can look
> back to a point at which I awoke, as it were, from a dream, and found
> myself as if hanging over fathomless perdition; and I can mark another
> point, a few days after, when, in conversation with a Methodist preacher,
> a dawn sprung up, that has been since often beclouded by disease, but
> which has never gone back.[31]

This version is the more dramatic: a "revolution" occurs. In the 1800 version, by
contrast, matters progress more slowly. At first, Knox's depression led him to
prayer, but:

---

27   Beckett, "Literature in English, 1691–1800," p. 466; *British Critic*, 14 (August 1799), p. 119. In
     contrast to the praise bestowed on the *Essays*, views of Knox's style in his theological writ-
     ings were more mixed. See below, p. 30.
28   Robert Stewart, Viscount Castlereagh (1769–1822), Chief Secretary of Ireland, 1798–1801.
     He went on to become British Foreign Secretary, 1812–22. The most complete account is
     Vane, ed., *Memoirs and Correspondence*.
29   *Remains*, Vol. 4, pp. 58, 31. Vane describes Knox as Castlereagh's assistant private secre-
     tary (*Memoirs and Correspondence*, Vol. 2, p. 44, note 4). The most detailed account of
     Castlereagh's secretaries in Dublin is furnished by H. M. Hyde in his *Rise of Castlereagh*,
     pp. 219–28. For his treatment of Knox, see pp. 224–27. It should be noted that Knox
     was more than simply Castlereagh's secretary; he was also his "confidential friend"
     (P. R. O. N. I., Hill of Brook Hall Papers, D642/A/10/19, Knox to Sir George Hill, letter
     [1798]).
30   For Knox's mental and physical health at this juncture, see N. L. I., Ms 8868, Brodrick
     Papers (folder 2), Knox to Charles Brodrick, letter, December 8, 1803; *Remains*, Vol. 4,
     pp. 57–58.
31   *Remains*, Vol. 4, pp. 128–29.

I found no relief for some days. I then, in my distress, went to the Methodist preacher; my pains having so far brought down my pride. His conversation brought me the first ease. I then began to pray with some hope ... But these feelings, in a few days, subsided also. Still, however, a seriousness remained, which I had not had for years; though not that uniform, practical seriousness, which implies a real work of God.[32]

This second version, written nearer the time and for his eyes alone, has the merit of sounding truer to life: a slow struggle, rather than a sudden conversion.[33] Whatever the exact nature of the case, it is nonetheless clear that Knox's religiosity had been rekindled and that, consequently, he was afraid if he accepted Castlereagh's offer, he "should again be drawn into the world."[34] Nonetheless, pressed by the Chief Secretary, he eventually gave way and joined the staff at Dublin Castle, the headquarters of the government administration. The very night after he had started work, the Rebellion of the United Irishmen broke out.[35] It was not, however, an event by which he was much perturbed. At the time, describing the arrival of James Napper Tandy as *having something funny about it*," he confessed: "I can't help being amused;" while later on he reminded Castlereagh of how he used "to triumph in the repeated defeats of the Rebels in the year '98."[36] By contrast, he was far less sanguine about the man dispatched from London to handle the situation, Lord Cornwallis. Writing "bluntly," as he put it, to his friend Sir George Hill, he declared: "Things do not go on to please me at all." Cornwallis was, in his opinion, too lenient towards the rebels, stubbornly refusing to heed advice on how to deal with them. But it could not be otherwise, Knox lamented: "I don't expect an English gentleman to understand Irish politicks [*sic*] by intuition. And I do not expect a general of between 60 and 70 who has fought in both hemispheres to be advisable."[37]

---

32   Ibid., p. 58.

33   One wonders, too, if Knox would have been so suspicious of "sudden revolutions of mind" (*Wesley*, p. 412), had he himself undergone one. See, also, *Remains*, Vol. 4, p. 147.

34   *Remains*, Vol. 4, p. 58.

35   Ibid., p. 59. The Rebellion began in the night of May 23–24. For a succinct account, see Curtin, *United Irishmen*, chapter 10, "Rebellion," pp. 254–81.

36   P. R. O. N. I., Hill of Brook Hall Papers, D642/A/10/16, Knox to Sir George Hill, letter, Thursday [1798] (emphasis in the original); D642/A/10/19, Knox to Sir George Hill, letter, [1798]; Knox to Lord Castlereagh, letter, February 23, 1802, in Vane, *Memoirs and Correspondence*, Vol. 4, p. 220. For James Napper Tandy (c. 1737–1803), who led an abortive invasion of Ireland in September 1798, see *O. D. N. B.*

37   P. R. O. N. I., Hill of Brook Hall Papers, D642/A/10/19, Knox to Sir George Hill, letter, [1798]; D642/A/10/26, Knox to Sir George Hill, letter, November 16, 1798; D642/A/10/19, Knox to Sir George Hill, letter, [1798]. For Lord Cornwallis (1738–1805), Lord Lieutenant of Ireland

Knox was not particularly suited to his position as Castlereagh's secretary. As Castlereagh complained to Lord Teignmouth, he was hopeless at filing papers, and unable to communicate when it came to "practical discourse with mankind."[38] Nonetheless, in a letter addressed in July 1798 to his friend George Schoales, Knox gave an idyllic picture of his life at the Castle. Although both the vagaries of his health and his spiritual development meant that he knew himself to be "but *in transitu*," he could still describe his situation as "for the time being ... not unpleasant ... I sit often, at my ease, and look from my window at the ebbing and flowing of the tide of men coming in and out of the castle-yard."[39] Yet, not all was indolence: much of Knox's time was taken up with preparations for the Act of Union, the British government's response to the Rebellion. Hannah More calls Knox a "grand instrument in accomplishing the great work of the Union," while Colby describes him as being a "warm advocate for a legislative union with Great Britain ... [and] a powerful assistant in effecting that measure."[40] Certainly, he was so involved in seeking to win over the reluctant Protestant populace to acceptance of the plan, that subsequently both Castlereagh and the Lord Lieutenant of Ireland at the time, Lord Camden, suggested that he should write a history of the period, an invitation which he declined.[41] Not that he appears to have doubted the wisdom of legislative unity. He was fully convinced, he told Hill, that it was "a measure dictated by soundest policy," and one that would contribute to "the welfare of the British Empire, and to the safety and happiness of Ireland." No longer would Protestants be a minority in Ireland, he maintained; they would be a majority in the United Kingdom.[42] Knox was also tasked with drawing up a report on the origins and causes of the Rebellion, an undertaking which, in the words of H. Montgomery Hyde, he "accomplished with conspicuous ability."[43]

---

and Commander-in-Chief, 1798–1801, see *O. D. N. B.* For the Londonderry politician Sir George Fitzgerald Hill (1763–1839), in 1798 Clerk of the Irish Parliament, see McGuire and Quinn, eds, *Dictionary of Irish Biography*, Vol. 4, pp. 699–700.

38   Teignmouth, *Reminiscences*, Vol. 1, p. 185.

39   *Remains*, Vol. 4, pp. 30–31.

40   Hannah More to William Wilberforce, letter, September 24, 1804, in Wilberforce, *Correspondence*, Vol. 1, p. 323; Colby, *Ordnance Survey*, p. 97. On the Union, see, e.g., Geoghegan, *Irish Act of Union*; also, Keogh and Whelan, eds, *Acts of Union*.

41   *Remains*, Vol. 4, pp. 539–41. Lord Camden, John Jeffreys Pratt (1759–1840) was Lord Lieutenant of Ireland, 1795–98. See *O. D. N. B.* For Protestant attitudes towards the Union, see Hill, *From Patriots to Unionists*, chapter 10, "The Constitution Defended: Opposition to Union, 1798–1814," pp. 257–82.

42   P. R. O. N. I., Hill of Brook Hall Papers, D642/A/10/26, Knox to Sir George Hill, letter, [1799].

43   Hyde, *Rise of Castlereagh*, p. 226. The report was presented by Castlereagh to the Irish Parliament, August 21, 1798; see *Report from the Committee of Secrecy*.

In the summer of 1799 Knox resigned his position.[44] Gunstone has suggested that the reason he did so was stress brought on by having to deal with the
Rebellion of the preceding year.[45] As we have seen, however, the Rebellion did
not occasion any concern on Knox's part. Rather, the reason he gave for his
resignation was his inability to ride, horsemanship being needed in the campaign to rally support for the Union.[46] Knox's lack of equestrian skill pointed to
a more fundamental problem, that of his ill-health, the fact that he was, as he
himself put it, "enfeebled and unfitted for active life, by protracted and severe
indisposition." To quote his obituary: "His bodily structure was so infirm ... as
to preclude all professional pursuit."[47] Combined with this, there was, it seems,
a certain disenchantment with the means used to secure Protestant acceptance of the Union, described by Cornwallis as "such dirty work."[48] Apart from
a declaration that he was sick of politics, Knox makes no allusion to this in his
writings, but the *British Critic* records that, although "he considered the Union
as a measure essential to the integrity of the empire, his pure and upright mind
revolted from the process by which it was accomplished: and, to his latest hour,
he was thankful for the bodily suffering which removed him from all temptation to join in the consummation of the work."[49] One may also note that
Knox had to endure what he termed the "rage of the Anti-Unionists," being
"obliged to listen to as stupid and as insolent an effusion against the *Union*, as
it was possible for exasperated vanity without knowledge or judgment to pour
forth."[50] And this, too, may have contributed to his decision. The chief motive
for Knox's resignation was, it would seem, religious: the desire to embrace a
life of devout retirement. As he told Brodrick, despite the loss of his early piety,
he had never ceased to pine after such an existence.[51] Castlereagh was loath to

---

44   There is no exact date for the cessation of Knox's employment, but in a letter to George
      Schoales, dated July 16, 1799, he speaks of his intention of leaving Ireland for England
      "in a very few days" (*Remains*, Vol. 4, p. 36). Hyde gives the date as August 1799 (*Rise of
      Castlereagh*, p. 226).

45   Gunstone, "Knox," p. 464. Gunstone is followed by Barrett, "Knox," p. 43.

46   Teignmouth, *Reminiscences*, Vol. 1, p. 185.

47   *Candid Animadversions*, p. 1; *Christian Examiner*, 11. 73 (July 1831), p. 562.

48   Lord Cornwallis to Major-General Ross, letter, June 8, 1799, in Ross, ed., *Correspondence
      of Cornwallis*, Vol. 3, p. 102.

49   *British Critic*, 17. 33 (January 1835), p. 159. For the declaration that Knox was sick of politics,
      see *Remains*, Vol. 4, p. 34. Compare Hannah More's remark to William Wilberforce that
      Knox had firmly "turned his back on politics and politicians": letter, September 24, 1804,
      in Wilberforce, *Correspondence*, Vol. 1, p. 323.

50   P. R. O. N. I., Hill of Brook Hall Papers, D642/A/10/26, Knox to Sir George Hill, letter,
      [1799].

51   N. L. I., Ms 8868, Brodrick Papers (folder 2), Knox to Charles Brodrick, letter, December 8,
      1803. See also: *Remains*, Vol. 4, pp. 59–60; *Dublin University Magazine*, 4. 21 (September 1834),
      p. 245; Nockles, "Knox," p. 2.

let Knox go, and, such was the esteem in which he held him, tried to persuade him to stand as M. P. for Londonderry.[52] But Knox was adamant. Henceforth, he declared, his concern was to be for τὸ πολίτευμα ἐν οὐρανοῖς [*to politeuma en ouranois*].[53]

Knox did not leave Dublin Castle wholly unrewarded in material terms. He accepted the position of Agent for the Roman Catholic college of Maynooth, which paid him an annual salary of £300. The Agent's function was to liaise between Dublin Castle and the college. Although Knox carried out an annual visitation, he regarded the office simply as a sinecure, a gift from Castlereagh which expressed personal friendship and also served as a reward for his service to the government.[54] There were only two occasions on which he carried out any actions of note. The first was in 1801: the government was worried about a lay-school annexed to the seminary, and Knox was dispatched by Charles Abbot, Castlereagh's successor as Chief Secretary, to convey this concern to the Catholic Archbishop of Dublin, John Troy. Knox seems to have mismanaged the business, receiving a reprimand, via Abbot, from the Lord Lieutenant, the Earl of Hardwicke, although no details of the incident have been preserved.[55] The second occasion was when he wrote to Castlereagh, seeking to secure a grant for the college from the estate of Lord Dunboyne, John Butler, for the education of professors. "The thing was done," Knox related, "but I by no means take upon myself to say that it was done through my application."[56] Knox seems to have enjoyed his relationship with the college, to which he left his "Benedictines" in his will.[57]

---

52   *British Critic*, 17. 33 (January 1835), p. 159; *Christian Examiner*, 11. 73 (July 1831), p. 562; *Dublin University Magazine*, 4. 21 (September 1834), p. 245. For Castlereagh's "warmest and most sincere regard" for Knox, see his letter of March 30, 1811, in *Remains*, Vol. 4, pp. 539–41, note. The admiration was mutual; see *Remains*, Vol. 4, pp. 31–32.

53   *Remains*, Vol. 4, p. 34. Knox quotes from the Greek of Philippians 3, 20, "the commonwealth of heaven" (my translation).

54   *Eighth Report of the Commissioners of Irish Education Inquiry*, pp. 444–45. St Patrick's College, Maynooth, was founded by the government for both lay and clerical students in 1795. See Corish, *Maynooth*. For Knox's annual visitation, see Teignmouth, *Reminiscences*, Vol. 1, p. 281.

55   *Eighth Report of the Commissioners of Irish Education Inquiry*, p. 445; *Diary and Correspondence of Charles Abbot, Lord Colchester*, Vol. 1, pp. 330–40; Corish, *Maynooth*, pp. 40–41. For Charles Abbot (1757–1829), Chief Secretary for Ireland, 1801–2, thereafter, Speaker of the House of Commons; John Thomas Troy (1739–1823), Archbishop of Dublin, 1786–1823; and Philip Yorke, third Earl of Hardwicke (1757–1834), Lord Lieutenant of Ireland, 1801–6, see O. D. N. B.

56   *Eighth Report of the Commissioners of Irish Education Inquiry*, p. 445. For Lord Dunboyne (1731–1800) and the dispute over his estate, see Corish, *Maynooth*, pp. 54–55.

57   P. R. O. N. I., T810/8, fol. 373, certified copy of Knox's Will. For the "Benedictines," see below, p. 132.

There is no evidence to support the assertion, first made by William Fitzpatrick, that Knox mutilated himself as a result of an unrequited passion for Robert Peel's wife, Julia. The allegation is undermined, first, by the fact of being made seventy years after the supposed event; even more by Peel having been unmarried when Knox is claimed to have fallen for his spouse.[58] Most importantly, the accusation fails to take seriously the significance of what Knox saw as his religious conversion. As a result of it, he affirms on several occasions, never once did he subsequently yield to the desires of the flesh.[59]

4   Religious Retirement

Having renounced what he termed the din of politics, Knox set out for England, where he spent about year, mainly frequenting the spa towns of the West Country. During his sojourn he encountered a number of leading Evangelicals, notably Hannah More.[60] Returning to Dublin in 1801, he settled down to a life of religious retirement at 46, Dawson Street, a large, somewhat melancholy end-of-terrace house near Trinity College.[61] Here Knox gave himself over to what More termed "contemplation and inward religion," something she described as being his "chief delight."[62] It was a life-style which he was able to afford owing to rents he received from properties he owned in Antrim and

---

58   For the initial allegation, see Fitzpatrick, *Sham Squire*, p. 225. The story is repeated by Hyde, *Rise of Castlereagh*, p. 227, and by Leigh, *Castlereagh*, p. 100. Robert Peel (1788–1850), who eventually became British Prime Minister (1834–35; 1841–46), started his political career in Ireland as M. P. for Cashel. He subsequently became Chief Secretary for Ireland, 1812–18. He did not marry Julia until 1820. See Gash, *Mr. Secretary Peel*, p. 260. For William John Fitzpatrick (1830–95), a Dublin writer on historical subjects, see O. D. N. B. For the whole incident, see also, Nockles, "Knox," p. 2.

59   *Remains*, Vol. 1, p. 184; Vol. 4, p. 58; N. L. I., Ms 8868, Brodrick Papers (folder 2), Knox to Charles Brodrick, letter, December 8, 1803.

60   For the phrase, "din of politics," see Bodleian, Ms. Wilberforce c. 52, fols. 77–82, copy of a letter from Knox to Samuel Whitbread, December 1, 1812, fol. 80. Details of Knox's trip to England may be gleaned from the letters he wrote during this period; see *Remains*, Vol. 4, pp. 35–40, 45–55, 61–71, 74–77, 79–84. See also, P. R. O. N. I., Castlereagh Papers, D3030/1595, Knox to Lord Castlereagh, letter, February 9, 1801.

61   For the phrase "religious retirement," see Hannah More's letter to William Wilberforce, September 24, 1804, in Wilberforce, *Correspondence*, Vol. 1, p. 323. For Knox's house, see Hornby, "Editor's Preface to the Third and Fourth Volumes," p. xix. See, too, Stokes, "Alexander Knox and the Oxford Movement," p. 205; also, Ewens, *Three Hermits*, p. 9, where the address is given as 56, Dawson Street. Hughes gives it as 65 ("Life and Work," p. 15).

62   Hannah More to William Wilberforce, letter, September 24, 1804, in Wilberforce, *Correspondence*, Vol. 1, p. 323.

Armagh, as well as his pension as Agent for Maynooth.[63] It is a life-style, too, in which one cannot help but see a parallel with that of the earlier figure of James Bonnell, another pious High Church Dublin layman. If Bonnell and Knox both belong to the same tradition, however, there is no substantive link between them.[64]

Although Knox described himself as a hermit, he did not live alone, being cared for by his devoted manservant, Michael McFeely, and his equally devoted housekeeper, Miss Ferguson.[65] Nor did he forsake the wider world. To quote his own words: "[M]ost certainly, I do not withdraw myself from society: on the contrary, I give myself very much to it."[66] As well as being a parishioner at St Ann's, the church opposite his home in Dawson Street, he would also frequent the chapel of near-by Trinity College. He likewise frequented the College library,[67] as well as attending lectures, at least those of George Miller, who taught history at Trinity between 1789 and 1811 before eventually becoming Headmaster of the Royal School, Armagh. Subsequently published as *Lectures on the Philosophy of Modern History*, Miller's discourses, which emphasized the role of divine providence in human affairs, had a discernible influence on Knox, who took in them a very lively interest.[68] The influence was not reciprocal. Miller, who saw Knox as a progenitor of the Tractarianism which he loathed, was at pains to point out that he paid little attention to Knox's religious opinions.[69] Knox was also acquainted with Thomas Elrington, Provost of Trinity from 1811 until 1820, though he and the anti-Catholic Elrington fell

---

63 For the sources of Knox's income, see P. R. O. N. I., T810/8, fol. 373, certified copy of Knox's Will.

64 For James Bonnell (1653–99), see Hamilton, *Exemplary Life and Character of James Bonnell.*

65 For Knox's description of himself as a hermit, see *Remains*, Vol. 4, p. 384. See also, ibid., pp. 129–30, where Knox describes the pleasure he derived from solitude. For Michael McFeely, Knox's servant from at least 1796 until his master's death in 1831, see *Remains*, Vol. 4, pp. 81, 165–66, 407–8; T810/8, fol. 373, certified copy of Knox's Will. For Miss Ferguson (died 1830), the recipient of a number of letters, see: *Remains*, Vol. 4, pp. 37, 318, 590–92; *Correspondence*, Vol. 1, p. 606, note; Vol. 2, pp. 582–83.

66 *Remains*, Vol. 1, p. 70–71. See, also, ibid., p. 152, where Knox speaks of "a man" who "has separated himself from the pollutions of the world, without withdrawing from its common intercourse." See, too, *Remains*, Vol. 4, p. 150.

67 B. L., Add. Ms 41163, Correspondence between Alexander Knox and John Jebb (1799–1811), fol. 197, Knox to John Jebb, letter, March 17, 1809; N. L. I., Ms 8868, Brodrick Papers, (folder 7), Knox to Charles Brodrick, letter, undated.

68 *The Church of England Magazine*, 26. 748, (February 10, 1849), p. 94. For Knox's interest in Miller's work, see, also: *Correspondence*, Vol. 1, pp. 374–75; and, below, pp. 231–32. For George Miller (1764–1848), see O. D. N. B.

69 *The Church of England Magazine*, 26. 748, (February 10, 1849), p. 94.

out over Knox's 1810 *Answer to Duigenan*, in which Knox argued the case for Roman Catholic Emancipation. Nonetheless, through their joint work for the Association for Discountenancing Vice (A. D. V.) and the Royal Irish Academy, they achieved a certain degree of reconciliation, fostered by their common High Churchmanship.[70]

Another don with whom Knox had a strained relationship was William Magee, Professor of Mathematics from 1800 to 1812.[71] The two men differed politically, Magee having been a staunch opponent of the Union, which Knox had been charged with promoting. Theologically, too, they were at odds, particularly in relation to the doctrine of the atonement. One of Magee's principal works had been a trenchant defence of Christ's death as an expiatory sacrifice, something which Knox's theology downplayed.[72] A further divergence occurred in 1803, over a tract which Knox produced for the A. D. V., a collection of writings by Bishop Gilbert Burnet entitled *Lives, Characters, and a Sermon Preached at the Funeral of the Hon. Robert Boyle*. In his preface to the tract, Knox spoke appreciatively of the Puritan Richard Baxter and this offended the High Church Magee, who thought that Knox was favoring Dissent.[73] This spat was followed in 1806 by a quarrel over the *Homilies*. It was the practice of the A. D. V. to distribute copies of the *Homilies* to children, something which Knox opposed, on the grounds that they contained an anti-Roman Catholic rhetoric which he judged inflammatory.[74] Magee, who like Knox was on the board of the Association, defended the *Homilies'* distribution with vehemence. "Dr. Magee has certainly done all in his power to *put me* down," Knox complained to Brodrick,[75] and one can imagine that matters only got worse once Knox carried the day, and the distribution of the *Homilies* was abandoned. Despite these repeated clashes, rapprochement was achieved in 1815 when

---

70 Thomas Elrington (1760–1835) held various academic posts in Trinity before becoming Provost. In 1820, he became Bishop of Limerick, before being translated to Leighlin and Ferns in 1822. See *O. D. N. B.* For his relationship with Knox, see B. L., Add. Ms 41164, Correspondence between Alexander Knox and John Jebb (1812–30), fols. 83–84, Knox to John Jebb, letter, April 28, 1816. For the A. D. V., see below, 28.

71 For William Magee (1766–1831), subsequently Dean of Cork (1813–19), Bishop of Raphoe (1819–22) and Archbishop of Dublin (1822–31), see *O. D. N. B.*

72 For Knox's teaching on the atonement, see below, pp. 157–60. For Magee's position, see his *Discourses on the Scriptural Doctrines of Atonement and Sacrifice* (1801).

73 *Correspondence*, Vol. 2, p. 229. No copies of the 1803 edition of the *Lives* appear to be extant. The preface, however, is preserved in Jebb's edition of Burnet's *Lives*, pp. xliii–xlvi. It will be cited hereafter as "Preface to the First Dublin Edition."

74 For the *Homilies*, see *Certain Sermons*. For Knox's views on the *Homilies*, see below, p. 44.

75 N. L. I., Ms 8868, Brodrick Papers, (folder 3). Knox to Charles Brodrick, letter, May 6, 1806. Emphasis in the original.

Knox brought out a second edition of Burnet's *Lives*, this time furnished with
a very High Church preface, which Magee found wholly admirable.[76] Richard
Graves, successively Professor of Laws (1809), Greek (1810), and Divinity (1819),
and Dean of Ardagh, 1814–29, was the Trinity man to whom Knox was personally closest. A frequent visitor to Dawson Street, Knox reported of him: "[H]e
loves our way of thinking as far as he knows it," although there is no indication
that either influenced the other's theology.[77]

Graves was by no means Knox's only visitor. Jebb applied to him the remark first made about John Hales: "His chamber was a church, and his chair
a pulpit."[78] Callers flocked to Knox, drawn by the bold and challenging nature
of his thought. As he noted concerning a visit to Bath in 1804, "[T]hose who
heard me were pleased; and surprised at having, as it were, religion presented
to them in so different a form from that to which they had been accustomed."[79]
It was not simply his ideas which attracted people, however, but also the eloquence with which he expressed them, a point frequently noted by contemporaries.[80] One, Daniel Parken, the editor of the *Eclectic Review*, describes Knox's
conversational abilities as follows:

> His manner of expression is natural and easy; fluent, in general, but not
> very fast; he hesitates, occasionally, for a word; and encumbers his diction
> with long, explanatory parentheses, from which, however, he returns duly
> to his proper topic. His language is commonly appropriate, and almost
> invariably pure; sometimes, exquisitely elegant; his imagery is copious,
> original, very suitable, and, mostly, well made out; occasionally, it is quite
> sublime. His voice is clear and pleasant, with a very little of the Irish tone.

---

76 *Correspondence*, Vol. 2, pp. 229–30. The second edition of *Lives, Characters, and a Sermon
    preached at the Funeral of the Hon. Robert Boyle by Gilbert Burnet, Lord Bishop of Sarum*,
    was published in Dublin by W. Watson in 1815. Knox's "Preface to the Second Dublin
    Edition" was reprinted in Jebb's 1833 edition of the *Lives*, pp. xlvii–lxx, and all quotations
    are taken from this source.

77 For Richard Graves (1764–1829), see Leslie, *Clergy of Dublin and Glendalough*, p. 677, as
    well as Graves's *Whole Works*. For Graves's relationship with Knox, see: *Remains*, Vol. 4,
    p. 380; *Correspondence*, Vol. 1, p. 210; Vol. 2, pp. 190–91; T. C. D., Ms 6396–6397, Jebb Papers,
    Correspondence 1795–1827, fol. 20, Charles Forster to John Jebb, letter, December 23, 1814;
    B. L., Add. Ms 41163, Correspondence between Alexander Knox and John Jebb (1799–1811),
    fol. 197, Knox to John Jebb, letter, March 17, 1809.

78 *Correspondence*, Vol. 1, p. 160.

79 *Remains*, Vol. 4, pp. 185–86. For Knox's visitors, see Vol. 2, pp. 220–21.

80 For testimonies to Knox's conversational powers, see, e.g., Bodleian, Ms. Eng. lett.
    d. 124, "Letters to C. A. Ogilvie, K-Z," fols. 101–2, Hannah More to C. A. Ogilvie, letter,
    July 19, [1815], fol. 101; *British Critic*, 17. 33 (January 1835), p. 160; *Christian Examiner*, 3. 35
    (September 1834), p. 632; *Correspondence*, Vol. 1, pp. 241, 478; *Dublin University Magazine*,
    4. 21 (September 1834), p. 243.

Parken also furnishes us with the following physical description of Knox:

> He is rather below the middle size, his head not large; his face rather long,
> rather narrow, and more rectangular than oval; his features interesting,
> rather than pleasing; his forehead high, but not wide; his eye quick, his
> eye-brow elevated; his nose aquiline; his under lip protruded; his muscles
> very full of motion; his complexion pale, apparently from ill health, but
> susceptible of a fine glow, when the subject of conversation became ani-
> mating ... He is small-limbed and thin. He wears spectacles, which very
> much become him. When highly interested, his countenance is full of
> action, his eye piercing, his cheek suffused, his gestures profuse and ener-
> getic, his whole form in motion and ready to start from his seat.[81]

As well as receiving visitors, Knox spent much of his time visiting other
people.[82] He was especially fond of Bellevue, the Delgany home of Peter La
Touche and his wife Elizabeth, and from 1803 until 1828, when Peter La Touche
died, he was there in almost constant residence. The beautiful setting and the
congenial company had a healing effect on his mental state: there was no former period of his life when he had known such composure, he related. As in
Dublin, Knox spent much of his time at Bellevue expounding his ideas to a
circle of admirers, passing "generally whole afternoons and evenings in the
parlour and drawing-room."[83] As well as talking, however, Knox also laboured
long hours in composing voluminous letters to his friends. Together with his
conversation, these letters made up what Gunstone describes as Knox's "method of personal influence." This topic of influence is the subject of chapter
thirteen, but for the moment it suffices to note that, despite his religious retirement, Knox nonetheless managed to propagate his ideas to what Gunstone
calls an astonishingly wide and varied audience.[84]

---

81 Both descriptions come from a letter dated September 5, 1809, and appear in Jebb's
    "Introduction" to Burnet's *Lives*, pp. xxxiii–xxxiv. For Daniel Parken (1785–1812), one of the
    founders of the *Eclectic Review*, which he edited from 1806 until his death, see Hiller, "The
    Eclectic Review, 1805–1868," p. 180. Parken mentions Knox wearing eye-glasses, whence his
    nick-name, "Spectacle" Knox.

82 B. L., Add. Ms, 41163, Correspondence between Alexander Knox and John Jebb (1799–
    1811), fol. 171, Knox to Jebb, letter, November 30, 1808.

83 For Knox's life at Bellevue, see: *Remains*, Vol. 4, pp. 124–25, 132, 318–19; *Correspondence*,
    Vol. 2, p. 53; Hornby, "Editor's Preface to the Third and Fourth Volumes," p. xix; Teignmouth,
    Reminiscences, Vol. 1, pp. 183–200, 281–82. Peter La Touche (1733–1828) was the scion of an
    important banking family of Huguenot extraction. Elizabeth (1759–1844) was his second
    wife. See McGuire and Quinn, eds, *Dictionary of Irish Biography*, Vol. 5, pp. 334–36.

84 For Gunstone's comments, see "Alexander Knox," p. 466.

Contemplation, conversation and correspondence were not Knox's only activities. "Association, Academy, charities, cut deeply into my time," he recorded.[85] The "Academy" was the Royal Irish Academy; the "Association," the A. D. V. Founded in 1792, and incorporated in 1800, its object was the distribution of Bibles and religious tracts.[86] Knox, as already noted, sat on the governing board, and also on the "Tract Committee." The "charities" were several. One was the Female Orphan House on North Circular Road, Dublin, of which, from 1809 onwards, Knox was "a very active governor," one who was "particularly anxious for the welfare of the establishment." This anxiety extended to the spiritual life of the orphans, to whom Knox sought to apply his High Church principles, by seeing that the chapel had "the external appearance and suitable appointments of a regular place of Church of England worship," with the services made "engaging and impressive."[87] Knox was also a governor of the Hospital for the Relief of Poor Lying in Women, in Great Britain Street; a member of the committee of the Dublin Institution; and a subscriber to the Magdalene Asylum, in Leeson Street. His main involvement, however, apart from the Orphan House, was with the Richmond Institution, founded in 1809, and located first on Great Britain Street, before moving to Sackville Street in 1814, and which provided employment for the blind.[88]

---

85   *Correspondence*, Vol. 2, p. 253. Compare Knox's complaint to Brodrick: "[B]usiness of the Association and of the R[oyal] I[rish] Academy has occupied me so as to leave no room for anything else," N. L. I., Ms 8868, Brodrick Papers, (folder 6), Knox to Charles Brodrick, letter, February 17, 1816.

86   See Nun, *Statutes Passed in the Parliaments held in Ireland*, Vol. 12, chapter lxvi, "An Act for incorporating the Association for discountenancing Vice, and promoting the Knowledge and Practice of the Christian Religion," pp. 234–37.

87   *Sixth Report of the Commissioners of Irish Education Inquiry*, "Appendix, No. 43, EXAMINATION of Mr. RICHARD MALINS, Monday, 29th of November 1824," p. 96; "Appendix, No. 45, EXAMINATION of Miss SARAH STEPHENS, Friday, 27th January 1826," p. 104; "Appendix, No. 46, EXAMINATION of ALEXANDER KNOX, Esq., Saturday, 28th January 1826," p. 107. For the Female Orphan House, see "Nemo," *Brief Record*.

88   For the institutions mentioned, see Warburton, Whitelaw, and Walsh, *History of the City of Dublin*, Vol. 2, pp. 669–82, 943–44, 770–73, 767–68. For Knox's association with them, see the *Treble Almanack* (1806), p. 136; (1815), p. 227; (1830), p. 198. The Richmond Institution is mentioned frequently in Knox's private papers: B. L., Add. Ms 41163, Correspondence between Alexander Knox and John Jebb (1799–1811), fol. 214, Knox to John Jebb, letter, December 27, 1809; Add. Ms 41164, Correspondence between Alexander Knox and John Jebb (1812–30), fol. 56, Knox to John Jebb, letter, May 20, 1815; fol. 82, Knox to John Jebb, letter, April 15, 1816; fol. 199, June 19, 1826; T. C. D., Ms 6396–6397, Jebb Papers, Correspondence 1795–1827, fol. 19, Charles Forster to John Jebb, letter, December 21, 1814.

5   Knox and John Jebb

We have seen that Knox's religious retirement did not mean isolation from other people. Friendships were important to him, and none more so than that which he enjoyed with John Jebb. Their "long intimacy," as Jebb termed it, began around 1790 in Londonderry, when Jebb was a pupil at the city's Free Grammar School.[89] It was a time which he was later to describe as the great hinge of his life, precisely because it brought him into contact with Knox, whom he described as being his "guide, philosopher, and friend."[90] They first met at a dinner held at the school and, despite an age-gap of some fifteen years, developed a close personal bond, a relationship perhaps best explained by the fact that Jebb was an orphan and Knox childless.[91] Their paths diverged for a short time after Jebb left school, but the friendship was subsequently renewed in Dublin. Guided by Knox, Jebb discovered that he had a call to ordination, and Knox introduced him to Charles Brodrick, then Bishop of Kilmore, in whose diocese Jebb started work as a clergyman, serving as curate of Swanlinbar. When Brodrick was translated to Cashel in 1801, Jebb followed him, becoming Rector of Abington, where he stayed until in 1822, when he was appointed Bishop of Limerick. In 1827 he suffered a stroke, as a result of which he moved to Wandsworth in England. Despite this, he did not resign his see, but continued to govern the diocese through a Vicar-General, James Forster, until his death in 1833.[92]

It was James Forster's brother, Charles, Jebb's biographer, who best summed up the symbiosis between the two men. "If Mr. Knox be Socrates," he wrote, "Mr. Jebb is Plato." By this Forster meant that Jebb was Knox's "pupil and voice."[93] His pupil, because it was to Knox that he was indebted for his theology;[94] his voice, because he was able to write about that theology with

---

89   For the phrase "long intimacy," see Forster, *Life of Jebb*, Vol. 1, p. 23, note. For Jebb (1775–1833), see, besides Forster, Acheson, *Jebb*.

90   *Correspondence*, Vol. 2, p. 111; Forster, *Life of Jebb*, Vol. 1, p. 23, note.

91   Forster speaks of Knox's "parental affection" for Jebb: T. C. D., Ms 6396–6397, Jebb Papers, Correspondence 1795–1827, fol. 184, Charles Forster to John Jebb, letter, September 15, 1819. See too, Jebb's remarks, in his "Introduction" to Burnet's *Lives*, p. xxix.

92   For James Forster (died 1861), Rector of Tankardstown and Aghadoe, Archdeacon of Aghadoe, 1834–61, see, Boase, *Modern English Biography*, Vol. 5, cols. 327–28.

93   Forster, *Life of Jebb*, Vol. 1, p. 87; Barrett, "Knox," p. 45. The two men's mutualism was already noted in the *Christian Examiner's* review of the *Correspondence*: "We can scarcely say that we have two writers" (3. 35, September 1834, p. 633).

94   G. T. Stokes calls Jebb "simply Knox's mouthpiece" (*Guardian*, September 14, 1887, p. 1382), while the *British Critic* notes: "[T]he formation of Bishop Jebb, as a divine, was principally the work of Knox" (17. 33, January 1835, p. 167). For Jebb's acknowledgement of the debt he

concision and clarity, whereas Knox had considerable difficulty expressing himself on paper. To quote the *Dublin University Magazine*:

> [Knox's] conversation was immeasurably beyond his composition. Nothing surprised his friends more than the felicity of his language, the happy arrangement of his thoughts, the exquisite richness and force of the imagery by which they were illustrated and adorned, except the fact, that, when he came to put the same matter into a written form, the production had all the appearance of a tame translation of himself.[95]

Knox freely acknowledged the problem, confessing his writing to be like "a Serbonian bog."[96] What was needed, he declared, was "a more digested, as well as [a] more systematized statement of all my views."[97] It was this that Jebb provided. As Gunstone says: "Jebb indeed mirrored Knox's teaching, but to its reflected light he added the clear outline of scholarly discipline."[98] As Jebb expressed it, he could "exhibit, with tolerable clearness and precision," Knox's theological principles, "and thus, in the end, the pair of us, may be enabled to do, what neither of us, separately, could have effected."[99] The negative view of Knox as a writer was not universal, however. Jebb, despite the remark just quoted, spoke of Knox's style as "true, luminous, and exquisitely English;" the *Eclectic Review* called it "easy, flowing, and often beautiful;" and the *British Critic* lauded its "vigour," "richness," and "loftiness."[100] The discrepancy is, perhaps, to be explained by the fact that most of Knox's extant writings were not intended for publication as they stood.[101] Knox did not therefore feel the need to polish them, as he did those works which he composed for public consumption.

---

owed to Knox, see: *Correspondence*, Vol. 2, pp. 59, 205–206, 479; "Introduction" to Burnet's *Lives*, pp. xxix–xxxii.

95   *Dublin University Magazine*, 4. 21, (September 1834), p. 242.

96   *Correspondence*, Vol. 2, p. 56. The Serbonian bog refers to a marshy region of Egypt. For self-deprecatory remarks by Knox about his style, see: *Remains*, Vol. 1, pp. 365–66; Vol. 4, pp. 473–75, 598; P. R. O. N. I., Castlereagh Papers, D3030/406, Knox to Lord Castlereagh, letter, December 12, 1798.

97   *Correspondence*, Vol. 2, p. 55.

98   Gunstone, "Alexander Knox," p. 467.

99   *Correspondence*, Vol. 2, p. 385.

100   Ibid., p. 2; *Eclectic Review*, new series, 13 (February 1835), p. 62; *British Critic*, 17. 33 (January 1835), p. 160. See, also: Gunstone, "Alexander Knox," p. 474; Maclagan, *The Grace of Sacraments*, pp. x–xi.

101   See below, pp. 107-8.

6   Roman Catholic Emancipation and Roman Catholicism

For Knox, life and religion were inseparably woven together. In subsequent chapters, we will explore his Anglicanism and his relationship to Methodism, as well as his theological ideas more generally. A word, however, must also be said about his attitudes towards Roman Catholicism. The *Christian Examiner* claimed that Knox was a "friend of Roman Catholics, both in a political and religious point of view."[102] The reality is more complex. Knox was, in his own words, "zealous ... for Roman Catholic enfranchisement." "My motives spread out would fill a volume," he told William Wilberforce.[103] They may, however, be summarized as follows. First, Knox believed that unless Roman Catholics were granted equal rights they would become disaffected, thus destabilizing Ireland and causing insecurity at the very heart of the British Empire. Emancipation, on the other hand, would, he held, guarantee their loyalty.[104] Second, Knox argued that the actual situation of Roman Catholics led them to distinguish themselves as much as possible from their Anglican neighbours. By contrast, Emancipation would bring about a reformation of Roman Catholicism, he argued. This reformation would then lead, he maintained, to reunification with the Anglican Church, something which he regarded as inevitable, being the will of Christ, as expressed in John 10, 16.[105] Knox was not alone in hoping for such a reconciliation. This was true even in Ireland, despite the general hardening of sectarian attitudes noted above.[106] Of particular significance was the proposal made in 1824 by James Doyle, the Roman Catholic Bishop of Kildare and Leighlin. Responding to a suggestion made in the House of Commons by the Chancellor of the Exchequer, Frederick John Robinson, that the Irish Catholic Church should unite with the Church of Ireland, Doyle suggested the

---

102   *Christian Examiner*, 3. 36, (October 1834), p. 718.
103   Knox to William Wilberforce, letter, March 23, 1817, in Wilberforce, *Correspondence*, Vol. 2, p. 361. For Wilberforce (1759–1833) see, as well as his *Correspondence*, Hague, *William Wilberforce*. For the background, see Hinde, *Catholic Emancipation*.
104   Bodleian, Ms. Wilberforce d. 13, fols. 310–11, Knox to William Wilberforce, letter, February 15, 1813, fol. 311; Knox to Lord Castlereagh, letter, February 9, 1801, in Vane, *Memoirs and Correspondence*, Vol. 4, pp. 29–33, at pp. 31–33.
105   Knox to William Wilberforce, letter, August 31, 1818, in Wilberforce, *Correspondence*, Vol. 2, pp. 397–410, at p. 401; Knox to Thomas Newenham, letter, July 7, 1824, in Doyle et al., *Letters on a Reunion*, pp. 26–31, at p. 31; *Remains*, Vol. 4, pp. 520–21; *Correspondence*, Vol. 1, p. 547; Vol. 2, p. 36.
106   For ideas about reunion in Ireland, see McBride, "The Common Name of Irishman." See, also, more generally on projects for reunion between the Church of England and the Roman Catholic Church in the late eighteenth and early nineteenth centuries, Ollard, *Reunion*, pp. 24–31.

establishment of a joint-commission of Roman Catholic and Anglican theologians, tasked with resolving disputed issues. Doyle's idea was eagerly taken up and promoted by the former M. P. for Clonmel in the Irish Parliament, Thomas Newenham.[107] Knox, by contrast, was more hesitant and made his views known in two letters, one to Newenham, and a second to James Dunne, the Rector of Delgany.[108] These letters joined an earlier missive concerning reunion addressed to Wilberforce in 1818. In it Knox, somewhat disingenuously, sought to distance himself from another reunion scheme, similar to Doyle's, set out by Samuel Wix in his *Reflections concerning the Expediency of a Council of the Church of England and the Church of Rome* (1818). Knox's fear was that, if he were to be identified with Wix's scheme, this would jeopardize his attempts to enlist Wilberforce's support for Roman Catholic Emancipation.[109]

Knox's position was that (as noted above) reformation had to precede reconciliation. Before then, while charity and understanding were to be encouraged, reunion itself would be impossible.[110] But what, for him, needed to be reformed? It is noteworthy that Knox virtually ignored many issues that were often seen by Protestants as obstacles to unity: purgatory, indulgences, the sacrifice of the Mass, and devotion to Mary and the saints. The reason for this was that he understood most of these issues to be not so much doctrinal problems as practical matters, and, thus, relatively easy to resolve. "[N]o embarrassment can arise, in altering mere matters of practice," he contended, "should motives occur for such alteration."[111] With regard to the eucharistic sacrifice, this was a doctrine that he himself held, so it was not a topic which he regarded as divisive.[112] As for the saints, his views, to a certain extent, tended towards the Roman Catholic position. Commenting on Ephesians 2.19, which speaks of Christians as συμπολῖται τῶν ἁγίων [*sympolitai tōn hagiōn*] "fellow-citizens of the saints," Knox observed that the following conclusions may be deduced:

1. That the ἁγίοι with whom we are συμπολῖται, *are peculiarly the invisible ἁγίοι*; 2. That to think of these, our fellow-citizens, and cultivate our

107   For James Doyle (1786–1834) see McGrath, *Bishop James Doyle*. For Doyle's reunion scheme, see *Letters on a Reunion*, pp. 1–10. For Thomas Newenham (1762–1831), see *O. D. N. B.*
108   For Knox's letter to Newenham see *Letters on a Reunion*, pp. 26–31. The letter to Dunne appears in the *Remains*, Vol. 3, pp. 314–30. For James Dunne (1767–1838), Rector of Delgany from 1810 until 1817, see Leslie, *Clergy of Dublin and Glendalough*, p. 598. (In the *Remains* Dunne is spelled without an "e.")
109   Wilberforce, *Correspondence*, Vol. 2, pp. 397–410. For Samuel Wix (1771–1861), High Church Vicar of St. Bartholomew-the-Less, London, see *O. D. N. B.*
110   Knox to Thomas Newenham, letter, July 7, 1824, in Doyle et al., *Letters on a Reunion*, pp. 26–31, at p. 30.
111   *Correspondence*, Vol. 2, p. 37. See, also, *Remains*, Vol. 4, p. 305.
112   See below, pp. 209–210.

relation to them, must be a true exercise of faith; and 3. That this very exercise, is a natural, if not an essential part, of the πολίτευμα ἐν οὐρανοῖς [*politeuma en ouranois*].[113]

The context of the passage shows that by cultivating a relationship with the saints Knox meant contemplating them, but the step from that to asking their prayers would seem to be a small one, especially as Knox held that the saints in paradise intercede for those on earth.[114] Concerning the Virgin Mary in particular, Jebb made the comment that Knox enjoyed hearing Roman Catholics speak of her as the Mother of God, since the epithet underlined the reality of the Incarnation.[115]

For Knox the issues of real contention between Anglicans and Roman Catholics were two: the supremacy of the Pope and the doctrine of transubstantiation.[116] With regard to the first, he viewed the papacy simply as an exercise in tyranny,[117] while transubstantiation he saw as a modern dogma, unknown to the Fathers, one whose materialism contradicted the spiritual nature of the sacrament.[118] "[W]e resist [it], and must resist [it]," he wrote in 1811; it would be the "last remaining barrier to coalescence."[119] The same stance is found in his 1824 *Inquiry on Grounds of Scripture and Reason into the Use and Import of the Eucharistic Symbols*, as well as in a letter addressed in 1826 to J. S. Harford.[120] Given these statements, it is a surprise to find Knox telling Newenham in 1824 that, if there were nothing else but transubstantiation dividing them, the Church of England and the Roman Catholic Church might easily come to an understanding.[121] Possibly the anomaly is to be explained by the caveat which Knox makes to Newenham, that he is talking about the doctrine of transubstantiation as elucidated by the Council of Trent, which may

---

113   *Remains*, Vol. 1, pp. 422–23. Knox alludes, at the end, to Philippians 3, 20, "citizenship of heaven" (my translation).
114   *Remains*, Vol. 4, pp. 427–28.
115   Jebb, "Introduction" to Burnet's *Lives*, p. xxxviii.
116   *Correspondence*, Vol. 1, p. 547.
117   *Remains*, Vol. 1, p. 418; Vol. 3, pp. 316–19, 324; Vol. 4, p. 243; *Answer to Duigenan*, pp. 62–63; Knox to Thomas Newenham, letter, July 7, 1824, in Doyle et al., *Letters on a Reunion*, pp. 26–31, at p. 28.
118   *Remains*, Vol. 2, pp. 157, 160, 168, 178–83, 190; *Correspondence*, Vol. 2, pp. 36–39.
119   *Correspondence*, Vol. 2, p. 37.
120   "Letter to John S. Harford, Esq., Prefatory to the Treatise on the Eucharist," *Remains*, Vol. 2, pp. 154–83. Dated July 19, 1826, the letter was clearly intended to be prefaced to a second edition of the "Treatise on the Use and Import of the Eucharistic Symbols." This second edition did not, however, appear in Knox's lifetime. For John Scandrett Harford (1785–1866), Clamphamite layman, see *O. D. N. B.*
121   Knox to Thomas Newenham, letter, July 7, 1824, in Doyle et al., *Letters on a Reunion*, pp. 26–31, at p. 28.

imply that he understood the Council to have taught something other than what he elsewhere termed "the gross doctrine of a literal transubstantiation."[122] Unfortunately, however, he did not clarify his meaning.

Despite his criticisms of the Roman Church, Knox nonetheless valued the way in which it had retained many elements of what he called "original Catholicity."[123] Even if these primitive elements had been overlaid by later innovations, they still continued to form, in his view, an integral part of the Roman system, making it more attractive to him than those many forms of Protestantism which he saw as having rejected what he called the "catholic verities."[124] As he told Jebb, "I prize what the church of Rome possesses, so deeply, as to make me prefer their religion to sectarianism, in whatever plausible form the latter may appear." Or, as he put it in his *Answer to Duigenan*, "[T]he *Catholic Roman* [is] ... a sounder Christian ... than an *uncatholic Protestant*." Writing to Newenham, he went even further and declared that when it came to controverted issues, there were many areas in which truth was to be found more on the Roman than on the Protestant side.[125] Conversely, the Catholic elements in the Roman Church made for what Knox termed "consanguinity" between it and Anglicanism.[126] This consanguinity was to be seen, he maintained, in the fact that Anglicans were indebted to the Roman Church for much of their liturgy, as well as for their episcopal constitution and their doctrine.[127] Thus, Knox argued, reunion would be of benefit to Anglicans by helping to restore to prominence certain parts of their own patrimony which had been obscured, not least by the growth of Pan-Protestantism.[128] But even before reunion was accomplished, there was much, he held, that Anglicans could already glean from the Roman Church, not least in the realm of spirituality, Roman authors in this area being, in his judgement, "cast in the mould of the very holiest of the Fathers."[129]

---

122   *Remains*, Vol. 2, p. 190.
123   Ibid., Vol. 3, p. 315.
124   On the term "catholic verities," see below, p. 112.
125   *Correspondence*, Vol. 1, p. 459; *Answer to Duigenan*, p. 61 (emphases in the original); Knox to Thomas Newenham, letter, July 7, 1824, in Doyle et al., *Letters on a Reunion*, pp. 26–31, at p. 28. See also, *Remains*, Vol. 4, p. 305, and below, p. 172.
126   N. L. I., Ms 8868, Brodrick Papers (folder 3), Knox to Charles Brodrick, letter, November 11, 1808.
127   *Remains*, Vol. 4, p. 482; *Correspondence*, Vol. 2, pp. 322–24; *Answer to Duigenan*, pp. 41–42; Bodleian, Ms. Eng. lett. d. 124, "Letters to C. A. Ogilvie, K-Z," fols. 85–87, Knox to C. A. Ogilvie, letter, January 23, 1827, fols. 85; 86.
128   *Remains*, Vol. 1, pp. 402–3, 406–7; Vol. 3, pp. 188–90; Vol. 4, p. 608; *Correspondence*, Vol. 1, p. 459; Bodleian, Ms. Eng. lett. d. 124, "Letters to C. A. Ogilvie, K-Z," fols. 85–87, Knox to C. A. Ogilvie, letter, January 23, 1827, fol. 86.
129   *Remains*, Vol. 3, p. 110. See, also: Vol. 1, p. 131; Vol. 4, pp. 249–50, 487.

7   Knox's Death

Knox died at his Dawson Street residence around nine in the morning on Friday, June 17, 1831.[130] He was buried a few days later at his nearby parish church of St Ann. But he did not rest for long in peace. In 1836 a controversy erupted over his last days which serves to illustrate his importance as a theological thinker.[131] The controversy began with a letter from the leading Evangelical, Thomas Kelly, to the *Christian Observer*, claiming that he had visited Knox, with whom he was well-acquainted, a little before his demise, and that Knox had told him, "I begin to suspect, my dear Mr. Kelly, that I have not been *sufficiently evangelical*." Kelly took this to mean that Knox had, in the face of death, abandoned his own theological "system," to embrace the more comforting tenets, as Kelly saw them, of the Evangelical understanding of Christianity. "Mr. Knox had found his theories, however ingenious, to fail him in time of need," Kelly declared.[132] The story was taken up by other Evangelical newspapers, but met with a vigorous rebuttal from Hornby, both in an advertisement in the *Times*, and in the preface to the third and fourth volumes of the *Remains*. Kelly, however, maintained his position. "That my statement is *true*, I know," he asserted. "And that my opinion is *well-founded*, I am confident."[133] Although he confessed this opinion to be an impression, it was nonetheless an impression which was, he claimed, shared by several of Knox's other acquaintances. The matter was important for Evangelicals, because they thought that it showed the weakness of Knox's "system," which they perceived as a serious challenge to their doctrine of justification by faith alone, and thus to their aspiring hegemony over the Irish Church.[134]

---

130   Hornby, "Editor's Preface to the Third and Fourth Volumes," pp. xxix–xxx; Forster, *Life of Jebb*, Vol. 1, p. 376.

131   For a full account, see Hornby, "Editor's Preface to the Third and Fourth Volumes," pp. xii–cvii. See, too, T. C. D., Ms 6398, Correspondence of the Reverend John Jebb (1805–1886), 1827–1869, fol. 53, John Jebb, junior to J. J. Hornby, letter, October 2, 1836. It is worth noting that rumours about Knox's repudiation of his own views had been circulating prior to his death, and were explicitly denied by him (*Remains*, Vol. 4, pp. 561–63).

132   *Christian Observer*, 36 (August 1836), pp. 491–92. For Thomas Kelly (1769–1855) see Carter, *Anglican Evangelicals*, pp. 69–77.

133   *Christian Observer*, 37 (April 1837), p. 226 (emphasis in the original); Appendix (1837), pp. 809, 811.

134   *Christian Observer*, 37 (April 1837), p. 226. See, also, O'Brien, *Justification*, 3rd edition, pp. 437–38. For Knox's teaching on justification, see below, pp. 168–89.

8   Conclusion

In 1861, a stained-glass window was erected at St Ann's Church, Dublin, in Knox's honour; it depicts the Matthean parables, which were the subject of one of his essays in the *Remains*. The church also houses a memorial tablet, which bears the following inscription:

> ALEXANDER KNOX, died June 17, A. D. 1831. He was a true and real, a spiritual and practical, an informed and enlightened, a primitive and catholic Christian. His intellect was of a high order of ardent and soaring genius: discursive, intuitive, imaginative, judicious, he communicated truth with great force of argument, and splendour of eloquence, in writing and speech. To a temperament constitutionally nervous, timid, refined, sensitive, the warmth of his affections supplied energy, which gave zeal and constancy to his friendships, and courage to sustained exertions in a good cause. At an early age he gave up the world and its distinctions, devoting every power to the immediate service of God and His Word: that Word, in its letter and spirit, in its principles and their effects, was the satisfaction of his heart and mind: it gave enlightenment to the whole man in all his faculties. Cultivating it diligently, and bringing forth its fruits, he realised to himself the great fact, that the Gospel of Christ, by a justifying and sanctifying efficacy, is, to everyone that believeth, the power of God unto salvation. A cordial adherent of the Church of England, he loved her best in her universal character as a living member of Christ's body; and gave the right hand of fellowship to all who under any form possessed her spirit; rejoicing that in Christ Jesus neither circumcision availeth anything nor uncircumcision, but a new creature. As he lived the life of faith, so he died in the sure Christian hope of a resurrection to glory.[135]

Such, then, was the life of Alexander Knox. Our account of it, however, is but a prelude to the study of what truly makes him a figure of abiding significance: his theological thinking. It is to this that we now turn, beginning in the following chapter with his understanding of Anglicanism.

---

135   *Journal of the Association for the Preservation of the Memorials of the Dead in Ireland*, 2. 1 (1892), p. 85.

CHAPTER 2

Alexander Knox and Anglicanism

Alexander Knox's epitaph describes him as a "cordial adherent of the Church of England." Gladstone said of him that "he almost adored" the Anglican Church.[1] So, in this chapter, I will consider Knox's Anglicanism. I will look particularly at the theoretical account that he gave of it, his appeal to antiquity and his treatment of the Prayer Book and other ecclesiastical standards. I will also describe his High Churchmanship and his relationship with English Evangelicals, especially with Hannah More.

1 Knox as a Theoretician of Anglicanism

That, as an Irishman, Knox should write about the Church of England may at first sight seem strange. However, not only were the Churches of England and Ireland legally united from 1801 to 1870, but also Knox himself regarded the English Church as extending beyond the Provinces of Canterbury and York to cover the entirety of the British Empire. Thus, he spoke of "the united Church of the whole Empire;" of "the only Church of the Empire;" and, in relation to it, of "our Irish branch of the Anglican church."[2] Knox's use of the term "Anglican" is noteworthy. The Church of England in the first quarter of the nineteenth century found itself confronted by two major transformative factors: global expansion and local contraction. With the growth of Empire, the Church had scions spread throughout the world, but at the same time, in England itself, it was in decline. The ties which bound it to the state were loosening, as "infidelity," Roman Catholicism, and Dissent all gained an ever-stronger position in society. The qualification "of England" seemed, therefore, no longer entirely adequate. A new term was needed, one which would, moreover, help to underline the distinctive character of the Church in relation both to Roman Catholicism and to other reformed churches.[3]

---

1 B. L., Add. Ms 44724, Gladstone Papers, DCXXXIX, fols. 73–76, "memorandum" on Knox's *Remains*, fol. 76.

2 P. R. O. N. I., Castlereagh Papers, D3030/1123, Knox, "Draft Comments on the Union of the Churches" [1798]; *Correspondence*, Vol. 2, p. 495.

3 In both this and subsequent chapters, "Church" with a capital C designates the Church of England: "church" with a small c designates the universal body of Christians.

© KONINKLIJKE BRILL NV, LEIDEN, 2020 | DOI:10.1163/9789004426986_004

"Anglican" was the term which eventually came to prevail, a designation which Knox was among the first to employ.[4] The earliest occurrence in his writings is to be found in a letter to Hannah More, dated 1806, "On the Design of Providence respecting the Christian Church," and thereafter he employs it frequently.[5] More important than the word, however, was the content which Knox gave to it. Although the term "Anglicanism" post-dates him, first appearing in 1836,[6] he nonetheless produced a coherent theory of what it means to be Anglican. This theory appears throughout his writings, but its clearest and most systematic formulation is in an appendix to Jebb's *Sermons On Subjects Chiefly Practical* (1815).[7] The theory holds that the Church of England is distinct from Roman Catholicism because of the authority which it gives to Scripture.[8] But, because the Church appeals to "antiquity" as well as to the Bible, it is distinct also from other reformed denominations.[9] It steers "a middle course," as Knox puts it, "equidistant from puritanism on the one hand, and from popery on the other."[10] Knox thus presages the via media position which Newman was later to make more famous;[11] but also, as Newman himself acknowledged, Knox had a significant impact on his own development of the concept.[12] By distancing the Church of England from other reformed bodies, Knox implied in the *Appendix* that it was not Protestant. Elsewhere, he was more explicit. Writing to Jebb, he asserted that the "nick-name of protestant" had had a "perverse influence" on Anglican self-understanding.[13] This rejection of the Protestant nature of Anglicanism distinguished Knox from the vast majority of contemporary High Churchmen. For them, the Church was both Catholic, because it held to the primitive faith, and Protestant, because it rejected the Roman innovations

---

4   For the history of the term "Anglican," see Podmore, *Aspects of Anglican Identity*, pp. 35–37.

5   For Knox's letter "On the Design of Providence," see *Remains*, Vol. 3, pp. 103–230. The term "Anglican" appears on pp. 115 and 189. For other instances of Knox's use of the term, see: *Remains*, 1, pp. 130; 132; 133; 289; 309; 310; 2, p. 281, note; 3, pp. 64; 290; 295; 297; 303; 328; 4, p. 482; *Correspondence*, 1, p. 576; 2, pp. 190; 495.

6   [Wiseman], "The Oxford Controversy," p. 264.

7   The *Appendix*, as it will be referred to hereafter, covers pages 357–98 of the *Sermons*. For Knox's contribution to the work, see: *Appendix*, p. 355; *Remains*, Vol. 4, p. 463; *Correspondence*, Vol. 2, pp. 225–26, 232, 245.

8   *Appendix*, p. 358.

9   Ibid.

10   Ibid., p. 397; *Remains*, Vol. 3, p. 329.

11   Newman, *Lectures on Certain Difficulties*, p. 307.

12   Nockles, "Church or Protestant Sect?" p. 464. For a fuller treatment of the issue, see Allen, *John Henry Newman and the Abbé Jager*. Allen deals at length with the influence of the *Appendix* on Newman, but says surprisingly little about Knox. For the relationship between Newman and Knox, see below, pp. 247-53.

13   *Correspondence*, Vol. 2, p. 125.

(as they saw them) by which that faith had been overlaid.[14] Knox's standpoint did, however, once again anticipate the attitude of the Tractarians, who held the Church to be, in Newman's words, "merely *reformed*, not Protestant."[15] Protestantism, for Knox, was as much a threat to Anglican identity as Roman Catholicism. "[I]f Popery can be a Charybdis," he wrote, "there is a Scylla, on the other side, not less dangerous."[16] The peril lay, he reasoned, in the doctrine of *sola scriptura*, the idea that "the Bible alone" was authoritative in matters of faith. Once this principle was allowed, and, consequently, the interpretative authority of Catholic antiquity was lost, then doctrinal disaster followed automatically. As confirmation, he argued that one had only to look at the other reformed churches and the heterodoxy into which they had fallen.[17] "The Church of England alone appears to have escaped this warping influence;" he contended, because it alone combined the "study of the sacred word ... with a reverent attention to Catholic consent."[18]

2   The Appeal to Antiquity

The idea of "Catholic consent," the *consensus omnium*, was derived by Knox from the *Commonitorium* of St. Vincent of Lérins, or "Vincentius Lirinensis," as he called him.[19] Seeking to establish a rule or "canon" by which the truth in religious controversies could be determined, Vincent had argued that "we must take care to hold what has been believed everywhere, always, and by all."[20] This rule, which Knox states in a slightly different form, was fundamental to his theology, for he saw it as providing the very definition of the Catholic faith.[21] Having been believed always, the *consensus omnium* was often also presented by Knox in terms of "antiquity," by which he meant the unanimous

---

14   Nockles, *Oxford Movement in Context*, p. 154. For an example of the standard pre-Tractarian High Church position, see Daubeny, *The Protestant's Companion*.
15   [Newman], *Tract 71*, p. 32 (emphasis in the original).
16   *Remains*, Vol. 1, p. 58.
17   *Appendix*, p. 367.
18   Ibid., pp. 367–68.
19   For the Latin text, see, besides Migne, *P. L.*, 50, cols. 637–686, Moxon, ed., *The Commonitorium of Vicentius of Lerins*. The word *commonitorium* might be translated "an aid to memory." Unless otherwise stated, all translations from patristic sources are my own. For Vincent (died c. 445), see, also, Guarino, *Vincent of Lérins*.
20   "[C]urandum est ut id teneamus quod ubique, quod semper, quod ab omnibus creditum est," Vincent, *Commonitorium*, 2, *P. L.*, 50, col. 640. In modern times the rule is usually cited, as in Knox, "*semper, ubique et ab omnibus*."
21   *Remains*, Vol. 3, pp. 67, 292.

teaching of the Fathers, the *consensus patrum*.[22] This did not, however, make him an inflexible traditionalist. He believed that Anglicanism was eminently balanced: "a combination," as he put it, "of mental freedom, and mental discipline; of adherence to all that has received the concurrent stamp of times that are past; and of openness to all those intellectual improvements, with which the goodness of Providence may yet be pleased to bless posterity."[23] Knox thus believed in the development of doctrine.[24] Without abandoning their fundamental teaching, Anglicanism had, in his view, "improved upon the fathers."[25] As he wrote in a letter to Daniel Parken:

> The Church of England, on the whole ... has carefully retained and preserved all the treasures of the ancients ... but she has not buried it [*sic*] in a napkin. She has traded with her five talents; nor is the time of occupying yet over: she may, in the end, have ten talents to deliver to the great Taskmaster. In the mean time [*sic*], what equal instance have we of approach to that description of the mystical 'householder, who bringeth forth out of his treasures things new and old?'[26]

Numerous editions and translations of the *Commonitorium* had been circulating in Europe since the seventeenth century, and Church of England writers had consistently invoked it, as they defended Anglican doctrine by an appeal to patristic tradition. The wish to keep the Church of England primitive was, Knox argued, the "uniform spirit and feeling of all the Anglican divines."[27] It was an assertion in evidence of which he furnished a catena of quotations from earlier authors.[28] Nonetheless, there was an important difference between Knox's teaching and that of other High Churchmen. As Newman's pupil, S. F. Wood, expressed it, Knox produced "in a modern shape the Anglican Rule of Faith."[29] For other High Churchmen, Anglicanism and antiquity were

---

22 For the *consensus omnium* and the *consensus patrum*, see, also, below, pp. 127–33.

23 *Appendix*, p. 368.

24 The idea of development is also present in Vincent, *Commonitorium*, 23, *P. L.*, 50, cols. 667–68.

25 *Remains*, Vol. 1, p. 299.

26 Ibid., pp. 299–300. Knox alludes to the parable of the talents, Matthew 25. 14–30, as well as to the logion of Matthew 13. 52.

27 *Correspondence*, Vol. 1, p. 576. Compare Newman's claim: "[T]he Anglican plea was antiquity" (*Apologia*, p. 102). For the use of the *Commonitorium* in Europe generally, see Pelikan, *Christian Doctrine and Modern Culture*, p. 80.

28 *Appendix*, pp. 388–96.

29 Wood, "Revival of Primitive Doctrine," p. 254. Wood is speaking of the *Appendix*, and does not mention of Knox at this point. A little later, however, he writes of Jebb's indebtedness

substantially identical because the Fathers were seen as espousing the doctrine of the Church of England; they were "marshalled in Anglican order and
costume," to borrow Tom Mozley's words.[30] For Knox, by contrast, the Church
of England was identical with antiquity because it espoused the doctrine of
the Fathers. "[O]ur Church follows the ancient Church," he contended; it was
this, in his view, that made its teaching authoritative.[31] Because of the identity
of the Church's teaching with that of antiquity, Knox held that, in order to be
properly understood, the Anglican formularies had to be interpreted by reference to the Fathers. No one could, he maintained, "understand the Church of
England, until they have recourse to the ancient Catholic church."[32] To quote
again from his letter to Parken: "[I]f we would understand our formularies,
we must resort to the sources from whence they were derived, and consult
[the] ancients."[33] The corollary of this was that, if anything were to be found
in the Church of England which was incompatible with Catholic antiquity, it
should be regarded as something foreign to the true genius of Anglicanism and
corrected accordingly.[34] All this is important because, once again, it set Knox
apart from contemporary High Churchmen, and marked him out as a precursor of the Tractarians. They, too, held as a fundamental principle:

> Reverence for and deference to the Ancient Church, of which our own
> Church is looked upon as the representative to us, and by whose views
> and doctrines we interpret our own Church when her meaning is ques-
> tioned or doubtful: in a word, reference to the Ancient Church, instead of
> the Reformers, as the ultimate expounder of the meaning of our Church.[35]

Despite his contention that the Church of England was subject to the judgement of antiquity, for Knox any dissonance between Anglican and patristic
teaching was merely hypothetical. He believed the Anglican Church to be

---

         to Knox (p. 262). For Samuel Francis Wood (1809–43), see Ker and Gornall, eds., *L. &. D.*,
         Vol. 2, p. 416.
30   Mozley, *Reminiscences*, Vol. 2, p. 400. Ironically, Mozley was talking about Newman's
         method of argumentation in *The Arians of the Fourth Century*. For Thomas Mozley
         (1806–93), clergyman and journalist, see *O. D. N. B.*
31   *Remains*, Vol. 1, p. 309.
32   N. L. I., Ms 8868, Brodrick Papers (folder 5), Knox to Charles Brodrick, letter, January 23,
         1812.
33   *Remains*, Vol. 1, p. 385.
34   For the enunciation of this principle, see: *Remains*, Vol. 3, p. 45; *Correspondence*, Vol. 1,
         pp. 562–63.
35   Liddon, *Life of Pusey*, Vol. 2, p. 140, quoting Pusey.

"radically primitive," entirely faithful to the Vincentian position.[36] "[N]ext to the explicit word of God, pious antiquity is the standard of the Church of England," he declared.[37] As he wrote in the preface to his second edition of Burnet's *Lives*: "[W]e, of the church of England, are only echoing the voices, repeating the movements, and tracing the footsteps, of the great body of the church militant, which has marched on before."[38] Anglicans, he affirmed, "are, in the justest and strictest sense, Catholic; that is, diligent inquirers after the united sense of the regular Christian church (in interpreting Holy Scripture), and steady adherents to what we thus find clearly avouched to us."[39] Although he could be more nuanced, Knox at times even went so far as to claim that the Church of England was the "exclusive providential conservatory of ancient Catholic faith and ancient Catholic piety."[40] As he told James Dunne: "[W]hat else did the Church of England at the Reformation, than follow the spirit of Vincentius's principle? And, it may even now be asked, Where, except by the Church of England alone, has this principle been practically and consistently maintained?"[41] Or, as he told Jebb, the Vincentian principle "at this day exists no where [*sic*], but in the genuine central essence of our own reformed episcopal church."[42]

3   The Prayer Book

Knox saw the primitive nature of the Church manifested in two main areas. The first was the episcopate, though this was not an idea that he developed.[43] By contrast, the Catholicity of the Prayer Book was a constant theme. "Were a Christian of the third or fourth generation to revisit the earth and be present at our public worship, what difference would he find?" he asked in a question

---

36   "Preface to the Second Dublin Edition," p. lxii; *Remains*, Vol. 3, p. 323.
37   *Remains*, Vol. 1, p. 384. The principle is often affirmed in Knox's writings; see, for example: *Remains*, Vol. 1, pp. 66–67; Vol. 2, pp. 167–68, 175; Vol. 3, pp. 43–45, 65–66, 295; Vol. 4, pp. 240, 402–3; *Correspondence*, Vol. 2, p. 125.
38   "Preface to the Second Dublin Edition," p. lxiii.
39   *Remains*, Vol. 4, p. 240.
40   Ibid., Vol. 2, p. 175. See also *Correspondence*, Vol. 2, p. 482. For Knox's more nuanced approach, see, e.g.: Bodleian, Ms. Eng. lett. d. 124, "Letters to C. A. Ogilvie, K-Z," fols. 85–87, Knox to C. A. Ogilvie, letter, January 23, 1827, fol. 86; *Remains*, Vol. 1, pp. 406–7; Vol. 3, pp. 211–12.
41   *Remains*, Vol. 3, p. 323.
42   *Correspondence*, Vol. 2, p. 125.
43   For the theme of the episcopate in Knox, see, e.g.: *Remains*, Vol. 3, p. 69; Vol. 4, pp. 482–83; *Correspondence*, Vol. 2, pp. 17–18; *Answer to Duigenan*, pp. 40, 63.

reminiscent to us of a comment later made by Newman.[44] For Knox , the Book of Common Prayer contained "every thing [sic] essential to Catholic theology, set forth in terms the most simple, luminous, and impressive."[45] It was "a body of practical theology" which served as "a standard ... of doctrine as well as of devotion."[46] Despite this high regard for the Prayer Book then in use, that of 1662, Knox expressed a preference for the original 1549 edition. This preference appears in his private correspondence with Jebb, as well as in his published writings, and is based on his belief that the 1549 Book provided a more acceptable expression of Eucharistic doctrine than that of 1662.[47] In all this, one is struck, once again, by Knox's foreshadowing of the Tractarians. For them, the liturgy was, in Newman's words, "the living authority, on which they based their theological system."[48] Like Knox, they also preferred 1549 to 1662 and, given their appreciation for Knox's teaching on the Eucharist, this predilection for the older liturgy may be another instance of his having influenced their views.[49]

4   The Other Anglican Standards

Knox held that the Thirty-Nine Articles were subordinate to the Prayer Book as the primary doctrinal standard,[50] a position where, again, we see him anticipating the Tractarians.[51] Knox's contention was that, while the Prayer Book embodied "the sublime piety of the primitive Church," the Articles drew their

---

44   *Christian Observer*, 15. 6 (June 1816), p. 360. The letter from which this quotation comes runs from pages 358 to 365. Signed "Amicus," it is a defence of the *Appendix*; the style and argumentation point to Knox as its author. Newman's later comment, made as a Roman Catholic, was: "Did St. Athanasius or St. Ambrose come suddenly to life, it cannot be doubted what communion they would mistake for their own" (*Essay on the Development of Christian Doctrine*, p. 138).

45   *Remains*, Vol. 3, p. 68.

46   Ibid., p. 63.

47   B. L., Add. Ms 41164, Correspondence between Alexander Knox and John Jebb (1812–1830), fol. 245, Knox to John Jebb, letter,? January 1816; *Remains*, Vol. 2, pp. 168–75.

48   Newman, *Lectures on Certain Difficulties*, p. 109.

49   For the Tractarian preference for the 1549 rite, see Härdelin, *Tractarian Understanding of the Eucharist*, p. 253. For the Tractarian appreciation of Knox's Eucharistic theology, see below, pp. 247–48, 250, 253, 254–55.

50   For the idea of "standards" in Anglicanism, see, e.g., Sykes, Booty, and Knight, eds, *The Study of Anglicanism*, Part IV: "Anglican Standards" (pp. 131–245).

51   For Knox's position, see *Remains*, Vol. 3, pp. 61–62. For the Tractarian position, see, e.g.,: [Newman], *Tract 38*, passim; *Remarks on Certain Passages in the Thirty-Nine Articles* (*Tract 90*), pp. 4, 80; Newman, *The Via Media of the Anglican Church*, Vol. 2, pp. 253–57.

"materials ... from later times."[52] Not only, however, were the Articles modern;
a number of them also suffered, in Knox's view, from doctrinal imperfections.
They contained "a series of hair-breadth 'scapes," by which he meant that they
came perilously close to "injuring the integrity of primitive truth."[53] Indeed,
writing to Brodrick, he went so far as to say that they were infected with the
fungi of Calvinism.[54] In spite of such strictures, Knox did appeal to the Articles
in his writings. Thus, in his teaching on the Eucharist, he cited Articles xxv,
xxviii and xxix, while in his work on justification, he quoted Articles xi
and xii.[55] He did so, first, because he did not think all the Articles unsound;
some he esteemed excellent. For example, he held that the Catholic doctrine of the sacraments "could scarcely be expressed with greater simplicity
or strength" than in the words of Article xxv.[56] Second, even those Articles
which he judged "pernicious" were "not poisonous."[57] They were capable of
being interpreted in an orthodox sense. Thus, discussing Articles xi and xii,
on the question of justification, he claimed that, once they had been care-
fully examined, "[t]he inference, on the whole, is, that justification (or acceptance with God), is most essentially, connected with moral obedience."[58] As
well as the Articles, Knox also appealed to the Church Catechism, which he
cited in his teaching on baptism and the Eucharist.[59] He appealed, likewise, to
the *Homilies*, although he declined to consider them as binding statements of
the Church's faith. They are "not ... in any respect, *authoritative* in the English
Church," he asserted.[60]

John Henry Newman to R. F. Wilson, letter, May 13, 1835, in Gornall, ed., *L. & D.*, Vol. 5, pp. 70–71, at p. 70.
52   *Remains*, Vol. 4, p. 302.
53   Ibid., Vol. 3, pp. 83, 84.
54   N. L. I., Ms 8868, Brodrick Papers (folder 3), Knox to Charles Brodrick, letter, November 11, 1808.
55   *Remains*, Vol. 2, pp. 189–91; Vol. 1, pp. 291–93.
56   Ibid., Vol. 2, p. 189.
57   N. L. I., Ms 8868, Brodrick Papers (folder 3), Knox to Charles Brodrick, letter, November 11, 1808.
58   *Remains*, Vol. 3, p. 85.
59   Ibid., Vol. 1, p. 496; Vol. 2, pp. 191–93.
60   "A Member of the Tract Committee" [Alexander Knox], *The Judgment of the Tract Committee*, p. 13 (emphasis in the original). See also: Bodleian, Ms. Eng. lett. c. 140, "Papers Relating to Thomas Burgess," fol. 97, copy of a letter from Knox to James Wilson, December 27, 1825; *Remains*, Vol. 1, pp. 293–98. Knox's attitude to the *Homilies* was the sub- ject of considerable controversy; see the *Christian Examiner*: 4. 21 (March 1827), pp. 216– 32; 22 (April 1827), pp. 292–311; 23 (May 1827), pp. 386–88; 26 (June 1827), pp. 434–61.

5   High Churchmanship

Previous studies of Knox have emphasized his ecclesiastical idiosyncrasy, and he himself insisted on his independence from all church parties.[61] Yet his individualism should not be pressed too far. Although he distanced himself from others who owned that designation, he defined himself as a High Churchman.[62] Or, as he told one correspondent, "I am a primitive Churchman; prizing in our system, most cordially, what it has retained from Christian antiquity, as well as what it has gained from the good sense of the Reformers in expurgating it from later abuses."[63] This churchmanship was manifested primarily in what Knox termed "just and adequate views of the sacraments, the church, and the Scriptures."[64] It was also, however, revealed in externals. "I love," he wrote, "Episcopacy, the surplice, festivals, the communion table set altar-wise, antiphonal devotions."[65] This was not just a question of taste. Knox believed that as well as appealing to the reason, Christianity had likewise to make an impression on the senses.[66] Even more importantly, he saw the outward trappings of liturgical worship as an aid to holiness. They helped to foster, in his words, "such habits and feelings of devotion, as must imply a constant commerce of the heart with heaven, and a gradual approximation to its purity, its serenity, and its happiness, through fresh and fuller infusion of that eternal life, which God has given us in his Son."[67]

It was the stress which Knox laid on holiness that caused him to distance himself from what he called "the old high Church race."[68] Deprecating their bigotry,[69] he was offended above all by their lack of sanctity. In his view, the majority of them were "mere men of the world," whose defining characteristic

---

61   Hunt, *Religious Thought in England in the Nineteenth Century*, p. 44; Reardon, *From Coleridge to Gore*, p. 38; B. L., Add. Ms 41163, Correspondence between Alexander Knox and John Jebb (1799–1811), fol. 71, Knox to John Jebb, letter, October 23, 1804.

62   Bodleian, Ms. Wilberforce c. 52, fols. 77–82, Knox to Samuel Whitbread, copy of a letter, December 1, 1812: "... a High Churchman such as I confess myself to be" (fol. 80). For an analysis of the term "High Church" at this time, see, Nockles, "Church Parties."

63   *Remains*, Vol. 4, p. 207. For Knox, the "good sense" of the Reformers, by which he meant the *English* Reformers, lay precisely in their appeal to antiquity, *Remains*, Vol. 1, p. 66.

64   *Correspondence*, Vol. 2, p. 457.

65   *Remains*, Vol. 4, p. 207.

66   *Correspondence*, Vol. 2, pp. 341–43.

67   *Remains*, Vol. 2, p. 272.

68   Ibid., Vol. 1, p. 54.

69   Ibid. See, also: *Remains*, Vol. 1, pp. 64–65; 4, pp. 328–29; *Correspondence*, Vol. 1, p. 198; Bodleian, Ms. Wilberforce d. 15, fols. 63–64, Knox to William Wilberforce, letter, January 9, 1801; Knox to Lord Castlereagh, letter, 96 February 9, 1801, in Vane, *Memoirs and Correspondence*, Vol. 4, pp. 29–33, at p. 31. See, also, below, p. 51.

was "unspiritual orthodoxy."[70] They were exemplified by "Mr. Testy," a satirical character Knox described in *The Flapper*, a short-lived Dublin journal to which he contributed several articles. "No man appears more attached to the established religion or is more zealous in its defence," Knox commented. "But notwithstanding all [his] great zeal for religion, it is remarkable that Mr. Testy uniformly forgets to go to church," nor can even a Bible be found in his house.[71] Instead of such cold and rigid orthodoxy, Knox espoused *"warmth of piety* – something like that described by the two travellers: Did not our hearts *burn within us*?"[72] Brilioth maintains that: "To have accomplished this fusion [of warmth and orthodoxy] is what gives Knox his importance in the history of English theology." (Though Knox's importance is undoubtedly more than simply this, it is this feature of his Churchmanship which, arguably, most made him a precursor of the Tractarians, of whom, doctrinally, he is so often seen as a forerunner.)[73]

6   Evangelicalism

"Warmth of piety" also enabled Knox to have a good relationship with English Evangelicals,[74] a number of whom, including John Venn, William Wilberforce and Henry Thornton, he met on his two extended trips to England in 1799–1801 and 1809.[75] Certainly there were what Jebb termed "differences of [doctrinal] opinion" between Knox and the Evangelicals;[76] nonetheless, he and they were united at a more fundamental level. As Knox explained:

---

70   *Remains*, Vol. 1, 54; *Correspondence*, Vol. 1, p. 339. On High Church spirituality, just prior to the Oxford Movement, see: Gilley, "John Keble and the Victorian Churching of Romanticism," pp. 227–29. See, also, Nockles, *Oxford Movement in Context*, pp. 190–98.
71   *The Flapper*, 15, (March 22, 1796), pp. 58–59. *The Flapper* ran from February 2, 1796, to February 4, 1797, (Hope, *Catalogue of a Collection of Early Newspapers and Essayists*, p. 123).
72   B. L., Add. Ms 41163, Correspondence between Alexander Knox and John Jebb (1799–1811), fol. 74, Knox to John Jebb, letter, March 20, 1805 (emphasis in the original). Knox alludes to Luke 24, 32.
73   Brilioth, *Anglican Revival*, p. 45. See below, p. 257.
74   For an introduction to early nineteenth-century Anglican Evangelicalism, as well as for the figures mentioned, see Hennel, *John Venn and the Clapham Sect*. Knox's relationship with Irish Evangelicals was not always so easy. See, pp. 35, 58, 182, 221.
75   T. C. D., Ms 6396–6397, Jebb Papers, Correspondence 1795–1827, fol. 9, [Miss Ferguson], "Itinerary," 1809; and, above, p. 23 For the 1809 trip, see, too, Forster, *Life of Jebb*, Vol. 1, p. 80–81.
76   *Correspondence*, Vol. 2, p. 338. See, also: *Correspondence*, Vol. 1, p. 171; 2, pp. 107; 341; Forster, *Life of Jebb*, Vol. 1, pp. 80–81. The differences were also perceived by the Evangelicals; see:

[W]e both make it our object to pass through the form of godliness to the power thereof. They who agree with us in this, – be they Calvinists or Remonstrants, Presbyterians, Independents, or even Anabaptists, – may have intercourse with us, useful and pleasant to us and to them. But between all anti-fanatics (as they deem themselves) and us, there is, as it were, a great gulf fixed. We have not any common ideas to exchange, nor any common ground whereon to meet. There may be kind and friendly converse, and real mutual regard; but no intermixture of hearts: for, in the mysterious difference of which I speak, it is the heart, and not the understanding, which is concerned; and there is want of harmony, not because the parties do not think, but because they do not feel, alike.[77]

In other words, there was between Knox and other High Churchmen, the "anti-fanatics," agreement in theology, but divergence spiritually; between him and the Evangelicals (including non-Anglican Evangelicals) there was a meeting of hearts, if not of minds.

Anne Stott has argued that, besides a shared heart religion, Knox cultivated the Evangelical world "partly to move it in a more High Church direction, partly to convert the parliamentary Claphamites to the cause of Catholic Emancipation."[78] The first of these objectives will be examined in a moment, when we come to look at Knox's relationship with Hannah More. As for the conversion of the Claphamites to the cause of Catholic Emancipation, this was certainly Knox's intention, although the extent to which he actually succeeded in realizing it is unclear. In the case of More, given their proximity, he may have aided the evolution of her views, although I have found no evidence for this. By contrast, although the full extent of his influence is impossible to gauge, there are several indications that Knox helped Wilberforce in his slow and laborious move from outright opposition to the measure to qualified support for it. Forster speaks of the impact that Knox made on Wilberforce by his "eloquence and genius," though he does not link this statement specifically to the topic of Emancipation. By contrast, the *Dublin University Magazine* is explicit in asserting its belief that Knox had "much to do in inducing Mr. Wilberforce to change his first impression ... and to become the advocate of emancipation." For his own part, Wilberforce simply wrote: "Knox is a wonderful creature, and so eloquent that you scarcely know how to refuse your assent to the strangest propositions which he pours forth most copiously.

More to Wilberforce, letter, September 24, 1804, in Wilberforce, *Correspondence*, Vol. 1, p. 323; Hennell, *John Venn and the Clapham Sect*, p. 179. See, also, below p. 50.

77   *Remains*, Vol. 4, pp. 174–75.

78   Stott, *Hannah More*, p. 262.

His opinions concerning the Roman Catholics you must, I think, have heard me mention. He declares, that ... the true policy is to quiet them ... and then to grant them all they desire."[79]

Although he was passionate about Roman Catholic Emancipation, Knox showed no interest in the social issues that so exercised the Evangelicals, describing Wilberforce's opposition to slavery as being the result, at least in part, of "over-earnest zeal."[80] His main disagreement with the English Evangelicals, however, concerned the British and Foreign Bible Society, founded in 1804. At first, Knox was supportive of the initiative; in 1805, we find him sketching a reply to a High Church attack on the Society.[81] Even after he had changed his mind on the issue, which he seems to have done fairly rapidly, he was still dismissive of the line taken by other orthodox critics. "They that oppose the Bible Society seem hitherto unhappy in their ground," he opined to Brodrick. "[T]hey are at a loss for a satisfactory reason [for their opposition]."[82] At first sight this seems a strange remark, since Knox's criticisms appear indistinguishable from those of other High Churchmen. He held, first, that the Society's Pan-Protestant structure blurred the distinction between the Established Church and other denominations. Making his own the strictures of William Phelan on the "latitudinarianism of the Bible Society," he argued that the Society's members had replaced the Church of England, the Catholic Church of the kingdom, with "a notional Church of their own, – consisting of those, in different denominations, who have adopted the same doctrinal language, and are engaged in the same active plans for diffusing what they conceive the true knowledge of our Saviour."[83] Consequent on this doctrinal error, Knox feared a practical danger. "[It] *votes down all establishments*," he warned. "It makes every man his

---

79   Forster, *Life of Jebb*, Vol. 1, p. 168; *Dublin University Magazine*, 4. 21 (September 1834), p. 257; William Wilberforce to "a friend," August 1809, in Wilberforce, *Correspondence*, Vol. 2, pp. 164–65.

80   Knox to Lord Castlereagh, letter, July 21, 1803, in Vane, *Memoirs and Correspondence*, Vol. 4, p. 294.

81   *Correspondence*, Vol. 1, p. 198. It does not seem that Knox ever published this riposte. For the Bible Society, see Canton, *A History of the British and Foreign Bible Society*, and more recently, Howsam, *Cheap Bibles*.

82   N. L. I., Ms 8868, Brodrick Papers (folder 5), Knox to Charles Brodrick, letter, January 23, 1812.

83   *Correspondence*, Vol. 2, p. 322 (quoting from Phelan, *The Bible, Not the Bible Society*, p. 21); *Remains*, Vol. 4, p. 437. Knox's concern was not without foundation, in so far as the Bible Society encouraged ecumenism among Evangelicals of all denominations. See Martin, *Evangelicals United*. For William Phelan (1789–1830), at this time a Fellow of Trinity College, Dublin, see Jebb's "Biographical Memoir," in *The Remains of William Phelan, D. D.*, Vol. 1, pp. 1–96.

own teacher. Therefore, good night Bishops and Presbyters!"[84] Knox further objected to the Bible Society's methods. He predicted that the indiscriminate distribution of Scripture would lead to "the Sacred Volume [being] exposed to depreciation, in one class, from disappointment, in another class, from familiarity."[85] He believed, moreover, that Scripture could not be understood without help; it was necessary, in his view, "to furnish due aids for reading the Scriptures with profit."[86] Where Knox differed from the orthodox, was on the way in which the false ecclesiology of the Bible Society was to be combatted. It should not be opposed by legislation, he held, but by a renewal of piety on the part of the clergy of the Established Church, which would render the need for Dissent obsolete.[87]

7   Hannah More

Knox's closet English Evangelical friendship was with Hannah More.[88] More was one of the most remarkable figures of her age and the connection between her and Knox is one which for that reason alone merits attention. At the same time, the friendship between Knox and More serves to illustrate the nature of Knox's relationship to English Evangelicalism as a whole. It is possible that Knox initially became acquainted with More through his work for the A. D. V., which printed and distributed her tracts in Ireland. They appear, however, to have actually met for the first time in February 1800.[89] Following this meeting, Knox was moved to write a pamphlet in More's defence against the High Church polemicist Charles Daubeny, who had attacked her in print the previ-

---

84   N. L. I., Ms 8868, Brodrick Papers, (folder 5), Knox to Charles Brodrick, letter, January 23, 1812 (emphasis in the original). This is presumably what most distinguished the Bible Society, in Knox's eyes, from the A. D. V., which also distributed Scripture. The A. D. V. acted under the supervision of the Church.

85   *Correspondence*, Vol. 2, p. 330. It is this conviction which perhaps helps explain his comment to Brodrick, that the Bible was not meant "for the vulgar and ignorant, but for the refined and enlightened" (N. L. I., Ms 8868. Brodrick Papers, folder 7, Knox to Charles Brodrick, letter, November 23, 1819).

86   *Correspondence*, Vol. 2, p. 322.

87   N. L. I., Ms 8868, Brodrick Papers, (folder 5), Knox to Charles Brodrick, June 22, 1812.

88   For More (1745–1833), see: Stott, *Hannah More*; Jones, *Hannah More*, and Roberts, *Memoirs*. Besides these secondary materials, there is an important collection of uncatalogued letters from More to Knox in the Clark Library, Los Angeles.

89   *Remains*, Vol. 4, pp. 63–65. Later (in 1802), Knox claimed to identify in a passage from More's tract, *The Shepherd of Salisbury Plain* "the substance of a conversation which took place one evening I was with her" (*Remains*, Vol. 4, p. 89). The tract in question was, however, published in 1795, which would make Knox's claim impossible.

ous year.[90] Four years later, in 1804, Knox paid an extended visit to More at her home, Barley Wood, near Wrington in Somerset. He had already described her as "one of the most truly evangelical divines of this whole age, perhaps almost of any not apostolic age."[91] Now, writing to Brodrick, he related that, having spent eight days in her company, she had only continued to rise in his estimation. He felt, he said, "emphatically at home with her."[92] The admiration was mutual. In a letter to Wilberforce written in September the same year, More described Knox as "almost the most intellectual and spiritual man I ever knew." "[B]ut," she continued, "he is not in all points in our way."[93] This "way" was that of Evangelicalism, and the differences of which More spoke were soon to become apparent. Knox arrived at Barley Wood in April 1804. At the time, More was working on her book, *Hints towards Forming the Character of a Young Princess*, a programme of education for George III's granddaughter, Charlotte.[94] The book was published the following year, and, as Anne Stott remarks, Knox had "much influence on the finished product."[95] More herself acknowledged this influence in only one area, that of her teaching on providence.[96] Nonetheless, the *Hints* contains a number of ideas so similar to Knox's as to suggest that his impact on her thinking was much greater. More presents Christianity as being not so much about doctrine as about practice, its aim being "to make us *love* what is *right*, rather than to occupy our understandings with its theory."[97] She thus defines faith as an "effectual and impressive apprehension of God," who, in Christ, is manifested to us so that "he might 'redeem us from all iniquity, and

---

90   "A Layman of the Established Church," *A Brief Confutation*; Daubeny, *Letter to Mrs. Hannah More*. For Daubeny (1745–1827), see *O. D. N. B.*

91   "Extract from a letter from Mr. Knox," in Roberts, *Memoirs*, Vol. 3, pp. 161–62, at p. 161. For Knox's early appreciation of More, see, also, *Remains*, Vol. 4, pp. 64–65.

92   N. L. I., Ms 8868, Brodrick Papers, (folder 2), Knox to Charles Brodrick, letter, April 11, 1804.

93   Hannah More to William Wilberforce, letter, September 24, 1804, in Wilberforce, *Correspondence*, Vol. 1, p. 323.

94   For Princess Charlotte of Wales (1796–1817), see *O. D. N. B.*

95   Stott, *Hannah More*, p. 261. Similarly, Jones comments: "It is not without significance that Alexander Knox ... was a guest at Barley Wood when Hannah More was writing the *Hints*" (*Hannah More*, p. 189). This collaboration is mentioned by Forster (*Correspondence*, Vol. 1, p. 191, note), as well as by More herself: Clark Library, Los Angeles, "Box 2: Hannah More Letters," Hannah More to Knox, letter, February 21, [1805]; Hannah More to Knox, letter, April 19, [1805]. See, also: Hannah More to Knox, letter, June 3, 1805, in Roberts, *Memoirs*, Vol. 3, pp. 227–27, at p. 227. The *Hints* were first published anonymously in two volumes by the London publishers Cadell and Davies in 1805.

96   More, *Hints*, Vol. 2, pp. 328–29, note. See also, Hannah More to Knox, letter, June, 1816, in Roberts, *Memoirs*, Vol. 3, pp. 450–451.

97   More, *Hints*, Vol. 1, p. 214 (emphasis in the original). For Knox's teaching, see, p. 111.

purify us unto himself a peculiar people zealous of *good works.'*"[98] For, she says, "faith, if real, must produce love."[99] Hence, she maintains, the best description of Christianity is *"faith which worketh by love."*[100] All this is strongly redolent of Knox, as is the idea that Christianity alone can make human beings truly happy, since it alone can satisfy all the exigencies of human nature.[101]

Of greatest significance, however, is the ecclesiology of More's book. Jones has remarked that More's teaching on the Church sits awkwardly in the *Hints*, appearing in it almost as an after-thought. Jones thus wonders if, rather than being an expression of More's own thinking, the ecclesiological teaching of the *Hints*, which is without parallel in her other writings, was included simply because she felt obliged to say something about the subject, given that Charlotte was in the direct line of succession to the throne, and thus destined to become "Supreme Governor of the Church of England."[102] This supposition is undoubtedly correct. More did not simply need to write about the Church, however; she needed to do so in a way that would avoid orthodox criticism. We have already seen that she had been savaged by Daubeny in 1799; but also from 1799 to 1803, in the so-called "Blagdon controversy", she had been, as Knox put it, "traduced and vilified by every acrimonious bigot."[103] One may therefore conjecture that she wanted someone with impeccably orthodox credentials to furnish her with a "correct" ecclesiology which no High Churchman could reproach.[104] This is what Knox apparently did, given the similarities, both of thought and language, between his ecclesiological teaching and that of the *Hints*. Most strikingly, the Church of England is called "the Anglican Church," which, as we have seen above, was an unusual term at the time, although habitually employed by Knox.[105] But there are other similarities, too. The Established Church is described as being animated by "liberal principles, and charitable feelings," "less polemical and more pious and practical"

---

98 More, *Hints*, Vol. 1, p. 216; Vol. 2, p. 223 (emphasis in the original). More cites Titus 2. 14, a verse which Knox often quotes in defence of his soteriology. For this teaching and for Knox's understanding of faith, see below, pp. 158, 171–72.
99 More, *Hints*, Vol. 1, p. 218.
100 Ibid., p. 215 (emphasis in the original). More is quoting Galatians 5. 6.
101 More, *Hints*, Vol. 1, pp. 226, 230–31, 240–48; Vol. 2, p. 206. For Knox's teaching, see below, pp. 95, 148–49.
102 Jones, *Hannah More*, p. 189. Princess Charlotte died prematurely, and thus did not accede to the throne.
103 "Extract from a letter from Mr. Knox," in Roberts, *Memoirs*, Vol. 3, pp. 161–62, at p. 161. For the background, see Stott, *Hannah More*, chapter 11, "The Blagdon Controversy 1799–1803" (pp. 232–57.)
104 Stott, *Hannah* More, p. 262. More "felt she needed Knox," Stott argues (p. 263).
105 More, *Hints*, Vol. 2, pp. 303, 313, 364–65.

than other denominations, careful "to distinguish between essentials and non-essentials."[106] Establishment is defended in the strongest terms as part of the divine plan, something demonstrated by an appeal to the parables.[107] The Prayer Book is lauded, its "devotional compositions" being, thanks to the conservatism of the English Reformers, "not more venerable for their antiquity, than valuable for their intrinsic excellence."[108]

Whatever influence Knox may have had on More, or whatever she may have borrowed from him, she did not simply reproduce his thinking, and although the *Hints* escaped censure from the orthodox more generally, the book failed to satisfy the demands of Knox's own High Churchmanship. In his public review of the *Hints* for the *Eclectic*, he was muted in his criticism.[109] In private, he proved much more plain-spoken. Writing to More in a letter dated May 30, 1805, he declared:

> Your omissions in what you had from me were quite what I wished you to do. But I should have endeavoured to argue you out of some of the additions; they not being, as I conceive, in my order of theological architecture. But, on this subject, I have no disposition to tease you. I love my own views for many reasons; and for this, among others, – that they do not dispose me to be over-eager in urging them; or to be much pained when I am a little thwarted in them.[110]

The tone may appear subdued, but it is clear nonetheless that Knox was dissatisfied with the *Hints*. Even so, he did not despair of winning More over to his ideas, and of the book undergoing a thorough revision prior to any new edition.[111] His motive was not simply to enlighten her personally; he also wanted to make her a conduit of his High Church teaching to a wider audience. For, as Jebb remarked, were "H. M. decidedly of your way of thinking, with the high character she has acquired, and the weight which attaches to her sentiments, among evangelical people, she might be an instrument of great good."[112]

---

106 More, *Hints*, Vol. 2, pp. 353, 312–13, 310. For Knox's teaching, see, pp. 112, 114, 117.
107 See especially More, "Of the established Church of England," *Hints*, Vol. 2, Chapter 34 (pp. 295–321). For Knox's teaching, see pp. 219–21. The use of the parables to bolster the idea of establishment is typical of Knox; see *Remains*, Vol. 1, pp. 447–67.
108 More, *Hints*, Vol. 2, p. 308. For Knox's view of the Prayer Book, see above, pp. 42–43.
109 *Eclectic Review*, 2.1 (January 1806), pp. 14–21; (February 1806), pp. 114–21. See also: *Remains*, Vol. 3, pp. 71–72 and Vol. 4, p. 206.
110 *Remains*, Vol. 4, p. 301.
111 *Correspondence*, Vol. 1, p. 199. See also, p. 197, where Knox says of the *Hints*: "I hope it will do good: but it still needs revising."
112 *Correspondence*, Vol. 1, p. 258.

Knox therefore sought to indoctrinate her with his High Churchmanship in a series of letters.[113] One wonders, however, if More gave anything other than a cursory glance to these virtual tracts.[114] It certainly seems that Knox suspected her of not reading them, for she had to assure him of the contrary. "Never entertain such unwarrantable distrusts any more," she urged, "but take it for granted that your friend has not so defective a taste as to want a relish for your writings."[115] Whether she read Knox's letters or not, More showed no sign of accepting his High Church thinking; and it is little wonder that, gradually, one finds Knox growing impatient with her. Writing to Miss Ferguson at the end of 1807, about a reply which More had sent in response to one of his letters, he complained that "where I wished her to be attentive, she makes scarcely the shadow of an observation."[116] The problem was that, in Stott's words, Knox was theologically "at the opposite pole from More."[117] As Jones puts it: "She was, at bottom, a Puritan ... He was 'not one whit puritanic.'"[118] Knox eventually admitted the unbridgeable distance between their views. As he wrote to Jebb in 1817, "We both value and wish for the same religious affections, the same, I mean, in substance; but we have quite different ideas of the best method of exciting them. And not only our views, but our habits of mind, put (at least circumstantial) agreement, wholly out of the question."[119]

The fundamental divergence between Knox and More concerned ecclesiology. As Stott remarks, Knox thought that More "had ignored the catholicity of the Church of England."[120] Jones has argued that it is impossible to read the *Hints* without becoming aware that More was influenced by Knox's doctrine of the via media.[121] But on this point Jones is mistaken. Knox's and More's views of the via media were radically distinct. For Knox, the Church of England stood mid-way between Protestantism and Roman Catholicism, and was fundamentally a Catholic church. For More it occupied "a kind of middle place" between

---

113 *Remains*, Vol. 3, pp. 71–102, 103–230; Vol. 4, pp. 231–53, 257–63, 323–35. Jebb also joined in the letter-writing campaign; see Hannah More to Knox, letter, 1805, in Roberts, *Memoirs*, Vol. 3, pp. 228–30, at p. 230.

114 "[*T*]*heses* would be the more appropriate term [than letters]," Jones comments on Knox's correspondence with More (*Hannah More*, p. 213; emphasis in the original).

115 Hannah More to Knox, letter, November 30, 1809, in Roberts, *Memoirs*, Vol. 3, pp. 302–7, at p. 302. See also Hannah More to Knox, letter, January 21, 1806, in Roberts, *Memoirs*, Vol. 3, pp. 235–40, at pp. 235–36.

116 *Remains*, Vol. 4, p. 227. For the letter in question, see *Remains*, Vol. 3, pp. 71–102.

117 Stott, *Hannah More*, p. 262. See also pp. 284–85.

118 Jones, *Hannah More*, p. 215. Jones is quoting *Remains*, Vol. 4, p. 207.

119 *Correspondence*, Vol. 2, p. 341.

120 Stott, *Hannah More*, p. 266.

121 Jones, *Hannah More*, pp. 213–14. See also p. 189.

Lutheranism and Calvinism, but essentially was no different from the "other national churches of the reformation."[122] Concomitant with this ecclesiological difference was a second issue, that of authority. For Knox, Anglicans were to look not to Scripture alone for guidance, nor to the principles of the continental Reformation, but to Scripture and Catholic antiquity.[123] He exhorted More, "[T]rust not to the uncertain sounds of scarcely three centuries, when you may listen to the concurrent voice of acknowledged wisdom and universal revered piety, through all the successive ages of the Catholic Church."[124] It was an appeal to which More was deaf. For her, theological authority resided solely in "the plain unadulterated Bible."[125] She thus eulogized Luther for what she called his "bold genius and adventurous spirit" in restoring what she saw as the primary truths of Scripture, of which one of the most fundamental was, in her view, "the doctrine of salvation by remission of sins through a Mediator."[126] The significance which More attributed to this "doctrine of salvation" was a point of further disagreement between her and Knox, who firmly rejected the idea that the atonement was a fundamental doctrine, to be ranked among the "catholic verities."[127] In making her case for the importance of the doctrine of the atonement, More appealed to three of the main authorities which he habitually invoked: Catholic consent, the Prayer Book and the demands of human nature.[128] The evidence strongly suggests that More had Knox in mind when she concluded her soteriological teaching with this admonition: "Let those, therefore, who have never felt [the conflicts of an afflicted conscience], beware how they despise what they may yet be impelled to resort to, as the only certain stay and prop of their sinking spirits."[129]

8   Conclusion

In this chapter we have seen that Knox was not only one of the first writers to employ the term 'Anglican', but also that he developed a theory of what

---

122   More, *Hints*, Vol. 2, p. 302. See on this point Stott, *Hannah More*, p. 266. For Knox's views, see, p. 38.
123   *Remains*, Vol. 4, p. 240. See, also, above, p. 39.
124   *Remains*, Vol. 4, p. 243.
125   More, *Hints*, Vol. 2, p. 269.
126   Ibid., p. 277. See also Vol. 1, pp. 211, 256.
127   *Remains*, Vol. 2, pp. 317, 358–59, and especially Vol. 4, pp. 259–60, where Knox raises the issue directly with More. For the "catholic verities," see below, pp. 112–113.
128   More, *Hints*, Vol. 1, pp. 256–59.
129   Ibid., p. 258.

Anglicanism means. Unlike Roman Catholicism, it accords the highest importance to Scripture; but, unlike other reformed churches, it does not appeal to
Scripture alone, but to Scripture interpreted by "Catholic consent," that which
has been taught, following the rule or canon of Vincent of Lérins, always, everywhere, and by all. Fidelity to this canon made the Church of England, for
Knox, essentially identical with the primitive church. Although the Church had
developed the thinking of the Fathers, it maintained their collective doctrine,
rather than simply appealing to them to bolster its own teaching. For this reason, the Church was bound to submit itself to the patristic consensus, and its
formularies were to be interpreted, and if necessary, corrected by reference to
it. For Knox, the identity of Anglicanism with the early church appeared most
clearly in the Book of Common Prayer. Although he expressed a preference for
the 1549 version over that of 1662, the latter was for him the Church's primary
standard. By contrast, he was critical of the Thirty-Nine Articles, which not
only came from a later epoch, but were also doctrinally suspect. Nonetheless,
he did appeal to them, as he did to the Catechism. The *Homilies*, by contrast,
although he occasionally used them, he held to be without authority.

Knox's ecclesiology marked him out as a High Churchman, as did his appeal to ceremonial. But he was a High Churchman *sui generis*, differing from
his contemporaries on a number of issues. Of these differences, two merit
particular attention. One was the normative authority which he gave to antiquity. The other was his rejection of cold formalism in favor of what he termed
"warmth of piety." Both points serve to highlight Knox as a precursor of the
Oxford Movement. But he anticipated it in other ways as well. His rejection
of the Protestant character of the Church; the primary authority given to the
Prayer Book; his disapprobation of the Thirty-Nine Articles: all foreshadow
the Tractarians. Knox did not, however, simply anticipate. He had a formative
influence on Newman's conception the via media; and it is probable that he
helped inspire the Tractarians' preference for 1549 Book of Common Prayer.

Despite his High Churchmanship, Knox enjoyed a good rapport with
English Evangelicals. This was founded on a shared affective piety, although, at
the same time, he also wanted to gain Evangelical backing for Roman Catholic
Emancipation, as well as moving Evangelicals in a more High Church direction.
He disagreed with them on social issues, but the greatest difference between
him and them concerned the Bible Society. Knox feared that the Society's
Pan-Protestantism would weaken the correct Anglican understanding of the
Church, and that allowing each person to interpret the Bible for themselves
would diminish the authority of the clergy. Moreover, the indiscriminate dissemination of the Scriptures would, he felt, devalue it in people's eyes and open
it up to misunderstanding and misinterpretation. Knox's closest Evangelical

friendship was with Hannah More. Her *Hints towards the Formation of the Character of a Young Princess* show a number of similarities to his thought, especially on the topic of ecclesiology, where she clearly sought his help, so as to avoid censure by the orthodox. There were, however, marked differences between her and Knox: on the nature of the English Church's via media; on the question of authority; and on the doctrine of the atonement. These differences between Knox and More arose from Knox's High Churchmanship, and it is to the origins of this Churchmanship that we now turn in the next chapter, as we examine the theological inheritance which Knox derived from his relationship with John Wesley.

CHAPTER 3

Alexander Knox and John Wesley

"A Church-of-England man of the highest tone."[1] Thus Alexander Knox describes John Wesley, and from Wesley it was that he largely derived his own
High Churchmanship. Such a claim may appear surprising, but it points us
to one of the reasons why Knox is significant: he bears important witness to
the nature of Wesley's religious convictions. He does this particularly in his
Remarks on the Life and Character of John Wesley and it is with a discussion of
this work that the present chapter begins, though prefaced by a brief examination of two earlier defences. The chapter then continues by seeking to assess
Wesley's influence on Knox's theology, exploring the differences and similarities in their thinking, before concluding with a look at Knox's relationship to
the Methodist movement, following Wesley's death.

1   Knox's First Two Defences of Wesley

The singular tenderness shown by Wesley to Knox as a young man has already
been noted. It was a tenderness which Knox repaid in later life by publicly
coming to Wesley's defence on three occasions. The first was in the summer
of 1789. Wesley had permitted services to be held in the Methodist chapel in
Whitefriar Street, Dublin, at the same time that worship was being conducted
in the local Church of Ireland parish church. This was an innovation, because
until then Methodist services had been held at different times from those of
the Established Church. Wesley's decision met with a great deal of criticism,
and was held up as a sign of his separatist intentions. Knox entered the fray
with a letter to the *Dublin Chronicle*, in which he conceded that a "growing
tendancy to a separation from the church has long been observable among the
Methodists." But, he argued, the reason why no actual schism had occurred was
Wesley's staunch opposition to such a move. Now, however, Knox demanded,
given that Wesley was eighty-six years old, "[is] it strange that he should in
many things *yield* rather than *contend* – that he should cease to *struggle* where
he cannot hope to *prevail*, and, as far as he can, acquiesce in the prejudices

---

1   *Wesley*, p. 445.

of his wayward children?"[2] Knox's second defence of Wesley was a tract entitled *Remarks on an Expostulatory Address*, published in Dublin in 1802. It was
written in reply to an intemperate attack on Methodism by the Evangelical,
John Walker, and was presented as an eirenicon, appealing for charity and
understanding. With regard to the main question at issue, the doctrine of
justification, the differences between the two sides were more verbal than substantial, Knox contended. In response, Walker issued a series of seven letters
insisting that this was not at all the case. The tenet of justification by faith
alone was essential to the Gospel, he claimed, and Wesley and Knox had both
abandoned it.[3]

2   Knox's *Remarks on the Life and Character of John Wesley*

In 1820 a *Life of Wesley* was produced by the then Poet Laureate, Robert
Southey.[4] The work dismayed Knox, who was particularly concerned with
Southey's portrayal of Wesley as motivated primarily by ambition. Southey
challenged Knox to convince him of the contrary and the result was the
Remarks on the Life and Character of John Wesley (1828). So impressed was
Southey by Knox's arguments that he confessed himself mistaken, and when
the third edition of the *Life* came out in 1846, Knox's essay appeared in it as
an appendix.[5]

To claim with Jebb that Knox knew "the very secrets of [Wesley's] heart,"
is doubtless an exaggeration. Nonetheless, as Knox himself pointed out repeatedly, he was intimate with Wesley over a long period, and to this intimate

---

2   *Dublin Chronicle*, June 27–30, 1789, pp. 206–7. The letter, signed "Humanus," was subsequently quoted both by John Whitehead and Henry Moore in their *Lives* of Wesley (Dublin edition, Vol. 2, p. 486; 2, pp. 455–56). For the background, see Rogal, *Wesley in Ireland*, Vol. 2,
pp. 591–97.
3   Walker's letters were subsequently collected in a single volume, *A Letter to Alexander Knox,
Esq.* (1803). In 1806, the letters were published together with Walker's 1802 *Expostulatory
Address to the Members of the Methodist Society in Ireland* (1802), and it is from this edition,
produced in Edinburgh, that quotations from both the *Address* and the letters are taken. For
Walker, see above, p. 15.
4   For Robert Southey (1774–1843), see *O. D. N. B.*
5   For the background see: *Wesley*, pp. 409–10, 425–27; *Remains*, Vol. 4, pp. 444–45;
Correspondence, Vol. 2, pp. 512–13; and, especially, Knox's two letters on the subject to
Hannah More, *Remains*, Vol. 3, pp. 457–80. See also: Robert Southey to Richard Watson, letter,
August 17, 1835, quoted Stevens, *History of Methodism*, Vol. 2, p. 515; and Nockles, "Reactions."

knowledge he added "deep reflection during thirty-six subsequent years."[6] It is this quality which, even today, makes Knox's essay (in the words of Henry Rack), one of "the most acute and penetrating studies of Wesley's character and theology." "[O]ne of the most probing of all the theological appraisals of Wesley by any of his own contemporaries," is the judgment of Albert C. Outler, who adds that it is also "one of the most unjustly neglected."[7] But, as well as shedding light on Wesley, the essay is important for our understanding of Knox. To quote his own words: "[I]n giving my views of John Wesley's religious principles, I have pretty largely developed my own."[8] In his "remarkable essay," as Rack dubs it,[9] Knox depicted Wesley as one who loved and valued "that pure spirit of faith and piety which the Church of England inherits from Catholic antiquity." More precisely, according to Knox, Wesley "formed his views in the school of the Greek fathers, and in that of their closest modern followers, the Platonic divines of the Church of England," whom Knox listed as Taylor, Smith, Cudworth, Worthington, and Lucas.[10] According to Knox, these formative influences guided Wesley's thinking for the whole of his life. Nonetheless, Knox continued, there was a period when, through his acquaintance with Moravianism, Wesley became "imbued with the doctrines of Luther," which Knox dismissed as "mere human theology." Knox claimed that "under the full influence of ... Lutheran dogma," Wesley defined faith as a "sure trust and confidence in God that by the merits of Christ [the Christian's] sins are forgiven, and he is reconciled to the favour of God." This allowed Wesley's true understanding of justifying faith to be, in Knox's word, "disguised." "[He] spoke on the subject of Faith," Knox complained, "in a manner which made it difficult to distinguish his sounder views from the questionable positions with which they were more or less intermingled."[11] This Lutheran period came to an end,

---

6   For Jebb's remark, see John Jebb to Robert Southey, letter, December 26, 1817, quoted in Forster, *Life of Jebb*, Vol. 1, pp. 179–85, at p. 185. For Knox's knowledge of Wesley see, for example: *Wesley*, pp. 415, 416, 423, 425, 429, 437, 447, 451, 452. See, too, *Remains*, Vol. 3, p. 479. For Knox's subsequent reflection on Wesley, see: John Jebb to Robert Southey, letter, December 26, 1817, quoted in Forster, *Life of Jebb*, Vol. 1, pp. 179–85, at p. 185; *Wesley*, p. 417.

7   Rack, *Reasonable Enthusiast*, p. 537; Outler, ed., *Works of John Wesley, Vol.* 1, p. 62, n. 28.

8   *Wesley*, p. 409.

9   Rack, *Reasonable Enthusiast*, p. xii.

10   *Wesley*, pp. 445, 419. For the authors mentioned, see below, pp. 82, 137, 175.

11   *Wesley*, pp. 474, 484–85, 496–97. The definition of faith as "sure trust and confidence" comes from "A Sermon of The Salvation of Mankind" (*Certain Sermons*, pp. 19–31, p. 29), but Knox believed that the influence of Lutheranism made Wesley misconstrue the meaning.

according to Knox, in 1767, its termination being marked by Wesley in his
Journal with the question: "[I]s it not high time for us ... to return to the plain
word: *He that feareth God and worketh righteousness is accepted with Him?*"[12]
Knox interpreted this as Wesley abandoning Lutheran views to return to
what was "native and essential" in his theology.[13] Even so, to Knox's chagrin,
there remained in Wesley's teaching a subliminal Lutheran understanding of
faith, which, according to Knox, surfaced from time to time to mar Wesley's
sounder views.[14]

Knox's view of the evolution of Wesley's thought is reflected in modern
scholarship, which commonly distinguishes three Wesleys: early, middle or
mature, and late.[15] Although it would be a mistake to make these distinctions
too rigid, or to be too dogmatic about the precise moments at which his thinking shifted, there can be no doubt that the Wesley who emerged at the end of
the 1760s proclaimed himself to be a High Churchman.[16] His religion was, as he
put it in a sermon preached in 1777: "the *religion of the Church of England*, as
appears from all her authentic records, from the uniform tenor of her liturgy,
and from numberless passages in her Homilies."[17] And this religion, he claimed,
he had always held. As he put it in his "Farther Thoughts on Separation from
the Church," published in 1790, the year before his death:

> From a child I was taught to love and reverence the Scripture, the Oracles
> of God: and next to these to esteem the primitive Fathers, the writers of
> the first three centuries. Next after the primitive church, I esteemed our
> own, the Church of England, as the most scriptural national church in the
> world ... In this judgment and with this spirit I went to America, strongly
> attached to the Bible, the primitive church, and the Church of England ...
> In this spirit I returned.[18]

---

12   *Wesley*, pp. 420 (emphasis in the original), 478. For Wesley's question, see his *Journal* entry
      for December 1, 1767 (Vol. 5, p. 244).
13   *Wesley*, p. 472; see also: pp. 420–21, 477; *Remains*, Vol. 3, p. 154.
14   *Wesley*, pp. 484–86.
15   See, for example: Maddox, *Responsible Grace*, p. 20; Outler, ed., *Works of John Wesley*,
      Vol. 1, pp. 65–66.
16   "I am an High Church man," John Wesley to Lord Dartmouth, letter, June 14, 1775, (*Letters*,
      Vol. 6, p. 156).
17   Wesley, Sermon 112, "On Laying the Foundation of the New Chapel," 2, 4, in Outler, ed.,
      Works of John Wesley, Vol. 3, pp. 579–92, at p. 586 (emphasis in the original).
18   Wesley, "Farther Thoughts on Separation from the Church," 1–2. Text in Baker, *John Wesley
      and the Church of England*, pp. 320–22 (punctuation slightly altered). Although composed
      in 1789, "Farther Thoughts" was first published in the *Arminian Magazine*, April 1790.

In other words, although there are obvious discontinuities between the "early" and "late" Wesley, there are also essential similarities. Wesley in 1767 is, in many ways, as much a High Churchman as the Wesley who had set out for Georgia thirty years earlier (something which will be demonstrated in subsequent chapters, when, in relation to Knox's theology, we come to look at his teaching on specific issues). Despite this evidence, a number of scholars have argued that Wesley should be seen as an Evangelical, especially on the issue of justification. This is the case, for example, with George Croft Cell in the *Rediscovery of John Wesley* (1935) and Harald Lindström in *Wesley and Sanctification: A Study in the Doctrine of Salvation* (1946). However, if these scholars can appeal to the "middle" Wesley, they do not seem to give sufficient weight to the "plain fact," as Alan C. Clifford calls it, that Wesley's "Lutheran view of justification underwent a significant change in the face of the antinomian challenge." "Wesley rejected solifidianism," Clifford concludes.[19] Following his death, Wesley's followers moved in a much more evangelical direction. This development, charted by Mats Selén in his book The *Oxford Movement and Methodism in England* (1992), is one of the main reasons that the image of Wesley as a churchman "of the highest tone" has been obscured, an obscurity which the study of Knox helps us to dispel.[20]

In his 2012 article on "Reactions to Robert Southey's *Life of Wesley* (1820) Reconsidered," Peter Nockles has suggested that Knox's *Remarks on the Life and Character of John Wesley* should be read as a subtle but nonetheless "devastating critique of Wesleyan theology."[21] I find this reading hard to accept. For Knox one of the main defects of Southey's book was (as he told Hannah More) the fact that Southey had overlooked the "revolutions," as he put it, which had occurred in Wesley's theology, ignoring his later views.[22] It seems to me, therefore, that, as well as defending Wesley from the charge of ambition, one of the intentions of Knox's essay was to correct what he saw as the "particularly defective" statement of Wesley's doctrine given by Southey.[23] Thus, while he was by no means blind to what he termed Wesley's "peculiarities" and the

---

19   Clifford, *Atonement and Justification*, pp. 60, 59. Clifford contends that Wesley was actually influenced by Calvin in his soteriology, a view, of course, diametrically opposed to Knox's. See especially *Atonement and Justification*, pp. 132–35.

20   David Hempton cautions that writers from each of the various traditions that influenced the eclectic Wesley are prone to claim him for one of their own (*Methodism: Empire of the Spirit*, p. 57). This warning heeded, the evidence nevertheless supports the conclusion that Wesley was a High Churchman. Even if his High Churchmanship was idiosyncratic, this idiosyncrasy was, we should note, revealed more in his actions than in his teaching.

21   Nockles, "Reactions," p. 75.

22   *Remains*, Vol. 3, p. 468.

23   Ibid.

"circumstantial extravagances" and "nebulous accompaniments" of his teaching, Knox in his essay identifies that teaching as essentially or "in substance" that of "the ancient Fathers, and the most eminent anti-Calvinist divines of the Church of England."[24] As we have seen, Knox argued that it was these authorities that formed Wesley as a theologian and that, although Wesley's thinking later suffered from an exposure to the ideas of the continental Reformers, he subsequently corrected himself.

3   Wesley's Influence on Knox

Because of Wesley's High Churchmanship, I also find myself in disagreement with Nockles when, in his *o. d. n. b.* article on Knox, he suggests that Knox's views on the primitive church, and the emphasis he gave to apostolic order and authority, were the result of his own independent thinking, rather than something he derived from Wesley.[25] Brilioth has suggested that Knox's High Churchmanship was "*perhaps* in no small degree a legacy from Wesley the High Churchman."[26] To my mind, Brilioth is too cautious. Even at his most "Catholic" Knox shows the influence of Wesley: he went beyond him, but the origin of his teaching lay in principles which he imbibed from Wesley, something that is already clear in Knox's three earliest published works: *Free Thoughts* (1785), *Considerations* (1794) and *Candid Animadversions* (1794). This theological debt is one which Knox himself acknowledged. "[W]hat do I not owe, subordinately, to [Wesley]?" he asked.[27] And, as we will see in looking more closely at Knox's teaching, there are a number of points on which he appealed expressly to him. Even when such an appeal is lacking, the similarities between the two men's views are clear.

The earliest evidence of Wesley's influence on Knox are his letters to him. In these letters one finds several themes which were later to become prominent in Knox's theology. One is the central tenet of God's love, felt and acted on. It was this love, Wesley wrote, which lay behind Knox's childhood sickliness. His ill-health was providential, Wesley argued, "a proof of God's watchful care," by which "Alleck" was being taught to "seek all [his] happiness in God."[28] A second feature of the letters is their anti-Calvinist tone. One urged "Alleck"

---

24   *Wesley*, pp. 412, 462, 472, 473, 455.
25   Nockles, "Knox," p. 1.
26   Brilioth, *Anglican Revival*, p. 46 (emphasis added).
27   *Remains*, Vol. 4, p. 159.
28   Ibid., pp. 1–2.

to be wary of "Predestinarians;" another warned him against being seduced by even *moderate Calvinism.* (Not that there can be any such thing as "moderate" Calvinism, Wesley insisted. "It is Stark Nonsense.")[29] More positively, the letters emphasized the cooperation of God and the individual in the process of salvation. "God works," Wesley affirmed, "and man believes. The power is God's; the act is man's." This act, Wesley made clear, is free. God may offer the gift of saving faith, but the individual "may or may not receive that Gift. He can so resist as to prevent God from Working."[30] Another fundamental idea is that of spiritual growth and development. At present, Wesley told "Alleck," he had only "a small spark" of love, the love of a servant, not yet of a son. What he needed was "to have the love of God fully shed abroad in [his] heart," to which end Wesley exhorted him to the practice of private prayer and the reading of Scripture.[31] Wesley likewise encouraged Knox to study history, poetry, and philosophy, as well as theology, or "divinity," as he called it, suggesting for this that Knox use "Bishop Pearson." The mention of Pearson is important. The High Church divine John Pearson held various academic posts before becoming Bishop of Chester in 1672. His *Exposition of the Creed*, first published in 1659, was, to quote Outler, "one of Wesley's most important [theological] sources," and it likewise proved influential on Knox, who described it as "the most perfect theological work that has ever come from an English pen."[32] Pearson insisted strongly on sanctification as the work of the Holy Spirit. "[H]e [*sic*] is ... called 'the Holy Spirit' or 'the Spirit of holiness' (Romans 1, 4)," Pearson wrote, "because of the three persons in the blessed Trinity, it is his particular office to sanctify or make us holy." It is a dictum which we find repeated almost verbatim by Knox, whose whole theology is marked by this tenet.[33] There is, however, no explicit evidence that Pearson influenced Knox's pneumatology. By contrast, with regard to ecclesiology, Knox invoked Pearson *nominatim*. He also invoked Pearson's appeal to the Fathers, commenting that Pearson's "incomparable selection of authorities, proves that VINCENTIUS could not have had a more active disciple."[34] If, however, Pearson was partially

---

29   O. C. M. C. H., B/Wes/J, letter 8, John Wesley to Knox, December 5, 1776; B/Wes/J, letter 9, John Wesley to Knox, March 19, 1777.

30   O. C. M. C. H., B/Wes/ J, letter 38, Wesley to Knox, December 7, 1783; B/Wes/J, letter 39, John Wesley to Knox, February 7, 1784.

31   *Remains*, Vol. 4, pp. 14, 6, 8.

32   *Remains*, Vol. 4, p. 8; Outler, ed., *Works of John Wesley*, Vol. 1, p. 83; *Remains*, Vol. 4, p. 339. For Knox's regard for Pearson, see, also: *Correspondence*, Vol. 2, p. 306; *Appendix*, p. 382; and below, pp. 164, n. 106, 222. For Pearson (1613–86), see O. D. N. B.

33   Pearson, *Exposition of the Creed*, p. 467. For the parallel in Knox, see *Remains*, Vol. 2, p. 327. More generally, for Knox's pneumatology, see below, pp. 162–66.

34   *Appendix*, p. 382.

responsible for Knox's interest in the Fathers, it seems more probable that this interest was initially sparked by Wesley himself, who, as we have already seen, Knox claimed several times to have been moulded by the Greek patristic tradition, a claim which has been confirmed by a substantial body of modern scholarship.[35] In particular, Wesley had a particular reverence for Clement of Alexandria, Pseudo-Macarius and John Chrysostom; and the fact that Knox, too, shared this reverence, is indicative of Wesley's influence on him.[36] We may furthermore suggest that this influence was not limited to an intellectual interest in patristics. Knox comments of Wesley that "to realise in himself the *perfect Christian of Clemens Alexandrinus* was the object of his heart," and this living out of the Fathers' teaching may also have had an impact on Knox, for whom Christianity was primarily a question of praxis rather than knowledge.[37]

Besides the Fathers, Knox presents "the Platonic divines of the Church of England" as a formative influence on Wesley. This has been confirmed by the work of John C. English, who concludes that Wesley was dependent on the moderates, as he terms them, for a portion of his ideas.[38] Once more, as with the Fathers, it seems highly probable that Knox, for whom the moderates

---

35   On the link between Wesley and the Greek Fathers, see: Maddox, "John Wesley and Eastern Orthodoxy: Influences, Convergences, and Differences," as well as the three volumes edited by S. T. Kimbrough, and published by St. Vladimir's Seminary Press: *Orthodox and Wesleyan Spirituality*; *Orthodox and Wesleyan Scriptural Understanding and Practice*; and *Orthodox and Wesleyan Ecclesiology*. See, also, Maddox, *Responsible Grace*, and Outler, *John Wesley*, both of whom make the connection between Wesley and the Greek Fathers a central theme. One must note, however, that Wesley did not follow the Fathers without reflection, but revised and adapted their teachings: see Campbell, *John Wesley and Christian Antiquity*. For Knox's claim of the influence of the Greek Fathers on Wesley, see, for example: *Remains*, Vol. 3, pp. 134–35, 138, 152; *Wesley*, p. 419.

36   The fullest treatment of the relationship between Wesley and Clement is given by Anderson, *Wesley's Appropriation of the Thought of Clement of Alexandria*, which includes a section on Knox, pp. 210–16. The clearest evidence for Clement's influence on Wesley appears in Wesley's *Character of A Methodist* (1742), which is a reworking of chapter seven of Clement's *Stromateis*; see Wesley, *Journal*, Vol. 5, p. 197, entry for March 5, 1767. For the influence of Pseudo-Macarius, see: Ford, "Saint Makarios of Egypt and John Wesley;" Outler, *John Wesley*, p. 9, n. 26; Snyder, "John Wesley and Macarius the Egyptian." Note also, Wesley's own remark, that he "read Macarius and sang" (*Journal*, Vol. 1, p. 254, entry for July 30, 1736). For the influence of Chrysostom on Wesley, see: McCormick, "John Wesley's Use of John Chrysostom" and Young's "Grace and Demand;" "Inner Struggle,"and "God's Word Proclaimed."

37   *Wesley*, p. 419 (emphasis in the original). For Knox's view of Christianity as practice rather than dogma, see below, p. 111.

38   English, "Wesley and the Anglican Moderates," p. 206. For the influence of the moderates on Wesley, see also, English, "The Cambridge Platonists in Wesley's 'Christian Library'." See also below, p. 87.

were of primary importance, received his first exposure to them from Wesley, although there is no definitive evidence of this.

4   Knox's Disagreements with Wesley's Theology

In light of the argument that Knox's theology was substantially derived from Wesley, it is disconcerting to find that, on a number of occasions, Knox insisted on his autonomy from Wesley. "I never called Mr. Wesley, Rabbi," he asserted.[39] Nonetheless, if one examines the points on which Knox distanced himself from Wesley one will find that, for the most part, they concerned what Knox called "circumstantial extravagances." These Knox explicitly distinguished from "the substance of John Wesley's religion." And, he wrote: "I as much love the one as I should shrink back from the other."[40] Apart from his criticisms of the "middle" Wesley, and the residual Lutheran understanding of faith which Knox perceived in his "late" phase, there were only two major doctrinal points on which Knox took issue with his mentor. The first concerned the sudden attainment of perfection.[41] Wesley taught that a person could become perfect in a moment: Knox denied this, arguing that perfection was a process. One should note, however, that Wesley qualified his doctrine of instantaneous perfection by affirming that there is "a *gradual* work, both *before* and *after* that moment. So that one may affirm, the work is *gradual*, another, it is *instantaneous*, without any manner of contradiction."[42] Allowing for this "gradual work" meant that Wesley could speak of perfection as something dynamic and admitting of "a continual increase"[43] and thus his difference from Knox on this point was less great than might be supposed. Otherwise, with regard to Wesley's doctrine of perfection, Knox held that, although Wesley's views of the subject had at one time been "excessive," he had subsequently corrected himself, so much so that Knox affirmed that a "more just or more delightful idea of matured piety could [not] easily be found." It was an idea to which he confessed himself personally beholden. "I think, to [Wesley] more than to any human instrumentality,

---

39   *Remains*, Vol. 1, p. 79 (as so often, Knox makes a scriptural allusion, in this case to Matthew 23, 8). For other statements of independence from Wesley, see: *Remains*, Vol. 1, p. 275; Vol. 3, pp. 78, 443; Vol. 4, pp. 278, 280, 282; *Wesley*, pp. 418–19, 481.

40   *Wesley*, p. 462; *Remains*, Vol. 4, p. 279.

41   *Remains*, Vol. 3, p. 468; *Wesley*, pp. 454–55.

42   Wesley, *A Plain Account of Christian Perfection*, p. 73 (emphasis in the original).

43   Wesley, Sermon 40, "Christian Perfection," 1, 9, in Outler, ed., *Works of John Wesley*, Vol. 2, pp. 97–124, at p. 104.

I am indebted for whatever light I have [on this subject]," he declared.[44] Knox's second point of disagreement with Wesley concerned the interior witness of the Holy Spirit.[45] Wesley taught that the Holy Spirit directly and immediately bestows "an inward impression on the souls of believers, whereby [it] directly testifies to their spirit that they are children of God." Gerald Cragg calls this doctrine "one of Wesley's distinctive contributions to the presentation of religious truth," while Thomas Lessmann goes so far as to describe it as the heart of Wesley's theology.[46] Knox, however, rejected the teaching, which he claimed to be based on "one single [Bible] verse ... the construction of which [Wesley] has really, though, I am certain, unconsciously, forced to his purpose."[47] Knox's opposition on this point was two-fold. First, he argued that the doctrine "opened a door for self-delusion," for there was no criterion by which the subjective sentiment of assurance could be shown to come directly from the Holy Spirit. Second, Knox asserted that reliance on "feeling" (which here he used, unusually, in a pejorative sense) risked impeding spiritual progress, since people would be tempted to trust in it for salvation, rather than striving to grow in holiness.[48] He therefore offered an alternative theory. Sure evidence, as he puts it, that we are actual objects of mercy is provided by the experience we have of the effects of grace, a transformation of our lives so radical that it can only be ascribed to divine agency.[49] In positing this theory as an alternative to Wesley's teaching, Knox seems to ignore Wesley's insistence that the direct witness of the Spirit is accompanied by the indirect witness of the fruit of the Spirit, which, Wesley says, immediately springs from the direct testimony, and is inseparable from it.[50] Since the fruit of the Spirit is for Wesley that described by St. Paul in Galatians 5, 22, love, joy, peace, and so forth, it appears once again that there is less difference between him and Knox than might initially appear.

The point on which Knox and Wesley most diverged was one which Knox does not mention as being a difference between them: their respective views of the atonement. For Knox, salvation was far less something accomplished

---

44   *Wesley*, pp. 454–55; *Remains*, Vol. 3, pp. 468–69; Vol. 4, p. 282. See also, *Correspondence*, Vol. 1, pp. 144–45.

45   *Wesley*, pp. 481–83.

46   Wesley, Sermon 11, "The Witness of the Spirit: 2," 5, p. 1, in Outler, ed., *Works of John Wesley*, Vol. 1, pp. 285–298, at p. 296; Cragg, *Reason and Authority in the Eighteenth Century*, p. 166; Lessmann, *Rolle und Bedeutung*, p. 47. On this aspect of Wesley's theology, see Yates, *Doctrine of Assurance*.

47   *Wesley*, p. 481. The verse in question is Romans 8, 16.

48   *Wesley*, pp. 482–483.

49   For Knox's statement of this doctrine, see, for example: *Remains*, Vol. 1, pp. 26, 516; Vol. 2, pp. 50–51, 336–37, 479; Vol. 4, pp. 127, 378; *Correspondence*, Vol. 2, pp. 108, 511, 527–29.

50   See, on this point, Wesley, Sermon 11, "The Witness of the Spirit, II," 2, 1; 7, in Outler, ed., *Works of John Wesley*, 1, pp. 285–98, pp. 286, 288.

in the past by Christ on the cross than an on-going process of healing, which Christ works here and now in believers' lives.[51] This position certainly mirrors one side of Wesley's teaching, and three times one finds Knox quoting Wesley's definition of salvation as "a present deliverance from sin; a restoration of the soul to its primitive health, its original purity; a recovery of the divine nature; the renewal of our souls after the image of God in righteousness and true holiness, in justice, mercy and truth."[52]

As well as "Christ reigning in us," Wesley held that "Christ dying for us" should be preached with equal insistence. He proclaimed both "salvation from sin *and* the consequences of sin ... a deliverance from guilt and punishment, by the atonement of Christ ... *and* a deliverance from the power of sin through Christ 'formed in [the] heart.'"[53] His treatment of "Christ dying for us" was particularly rich and multifaceted. It included a subjective element: Christ crucified was (in the words of Randy Maddox) "the Representative of God's pardoning and restoring love," a love which as such attracted and drew souls.[54] And it is in this way that Knox, when he does speak about the atonement, explains the salvific significance of the cross. But the subjective theory by no means exhausted Wesley's understanding of Christ's death. Harald Lindström, for example, cogently demonstrated in his book *Wesley and Sanctification* (1950) that Wesley's primary understanding of atonement was as a work of satisfaction. It was, ironically, this emphasis in Wesley's teaching that was taken up by the Evangelicals against whom Knox's soteriology was intended as a direct counterblast.[55]

5   Knox's Agreement with Wesley's Theology

The differences between Knox and Wesley were minor, compared with what they held in common. When it came to what Knox designated as "the very pith and marrow of Mr. Wesley's views, and ... those matters which through life he most prized, most dwelt upon, and which lay nearest his heart," it was Knox's persuasion that "there is not one of his own nominal followers who

---

51   For Knox's teaching on the atonement, see below, pp. 157–62.

52   Wesley, *A Farther Appeal to Men of Reason and Religion*, 1, 1, 3, in Cragg, ed., *Works of John Wesley*, 11, pp. 105–202, at p. 106. Knox cites the passage: *Remains*, 1, pp. 180; 278–79; *Wesley*, p. 421.

53   Wesley to Charles Perronet, letter, December 28, 1774, *Letters*, 6, p. 134; Wesley, Sermon 1, "Salvation by Faith," 2, 7, in Outler, ed., *Works of John Wesley*, 1, pp. 117–30, at p. 124 (emphases added).

54   Maddox, *Responsible Grace*, p. 109.

55   Bebbington, *Evangelicalism in Modern Britain*, p. 14.

agrees with him more identically than I do."[56] The reason for this was that Knox saw Wesley as perfecting one of the two great traditions into which, Knox believed, Christianity been divided since post-Apostolic times: the tradition of holiness, which Knox identified with Christian Platonism.[57] As he wrote to Jebb in a letter dated July 19, 1804: "In John Wesley's views of christian perfection are combined, in substance, all the sublime morality of the greek fathers, the spirituality of the mystics, and the divine philosophy of our favourite platonists. Macarius, Fénelon, Lucas, and all their respective classes, have been consulted and digested by him; and his ideas are, essentially, theirs."[58] As Knox told Hannah More, Wesley's teaching was "the very spirit of Macarius and Chrysostom, of Smith and Cudworth, of De Sales and Fénélon, simplified, systematised, rationalised, and evangelised!"[59] Evangelized, because in Knox's estimation, Wesley had succeeded in harmonizing the Platonic tradition of holiness with what Knox held to be the other great school of Christian thought, that of divine grace. Exemplified for Knox by St. Augustine, this school emphasised, in Knox's view, the depth of sin's depravity, and the consequent necessity of God's aid to remedy the human situation. It taught, as Knox put it, how the foundations of the Christian life were to be laid, just as Platonism taught how to raise up on this foundation the superstructure of good works. Hence, Knox's encomium of Wesley: "[N]ever, elsewhere, except in the Apostles themselves, and in the sacred books they have left, were the true foundation, and the sublime superstructure of Christianity so effectually united."[60]

6   Knox and Methodism

Knox's esteem for Wesley was matched by his opposition to those whom he decried as "Separating Methodists."[61] As early as 1785, he produced a tract, *Free Thoughts*, directed against them. In this pamphlet, Knox appealed to Wesley

---

56   *Remains*, 1, p. 80.
57   On Christian Platonism, see chapter 4.
58   *Correspondence*, Vol. 1, p. 145 (lack of capitalization in the original). For those mentioned, see chapter 4.
59   *Remains*, Vol. 3, p. 138.
60   Ibid., Vol. 1, p. 83. See, also, for examples of this theme: *Remains*, Vol. 1, pp. 179–82; Vol. 3, 78–79, 134–35, 152–53, 170, 226, 483. Knox claims inspiration for the distinction from Wesley (*Remains*, Vol. 1, p. 77), although it first appears in his writings in a letter to Jebb, dated June 21, 1804 (*Correspondence*, Vol. 1, pp. 134–35). One may note that, despite his effusive praise of Wesley's synthesis, Knox believed that this synthesis needed further development. See below, p. 88.
61   *Candid Animadversions*, p. 7.

to remind his readers that Methodism had been raised up not to proclaim any new doctrine or to change people from one religious opinion to another, but to bring them "from sin and Satan to the living God."[62] Luke Tyerman describes the tract as "important," because it sums up so clearly the debate in the Methodism of the period between those who wanted to break with the Church of England, and those who wanted to remain within it.[63] Tyerman did not identify the author of the tract, and perhaps he did not know his identity, because Knox wrote simply as "A Layman of the Methodist Society." When Knox next dealt with the topic of separation, in 1794, it was significantly as "A Member of the Established Church." His *Considerations on a Separation of the Methodists*, soon followed by a second pamphlet, *Candid Animadversions* (also 1794) was directed against his former friend and fellow-Irishman, Henry Moore.[64] Moore was favorable to those Methodists who desired to receive the sacraments from ministers of their own, rather than from the clergy of the Church of England. The trustees of the "Old Room" chapel in Bristol, where Moore was a preacher, were opposed to any such move, and sought to inhibit Moore's ministry. Abel Stevens notes: "The dispute soon involved the whole Methodist community, and pamphlets and printed circulars were scattered 'almost from John O'Groat's to Land's End.'" Knox's tracts were included in these, and, according to Stevens, they were among the most important contributions made to the debate.[65]

In 1795 the governing body of English Methodism, the Conference, approved the so-called "Plan of Pacification," which allowed preachers not ordained in the Church of England to celebrate Holy Communion. Despite the provisos with which this permission was hedged, the Plan represented, to quote Richard P. Heitzenrater, "an acknowledgment of British Methodism's final ecclesiastical separation from the Church of England," and it is from this decision that the existence of Methodism as a separate denomination in England is dated.[66] Seeking to help avert a similar split in Ireland, Knox visited

---

62 *Free Thoughts*, p. 3.
63 Tyerman, *Life and Times of Wesley*, Vol. 3, pp. 468–69.
64 Henry Moore (1751–1844), a native of Dublin, was a close associate of Wesley. He arrived as a preacher in Londonderry in 1779 and became a friend of the Knox family, although, as noted in the text, at the time of his conflict with Knox he was stationed in Bristol. It was his *Reply* to Knox's *Considerations* (1794) which occasioned *Candid Animadversions*. Moore and Knox were eventually reconciled. See Smith, *Life of Moore*, especially pp. 49, 76, 130–32.
65 Stevens, *History of Methodism*, Vol. 3, pp. 57–58.
66 Heitzenrater, *Wesley and the People Called Methodists*, p. 316.

the Irish Methodist Conference annually between 1806 and 1809.[67] Right up
to the eve of the 1809 Conference he remained optimistic that he could persuade the Methodist leadership to remain part of the Established Church,
but his hopes were dashed when the Conference gave its support to Adam
Averell, who, although only a deacon, had taken it upon himself to start admin-
istering the Eucharist.[68] Knox's feelings on the matter appear in a letter which
he wrote shortly afterwards to Hannah More. He began by describing what he
called a "most unpleasant" circumstance, "the adoption of a clear dissenting
principle by the Irish Wesleyan Methodists." "I take it to be fixed past recall,"
he lamented. "The apparent effects of this change will, probably, not be sudden; but they must be certain." Knox then explained how Averell had started
celebrating "the Lord's Supper," as he termed it, before continuing:

> [T]he body of Methodist preachers, at their yearly conference last July,
> having fully heard the matter, were pleased to sanction Mr. A.'s proceed-
> ings. So that his violation of the established order, in its most central prin-
> ciple, is now the common act of the fraternity. This occurrence has given
> me no surprise: it has only disappointed a very faint hope. I knew well the
> Irish Wesleyan Methodists had no steady principles. But, inferring, from
> this obvious fact, that Providence alone could have kept them in their
> subordinate state for fifteen years, in spite of the example of their breth-
> ren in England, I thought it possible that the same restraint upon them
> might still be continued. My hope of this, however, grew less and less, in

---

67 These are the years for which there are mentions of Knox's presence at the Conference;
    see *Correspondence*, Vol. 1, pp. 264, 348–50, 426–27, 552. On Knox's attendance at the
    Conference see also, Ewens, *Three Hermits*, pp. 48–51, and for the background, Cooney,
    The Methodists in Ireland, pp. 58–62. With regard to the Conference: in 1789, when, owing
    to political circumstances, there was a ban on public assemblies, it was at least in part
    thanks to Knox that the Conference was able to meet (Crookshank, *History of Methodism
    in Ireland*, Vol. 2, p. 147; Cooney, *The Methodists in Ireland*, p. 52). This was one of at
    least three occasions when Knox sought to aid Methodism from behind the scenes. In
    February 1801 he wrote to Castlereagh opposing the hostility of the English episcopate to
    Methodism (letter, February 19, 1801, in Vane, *Memoirs and Correspondence*, Vol. 4, pp. 53–
    60). In July 1803, in a letter on Presbyterianism in Ireland, he added a plea for Castlereagh
    to look into a measure passed by the government of Jamaica to prohibit Methodist
    preachers evangelizing slaves (letter, July 18, 1803, in Vane, *Memoirs and Correspondence*,
    Vol. 4, pp. 284–90).
68 For Adam Averell (1754–1847), see Stewart and Revington, *Memoir of Adam Averell*. Averell
    was Knox's cousin (*Correspondence*, Vol. 1, p. 264). For Knox's hopes for averting a split
    between Methodists and the Church, see *Correspondence*, Vol. 1, pp. 426–27, 437, 552.

proportion as I saw the Irish Methodists becoming more and more spirit-
less and formal. Principles of corruption were, self-evidently, extending
themselves within; and tokens of morbidness must, at length, appear on
the surface. That event has clearly come ...[69]

Despite these gloomy sentiments, Knox did not abandon hope entirely,
and even as late as 1813 one finds him refusing to account Irish Methodists
as schismatics on the grounds that they did exhibit "*separate communion.*"[70]
Three years later, however, the Conference of 1816 authorized the celebration
of baptism and the Eucharist by Methodist ministers and with this step the
Methodist Church in Ireland was born, although the "Primitive Methodist
Wesleyan Society" was established at the same time by those who wished to
remain members of the Church.[71]

In part, Knox opposed separation on extra-theological grounds. First,
separation would injure the interests of the Established Church, depriving
it of a much-needed leaven, while at the same time giving joy to the forces
of "infidelity."[72] Secondly, he predicted that separation would injure the
Methodists themselves. It would remove them from the haven of doctrinal
safety provided by the Church's formularies and leave them exposed to every
current of heterodox opinion, as well as inculcating a religious formalism instead of spiritual ardour, if not downright scepticism.[73] Thirdly, separation
was contrary to the express wishes of John Wesley, who "[e]very where, and
on all occasions ... had inculcated on his people the strictest attachment to
the established communion." If Wesley had subsequently acted in "direct contradiction to the whole tenor of [his] language through life," it was at a time
when "his strength [was] failing, his memory decaying, and his whole frame
rapidly sinking into the grave," and he could easily be led astray "by subtility
and management."[74] Whatever force Knox's other arguments may have had,
this last one, for all its rhetoric, was weak, betraying an apparent ignorance on
Knox's part of how many ordinations Wesley had been performing. Knox spoke

---

69   *Remains*, Vol. 4, pp. 231–33 (layout altered). Knox also wrote to Brodrick on the subject:
     N. L. I., Ms 8868, Brodrick Papers, (folder 4), Knox to Charles Brodrick, letter, December 6,
     1809.
70   *Correspondence*, Vol. 2, p. 172. Emphasis in the original.
71   See Cooney, *The Methodists in Ireland*, pp. 61–62.
72   *Correspondence*, Vol. 1, p. 140; *Considerations*, pp. 11–12, 34–35.
73   *Considerations*, pp. 27, 7, 32.
74   *Candid Animadversions*, pp. 17, 20.

of "a single contradictory act,"[75] whereas Wesley had carried out a whole series of ordinations, clearly after careful deliberation.[76] Knox was, however, right to say that Wesley constantly urged his followers to remain united to the Church of England.[77] The dichotomy exemplifies the ambivalent nature of Wesley's relationship to Anglicanism. To use a simile which Frank Baker borrows from Joseph Beaumont, Wesley was like a rower, looking one way while moving another, in theory desiring to "live and die a member of the Church of England," while in practice pulling away from it.[78] Knox was aware of this dichotomy. He fully understood "that two dissonant principles wrought in Mr. Wesley's mind; that he was unfeignedly attached to the Church of England, but that he was more sensitively and practically united to his own society." Knox argued that, being convinced the Methodist movement was "indispensable" to the "good [of] many thousands of human beings," Wesley would, "in a case of absolute necessity," have chosen his society over the Church of England, although, in fact, he was wholly opposed to "a gratuitous separation," assuring Knox shortly before his death that in the event of such a separation, his friends should "adhere to the Church, and leave the Methodists."[79] Knox's main opposition to the Methodists leaving the Established Church was, however, theological, showing, incidentally, that, even at this early stage, Knox was possessed of a High Church ecclesiology. Knox does not employ the word "schism," but the term "separation," is its equivalent in his vocabulary and is constituted, in his view, by the creation of a separate sacramental system, and a separate hierarchy to administer it. Separation, "in the opinion of all the fathers of the Church, and indeed self-evidently, consists in *Altare contra Altare*, i.e., one altar opposed to another; in other words, in an *independent ordination* and *administration of the sacraments*." Thus "[i]*ndependent Ordination* and administration of the *Sacraments* constitute an Independent, Separate Church," he argued.[80]

---

75   Ibid., p. 20.

76   For Wesley's ordinations, see Baker, *John Wesley and the Church of England*, chapter 15, "1784 (III): Ordination is Separation," pp. 256–82. Wesley ended up ordaining twenty-seven presbyters and two "superintendents" (ibid., p. 282).

77   "I am a Church-of-England man and ... in the Church I will live and die" (John Wesley to Henry Moore, letter, May 6, 1788, *Letters*, Vol. 8, p. 58).

78   Baker, *John Wesley and the Church of England*, p. 2.

79   *Wesley*, pp. 438, 446, 439; *Considerations*, p. 36.

80   *Considerations*, p. 31.

7   **Conclusion**

This chapter has explored in greater depth the link between Knox and Wesley. We began by looking at Knox's defences of Wesley, especially his *Remarks*, a work whose importance has been recognized by several modern scholars because of the light which it sheds on its subject, whom Knox portrayed as a High Churchman inspired by the Christian Platonic tradition. But Knox's essay also tells us about its author, indicating the influence which Wesley had on him, as well as Wesley's contribution to his formation as a High Churchman. Wesley's influence on Knox began early, in the letters Wesley wrote to him, which already contained in germ a number of themes which would fructify in Knox's later theology. Wesley's influence is to be seen likewise in Knox's admiration for the Greek Fathers and the Anglican moderates, to whom Knox was, in all probability, first introduced by Wesley. Despite Knox's declarations of independence from Wesley, the differences between the two were, in the main, over circumstantial issues. Nonetheless, differences over matters of substance did exist. Knox objected to what he regarded as a flawed view of the nature of faith in some of Wesley's statements, which he saw as a remnant of Wesley's Lutheran phase, at odds with the sounder understanding which Wesley had inherited from the Fathers and the moderates. Knox rejected, too, Wesley's doctrine of sudden conversion to perfection, as well as his teaching on the interior witness of the Holy Spirit. On both these points, however, there seems to be less distance between Knox and Wesley than Knox implied. More significant was the soteriological divergence between the two, which Knox nonetheless ignored. Wesley held that salvation was a present work of Christ, effected in the believer's heart; and Knox shared this view, explicitly invoking Wesley's authority in support of it. But Wesley was equally emphatic that Christ's death was salvific, an atonement wrought for the human race, and this aspect of Wesley's teaching is absent from Knox, who wanted to minimize the importance of the cross, which he believed to have been exaggerated by Evangelicals. Despite these differences, when it came to what Knox termed "the very pith and marrow" of Wesley's teaching, the two men were, Knox claimed, in harmony. Knox deemed Wesley to have perfected what Knox saw as one of the two great traditions of Christianity, the tradition of holiness, above all by uniting it to the other great tradition, that of grace. The chapter closed with an examination of Knox's attitude towards the Methodist movement, which he consistently strove to keep within the pale of the Established Church. His earliest published writings, *Free Thoughts*, *Considerations* and *Candid Animadversions*, were significant contributions to the debate over separation, and, after English

Methodism became its own denomination, he sought, by personal contact, to avert the same outcome in Ireland. His motivations in so doing were several. He argued that such a move would be detrimental to Anglicans and Methodists alike, as well as being in opposition to Wesley's own wishes. Knox's main objection to separation was, nonetheless, theological: he saw it as an act of schism. Having examined the relationship between Knox and Wesley, we now turn in the next chapter to examine more fully the theological and philosophical tradition to which they both belonged, the tradition of Christian Platonism.

CHAPTER 4

Alexander Knox and the Christian Platonic Tradition

As we saw in the previous chapter, Knox regarded John Wesley as belonging to the Christian Platonic tradition. This was the tradition to which Knox himself belonged, so in the present chapter we will analyse the nature of Christian Platonism and Knox's understanding of it. We begin with a brief summary of the tradition, before examining those whom Knox regarded as its chief representatives: Clement of Alexandria; Pseudo-Macarius; Chrysostom; the Anglican moderates; and Wesley himself; as well as those whom Knox viewed as deforming the tradition, the "modern mystics," as he labelled them. The chapter closes with a section on Knox's own Platonism.

1   The Platonic Tradition

The origin of Christian Platonism lies in an initially somewhat obscure phrase from Plato's dialogue *Theaetetus*, that the goal of human life is ὁμοίωσις θεῷ κατὰ τὸ δυνατόν (*homoiōsis theōi kata to dynaton*: assimilation to God as much as is possible) and δίκαιον καὶ ὅσιον μετὰ φρονήσεως γενέσθαι (*dikaion kai hosion meta phronēseōs genesthai*: to be righteous, and holy, and wise).[1] This teaching was picked up by Eudorus of Alexandria and the Middle Platonist school, and subsequently adopted by a number of patristic writers, specifically those of Alexandria and Cappadocia, who saw it as corresponding to the teaching of the Bible, particularly 2 Peter 1, 4, which speaks of Christians being made "partakers of the divine nature." The doctrine is encapsulated by Gregory of Nyssa in his formula: "The end of the virtuous life is likeness to God." This God-likeness, or θέωσις (*theōsis*), as it eventually came to be called, was achieved, the Fathers taught, by the Holy Spirit dwelling in the hearts of believers, a theory which continued to be maintained in the Christian East, but gradually disappeared in the West.[2] In the sixteenth century, however, it was revived by, among others,

---

1   Plato, *Theaetetus*, line 176b (my translation).
2   There is a fairly extensive literature on the subject of *theosis*. For the pre-Christian development, see Dillon, *The Middle Platonists*. For the doctrine in general, and especially in Christianity, see, besides Russell (fn 6, below): Christensen and Wittung, eds., *Partakers*

© KONINKLIJKE BRILL NV, LEIDEN, 2020 | DOI:10.1163/9789004426986_006

several scholars at the University of Cambridge. Cambridge was also the scene
of a second revival in the seventeenth century, and from these Cambridge
Platonists it was mediated, at least in part, to Wesley.

2   Clement of Alexandria

Knox referred to the Platonic tradition several times, most notably in a letter to
Hannah More, dated December 27, 1806.[3] His description of it is historically accurate, broadly speaking, though it includes certain interpretations of his own,
which are open to question. Knox held that Platonism was "prepared providentially ... as [a] preliminary to christian [*sic*] piety,"[4] and thereafter introduced into the church by Clement of Alexandria. To quote the metaphor Knox
uses, "Clemens Alexandrinus" was the first to bind "the tender vine of Christian
spirituality to the deeply-rooted elm of Platonism."[5] The observation is one
with which modern scholarship would concur. Norman Russell, for example,
identifies Clement as "the first to use the technical vocabulary of deification."[6]
Likewise, Eric Osborn writes that Clement was the first Christian author after
the New Testament to deal at length with Christian spiritual life; and that, in
so doing, he became the first to expound the doctrine of God-likeness in a sustained fashion. Indeed, as Osborn notes, "The veritable leitmotif of Clement's
moral teaching is assimilation to God."[7] For Clement, Christians are called to
fulfil the ideal of Genesis 1, 26 and become like God. Thus, the true Christian

---

of the Divine Nature; Kärkkäinen, *One with God*; Louth, *Origins of the Christian Mystical Tradition*. Older, but still useful, are Lossky, *Mystical Theology*, and Lot-Borodine, *Déification de l'Homme*. The citation from Gregory of Nyssa is from *Homily 1 on the Beatitudes*, 6, *P. G.*, 44, col. 1200.

3   *Remains*, Vol. 3, pp. 103–230. See also: *Correspondence*, Vol. 1, p. 145; *Eclectic Review*, 6 (May 1810), p. 394.
4   *Correspondence*, Vol. 1, pp. 300–301.
5   *Remains*, Vol. 3, pp. 141–42. For Clement see: Ferguson, *Clement of Alexandria*; Lilla, *Clement of Alexandria*; and Osborn, *Clement of Alexandria*. Much that is useful in Osborn's book, from the point of view of the present section, is summarized in his essay, "The Bible and Christian Morality in Clement of Alexandria." More specific treatments of Clement's "practical theol-ogy," which is where Knox has most affinity with him, are: Behr, *Asceticism and Anthropology*, especially chapter five, "Rebirth and Christian Life," pp. 152–84, and chapter six, "The Higher Christian Life: *gnōsis, apatheia, agapē*," pp. 185–208; and Karavites, *Evil, Freedom, and the Road to Perfection in Clement of Alexandria*, especially chapter five, "Clement's Gnostic," pp. 139–74. The most recent treatment of the subject is Ashwin-Siejkowski, *Clement of Alexandria*.
6   Russell, *Deification in the Greek Patristic Tradition*, p. 1. See, also, pp. 52, 85.
7   Osborn, "The Bible and Moral Theology in Clement of Alexandria," p. 114. See, also, Osborn, *Clement of Alexandria*, p. 140.

or, in Clement's terminology, the Gnostic, is one who serves the Lord in cease-less love, assimilated to God as far as is humanly possible, through the practice of virtue. "Perfected according to the image of the master, the Gnostic be-comes divine while still living in the flesh."[8] This divinisation is accomplished, first, through the reading of Scripture, where, according to Clement, Christ "makes human beings divine by heavenly teaching, putting his laws into their minds, and inditing them upon their hearts."[9] Thus it is through the Bible that Christians learn how to be disciples, and imitate the life of Christ – though, as Russell notes, this learning demands that the Bible be interpreted according to the church's teaching. As Russell puts it, for Clement, "[i]t is divine *gnosis* received in accordance with the ecclesiastical rule of faith that deifies."[10] Knowledge alone, however, is not enough. As Osborn notes, "virtue calls for human effort *and* divine grace."[11] Clement made the activity of the Holy Spirit in the life of the believer an essential element in his teaching: "[F]or Clement only re-birth in baptism and the gift of the spirit can produce ... transforma-tion into God's likeness."[12] As Antonio Orbe writes, in baptism there descends on the Christian "the same divine life that descended fully on Jesus ... The one difference resides in the quantity: On Jesus descended *omnis fons Spiritus Sancti*; on the neophyte a participation in it. But it is always the same Spirit, the perfect Life of God."[13] All the same points appear in Knox, who, while regard-ing Clement's language as extravagant and hyperbolic, had no issues with the essential elements of Clement's teaching.[14]

3   Pseudo-Macarius

A second patristic example of Christian Platonism that was invoked by Knox was the author of the *Fifty Spiritual Homilies*, whom Knox believed, like the vast majority of his contemporaries, to have been Macarius the Great,

---

8   Clement, *Stromateis*, 7, 16, *P. G.*, 9, col. 540.
9   Clement, *Protrepticus*, 11, *P. G.*, 8, col. 233. Clement alludes to Jeremiah 31, 33.
10   Russell, *Doctrine of Deification*, p. 126.
11   Osborn, *Clement of Alexandria*, p. 237 (emphasis added).
12   Ibid., p. 234. See also pp. 152–53.
13   Orbe, "Teologia Bautismal," p. 444, note, quoted by Ferguson, *Baptism in the Early Church*, p. 311, n. 13. The Latin phrase which Orbe employs means "the whole fountain of the Holy Spirit" (my translation). For the emphasis in Clement on the importance of the church and sacraments, see Russell, *Deification in the Greek Patristic Tradition*, p. 138.
14   *Remains*, Vol. 1, pp. 351, 353; *Wesley*, p. 460. Knox is not alone in his criticism of Clement's language; as Russell notes, some of the latter's expressions are "startling to Western ears" (*Doctrine of Deification*, p. 121).

"an Egyptian monk of the 4th century."[15] Modern scholarship, however, designates the author of these *Homilies* as Pseudo-Macarius, usually identified as a Syrian ascetic, writing somewhere in the 380s.[16] Despite his location in Syria, many aspects of Pseudo-Macarius's thought are, as Marcus Plested notes, "rooted in the Alexandrine theological tradition, doubtless due in part to the influence of the Cappadocian Fathers, into whose orbit he fell," Cappadocia having been evangelised by St. Gregory Thaumaturgos, a disciple of Origen.[17] Although Knox taxed Pseudo-Macarius, like Clement, with extravagance of language, he still hailed him as being among "the most excellent of the Fathers." He was, he observed, "a wonderful spiritualist; no Greek Father is so (strictly speaking) experimental."[18] By this Knox meant both that Pseudo-Macarius was interested in praxis rather than abstract speculation, and that he was concerned with the inward experience of God. In both these senses, Knox's assessment of Pseudo-Macarius as an "experimental" theologian once again accords with the verdict of modern scholarship, which sees Pseudo-Macarius as a deeply practical theologian, central to whose teaching was the direct experience of the triune God. He conceived of Christianity not primarily in terms of assent to reasoned arguments or outward conformity to a moral code, but as the progressive sanctification and deification of the believer, which saw a move from a heart possessed by evil to a heart indwelt by both sin and grace, and then, finally, to a heart from which sin has been wholly cast out, one that belonged to God alone. This progression represented (in Stewart's phrase), "the co-operative triumph of human will and divine Spirit", for only by the indwelling of the Holy Spirit was the Christian enabled to obey God spotlessly and perfectly. Thus the believer could not but be πνευματικός (*pneumatikos*), one who lived in and through the Spirit.[19]

---

15   B. L., Add. Ms 41163, Correspondence between Alexander Knox and John Jebb (1799–1811), fol. 66, Knox to John Jebb, letter, March 20, 1805.

16   For Pseudo-Macarius, see: Maloney, *Pseudo-Macarius*; Plested, *Macarian Legacy*; and Stewart, *Working the Earth of the Heart*. See also, for a briefer introduction, Golitzin, "Testimony." For references to Pseudo-Macarius in Knox, see: *Remains*, Vol. 1, pp. 350–53, 360; Vol. 3, pp. 109, 138, 281–82; Vol. 4, p. 333; *Correspondence*, Vol. 1, p. 302; B. L., Add. Ms 41163, Correspondence between Alexander Knox and John Jebb (1799–1811), fol. 66, Knox to John Jebb, letter, March 20, 1805.

17   Plested, *Macarian Legacy*, p. 14. On the specific issue of the links between Pseudo-Macarius and the Alexandrian tradition, see: Golitzin, "Testimony," pp. 130–31, 133; Maloney, *Pseudo-Macarius*, pp. 3, 9–11. For the doctrine of deification in Pseudo-Macarius, see Russell, *Deification in the Greek Patristic Tradition*, pp. 241–45.

18   *Remains*, Vol. 1, p. 352; Vol. 4, p. 333; Vol. 3, p. 281.

19   Plested, *Macarian Legacy*, pp. 2–3, 36; Ware, "Preface" to Maloney, p. xiv Maloney, *Pseudo-Macarius*, p. 27; Stewart, *Working the Earth of the Heart*, pp. 74–75, 80, 81, 109; Russell, *Deification in the Greek Patristic Tradition*, p. 242.

4   John Chrysostom

"I love Macarius," Knox once wrote to Jebb, "but I rejoice in Chrysostom."[20] For Knox, Chrysostom was the patriarch of the holiness tradition, completing the work of synthesis between Christianity and Platonism which Clement had begun.[21] The idea is not immediately compelling, since there is no direct link to be discerned between the Alexandrian Clement and the Antiochene Chrysostom, in whom the language of deification is by no means explicit. To quote Russell: "The great Antiochene fathers never use the term 'deification' at all."[22] Nonetheless, if the language of deification is not present in Chrysostom, the idea is. Christ, observed Chrysostom, "discoursed of doctrine only seldom ... but often, indeed always, of life;" and it was with life that Chrysostom concerned himself, too. As J. N. D. Kelly says, he was "much more a practical than a dogmatic theologian."[23] He preached a life of holiness, of total commitment to the Gospel, involving (in Gus George Christo's words) "a complete change and renewal of heart and mind; from the heart and mind of sin to *the mind of Christ*."[24] In this sense, therefore, "Christian salvation, for Chrysostom, is understood primarily in terms of deification, that is, the attainment of divine likeness."[25] This likeness, however, can only be attained with the help of the Holy Spirit, which God has poured out abundantly on believers, dwelling permanently in them, making them not only temples, but instruments of righteousness, guiding their lives, as a helmsman does a ship, or a driver his chariot.[26] It is this which must make one leery of what appears to be Knox's too rigid distinction between the two traditions into which he argues Christianity has been divided, exemplified by Chrysostom and Augustine respectively.[27] Knox taxes Chrysostom and those like him with being "too little

---

20   *Correspondence*, Vol. 1, p. 302. For Knox's appreciation of Chrysostom, see: *Remains*, Vol. 1, pp. 101–2; Vol. 3, pp. 45–47, 75–78; Vol. 4, pp. 333, 438–39; and Hannah More to Knox, letter, November 30, 1809, in Roberts, *Memoirs*, Vol. 4, p. 306, where More speaks of "Your own Chrysostom." For an introduction to Chrysostom himself (c. 347–407), see Kelly, *Golden Mouth*.

21   *Remains*, Vol. 3, pp. 75, 127, 143–44.

22   Russell, *Doctrine of Deification in the Greek Patristic Tradition*, p. 237. See, also, his remarks on p. 14.

23   Chrysostom, "Homily 64 on Matthew," 4, *P. G.*, 58, col. 614; Kelly, *Golden Mouth*, p. 195.

24   Christo, "Introduction" to *St. John Chrysostom: On Repentance and Almsgiving*, p. xiv (emphasis in the original). See, also: Kelly, *Golden Mouth*, pp. 35, 43; and Young, "God's Word Proclaimed," p. 143.

25   Lai, "John Chrysostom and the Hermeneutics of Exemplar Portraits," p. 143.

26   Chrysostom, "Homily 11 on Matthew," 4, *P. G.*, 57, col. 197; "Homily 13 on Romans," 9, *P. G.*, 60, col. 520; Wenger, ed., *Huits Catechèses Baptismales*, p. 153; Chrysostom, "Homily 14 on Romans," 2, *P. G.*, 60, col. 525.

27   See, above, p. 68.

aware that we are not sufficient so much as to think any thing [*sic*] as of ourselves, but that it is God that worketh in us."[28] In fact, as David Rylaarsdam has
pointed out, according to Chrysostom, "grace is absolutely necessary [for salva-
tion]." For Chrysostom, "free will and the commandments are insufficient," as
are the "human striving and accomplishment characteristic of Greek *paideia*."[29]
Where Knox is right, however, is in his claim that Chrysostom has a different view of the plight of humanity from that of Augustine and his followers.
For Chrysostom, the consequence of Adam's sin is not, to use Knox's words,
"human depravity and human weakness," but subjection to mortality.[30]

5   Mysticism

For Knox, Chrysostom signaled a high point in the history of the Platonic tradition. After him came a period of decline, lasting, in Knox's estimation, for
centuries.[31] This period was marked by the emergence of mysticism, which he
castigated as "Platonic Christianity ... disfigured."[32] Such a negative judgement
on mysticism may at first sight appear surprising, if one defines mysticism
with Bernard McGinn as that part of Christianity's beliefs and practices which
"concerns the preparation for, the consciousness of, and the reaction to what
can be described as the immediate or direct presence of God."[33] On this definition, Knox might well be classed as a mystic, but it is a designation which
he would almost certainly have refused. This is clear from a letter he wrote
in 1810 to Daniel Parken. Parken had wanted Knox to write a piece on Charles
Butler's recently-published *Life of Fénelon* for the *Eclectic Review*, a request
with which Knox felt unable to comply, since he disagreed with the *Review*'s
evangelical theology. Nonetheless, since Parken had sent him a free copy of
Butler's book, Knox considered himself obliged to offer something more than
a simple refusal, and replied to Parken with a detailed account of his views on

---

28   *Remains*, Vol. 3, p. 79. Knox conflates 2 Corinthians 3, 5, and Philippians 2, 13. See, also, for
     this criticism of Chrysostom, *Correspondence*, Vol. 1, p. 135.
29   Rylaarsdam, *John Chrysostom on Divine Pedagogy*, pp. 144, 146. See also, for Chrysostom's
     teaching on what Edward Nowak calls "the benefits of Christ's suffering for humanity,"
     Nowak's book, *Le Chrétien devant la Souffrance*, pp. 114–25.
30   *Remains*, Vol. 3, p. 79. See on this point, Papageorgiou, "Chrysostom and Augustine."
31   *Remains*, Vol. 3, pp. 198–99.
32   Ibid., p. 145. See also p. 127.
33   McGinn, *Foundations of Mysticism*, p. xvii.

mysticism.[34] Describing Fénelon as a "modern mystic," a class in which he also included Miguel de Molinos, William Law, Madame Guyon and "all the German mystics,"[35] Knox contended that their methods were contrary to and, in fact, a suppression of "*that* nature, which God has formed us with." What mattered to the modern mystics was, Knox alleged, "the mere mind itself." For them, he believed, every other aspect of humanity was to be suppressed and even the mind was to be "absorbed in God."[36] But the contemplation of "the infinite, essential Godhead" is beyond the power of the human intellect. Attempting to leave all else aside and focus on it, renders the soul "bewildered and lost."[37] And that is why, he argued, "mirrors of God's own preparation" had been provided for humanity, the divine works of creation, providence, and redemption, which allow us to know God in a manner adapted to our nature.[38] This, Knox maintained, was especially true with regard to God's plan of redemption through the incarnation, which is why Knox could go so far as to say that mysticism was "hostile to Christianity." In turning themselves to the direct contemplation of the divine essence, the mystics were turning away from the manifestation of God in Christ.[39] Gunstone has suggested that the nature of Knox's mental affliction contributed to his distrust of mysticism: "The Quietist movement did give the impression, at least to Knox, that to be a mystic you were taken to realities beyond scripture and reason and personal control, something which would have been very threatening to someone who had a history of nervous complaints."[40] Whatever the truth of this suggestion, Knox's views on

---

34 *Remains*, Vol. 1, pp. 318–66. See, also, *Correspondence*, Vol. 2, pp. 30–31, where Knox summarizes the letter for Jebb, as well as giving the background to it. See also, *Correspondence*, Vol. 1, pp. 512–19, where Knox discusses mysticism with Jebb.

35 For the designation "modern mystic," see *Remains*, Vol. 1, pp. 322, 351. For those whom Knox includes in this class, see pp. 344, 363; *Correspondence*, Vol. 2, p. 31. François Fénelon (1651–1715) appears a number of times in Knox's writings, usually in a negative light. Despite his rejection of what he termed Fénelon's "peculiarities," however, Knox still found in him "much ... to admire and love," describing his piety as "pure and exalted" (*Remains*, Vol. 1, p. 321). For Fénelon, see, besides Butler, Raymond, *Fénelon*. For Miguel de Molinos (c. 1628–96), see Cross, ed., *O. D. C. C.*, p. 913. For William Law (1686–1761), see *O. D. N. B.* For Jeanne Guyon, (1648–1717), see Cross, ed., *O. D. C. C.*, p. 598. For the medieval German mystics, see McGinn, *Harvest of Mysticism*.

36 *Correspondence*, Vol. 2, p. 30 (emphasis in the original). The accusation that mysticism is unnatural is repeated throughout the letter to Parken; see *Remains*, Vol. 1, pp. 321, 329, 339–41.

37 *Remains*, Vol. 1, p. 327.

38 Ibid., p. 323.

39 Ibid., p. 333.

40 John Gunstone, letter to David McCready, March 19, 2008.

mysticism are one of the areas in which he could, and did, claim the influence
of Wesley. Wesley, Knox wrote, "considered the supposed self-annihilation
of mysticism to be in opposition to the tenor of Holy Scripture, which uniformly addresses itself to man's natural thirst for happiness." To such testimony, Knox (to quote his own words) could not "but attach inexpressible value
and importance."[41]

6   The Anglican Moderates

Knox made a clear distinction between modern writers such as Fénelon and
the "old mystics" or "ancient spiritualists," such as Clement of Alexandria
and Pseudo-Macarius.[42] Their legacy, long neglected, he saw as being at last
revived in the seventeenth century. In the van of this revival, Knox placed,
first of all, the Cambridge Platonists, of whom he cites four in particular:
Ralph Cudworth, John Smith, Benjamin Whichcote and John Worthington.[43]
Together with them, Knox associated a number of other figures, who shared
a similar theological outlook. To refer to the whole group, the Cambridge
Platonists and those whom Knox connected with them, a suitable designation
is English's term, the Anglican moderates of the seventeenth century.[44] Knox
himself spoke of them as Latitudinarians, but he did not include among them
several significant figures to whom this descriptor is usually applied, such as
John Tillotson and John Wilkins. On the contrary, these men and their ilk had,

---

41   *Wesley*, pp. 454, 472. Cf. Rattenbury, *Wesley's Legacy to the World*, chapter XI, "Methodism
     and Mysticism," pp. 117–36.
42   *Remains*, Vol. 1, p. 351.
43   Although the Cambridge Platonists are the subject of a fairly extensive literature, schol-
     ars have tended to concentrate on their philosophical views rather than their religious
     teaching. For this teaching see: Jones, ed., *The Cambridge Platonists*; Patrides, ed., *The
     Cambridge Platonists*; de Pauley, *The Candle of the Lord*; and Taliaferro and Teply, eds.,
     Cambridge Platonist Spirituality. For Ralph Cudworth (1617–88), see *O. D. N. B.*; for refer-
     ences to him in Knox's writings, see: *Remains*, Vol. 1, pp. 44, 153–55; Vol. 3, pp. 75, 109, 224,
     469, note; Vol. 4, pp. 146, 330; *Correspondence*, Vol. 1, p. 259. For John Smith (1618–52), see
     O. D. N. B.; for references to him in Knox's writings see: *Remains*, Vol. 1, pp. 77, 105–6,
     153–55, 270; Vol. 3, pp. 75, 80, 109, 221, 223; Vol. 4, pp. 91, 146, 158, 330; *Correspondence*,
     Vol. 1, pp. 28–29, 259; *Eclectic Review*, 6 (May 1810), p. 394. For Benjamin Whichcote (1609–
     83), see *O. D. N. B.*; for references to him in Knox's writings, see: *Remains*, Vol. 1, p. 73;
     Vol. 4, p. 146; *Correspondence*, Vol. 1, p. 259. For John Worthington (1618–71), see *O. D. N. B.*;
     for references to him in Knox's writings, see: *Remains*, Vol. 1, pp. 103–5, 154–55; Vol. 3,
     p. 469, note; Vol. 4, pp. 146–47, 158; *Correspondence*, Vol. 1, p. 27; Vol. 2, pp. 89–92; *Eclectic
     Review*, 6 (May 1810), p. 394.
44   See, above, p. 64.

according to Knox, reduced Christianity to nothing more than mere morality, following the example of Episcopius and the Dutch Remonstrants.[45]

The Cambridge Platonists were, for the most part, associated with Emmanuel College, a Puritan foundation, which during the sixteenth century, and much of the seventeenth, was dominated by a strict and uncompromising Calvinism. It was in reaction to this that the Platonists sought for a different theology. Although they are not generally seen as such, they were in many ways High Churchman, something made apparent by "S. P.," in his *Brief Account of the New Sect of Latitude-Men* (1662), in which he cautions: "[L]et no man accuse them of harkening too much to their own reason, since their reason steers by so excellent a compass: the ancient Fathers and the councils of the church." Describing the Platonists' theological position, "S. P." writes that it derives:

> not from the *spinose school-men*, or *Dutch systematicks*, neither from *Rome* nor *Geneva*, the Council of *Trent*, nor Synod of *Dort*, but from the sacred writings of the apostles and evangelists; in interpreting whereof, they carefully attend to the sense of the antient church, by which they conceive the modern ought to be guided: and therefore they are very conversant in all the genuine monuments of the antient Fathers, those especially of the first and purest ages.[46]

These "antient Fathers" were, above all, those of the east, particularly Alexandria, such as Clement, and from them the "latitude-men" took the idea that Christianity was, as Smith described it, a "*divine life*" rather than a "*divine science*," a religion in which one is called, in Whichcote's words, to "imitate God in his holiness and righteousness; in his truth and faithfulness." As Cudworth

---

45   *Correspondence*, Vol. 1, pp. 26, 259. The Remonstrants were the Dutch Arminians of the seventeenth century, a group whose views became increasingly less orthodox with the passage of time. For them and their leader, Simon Episcopius (1583–1643), see Ellis, *Simon Episcopius*, especially chapter 1, "Arminius and Episcopius in Historical Context," pp. 25–41. For Latitudinarianism, see Griffin, *Latitudinarianism in the Seventeenth Century Church of England* and Spellman, *The Latitudinarians and the Church of England*. For Knox's designation of the moderates as Latitudinarians, see *Remains*, Vol. 4, pp. 147, 158; *Correspondence*, Vol. 1, p. 170.

46   "S. P.," *Brief Account*, pp. 10, 9 (italicization in the original). "Spinose" means "thorny;" the Dutch "systematicks" are the Calvinist theologians of the Dutch Reformed Church, and maybe also the Arminian Remonstrants; the Synod of Dort (1618–19) is where the two parties clashed, the Synod upholding a strict Calvinism. For Dort and the contending parties, see Ellis, *Simon Episcopius*, pp. 35–36. "S. P." is usually identified as Simon Patrick (1626–1707). For him, as for John Tillotson (1630–94), Archbishop of Canterbury, and John Wilkins (1614–72), Bishop of Chester, see *O. D. N. B.*

expressed it, "[W]e must not judge of our knowing of Christ by our skill in books and papers, but by our keeping of his commandments."[47] This one is enabled to do, the Cambridge Platonists taught, through the Holy Spirit dwelling in the heart. To quote again from Smith:

> When the Divinity united itself to human nature in the person of our Saviour, he then gave mankind a pledge and earnest of what he would further do therein, in bringing it into as near a conjunction as might be with himself, and in dispensing and communicating himself to man in a way as far correspondent and agreeable as might be to that first copy. And therefore we are told of "Christ being formed in us" and "the Spirit of Christ dwelling in us" ... and the like: because indeed the same Spirit that dwelt in him, extends itself in its mighty virtue and energy through all believing souls, shaping them more and more into a just resemblance and conformity to him as the first copy and pattern ... And all this is done for us by degrees, through the efficacy of the eternal Spirit ...[48]

Knox is thus correct to claim that the Cambridge Platonists followed in the footsteps of the Fathers. As he put it, somewhat less correctly, they were a "band of Chrysostomians."[49] He also claimed, however, that the Platonic tradition was progressive, and that the 'Cambridge men' had improved on the Fathers through using more sober language.[50] Even so, they were not perfect, being in Knox's estimation, "too much philosophical" and "not enough evangelical."[51] "[T]he excesses of some of the puritanical men of [their] age, led them to be much on the reserve, as to some of the peculiar doctrines of

---

47   Smith, Discourse 1, "A Prefatory Discourse Concerning The True Way or Method of Attaining to Divine Knowledge," *Select Discourses*, pp. 3–25, at p. 3; Whichcote, Discourse XXIV, "The Practice of those who are improved," *Works*, Vol. 1, pp. 373–96, at p. 382; Cudworth, "Sermon I," *Works*, Vol. 4, pp. 289–350, at p. 296. For the Cambridge Platonists and the Fathers, see Dockrill, "The Fathers and the Theology of the Cambridge Platonists" and Panichas, "The Greek Spirit and the Mysticism of Henry More."

48   Smith, Discourse 7, "A Discourse of Legal Righteousness and of the Righteousness of Faith," *Select Discourses*, pp. 307–74, at p. 368.

49   *Remains* Vol. 3, p. 194: "... a band of Chrysostomians, (not avowedly such, I grant, but more substantially agreeing to this character than any who had preceded them)." Knox's parenthetical qualification seems to recognize that the Platonists were less influenced by Chrysostom than by the Alexandrian tradition.

50   For Knox's view that the Platonic tradition is progressive, see: *Remains*, Vol. 3, pp. 150, 199; cf. Vol. 1, p. 360 for the idea of the "sobriety" of the moderates' language compared to that of the Fathers.

51   *Remains*, Vol. 3, pp. 149–50. It is an allegation which Knox makes repeatedly: *Remains*, Vol. 1, pp. 77, 100; Vol. 3, p. 109; Vol. 4, pp. 146, 158; *Eclectic Review*, 6 (May 1810), pp. 389–90.

christianity," he alleged.[52] More concerned to stress the importance of good works, "the christian μετανοια [*metanoia*, repentance], and its most precious fruits," they were, Knox wrote, "respecting the christian πιστις [*pistis*, faith], its nature, and its exercise ... perhaps somewhat deficient."[53] Nor, he contended, did they take into sufficient account the depth of fallen humankind's depravity.[54] He thus repeats against them the same charges which he made against the Fathers. And, because they followed the Greek Fathers rather than Augustine, it is certainly true that we do not find the doctrine of original sin in the moderates.[55] Nonetheless, Knox does not seem to do the moderates justice, when he taxes them with being "not enough evangelical." If one of the main features of an evangelical faith is a focus on the cross of Christ, then this is clearly present in their teaching.[56] One finds, for example, Cudworth describing the cross as "a propitiatory sacrifice" by which Christ paid for humanity "the debt which was owing to ... Divine justice."[57] Cudworth balances this by stressing that salvation did not simply mean a forensic declaration of forgiveness, but also an actual, ontological change in the soul. This change is not, as Knox seems to suggest, a quasi-Pelagian accomplishment of unaided human nature, but something wrought by Christ. Christ, Cudworth proclaims, did not suffer on the cross

> merely to bring in a notion into the world, without producing any real substantial effect at all; without the changing, mending, and reforming of the world; so that men should still be as wicked as they were before, and as much under the power of the prince of darkness, only they should not be thought so; they should still remain as full of all the filthy sores of sin and corruption as before, only they should be accounted whole ... No, surely: the end of the gospel is life and perfection; it is a Divine nature; it is a godlike frame and disposition of spirit; it is to make us partakers of the image of God in righteousness and true holiness, without which salvation itself were but a notion.[58]

---

52 *Correspondence*, Vol. 1, p. 29.

53 Ibid. There is, I think, an allusion here to the Prayer Book Catechism, which speaks of faith and repentance; see *B. C. P.*, p. 215.

54 *Remains*, Vol. 3, p. 79.

55 Patrides, ed., *The Cambridge Platonists*, p. 38: "[S]triking is their unwillingness so much as to mention 'original sin.'"

56 For "crucicentrism," as he calls it, as a mark of evangelicalism, see Bebbington, *Evangelicalism in Modern Britain*, pp. 2–3.

57 Cudworth, "Sermon II," *Works*, Vol. 4, pp. 351–99, at p. 351. See, also, "Sermon I," *Works*, Vol. 4, pp. 289–350, at p. 314.

58 Cudworth, "Sermon I," *Works*, Vol. 4, pp. 289–350, at pp. 324–25.

A similar instance of the same doctrine is provided by Whichcote, writing to Anthony Tuckney, the Calvinist Master of Emmanuel College:

> [S]cripture holds forth Christ to us under a double notion. First, to be felt in us as the new man, in contradiction to the old man; as a divine nature, in contradistinction to the degenerate and apostate nature; and as a principle of heavenly life, contrary to the life of sin and spirit of the world. Second, to be believed on by us, as a sacrifice for the expiation and atonement of sin; as an advocate and means of reconciliation between God and man ... They therefore deceive and flatter themselves extremely, who think of reconciliation with God by means of a saviour acting upon God on their behalf, and not also working in or upon them to make them God-like.[59]

Again, therefore, salvation is presented by the moderates as much more than a merely moral, human quest. It is the work of Christ, accomplished by the Holy Spirit. Cudworth, for example, described justification variously as: "wrought or infused by the Spirit of Christ;" "the delivering of us from the power of sin, by the Spirit of Christ dwelling in our hearts;" our renovation "by the quickening and enlivening spirit of Christ."[60] Or, as Simon Patrick sums up John Smith's teaching: "[H]e was always very urgent upon us, that by the grace of God, and the help of the mighty Spirit of Jesus Christ working in us, we would endeavour to purge out the corruption of our natures, and ... as Plotin speaks, Θεόν εἶναι [*Theon einai*], to come to the true likeness of God and his Son, or, in the apostle's language, 'to be partaker of the divine nature.'"[61]

7   Wesley and the Platonic Tradition

We have seen that Knox places Wesley in the Platonic tradition and argues that he improved it, through the creation of an "unprecedented union of the

---

59   Whichcote, "Dr. Whichcote's First Letter," *Aphorisms*, pp. 6–16, at pp. 13–15 (spelling and punctuation modernized). For Anthony Tuckney (1599–1670), see *O. D. N. B.*

60   Cudworth, "Sermon II," *Works*, Vol. 4, pp. 351–99, at p. 369; "Sermon I," *Works*, Vol. 4, pp. 289–350, at p. 314; "Sermon II," *Works*, Vol. 4, pp. 351–99, at p. 371.

61   Patrick, "A Sermon Preached at the Funeral of Mr. John Smith," in Smith, *Select Discourses*, pp. 523–557, at pp. 544–45 (emphasis added). The quotation from Plotinus to which Patrick alludes comes from *Enneads*, 1, 2, 6, where Plotinus says that "our concern is not only to be free from sin but to become divine" (my translation).

doctrines of grace and holiness."[62] Having looked at the Platonic tradition in greater detail, we are now in a position to examine these claims. Was Wesley a Christian Platonist? The answer is, I maintain, a qualified yes. In spite of the arguments adduced by Knox in his *Remarks on the Life and Character of John Wesley*, it would be difficult to uphold the position that Wesley was simply a Christian Platonist, formed uniquely by the Anglican moderates and the Fathers of the Greek Church. It is patent that Wesley drew the materials for his theology from what David Hempton calls "a bewildering array of Christian traditions."[63] Nonetheless, as we have seen, the influence of the Platonic tradition on Wesley, in the form of the Fathers and of the moderates, has been clearly established. This influence is manifested in the fact that Wesley made their cardinal doctrine of deification central to his own teaching. Certainly, he did not use the term *theosis*; but even so, to quote Michael J. Christensen, "what John Wesley taught as Christian perfection, holiness, or entire sanctification is both historically and theologically *derivative* and *dependent* on the more ancient doctrines of deification as taught by theologians in the Greek patristic tradition of the first four centuries."[64] Wesley himself summed up his teaching on sanctification in section eight of his *Letter to a Roman Catholic* (1749). His words are a perfect definition of what deification means in the Platonic tradition: "[The Holy Spirit is] the immediate cause of all holiness in us: enlightening our understandings, rectifying our wills and affections, renewing our natures, uniting our persons to Christ, assuring us of the adoption of sons, leading us in our actions, purifying and sanctifying our souls and bodies to a full and eternal enjoyment of God."[65]

As Knox comments, "[A]ll [Wesley] says of the operation of Divine grace on the heart, from first to last, is but an expansion of that single position of St. Peter, 'Whereby are given unto us exceeding great and precious promises, that by them we might become partakers of the Divine nature,'" exactly the text that the Christian Platonic tradition took as its key proclamation.[66] But what of Knox's second claim, that Wesley improved the Platonic position by making it more evangelical? Given the evidence which we have seen, it appears hard to agree with Knox that either the Fathers or the moderates were more "philosophical" and less "evangelical" than Wesley, if by evangelical one means a religion which emphasises the importance of the cross, and the

---

62   *Remains*, Vol. 3, p. 152. See, above, p. 68.
63   Hempton, *Methodism: Empire of the Spirit*, p. 56.
64   Christensen, "John Wesley," p. 223 (emphasis in the original).
65   Wesley, *Letter to a Roman Catholic*, 8; text in Outler, *John Wesley*, pp. 493–99, at p. 495.
66   *Remains*, Vol. 3, p. 162.

necessity of grace. This said, Knox included under the rubric "evangelical" a firm emphasis on the depravity of fallen human nature, and this was something that Wesley clearly taught, in contradistinction to both the moderates and the Fathers.[67]

8   Knox and the Platonic Tradition

Knox confessed himself to be the "humble disciple" of the Anglican moderates, as well as avowing the influence of the Platonic tradition on him through Wesley.[68] Thus, despite his boast of being simply a "Catholic Christian," owing no allegiance to any particular school or party in the church, we may certainly concur with Hannah More, that Knox was "of the Platonic Christian school."[69] This conclusion will be confirmed when we come to examine Knox's theology in more detail, especially his teaching on sanctification and perfection, which, as we will show, corresponds exactly to the doctrine of *theosis*. Like Wesley, he does not use the word, perhaps because he thought it hyperbolic, extravagant-sounding to nineteenth-century English ears, but, again like Wesley, he clearly teaches the concept. For him – and this perhaps explains why he could call himself simply a Catholic Christian, and yet adhere to the Platonic tradition – Christianity itself meant "a real participation of the divine nature; the very image of Christ, drawn upon the soul; or, as it is in the Apostle's phrase, CHRIST FORMED WITHIN US."[70]

Although Knox regarded Wesley as having developed Christian Platonism significantly, he still believed that the tradition needed to progress further. It had, ultimately, to cease being Platonist, and become wholly Christian, leaving the support to which Clement had tethered it, to finally stand alone by its own strength. To this end, he insisted that a "full development of the true philosophy of the Gospel" was needed. Although he never says so explicitly, one may speculate that he saw his own teaching as a contribution to that goal.[71]

---

67   For Wesley's teaching on original sin, see Maddox, *Responsible Grace*, pp. 74–90, and Cox, "John Wesley's Concept of Sin," which concludes that Wesley's picture of fallen humanity was "very dark indeed" (p. 19).

68   *Remains*, Vol. 4, p. 101; Vol. 3, p. 138.

69   Ibid., Vol. 3, p. 172; Hannah More to William Wilberforce, letter, September 24, 1804, in Wilberforce, *Correspondence*, Vol. 1, p. 323.

70   *Correspondence*, Vol. 1, 31. Knox's words here are a quotation from Scougal, *The Life of God in the Soul of Man*, p. 5.

71   *Remains*, Vol. 3, p. 141; cf. p. 150; Vol. 4, p. 147, where Knox seems to hint that he is aiming to produce a theology that is both evangelical and philosophical, appealing alike to the understanding and the heart.

9   Conclusion

In this chapter we have set Knox's theology in the context of Christian Platonism. After a brief overview of this tradition, which we saw was characterised primarily by the doctrine of *theosis* or deification, we explored Knox's understanding of it. He was, we discovered, correct in his presentation of the tradition's broad historical outline, which he saw as beginning with Clement of Alexandria, Pseudo-Macarius and Chrysostom, before being revived in the seventeenth century by the Anglican moderates and then carried on by Wesley. Where we would argue that Knox is mistaken is in seeing the tradition as progressive, moving from a more philosophical to a more evangelical basis. While it is true that the Fathers and the moderates do not hold the doctrine of original sin, they are insistent that the process of salvation is always a divine initiative, dependent on grace. The moderates and Chrysostom also place the cross at the center of their soteriology, seeing it as a sacrifice for sin. The chapter also examined Knox's understanding of mysticism which, in what he termed its "modern" form, he saw as a deformation of the Platonic tradition, to be rejected as contrary to human nature, as well as to the divine provisions made for that nature. The chapter closed by confirming Knox's own attachment to the "Christian Platonic School," manifested in the centrality which (while avoiding the term), he gave to the concept of *theosis*. Having situated Knox diachronically in the tradition of Christian Platonism, we turn next to the age in which he lived, to see how his theology reflected the period, on the cusp of the Enlightenment and Romanticism.

CHAPTER 5

Alexander Knox in the Context of His Times: Heart Religion, the Enlightenment and Romanticism

In *Protestant Thought in the Nineteenth Century*, Claude Welch writes: "The immediate background of Protestant theology in the nineteenth century must be described by reference to at least three broad movements ... commonly labelled pietism, rationalism, and romanticism."[1] The aim of this chapter is to examine how Knox's theology fits in to the context of these three movements. We look, first, at how, in the realm of spirituality, he is an example of heart religion; next, we examine the roots of his thought in the Enlightenment, to which, in part, he was reacting, but by which, also, in part, he was formed. The chapter then goes on to explore the meaning of Romanticism, looking at the traits by which it is characterised. We then see how these traits mark Knox as a Romantic theologian, before closing with a comparison between Knox and two writers to whom this designation is habitually given, Samuel Taylor Coleridge, and Friedrich Schleiermacher.

1   Heart Religion

"True religion is that of the heart," Knox proclaimed in the *Brief Confutation*; the phrase "heart religion" or "religion of the heart" occurs extensively in his writings.[2] The same phenomenon as Welch's "pietism," this heart religion may be defined as the type of Christianity which emphasises the affective and experiential, rather than the dogmatic and cerebral. Such religion, of which Knox's Christian Platonism is one type, has undoubtedly existed within the church from the beginning, but it emerges with special prominence in the seventeenth and eighteenth centuries, where it took on various forms, in Protestantism, Roman Catholicism and Orthodoxy, with an analogous development appearing at the

---

1   Welch, *Protestant Thought in the Nineteenth Century*, p. 22.
2   *Brief Confutation*, p. 25. See, also, *Remains*, Vol. 4, p. 359: "Christianity is, essentially, the discipleship of the heart." For Knox's use of the term, see, for example: *Remains*, Vol. 3, pp. 288; 362; Vol. 4, pp. 43, 118; 154; 172, 190, 301, 510, 563 625; *Correspondence*, Vol. 1, p. 29.

same time in Judaism, in the guise of the Hasidic movement.[3] There are several
reasons for the emergence of heart religion at this period. One was reaction
to the rationalism of the Enlightenment, something which will be discussed
in detail below. Second, the rise of heart religion should be seen against the
background of the so-called wars of religion.[4] The period 1616–48 witnessed
the Thirty Years' War, which pitted the Catholic League against the Protestant
Union. The 1620s were marked in France by a series of Huguenot rebellions
against the Roman Catholic King Louis XIII and 1642–51 saw the (in part)
religiously-motivated Civil War in the British Isles. Heart religion provided an
opiate to the miseries engendered by these conflicts. At the same time, the view
that doctrinal disputes were the cause of so much pain and suffering led to a
premium being placed on holiness of life rather than on orthodoxy of dogma.
The words which Robert Crocker uses of the Cambridge Platonists in England
may be applied to groups across Europe: "[I]nfluenced by ... turbulent religious
wars and conflicts ... [they took] the conscious step of rejecting the dogmatism
of their upbringing or education."[5] Third, heart religion was motivated by "an
earnest desire for reform," a longing to reverse what its adherents saw as the
decline of piety in society at large.[6] As Hartmut Lehmann remarks, the various
movements of seventeenth-century piety "represented the first attempts to re-
christianize European societies threatened by de-Christianization."[7] Finally,
there was what one might term the "mobility of ideas." The printed word carried the doctrines of heart religion across not only geographical boundaries
but also denominational ones. At the same time, the period was likewise one
of mass migration; populations from the areas touched by Pietism carried their
fervour throughout Europe and North America.[8] All four of these factors were
still present, at least to some degree, in the late eighteenth and early nineteenth centuries and appear in the background to Knox's theology, albeit with
varying degrees of prominence. That his thought was, in part, a reaction to

---

3   See Campbell, *Religion of the Heart*; also, more briefly, Walton, *Jonathan Edwards*, pp. 221–23.
4   Stoeffler, *The Rise of Evangelical Pietism*, p. 180. Stoeffler is speaking about Pietism in particu-
    lar, but his words apply to the phenomenon of heart religion more generally.
5   Crocker, *Henry More*, p. xviii.
6   The phrase "an earnest desire for reform" comes from the sub-title of Philip Jakob Spener's,
    Pia Desideria oder herzliches Verlangen nach gottgefälliger Besserung (1675). With its call for
    a religion not of the head, but of the heart, the *Pia Desideria* is commonly seen as inau-
    gurating the Pietist movement. For an introduction to Spener (1635–1705), see Ward, *Early
    Evangelicalism*, Chapter 2, "Spener and the origins of church pietism," pp. 24–39.
7   Lehmann, "Pietism in the World of Transatlantic Religious Revivals," p. 16.
8   For the circulation of religious literature, see: Damrau, *The Reception of English Puritan
    Literature in Germany*; and Melton, "Pietism, Print Culture, and Salzburg Protestantism on
    the Eve of Expulsion." For the impact of migration, see Ward, "Power and Piety."

the Enlightenment will be considered in a moment; we have already seen that he was writing at a period of heightened sectarian tensions between Roman Catholics and Protestants. At the same time, there was what Knox termed a "declension of piety" in society. To quote from a sermon preached by Jebb in 1806: "[M]any ... regard Christianity with a sort of supercilious scorn." It was a situation which Knox believed could only be remedied by heart religion.[9] Finally, Knox was an inveterate reader; in the *Remains* and *Correspondence* he included numerous references to works of heart religion, from various different sources. The single most decisive cause of Knox's heart religion undoubtedly lay, however, in his up-bringing: the piety of his parents and the influence of John Wesley, whose religion Knox described as *"the religion of the heart."*[10]

2   Knox and the Enlightenment

"There can be no real question," writes Bernard Reardon, "but that the first four decades of the nineteenth century constitute ... the Romantic era *par excellence.*"[11] As a theologian who flourished in this era, Knox was strongly marked by Romanticism. This means, however, that *ipso facto* he was also marked by the Enlightenment, in which the roots of Romanticism lay.[12] For this reason, before looking at Knox as a Romantic theologian, we will first explore his relationship to the Enlightenment, Welch's "rationalism." Historiography before the last two decades of the twentieth century portrayed the Enlightenment as a secular phenomenon, resolutely anti-religious.[13] This view was challenged at the start of the 1980s in the book *Enlightenment in National Context* (1981), edited by Roy Porter and Mikuláš Teich, which argued the case for distinguishing several different Enlightenments. Amongst these different Enlightenments was a "religious Enlightenment," something illustrated especially clearly in England, where, as Porter notes, the Enlightenment "throve ... *within* piety."[14]

---

9   *Remains*, Vol. 4, p. 145; Jebb, *Practical Theology*, Vol. 1, p. 244. See, also, *Remains*, Vol. 1, p. 6.
10   "Humanus," letter, *Dublin Chronicle*, June 27–30, 1789, pp. 206–7, at p. 206 (emphasis in the original). On the subject of Wesley and heart religion, see Steele, ed., *"Heart Religion" in the Methodist Tradition*, and, more recently, Clapper, *Renewal of the Heart*.
11   Reardon, *Religion in the Age of Romanticism*, p. 2.
12   See below, pp. 96–97.
13   See, for examples of this approach: Chadwick, *Secularization of the European Mind*; Gay, *The Enlightenment: An Interpretation*.
14   Porter, "The Enlightenment in England," p. 6 (emphasis in the original). For further development of the point, see: Spadafora, *The Idea of Progress in Eighteenth-Century Britain*; and Young, *Religion and Enlightenment in Eighteenth-Century England*. What is said here about England applies equally to Knox's Ireland. For the idea of a religious Enlightenment, see Sorkin, *The Religious Enlightenment*.

Despite this, the Enlightenment posed two major problems for Christianity. One was theological, and came from Immanuel Kant, who, in his *Critik der reinen Vernunft* (1781), brought down, as Stephen Prickett puts it, "an iron curtain between the phenomenal world, where knowledge is possible, and the noumenal world, about which we must remain agnostic."[15] According to Kant, the only things that we can know are "phenomena," the objects of our direct sense-experience. Thus there could be no natural knowledge of God, a position that Kant reinforced by refuting the traditional arguments for the existence of a deity. Theology was thus left with a problem which it could not ignore: the problem of the knowability of God; and the quest for a solution to this problem was what dominated Protestant theological thought during the first quarter of the nineteenth century.[16] The strategy adopted by many theologians was to enlarge the category of direct experience; as Pelikan puts it: "The current 'experimental philosophy' was to find its counterpart in a genuinely experimental theology."[17] We have already seen that Knox's theology was of this experimental type. As he put it: "Religion is experience."[18] Nonetheless, raised from his childhood in a milieu of faith, he showed no sign of being perturbed by questions concerning the knowability of God. Rather, the role that Knox gave to experience had more to do with the second problem which the Enlightenment posed for Christianity. This problem was not intellectual, but spiritual: the accent which the *zeitgeist* placed on reason meant that much religion became arid and lifeless. 'The dry details of meagre morality ... pronounced from most parochial pulpits,' is how Knox described it.[19]

By emphasizing the role of experience in religion, Knox was reacting against the Enlightenment. But in a number of other ways he showed himself more positively marked by the spirit of his age. For instance, one feature of the Enlightenment period was the high value placed on science and, coupled with this, what Clare Jackson calls an "insatiable optimism."[20] The use of the scientific method had led to a dramatic increase in knowledge about the natural world, and the belief was prevalent that the same method could be applied to all aspects of human existence, yielding similar results. An example of this

---

15   Prickett, *Romanticism and Religion*, p. 21. For the impact of Kant (1724–1804) on theology, see Reardon, *Kant as Philosophical Theologian*.

16   "At the beginning of the nineteenth century the theological problem was, simply, 'How is theology possible?'" (Welch, *Protestant Thought in the Nineteenth Century*, p. 59).

17   Pelikan, *Christian Doctrine and Modern Culture*, p. 172. See also Welch, *Protestant Thought in the Nineteenth Century*, pp. 48, 59–60.

18   *Remains*, Vol. 4, p. 458.

19   Ibid., p. 102.

20   Jackson, "Progress and Optimism," p. 117. For more detail, see Spadafora, *The Idea of Progress*.

attitude is furnished by Jebb, who in his *Sermons on Subjects Chiefly Practical* held up the vision of "an unbounded prospect of intellectual improvement to future ages ... encouraged by the past history of all sciences." "[W]hat limits can be placed to the possible progress of those future theologians who shall engage in sacred studies, with humble, yet with philosophic minds?" he demanded.[21] The same respect for science and belief in progress run throughout Knox's work. He conceived of theology in scientific terms; it was for him "the science of true piety," no different in its methodology from astronomy, chemistry or mathematics, and, like these disciplines, capable of yielding ever-greater knowledge.[22] This growth in knowledge, Knox believed to be part of the divine plan for humankind. He was convinced that "the Christian dispensation, though perfectly and immutably defined in the New Testament, yet in actual development, was intended to be progressive."[23] This conviction was one of Knox's main motives for studying the Bible. "[M]y mind," he declared, "is generally full of thought on the yet unsettled meanings and unsuspected depths of the New Testament." Once these were uncovered, Knox hypothesized, they would prove of immense apologetic value, as well as nourishing piety.[24]

Optimism about knowledge was matched by optimism about human nature. Roy Porter remarks: "Central to the aspirations of enlightened minds was the search for a true 'science of man.'" As it was expressed by Alexander Pope, whose work is a résumé of English Enlightenment thinking: "The proper study of mankind is man."[25] A number of Enlightenment writers postulated, in the words of Adam Ferguson, that "man is susceptible of improvement, and has in himself a principle of progression, and a desire of perfection."[26] Knox's theology reflected the Enlightenment interest in anthropological questions. Not everything he taught about humanity was in keeping with the spirit of the Enlightenment. The emphasis which he placed on the fallenness of human nature may, in fact, be seen as a reaction to Enlightenment's dismissal of the idea of innate sinfulness as "unscientific and without foundation."[27] On the

21   Jebb, *Sermons on Subjects Chiefly Practical*, p. 348. Jebb quotes the Enlightenment philosopher Dugald Stewart (1753–1828), *Elements of the Philosophy of the Human Mind*, p. 222. See also Jebb, *Correspondence*, Vol. 2, p. 136.
22   *Remains*, Vol. 1, pp. 251, 246–48.
23   *Wesley*, p. 487.
24   *Remains*, Vol. 4, pp. 547–48; cf. Vol. 1, pp. 244, 447–48, 481; Vol. 3, pp. 201–3; Vol. 4, p. 615; and below, pp. 125–26.
25   Porter, *The Enlightenment*, p. 11; Pope, *An Essay on Man*, Epistle 2, line 2. For the Enlightenment's interest in human nature see, Knellwolf, "The Science of Man."
26   Ferguson, *An Essay on the History of Civil Society*, p. 12.
27   Porter, *The Enlightenment*, p. 17.

other hand, the emphasis which Knox placed on perfection, one of the most important and distinctive tenets of his theology, can be understood as being, in part, a reflection of the contemporary belief in the perfectibility of human nature.[28]

Connected to the idea of perfection was that of happiness – "happiness! our being's end and aim," to quote again from Pope.[29] "[T]he highest perfection of intellectual nature lies in a careful and constant pursuit of true and solid happiness," affirmed John Locke in his *Essay Concerning Human Understanding* (1690), where he defined happiness as, "in its full extent ... the utmost pleasure we are capable of."[30] Knox made this idea of "utmost pleasure" an essential feature of his thinking. With its title, "On Christianity, As the Way of Peace and True Happiness" (1805), the first essay in the *Remains* enunciated a theme which was constant through all four volumes, as well as in the *Correspondence*. In the essay, Knox spoke of:

> the happiness of loving God, and of exercising that love in devotional intercourse with him: happiness, not merely in the good effects which these habits produce, but in that sweet, rational, self-complacential, yea, direct, disinterested, delight, which they involve. To these sensations, I think religion owes its energy. We are made to love pleasure, and it is in virtue of a delectatio victrix, that christianity [*sic*] makes us its own.[31]

A final characteristic of the Enlightenment which marked Knox's thinking was the "brave attempt," as James Byrne puts it, "to focus on what unites, rather than divides us; a rejection of 'prejudice' in all its forms; an emphasis on toleration and the search for simplicity of religion." To borrow David Sorkin's words, the religious Enlightenment represented "a renunciation of Reformation and Counter-Reformation militance, an express alternative to two centuries of

---

28   For Knox's teaching on perfection, see below, pp. 178–82.
29   Pope, *An Essay on Man*, Epistle 4, line 1. For the theme of happiness in the Enlightenment see: Hazard, *La Pensée Européene au XVIIIème Siècle*, Vol. 1, chapter 2, "*Le Bonheur*," pp. 17–33; and, more recently, McMahon, "Happiness from deism to materialism to atheism."
30   Locke, *An Essay Concerning Human Understanding*, Book 2, Chapter 21, section 51; Book, 2, Chapter 21, section 42.
31   *Correspondence*, Vol. 1, p. 283. "Complacential" means "pleasing." *Delectatio victrix* is a phrase derived from Augustine, much used by the Jansenists, whom Knox had been discussing in the letter from which this passage is quoted. Literally meaning "conquering delight," it is the joy which, according to Augustine, the soul finds in God, making it able to resist the delight of earthly things. See Harrison, "*Delectatio Victrix*: Grace and Freedom in St Augustine." For a fuller treatment of the theme in Knox, see below, pp. 148–49. For Knox's essay on happiness, see *Remains*, Vol. 1, pp. 1–52.

dogmatism and fanaticism, intolerance and religious warfare."[32] This pacific spirit suffused Knox's writing. He constantly opposed bigotry and sectarian hostility; the virtues of humility, meekness, purity, and love were much more important than any particular doctrinal position, he held.[33]

The same Enlightenment traits which have just been enumerated appear in eighteenth-century evangelicalism, something which has led David Bebbington to argue that the evangelical version of Protestantism was created by the Enlightenment.[34] Could the same be said of Knox's theology? The answer must be a qualified no. As we have seen, Knox's theology is rooted in the tradition of Christian Platonism, a tradition which dates back to the second century. Nonetheless, if Knox's theology was not a "creation" of the Enlightenment, in the sense of being formed by it, of depending on it for its existence, it was shaped by the intellectual milieu in which it was articulated. The way in which Knox expressed his thinking and the issues that he addressed were inevitably, even if perhaps unconsciously, both moulded by and reflected the world in which he lived.

3   Romanticism

What does the term "Romanticism" signify? Some scholars, like Arthur O. Lovejoy, have argued that to speak of "Romanticism" at all is fatuous. Nonetheless, as Michael Ferber notes, the term continues to be employed, for it is possible to identify certain common characteristics, "family resemblances," which can contribute to a meaningful definition of the word.[35] Of these characteristics, the foremost is often seen as reaction against the Enlightenment's supposedly arid concept of reason. Nonetheless, to quote Richard Crouter, although "the Enlightenment" and "Romanticism" are useful categories for cultural periodization, they are misleading "if we suppose they signify a sharp divide that utterly separates two distinct eras."[36] This is because, first, as Frederick C. Beiser recalls: "If the Romantics were critics of the *Aufklärung*,

---

32 Byrne, *Religion and the Enlightenment*, p. 229; Sorkin, *The Religious Enlightenment*, p. 6.

33 *Candid Animadversions*, p. 30. See, also, pp. 115–16.

34 Bebbington, *Evangelicalism in Modern Britain*, p. 74.

35 Ferber, "Introduction" to *European Romanticism*, pp. 1–9, p. 6. Ferber takes the phrase "family resemblances" from Wittgenstein. For Lovejoy's position, see his essays "On the Discrimination of Romanticisms" (1924) and "The Meaning of Romanticism for the Historian of Ideas" (1941).

36 Crouter, *Schleiermacher*, p. 40.

they were also its disciples."[37] Second, rather than negate, the Romantics strove
to enlarge the vision of the eighteenth century.[38] The thoughts and ideas of the
two periods thus intersect and intertwine, and so, if Romanticism involved a
protest against what C. R. Cragg calls "the arid intellectualism of an excessively
intellectual age,"[39] reason was not by any means rejected. Instead, the appeal
to reason alone was balanced by a plea to what Keats called "the Heart's affections and the truth of Imagination."[40]

"Affections" meant, in the language of the Romantic era, what today would
be termed "emotions" or "feelings." And it is in the emotions that the origins
of Romanticism can be argued to lie. To the entire movement might be applied the description of poetry given by William Wordsworth: "the spontane-
ous overflow of powerful feelings."[41] But, if Romanticism was engendered by
the emotions, it also sought to stimulate them. As Wordsworth expressed it in
his poem *The Prelude* (1850):

> .... What we have loved,
>   Others will love, and we will teach them how;
>   Instruct them how the mind of man becomes
>   A thousand times more beautiful than the earth
> On which he dwells ...[42]

The words recall those of Mill in his essay on "Tennyson's Poems" (1835), where
he speaks of the "noblest end of poetry" being to act "upon the desires and
characters of mankind through their emotions, to raise them towards the perfection of their nature."[43] For the Romantics, the means to achieve this end
was the imagination, which James Engell has called "the core and *sine qua
non* of Romanticism."[44] Through the imagination, all the English Romantics,
whether poets, philosophers or theologians, were enabled to set out on
the epistemological quest to go beyond observable phenomena, to pierce,

---

37   Beiser, "Early Romanticism and the *Aufklärung*," p. 318.
38   See, on this point, Livingston, *Modern Christian Thought*, pp. 83–84.
39   Cragg, *Reason and Authority in the Eighteenth Century*, p. 176.
40   John Keats to Benjamin Bailey, letter, November 22, 1817, in Scott, ed., *Selected Letters of
     John Keats*, p. 54.
41   Wordsworth, *Lyrical Ballads*, p. xiv.
42   Wordsworth, *Prelude*, p.371.
43   Mill, "Tennyson's Poems," p. 261.
44   Engell, *Creative Imagination*, p. 4. Note also Engell's remark that "the idea of the imagina-
     tion, as understood in the Romantic period and as we still understand it today, was actu-
     ally the creation of the eighteenth century" (p. vii).

one might say, Prickett's iron curtain.[45] Imagination, which Mary Warnock defines with respect to the Romantics as "the power of seeing things as they are, namely as symbolic," enabled them to perceive in nature what Wordsworth termed the "types and symbols of Eternity;" or, to quote William Blake:

> To see a World in a Grain of Sand
> And a Heaven in a Wild Flower.[46]

With its stress on the world as symbolic, one is not surprised to find that a further feature of the Romantic era was a revival of Platonism. "Plato," Grierson famously claimed, "[was] the first great romantic," and "it is to Plato that the greatest romantics have always turned to find philosophical expression for their mood." Grierson's thesis finds ample verification in the case of post-Enlightenment England, which saw at the same time a renewed interest in Hellenism more generally.[47] Indeed, with Harry Levin, one may speak of the phenomenon of "Romantic Hellenism," a phenomenon reflected alike in art, architecture, literature, and even politics.[48]

From what has been said so far, it will be seen that the Romantic period was strongly marked by subjectivism. But, as Michael Löwy and Robert Sayre have remarked, "the demand for community is just as essential to the definition of the Romantic vision as its subjective and individualistic aspect [is]." As they note, this demand was expressed in a number of ways: "in authentic communication with others, in participation in the organic whole of a people (*Volk*) and its collective imaginary as expressed in mythology and folklore, in social harmony, or in a classless society."[49] In the Christianity of the Romantic period, it was reflected in a fresh interest in ecclesiology, as exemplified, for instance, by Johann Adam Möhler at Tübingen, Giovanni Perrone in Rome, the Slavophile, Alexei Khomiakov and, in Britain, Coleridge, William Palmer, and the Tractarians.[50] Linked to this interest in the church was a renewed concern

---

45   See Newsome, *Two Classes of Men*, p. 2.

46   Warnock, *Imagination*, p. 70; Wordsworth, *Prelude*, p. 161; Blake, "Auguries of Innocence," lines 1–2.

47   Grierson, "Classical and Romantic," p. 45. On revived Hellenism, see Jenkyns, *The Victorians and Ancient Greece* (despite its title, the book covers the later Hanoverian period). Jenkyns also deals with the revival of Platonism; see Chapter 10, pp. 227–63. For the theme of Platonism and English Romanticism, see Newsome, *Two Classes of Men*, especially chapter 1, pp. 8–24, "Plato and the Romantics."

48   For the term, see Levin, *Broken Column*.

49   Löwy and Sayre, *Romanticism Against the Tide of Modernity*, p. 26.

50   For Möhler (1796–1838) see Riga, "The Ecclesiology of Johann Adam Möhler;" for Perrone (1794–1876) see Kasper, *Die Lehre von der Tradition in der Römischen Schule*; for

for tradition, mirroring the attention given in the secular sphere to those things from the past which could aid the community to define its identity. Despite the emphasis laid on community, as far as Christianity was concerned, it was primarily the subjectivization of religious truth which distinguished theology in the Romantic period, the immanentizing of the spiritual, "[t]he self's involvement in theological assertions," to borrow Welch's term.[51]

4   Knox as a Romantic Theologian

All the characteristics of Romanticism enumerated above are found in Knox. First, there is what Coleridge calls the reconciliation of the heart with the head.[52] While not denying the importance of reason, Knox believed that "[r]eligion must, in order to work its full effect, give employment to every mental faculty."[53] He especially stressed the role of the affections and the imagination. His teaching on the affections will be discussed later, when we come to examine his anthropology.[54] For the present, we will confine ourselves to a discussion of his view of the imagination. "[P]ure poetry and vital religion are wonderfully akin," Knox wrote, and his understanding of imagination was that of the Romantic poets.[55] He spoke of it as the "mind's eye," an eye which had as its object of vision "what is sublime, or vast, or beautiful."[56] Thus, for example, in a scene which surely sums up the Romantic era, Knox related how, on holiday in the Welsh Marches, his man-servant Michael had "been particularly attracted by ruins and old castles; and will carry back with him a large set of new pictures in his imagination." For Knox, however, the great object of the

---

Khomiakov (1804–80) see Smith, *All God's People*, pp. 138–39; for Coleridge, Palmer, and the Tractarians, see below, pp. 101–4, 216, 246–57. It would be an oversimplification to see the nineteenth-century concern with ecclesiology simply as the result of Romanticism, but it certainly was one of the factors which contributed to the prominence given to the topic during this period. See Franklin, *Nineteenth-Century Churches*.

51   Welch, *Protestant Thought in the Nineteenth Century*, Vol. 1, p. 60. See, also, Reardon, *Religion in the Age of Romanticism*, p. 10.

52   Coleridge, *Biographia Literaria*, 1, p. 25.

53   *Remains*, Vol. 1, p. 419.

54   See, below, p. 148.

55   *Remains*, Vol. 4, p. 212. Cf. Keble: "[I]t is hard to believe that ... poetry and theology would have proved such true allies, unless there was a hidden tie of kinship between them" (Francis, trans., *Keble's Lectures on Poetry*, Vol. 2, pp. 479–80). For the original text, see Keble, *Praelectiones*, Vol. 2, p. 813.

56   *Remains*, Vol. 1, p. 481. See also: Vol. 1, p. 474; Vol. 4, p. 213. For examples of the imagination as the "mind's eye," see: *Remains*, Vol. 2, p. 337; Vol. 3, p. 406; Vol. 4, p. 268.

imagination was not "ruins and old castles," but God, "the original of all sublimity and beauty."[57] "[T]he imagination will, of necessity, find in that object,
both its amplest range and its noblest exercise," he affirmed.[58] But as well as
contemplating the divinity, the imagination also served, for Knox, to lead the
soul to God through a symbolic reading of the material world, "every image of
the sublime being, in my mind," as he wrote, "a reflected ray of Deity."[59] It is
an idea expressed by the Evangelical poet William Cowper in *The Task* (1785),
from which Knox quoted the following lines:

> The soul that sees him, or receives, sublim'd,
> New faculties, or learns, at least, t'employ
> More worthily the pow'rs she own'd before:
>   Discerns in all things – what with stupid gaze
> Of ignorance till then she overlook'd -
> A ray of heavenly light gilding all forms
> Terrestrial, in the vast and the minute,
> Th'unambiguous footsteps of a God,
> Who gives its lustre to th'insect's wing
>   And wheels his throne upon the rolling worlds.[60]

For Knox, however, imagination alone was not enough. There were, he argued, two, as he called them, "perceptive faculties," the imagination and the
understanding, and both needed to be employed in the service of religion.[61]
Neither faculty, however, availed without love. "Devotion," Knox wrote, is not "a
mere business of the imagination;" it calls also for "an affection of the heart."[62]
The same with understanding: it needed to be joined with love. Knox prayed,

---

57   *Remains*, Vol. 4, pp. 165–66; Vol. 1, p. 476.
58   Ibid., Vol. 1, p. 476.
59   Ibid., Vol. 1, p. 16. See also p. 17, where Knox speaks of "every species of the sublime" as "a
     shadowing of Deity ... [exciting] in the mind some tendency, however vague, toward the
     mysterious archetype of greatness."
60   Ibid., Vol. 3, p. 366. The quotation is from *The Task*, 5, lines 806–14. For William Cowper
     (1731–1800), see *O. D. N. B.* Knox penned an essay "On the Poetry of William Cowper,"
     (1802), whom he greatly admired. The essay was included in the *Remains* (Vol. 3, pp. 331–
     67); part of it had previously been published, anonymously and untitled, by William
     Hayley in the fourth, 1812, edition of his *Life and Letters of William Cowper* (Vol. 4,
     pp. 409–13).
61   *Remains*, Vol. 4, pp. 435–36.
62   Ibid., Vol. 1, pp. 476–77.

"Oh! work upon my understanding; and work upon my heart!" "[O]pen my understanding, that I may understand ... and quicken my heart, that I may feel."[63] Nothing could better illustrate the subjective element in Knox's theology, an element derived from his Christian Platonism, the latter indicative of the Hellenism which he shared with his contemporaries. His subjectivism was, however, balanced by a strong concept of the church and the importance of tradition, something at which we have already looked at in part, and which will be further illustrated in subsequent chapters.

5   Knox and Coleridge

As a Romantic theologian, Knox invites comparison with others to whom this epithet is usually given. These include the Tractarians, Tractarianism being, according to Aidan Nichols, "the ecclesial form of the Romantic movement in England" and, according to Prickett, "a religious flowering of the English Romantic movement."[64] Such, however, is the importance of the topic of Knox's relationship to the Tractarians that we will leave discussion of it to a later chapter.[65] For now, let us examine, first, the similarities between Knox and the theologian who has been held to represent "better than any other figure in England the Romantic protest against rationalism in the early decades of the nineteenth century," Samuel Taylor Coleridge.[66] Given that they were contemporaries and both prominent lay-theologians of the Anglican Church, it is surprising that no evidence appears to exist of any contact between Knox and Coleridge. This is even more surprising given the points which, despite significant differences, they held in common. Of these commonalities, several stand out as particularly worthy of note. First, like Knox, Coleridge attacked the narrow rationalism of the Enlightenment. Rationalism in religion was, for Coleridge, the great error of his age, and against this error he was resolved to strive with all his power. "I believe myself bound in conscience to throw the whole force of my intellect in the way of this triumphal car," he declared. The result was, to quote James Livingston, the articulation of a vital theology

63   Ibid., Vol. 4, pp. 78, 633.
64   Nichols, *The Panther and the Hind*, p. 118; Prickett, *Romanticism and Religion*, p. 170. Note also Brilioth, *Anglican Revival*, Chapter 5, "The Romantic Movement and Neo-Anglicanism," pp. 56–76.
65   Chapter 13, below.
66   Livingston, *Modern Christian Thought*, p. 86. For Coleridge (1772–1834) as a theologian, see Barth, *Coleridge and Christian Doctrine*; and Hedley, *Coleridge, Philosophy and Religion*. For a briefer introduction, see Hedley, "Coleridge as a Theologian."

quite different from the cold orthodoxy and rationalism of the late eighteenth-century.[67] Second, Coleridge and Knox held similar views of both the fall and of justification. Like Knox, Coleridge saw the fall of humankind as a calamity, "the corruption and disharmony of the human soul," rather than something to be considered in forensic terms as a crime deserving punishment. Like Knox, too, Coleridge viewed humanity as weak, but not totally depraved.[68] The corollary of this hamartiology is, in Coleridge, as in Knox, a rejection of the theory of the atonement as satisfaction. Indeed, Coleridge, like Knox, is far more concerned with our present redemption here and now, than with the past action of the Redeemer.[69] Like Knox, he sees justification as a dynamic process, through which, by the working of the Trinity, Christians are deified.

> We, according to the necessity of our imperfect understandings, must divide and distinguish. But surely justification and sanctification are one act of God, and only different perspectives of redemption by and through and for Christ. They are one and the same plant, justification the root, sanctification the flower; and, (may I not venture to add?), transubstantiation into Christ the celestial fruit.[70]

Although Coleridge nowhere treats at length of justification and grace, one thing is clear throughout his writings. To quote J. Robert Barth: "[H]is emphasis is constantly on the action of God, indwelling and working within man." This God is the Trinity; as Douglas Hedley has underlined, for Coleridge "the doctrine of the Trinity is at the very heart of Christian belief;" a point also made by Coleridge's nineteenth-century American editor, W. G. T. Shedd.[71] In the case of both Coleridge and Knox, the idea of God indwelling to sanctify human beings derived from a shared tradition, for Coleridge, like Knox, was a Christian Platonist, his theology being rooted in the English seventeenth century and the teaching of the Cambridge Platonists, although it went back beyond them to the Fathers and, further still, to the Middle Platonists, whom, even

---

67   Livingston, *Modern Christian Thought*, p. 86. The quotation from Coleridge comes from his *Aids to Reflection*, p. 408.

68   For Coleridge's hamartiology, see Barth, *Coleridge and Christian Doctrine*, pp. 114–21. Barth quotes Shedd, "Coleridge as a Philosopher and Theologian," p. 330.

69   For Coleridge's soteriology, see Barth, *Coleridge and Christian Doctrine*, pp. 139–47. See, too, Barbeau, *Coleridge, the Bible, and Religion*, pp. 20–23.

70   Coleridge, "Notes on Luther's Table Talk," *Literary Remains*, Vol. 4, pp. 1–65, at p. 32.

71   Barth, *Coleridge and Christian Doctrine*, p. 148; Hedley, *Coleridge, Philosophy and Religion*, p. 20; Shedd, "Coleridge as a Philosopher and Theologian," p. 321.

as a boy, Coleridge was reading at Christ's Hospital.[72] Also derived from Plato was a shared view of the world as symbolic. Coleridge, explains Nicholas Reid, "thinks of Nature as ... a (divine) *mythos*, a well-spring and system of symbols expressing the divine nature," the right reading of which meant, in Coleridge's own words, the "awful Recalling of the drowsed soul from the dreams and phantom world of sensuality to *actual* Reality."[73] This reading was done, for Coleridge, through the imagination, which is why , as Jonathan Wordsworth says, "imagination is for Coleridge an act of faith."[74] It gives to us "the power of discerning the *Cause* in the *Effect*," so that we can see God everywhere. Through its exercise the universe can be seen as a "written Language" proclaiming the Creator.[75] To be known rightly, however, the truths apprehended by the imagination need, according to Coleridge, to be experienced. "TRY IT," as he urged in his *Aids to Reflection* (1825). Coleridge defined Christianity not as "a theory, or a speculation; but a life; – not a philosophy of life, but a life and a living process."[76] All this is, as we have seen, in Knox, as well.

Like Knox, Coleridge had a high ecclesiology; in fact, the revival of the notion of the church as "first and foremost and above all things, essentially a religious society of divine institution" has been ascribed to him.[77] This notion appeared clearly in Coleridge's *On the Constitution of the Church and State* (1830), in which he spoke of the Christian church as being "no state, kingdom, or realm of this world; nor is it an Estate of any such realm, kingdom, or state." Rather, quite literally, the church for Coleridge is a "GOD-SEND." Its origin is supernatural and divine, although Coleridge was at pains to point out that this did not make it a hidden, unseen society. On the contrary, the church was "visible and militant under Christ."[78] He insisted too, like Knox, that the church was the proper interpreter of Scripture; he was, as Barth remarks, very Anglican in his firmness on this point. "My fixed principle is," he wrote, "that a Christianity without a Church exercising spiritual authority is vanity and dissolution." Thus, like Knox, he condemned in no uncertain terms what he deemed "the pretended right of every individual, competent and incompetent, to interpret

72   Hedley, "Participation in the divine life," p. 243; "Coleridge as a Theologian," p. 471.
73   Reid, *Coleridge, Form and Symbol*, p. 3; Coleridge, *Aids to Reflection*, p. 407 (emphasis in the original). For a full discussion, see Barth, *Symbolic Imagination*.
74   Wordsworth, "The Infinite I AM," p. 46. Barth insists that, for Coleridge, "imagination ... is a cognitive faculty." "Romanticism," Barth writes, "is not subjectivism. It is not simply a way of feeling, but a way of knowing" (*Symbolic Imagination*, pp. 21, 137–38).
75   Coleridge, "Fragment of Theological Lecture," in Patton and Mann, eds., *The Collected Works of Samuel Taylor Coleridge*, Vol. 1, pp. 338–39.
76   Coleridge, *Aids to Reflection*, p. 202.
77   Church, *Oxford Movement*, p. 129.
78   Coleridge, *On the Constitution of the Church and State*, pp. 114, 55, 116.

Scripture in a sense of his own, in opposition to the judgment of the Church ...
in contempt of uninterrupted tradition, the unanimous consent of the Fathers
and Councils, and the universal faith of the Church in all ages."[79] Thus there
is in Coleridge, as in Knox, a combining of the objective with the subjective.
As Coleridge wrote: "Religion [has] its objective, or historic and ecclesiastical
pole, and its subjective, or spiritual and individual pole."[80] One may note, finally, a rejection in both men of sectarianism and intolerance, combined with the
idea that, as Barth puts it, "the Church is one, despite its seeming division ...
into particular Christian sects."[81]

6   Knox and Schleiermacher

If Coleridge has been seen as the great theologian of English Romanticism, the
same accolade has likewise been accorded to Friedrich Schleiermacher with
regard to continental Europe, or, at least, to European Protestantism. To quote
Martin Kähler: "Schleiermacher is the Protestant theologian of the Romantic
movement."[82] Certainly, as Crouter has observed, Schleiermacher became less
"Romantic" over time;[83] nonetheless, in his early works especially, he invites
comparisons with Knox. This is especially clear if one examines the 1799 edition of his speeches *On Religion* (*Ueber die Religion: Reden an die Gebildeten
unter ihren Verächtern*). Here Schleiermacher, like Knox, is, in Crouter's words,
reacting to the "Enlightenment view of religion as rational or moral teachings." Schleiermacher rejects both a cerebral theology, which he characterized
as "cold argumentation," and a religion that was merely moral, "a system of
duties." Rather, his approach to religion is experiential. "Religion's essence is
neither thinking nor acting but intuition and feeling," a feeling which he defines as "sensibility and taste for the infinite."[84] For this reason, Schleiermacher

---

79   Coleridge, *Aids to Reflection*, p. 298; cf. Barth, *Coleridge and Christian Doctrine*, p. 81.
         Coleridge, like Knox, used the term "mystical" in relation to the church. This was not,
         however, developed in Coleridge's teaching (Barth, *Coleridge and Christian Doctrine*,
         pp. 135–36). For Coleridge's ecclesiology, see, besides Barth, Barbeau, *Coleridge, the Bible,
         and Religion*, Chapter 6, "The Church: Tradition as the Master-Key of Interpretation,"
         pp. 111–26; also, pp. 7–8.
80   Coleridge, *Confessions of an Inquiring Spirit*, p. 92.
81   Barth, *Coleridge and Christian Doctrine*, pp. 197, 167.
82   Quoted Crouter, ed., Schleiermacher, *On Religion*, p. vi. Cf. Reardon, *Religion in the Age of
         Romanticism*, pp. 29–30. For Schleiermacher (1768–1834) see the extensive bibliography in
         Mariña, ed., *The Cambridge Companion to Friedrich Schleiermacher*, pp. 319–24.
83   Crouter, "Rhetoric and Substance," p. 289.
84   Crouter, ed., Schleiermacher, *On Religion*, pp. xxx, 13, 20, 22, 23.

exercised a tolerant spirit towards dogmatic differences, roundly rejecting what he called the "malicious spirit of sectarianism and proselytizing, which always leads further away from the essence of religion."[85]

If it is misleading to declare outright that in his *On Religion*, Schleiermacher appears as a Platonist, the Platonic element in the speeches is nonetheless clear.[86] Nor should this surprise us. Schleiermacher was a classical scholar of considerable importance, his contribution to the study of Plato being arguably equal to his contribution to theology.[87] His philosophical Platonism certainly differed from the mystical form of the tradition espoused by Knox, but it does demonstrate a shared Hellenism. Shared, too, was the Romantic emphasis which Knox and Schleiermacher alike placed on the individual, balanced though it was by an insistence on the communal nature of religion. "Religion hates to be alone," Schleiermacher declared. "Once there is religion, it must necessarily also be social." For him, the social and the individual aspects of religion were not opposed, but reciprocal. "[T]he most proper object of [the] desire for communication is undoubtedly that where man originally feels himself to be passive, his intuitions and feelings."[88] Of note, too, is the centrality of the imagination to Schleiermacher's speeches. For him, imagination is "the highest … element in us," the means by which we intuit the infinite. Also striking is the optimistic spirit which runs throughout the speeches, what Crouter calls their "positivist and progressive understanding of human nature and the march of history." No less than Knox, Schleiermacher insists that "an infinite holiness is the ultimate goal of Christianity;" the truly religious individuals are, for him, never satisfied with what they have attained, but must ever press onwards.[89]

Despite these commonalities, Knox and Schleiermacher are ultimately very different theologians. Even when they use similar language, their thought stands poles apart. For example, although Schleiermacher insists on the social nature of religion, he roundly rejects what he terms the "monstrous association of institutional religion," especially when allied to the state. Again, while Knox sees imagination as a means of uniting us to the Triune God, for Schleiermacher it makes possible "innumerable forms of religion," even perhaps, a religion without God. For, says Schleiermacher, "whether we have God

---

85   Ibid., p. 91.
86   Beiser, *Romantic Imperative*, p. 70.
87   See, on this point, Lamm, "Schleiermacher as Plato Scholar;" also Tigerstedt, *Decline and Fall of the Neo-Platonic Interpretation of Plato*.
88   Crouter, ed., Schleiermacher, *On Religion*, pp. 124, 73.
89   Ibid., pp. 53, xxxviii, 117.

as part of our intuition depends on the direction of our imagination."[90] In fine, Schleiermacher is radically innovative, taking the human subject as his starting-point.[91] Knox, by contrast, is an avowed traditionalist. His starting-point is the biblical revelation, interpreted by the *consensus omnium*, which the believer then comes to know personally and experientially.

7   **Conclusion**

This chapter has shown how Knox exemplifies the age in which he lived, reflecting in his theology the spiritual and intellectual concerns of his time. First, he is an exemplar of heart religion, something about which he often spoke explicitly in his writings, which are marked throughout by the defining characteristic of such religion, which is the primacy of the affective and experiential over the cerebral and doctrinal. But his work is marked, too, by the Enlightenment. Numerous traits in his theology reflect the Age of Reason: an interest in science; the idea of progress; optimism, not least about the perfectibility of human nature; the theme of happiness; a spirit of tolerance. Yet, if his thinking is rooted in the Enlightenment, it flowers in Romanticism. He reacts to rationalism, not rejecting it, but adding to its perceived imbalance an emphasis on affection and imagination, the latter reading the world as symbolic. He reveals, in his Christian Platonism, a concern for Hellenism; he strongly insists on the subjective element in Christianity – "religion is experience" – yet there is an equal firmness on the church and on tradition. All these traits mark Knox out as a Romantic theologian, akin to those to whom that epithet is often given: Coleridge in England and Schleiermacher on the European continent. Yet, Knox is not a Romantic theologian *tout court*. His thought is "more than the 'churching of Romanticism,'" to borrow James Pereiro's words about the Oxford Movement. Romanticism is one element in his theology, of less importance to him than his constant appeal to "the judgment of the Church, ancient and Anglican."[92]

---

90   Ibid., pp. 85, 123, 53.

91   See, however, Schleiermacher's statement that all intuition proceeds from "an influence of the intuited on the one who intuits, from an original and independent action of the former, which is then grasped by the latter" (ibid., pp. 24–25). There is an interesting similarity here with Knox's thinking about divine attraction (see, pp. 125, 159, 167).

92   Pereiro, *Ethos and the Oxford Movement*, pp. 79–80; *Remains*, Vol. 1, p. 309 (punctuation modified).

CHAPTER 6

The Characteristics of Alexander Knox's Theology

Before looking at Alexander Knox's thought in detail, I would like to consider two general points. The first concerns the characteristics of his theology, which I would describe as coherent, consistent, practical, consensual, eclectic and "philosophic." In examining each of these characteristics, I will also underline the instances in which they reflect Knox's Christian Platonism, his historical situation in the post-Enlightenment period, his rootedness in the Fathers, and his understanding of Anglicanism.

1   A Coherent Theology

Knox's thought is sometimes described – by himself and by others – as his "system."[1] The term denotes what, in a letter to George Schoales, Knox called a "particular way of thinking;" or, to use a phrase from the *British Critic*, a "theological *panorama*."[2] "System" also implies, however, a certain order and cohesion, so it seems rather a misnomer when applied to Knox's rather untidy *oeuvre*. Knox professed to seek a "clear, definite, unprejudiced view of the plan of Christianity," and he bemoaned the lack of a "single book which directly and distinctly, simply and comprehensively, introduces an inquirer to the sacred science of Christianity." "[W]e have no adequate guide to theological studies; nor any competent key to the understanding of Holy Scripture."[3] He never seems to have thought of filling these lacunae himself; all his work was of an occasional nature, much of it never intended for publication in its present,

---

1   For the description of Knox's thought as a system see, for example: *Correspondence*, Vol. 2, pp. 61, 63, 101, 353; *British Critic*, 23.45 (January 1838), p. 14; Gunstone, "Alexander Knox," p. 469; Hornby, "Editor's Preface to the Third and Fourth Volumes," p. cxvii; *Christian Observer*, 3.36 (October 1834), pp. 396, 398.
2   *Remains*, Vol. 4, p. 117; *British Critic*, 23.45 (January 1838), p. 3 (italics original).
3   *Remains*, Vol. 4, pp. 208–9; Vol. 3, p. 278; Vol. 4, p. 336. Knox was not alone in voicing such complaints. For similar remarks made by his contemporaries, see Sykes, *Church and State in England in the Eighteenth Century*, p. 108. Compare Newman's statement: "We have a vast inheritance, but no inventory of our treasures. All is given us in profusion; it remains for us to catalogue, sort, distribute, select, harmonize, and complete" (Newman, *Lectures on the Prophetical Office of the Church*, p. 30).

sometimes confused note form.[4] Yet, in spite of this, one can apply to Knox's writings what he says about the Scriptures: they may appear to be a "miscellaneous assemblage," but in reality they form "a most regular system, in which one part is strictly dependent on another, and all the parts meet together in one grand central principle," like a plant whose disparate roots and branches are all connected to a single stem.[5] Thus, while they are not systematic, Knox's writings can be systematised; a clear and coherent structure may be drawn from their apparent disorder.[6] Knox hinted at this possibility, when he commented in the *Remains*: "[W]hat I generally insist upon, is, the victory of Divine grace over human depravity; the filial access to God, and delight in Him which flows therefrom; the Divine faith (or knowledge of God, and of Him whom He hath sent,) which is the root of this religion; and the true virtue, and genuine happiness, which are its fruits."[7]

The core of Knox's thought, its "one grand central principle," is the doctrine of justification (which is what "the victory of Divine grace over human depravity" in the above quotation signifies).[8] This is not to say that Knox focused uniquely on justification. As he asserted in a letter to the *Christian Observer*: "A science is not composed of one truth, but of many truths; and to fix upon one of them is to destroy the proportion, beauty, and perfection of the science."[9] Nonetheless, almost all of Knox's teaching can be related to justification. The exception is his teaching on providence, which he viewed as analogous. "By divine grace, God influences our minds and hearts. By divine providence, he disposes and arranges all our circumstances, as inhabitants of this world."[10] In other words, for Knox providence concerns God's activity exterior to human beings, justification God's activity within the soul.

---

4   Hornby, "Editor's Preface," p. vii; "Editor's Preface to the Third and Fourth Volumes," pp. ix–x; *Remains*, Vol. 1, p. 369; *Correspondence*, Vol. 2, p. 532.

5   *Remains*, Vol. 3, pp. 1, 3–4. See also, Vol. 1, p. 184, where Knox applies the metaphor of "inward vegetation" to his thinking.

6   Cf. *Remains*, Vol. 3, p. 137–8, where Knox expresses a similar view of Wesley's thought: that properly edited and arranged it would form an excellent compendium of theology.

7   *Remains*, Vol. 4, p. 136.

8   For Knox's teaching on justification, see below, pp. 168–73.

9   *Christian Observer*, 15.2 (February 1816), p. 78. The letter from which this quotation comes (pp. 76–80) is signed "Talmidon," but its style and content argue strongly for Knox as the author. The letter may very well be the "paper" mentioned by Jebb, *Correspondence*, Vol. 2, p. 279.

10   *Remains*, Vol. 2, p. 286.

2   A Consistent Theology

One of the most striking features of Knox's thought is its consistency. "[A]s far as man can be immutable, I am,'" he told Jebb in 1811. It was a claim which he repeated two years' later: "The whole tissue of my writing and talking, has been one and the same." Hornby noted: "If ever there was unbroken consistency of opinion, it existed in the case of Mr. Knox."[11] This claim of consistency may initially seem surprising, given that Knox spent more than thirty years reflecting on theological subjects, tirelessly reading authors of many different backgrounds and approaches. It also appears to be contradicted by several of his own statements. One of these is the confidence to Joseph Cooper Walker, that he did not want to publish anything, because while his writings were in manuscript, he could still revise them, but once they were fixed in print, he would not be able to correct their "inaccuracies or imperfections."[12] This comment may refer to changes of theological opinion, though given Knox's already-noted doubts about his prose, it probably refers to issues of style. There was no such ambiguity, however, in his avowal to Jebb: "My thoughts grow; new lights seem, every now and then, to open upon me; and to show some fresh object of admiration, in the great temple of truth." "My mind," he assured Jebb in another letter, "has moved onward and seen things, as I have proceeded, in something of a different light."[13] How can Knox's apparently discrepant statements be harmonized? The answer is that his work displays a remarkable stability with regard to principles: the substance of what he believed remained constant. One can, however, discern an expansion or unfolding of these basic principles. As Knox explained to Joseph Butterworth: "Doubtless, many thoughts have presented, and are still presenting, themselves to my mind, which once I had no idea of: but these in, I believe, every instance, are as much the growth of former rooted principles, as multiplied branches grow from one and the same main stem."[14] As he wrote in 1808 with regard to his correspondence:

---

11   *Correspondence*, Vol. 2, pp. 35, 139; Hornby, "Editor's Preface to the Third and Fourth Volumes," p. lxxiv. See, also, on this topic, "Editor's Preface," pp. viii–xi.

12   T. C. D., Ms 1461, volume 7, Correspondence of Joseph Cooper Walker (1761–1810), fol. 144, Knox to Joseph Cooper Walker, letter, May 18–19, [1802].

13   *Correspondence*, Vol. 1, p. 491; Vol. 2, p. 370.

14   *Remains*, Vol. 1, p. 184. Joseph Butterworth (1770–1826) was founder of the legal publishing house that still bears his name. A member of the 'Clapham Sect' and Treasurer of the Wesleyan Missionary Society, he was M. P. for Coventry, 1812–1818, then for Dover, 1818–26. See *O. D. N. B.*

From some such records I am now able to ascertain, to myself, that,
though I have been as busy a thinker as most people, my mind has always adhered to the same radical principles, and that changes in me have
either been circumstantial, or merely progressive; I should also say, perhaps, expansive. But, certainly, in no essential point do I seem to myself
to have veered about, from the age of eighteen to the present hour. My
conduct varied much, from that time, until I was thirty-nine; but not my
principles: and yet I was ever, I believe, open to conviction, and ready to
have embraced whatever could have been proved true.[15]

There is a similar statement in a letter to Knox from Jebb. Looking back in 1812
over their past exchanges, Jebb reflected:

It has brought before me, the gradual development of your system, and
shown you always at unity with yourself, though happily progressive
in your views; your mental horizon, enlarging itself on all sides, as you
advance. I am particularly interested by observing in the earlier parts, not
inconsistency, but deficiency of view; which, however, is always amply
supplied, either from more advanced stages of the correspondence, or
from recollections of our many conversations.[16]

If Knox's theology was consistent it was not static. It developed, but this
development was harmonious and organic, rather than constituting a substantial change.

The reason for the consistency of Knox's views is explained by Hornby as an
expression of the Church's unchanging faith. Knox's doctrines were, Hornby
says, "not singular, or his own; but held in common with the primitive and universal church." "There could be nothing of fluctuation in a mind that was anchored on catholic principles," Hornby maintained.[17] To the extent that Knox
viewed his teaching as nothing more or less than the faith held *semper, ubique,
et ab omnibus* and as such immutable, this is a conclusion with which one can
easily concur. As Knox put it: "[N]othing can be more settled, than the grounds
and reasons of my being what I am."[18]

---

15   *Remains*, Vol. 1, pp. 183–4.
16   *Correspondence*, Vol. 2, p. 63.
17   Hornby, "Editor's Preface to the Third and Fourth Volumes," p. lxxv.
18   *Correspondence*, Vol. 2, p. 35.

3 A Practical Theology

Knox presented himself as a "Christian philosopher," one whose days were devoted to rational reflection on his faith.[19] Yet, at the same time, he strenuously rejected what he dubbed "metaphysical divinity" and "dogmatic ratiocination."[20] The dichotomy is explained by seeing him as a practical, rather than a speculative theologian. His reflection was not concerned with abstractions, but with the Christian life, the stated goal of his philosophy being "*maturity* in goodness" and "the increase of piety."[21] And piety or "religion" was what the Christian life was all about, "THE GRAND OBJECT," which he equated with love, quoting 1 Timothy 1, 5: τὸ τέλος τῆς παραγγελίας, ἐστὶν ἀγάπη (*to telos tēs parangelias, estin agapē*: the goal of [the] commandment is love).[22] He informed George Schoales:

> By religion, I mean a steady choice of, and affectionate adherence to, God, as the paramount object of our hearts, and the supreme sum and centre of our happiness; and, by the religion of the Gospel, I mean the same great end pursued under those more familiarising, yet more elevating, views, and with an adequate knowledge of, and cordial relish for, those multiplied and invaluable aids, which the grand and gracious system of "God manifest in the flesh" implies.[23]

Or, as he put it elsewhere, more succinctly: "[T]he essence of true religion [is] the supreme love of God."[24]

Knox occasionally employed the word "spirituality" and its cognates in relation to the Christian life, being one of the first English writers to do so. For example, in his letter to Parken on mysticism, he used the word "spirituality" and the phrase "spiritual writer" once each, while twice speaking of the "ancient spiritualists."[25] The word was extant in English prior to Knox, in the sense of what pertains to the supernatural life. For example, we find it used throughout the tract "An Account of the Beginnings and Advances of A Spiritual Life,"

---

19   *Remains*, 3, p. 151. See, also: Jebb, "Introduction" to Burnet's *Lives*, p. xxix; and below, pp. 121–22.

20   *Remains*, Vol. 3, pp. 3, 38.

21   Ibid., Vol. 1, pp. 240, 375 (emphasis in the original).

22   Ibid., p. 407.

23   Ibid., Vol. 4, p. 140. One may note how Knox's use of the terms "piety" and "religion" recall the language of his contemporary Schleiermacher. See above, pp. 104–5.

24   *Remains*, Vol. 1, p. 469.

25   Ibid., pp. 350–2, 355.

annexed to one of Knox's favourite books, Henry Scougal's *Life of God in the Soul of Man* (1677). It is possible, however, that Knox's use of the word derived from the French, where *spiritualité* was widely employed in the seventeenth century, prior to *le crépescule des mystiques*.[26] Possibly also, Knox took the word directly from the Greek term πνευματικός (pneumatikos), used by Paul in 1 Corinthians 3, 1, to which Knox appealed when distinguishing between Christians simply in a state of grace and those who had moved on to "perfect love."[27] He would have found the word frequently in the Fathers, not least his favourites, Clement, Pseudo-Macarius and Chrysostom. From whatever source he derived it, describing the Christian life as "spiritual" fitted in well with Knox's understanding of that life as one animated by the Holy Spirit.

Concomitant with his practical approach to theology, was Knox's limitation of dogma to "a few radical truths,"[28] or the "catholic verities."[29] These truths were the "fundamentals" of the faith, because they belonged to "the essence of vital Christianity."[30] And here it is the word "vital" that needs to be noted.[31] "Fundamentals" and the "essence of Christianity" were both terms which had been used and discussed by Anglican theologians prior to Knox, but his treatment of them is distinctive.[32] For Knox, as we have just seen, the "essence of true religion" was "the supreme love of God" and accordingly, the only necessary doctrines were those implied by such love; those doctrines which "the Universal Church holds in common:"[33] "The Trinity in Unity, the incarnation

---

26   See on this point, McGinn, "The Letter and the Spirit," pp. 27–28.

27   *Remains*, Vol. 4, p. 331.

28   Ibid., p. 240.

29   Ibid., Vol. 2, p. 341. Prior to Knox, the plural "catholic verities" is rare in theological usage. Knox, however, employs it several times (*Remains*, Vol. 2, pp. 317, 341, 358; Vol. 3, p. 301; *Correspondence*, Vol. 2, pp. 161, 189), and subsequently it appears as a standard expression in Anglo-Catholic discourse, beginning with the Tractarians. It occurs in Tracts 61 and 81, the latter penned by Pusey who also used it in the introduction to his translation (1838) of Augustine's *Confessions*, the first volume in the "Library of the Fathers" (p. vii). This change may indicate the influence of Knox.

30   *Remains*, Vol. 3, p. 43; Vol. 2, p. 341. See also: Vol. 3, p. 8; Vol. 4, p. 244 ("fundamentals" capitalized in the original).

31   The theme of "vital Christianity" occurs several times in Knox: *Remains*, Vol. 2, pp. 341, 351; Vol. 3, p. 280; Vol. 4, pp. 326, 586. It was "the one thing needful" (Luke 10, 42), a phrase he often employed. See, e.g.: *Remains*, Vol. 1, pp. 7, 248, 269, 461, 474; Vol. 4, pp. 226, 259, 331, 401, 416.

32   On the fundamentals see Sykes, "The Fundamentals of Christianity," in Sykes, Booty, and Knight, eds., *The Study of Anglicanism*, pp. 262–77; and Avis, *Anglicanism and the Christian Church*, throughout which the doctrine of fundamentals is a running theme. On the "essence of Christianity," see Sykes, *Identity of Christianity*. As will be noted below, Knox's treatment of fundamentals echoes the thought of Wesley.

33   *Remains*, Vol. 4, p. 302. See also Vol. 2, p. 358.

of the second Person, and the efficacious grace of the third, together with the undeniable results of those two latter verities, in the salvation of man."[34] As long as these "supreme and essential matters" were accepted, then, Knox held, "let the individual Christian make his best use of the particular ideas which he may have been providentially led to entertain."[35]

Knox's concern with praxis rather than dogma reflected the attitude displayed by Wesley, who, in his own words, abstained "from all nice and philosophical speculations [and] all perplexed and intricate reasonings." Instead, Wesley's focus was on "one thing, the way to heaven – how to land safe on that happy shore."[36] This is not to say that he held back from theological reflection, but rather that, like Knox, he wished such reflection to serve a practical purpose. As he put it in his sermon on "The Danger of Riches" (1781): "[W]hat avails the clearest knowledge, even of the most excellent things ... if it go no farther than speculation, if it be not reduced to practice?"[37] Like Knox, Wesley limited the scope of dogma to a few essentials, vital for salvation.[38] Although he eschewed the term "fundamentals", he believed that there are some truths "which it nearly concerns us to know, as having a close connection with vital religion," among them the doctrine of the Trinity.[39] Similar language appeared in the "Minutes" of the 1746 Methodist Conference, where Wesley spoke of salvation by faith as constituting "the very vitals, the essence of Christianity."[40]

As we have seen above, the moderates were adamant that religion is not primarily a question of doctrine but of practice;[41] and therefore, they held, to quote Whichcote, that "Vitals in religion are few."[42] In his defence of practical theology over dogmatic speculation, Knox did not, however, appeal either to the moderates or to Wesley. Rather, he cited the twin examples of the primitive church and the Church of England. In the patristic period, Knox

---

34   Ibid., Vol. 2, p. 317. See, also, *Answer to Duigenan*, p. 60. Cf. Jebb, *Sermons on Subjects Chiefly Practical*, p. 293.

35   *Remains*, Vol. 2, p. 315.

36   Wesley, "Preface" to *Sermons on Several Occasions*, 3 in Outler, ed., *Works of John Wesley*, Vol. 1, pp. 103–7, at pp. 104–5.

37   Wesley, Sermon 87, "The Danger of Riches," 2, 1, in Outler, ed., *Works of John Wesley*, Vol. 3, pp. 228–46, at p. 236.

38   For Wesley, "an essential doctrine was one vital to salvation. Everything else represented speculative theory, and therefore held a very marginal place in his interest" (Cragg, ed., *Works of John Wesley*, Vol. 11, p. 23).

39   Wesley, Sermon 55, "On the Trinity," 2, in Outler, ed., *Works of John Wesley*, Vol. 2, pp. 374–86, at p. 376.

40   See Outler, *John Wesley*, pp. 159–60.

41   See above, p. 83–84. See also, English, "Wesley and the Anglican Moderates," pp. 214–19.

42   Whichcote, Aphorism 1008, *Aphorisms*, p. clx.

maintained, the "fire of divine love [glowed] without the smoke of dark dogmas."[43] At first sight, this contention might seem somewhat misjudged, given the Fathers' theological endeavours. Nevertheless, as Maurice Wiles points out, it would be wrong to think of the Fathers as academic theologians, whose theorizing was only remotely connected to the realities of the spiritual life. Rather, they were "passionately concerned … to propagate the gospel of salvation." This was true even when they seemed to be at their most speculative. To quote Nicolas Lossky:

> One of the first and main characteristics of [the] patristic approach to theology is that it is 'practical', not speculative. This, of course, is not to say there is never any speculation in the writings of such theologians; but the speculative elements always aim at redirecting people's attention to the central truth of the Christian faith, which is Christ Himself and the salvation offered in Him. Patristic theology is 'practical', one might even say 'utilitarian', in that it is salvational.[44]

Lossky's words could equally well be applied to Knox's understanding of Anglicanism, "so undogmatic, so purely devotional and spiritual a system," as Knox described it. Anglicanism has been historically, in the words of Paul Avis, "a practical, not a speculative faith." As an example of this, one may point to the Prayer Book Catechism. In contradistinction to similar documents in other traditions, the Westminster Catechism, for instance, or the Catechism of the Council of Trent, the Catechism of the Church of England limits itself, like Knox, to "a few radical truths," reducing the Christian *Credo* to a statement of belief in: "God the Father, who hath made me, and all the world … in God the Son, who hath redeemed me, and all mankind … [and] in God the Holy Ghost, who sanctifieth me, and all the elect people of God."[45]

4   A Consensual Theology

Speaking of Knox, William Ewart Gladstone observed: "[His] religion is very much individualised.… It has a [*sic*]intercourse with the Almighty, but the communication is with his own mind alone; it has no witnesses nor partners."

---

43   *Remains*, Vol. 4, p. 240; Vol. 3, p. 108.
44   Wiles, *The Christian Fathers*, p. 83; Lossky, "The Oxford Movement and the Revival of Patristic Theology," pp. 77–78.
45   *Remains*, Vol. 3, p. 131; Avis, "Keeping Faith with Anglicanism," p. 15; B. C. P., pp. 212–13.

It is "an isolated method of religion."[46] This is not so. Not only did Knox seek to anchor his theology in the context of Anglicanism, but he was also someone who discussed his thought with others. "[U]ntil my notions have been examined strictly by some competent judge," he wrote, "I have no right to esteem them more than probable conceptions." As he told Daniel Parken: "I am ready to hope that some of my conceptions may not be wholly useless: but I can have no assurance on this, unless they pass the trial of other minds." Nor were these minds simply those of people who agreed with him. Knox was keen to engage in discussion with those who held opinions different from his own. "It is always my wish to look at both sides of a question," he declared, thus belying the assertion of the *British Critic* that he shared his views only with "a chosen circle of admiring hearers."[47] The *Critic* is, however, right when it says that Knox avoided the "*collision* of mind with mind,"[48] for a further characteristic of Knox's thought is its consensual nature. In his theology Knox aimed, as he himself put it, "to combine apparently opposite truths."[49] Thus, for example, he held that if we are justified by faith, true faith is always productive of good works; if righteousness is imputed to the sinner, it is also imparted; if Scripture is the supreme authority in matters of religion, it also needs to be interpreted by Catholic tradition.[50]

Knox sought to demonstrate that most differences in theology were verbal rather than substantial, and that therefore they could, and should be, resolved. As he explained to Jebb, he would, when dealing with those of dissimilar views, seek "to show how far [their opinions] ... might be reconciled with those I wished to inculcate." Thus, he told Jebb, when discussing the doctrine of perfection with an old Methodist preacher, he had managed to persuade the man that their differences had nothing to do with issues of substance, but were merely "a dispute of words."[51] We have seen a similar approach in his early work, the *Remarks on an Expostulatory Address*.[52] Two further examples may be given from the *Correspondence*. In a letter dated November 12, 1805, Knox recounted to Jebb how he had endeavored to show the dissenting minister, Samuel Greatheed, editor, at that time, of the *Eclectic Review*, that their ideas

---

46   B. L., Add. Ms 44724, Gladstone Papers, DCXXXIX, fols. 73–76, "memorandum," March 24, 1835, fol. 74.

47   *Correspondence*, Vol. 2, p. 532 (= *Remains*, Vol. 4, p. 460); *Remains*, Vol. 1, p. 369; *Correspondence*, Vol. 1, p. 141; *Remains*, Vol. 4, p. 505; *British Critic*, 17.34 (April 1835), p. 295.

48   *British Critic*, 17.34 (April 1835), p. 295.

49   *Correspondence*, Vol. 1, p. 170 (emphasis added). See, too, Gunstone's comments, "Alexander Knox," p. 469.

50   See pp. 171–72, 170–71, 39.

51   *Correspondence*, Vol. 1, pp. 141–2.

52   See above, p. 58.

diverged "in words chiefly." Despite "a good deal of verbal and circumstantial dissonance," there was, Knox argued, "much substantial agreement" between Greatheed and himself.[53] In another letter, written in October 1807, Knox spoke of his discussions about grace with those whom he termed "honest calvinists," discussions which, he related, habitually resulted in an agreement being reached between both sides.[54] Even when others did not agree with him, Knox was not prepared to condemn them automatically. If people erred doctrinally, this could simply be a sincere intellectual mistake. "[T]hey may be upright in their affections; and however dark in their understandings, they may have the substance of divine love in their hearts."[55] In spite of this eirenicism, however, Knox did not avoid controversy. Not only did he receive censure for his own views, but he was also outspoken in his criticism of opinions which he believed to be genuinely wrong and harmful to spiritual growth.

Knox's open and tolerant attitude to doctrinal difference was a reflection of his age – a point which has already been made. It reflected, too, the position adopted by Wesley. The axiom "Think and Let Think," his "slogan for theological pluralism," as Outler calls it, occurs several times in his works.[56] One instance comes from his sermon on the death of George Whitefield:

> And, first, let us keep close to the grand scriptural doctrines which [Whitefield] everywhere delivered. There are many doctrines of a less essential nature, with regard to which even the sincere children of God (such is the present weakness of human understanding!) are and have been divided for many ages. In these we may think and let think; we may 'agree to disagree'. But meantime let us hold fast the essentials of the 'faith which was once delivered to the saints', and which this champion of God so strongly insisted on at all times and in all places.

"However confused their ideas may be," Wesley proclaimed, with regard to those from whom he differed theologically, "however improper their language, may there not be many of them whose heart is right toward God and who

---

53   *Correspondence*, Vol. 1, p. 217. Samuel Greatheed (1759–1823) was a Congregationalist minister at Newport Pagnell and co-founder of the *Eclectic Review* which he edited 1805–6. See *Notes and Queries*, 11th series, Vol. v.109, January 27, 1912, pp. 71–3. The name is spelled "Greathead" in the *Remains*.

54   *Remains*, Vol. 1, p. 381.

55   Ibid., Vol. 2, p. 352. Compare Wesley's words in "The Lord our Righteousness" (2, 16), quoted below.

56   Outler, ed., *Works of John Wesley*, Vol. 1, p. 220, note 7.

effectually know 'the Lord our righteousness?'"[57] Wesley was not simply tolerant of doctrinal difference, however. Like Knox, he also sought to unite oppos-
ing views. This is seen pre-eminently in what George Croft Cell has termed
Wesley's "synthesis of the Protestant ethic of grace with the Catholic ethic of
holiness." Another example is Wesley's teaching on baptism, in which he strove
to combine the High Church doctrine of regeneration with Evangelical concern for personal conversion.[58] The moderates, likewise, rejected what Henry
More termed "that wolfish and ferine humor of persecuting others." They desired rather, as English says, "peace and unity among Christians," believing
that, in Whichcote's words, "[t]hose, who *are* united by *Religion should be* united by *Charity*," a position which he aphorized as: "I *must* not be dogmatical."[59]
For Knox, however, eirenicism was, yet again, not something he derived sim-
ply from Wesley or the moderates, but from the Church of England itself.
For him, the "principles of liberality" were "planted in the very bosom of our
Establishment,"[60] an analysis in which he does not stand alone. As Andrew
Pierce has noted, "comprehensiveness has often been considered a typically
Anglican theological trait,"[61] which arose from the fact that the Church of
England was intended to embrace the entire nation.

5   An Eclectic Theology

"I am an eclectic," Knox declared. "I seem to myself to enjoy a most pleasant liberty of mind, ranging without restraint, *apis Matinae more modoque*."[62]
Theology, for him, he claimed, was an "unfettered plan."[63] He felt free to draw
from a broad variety of sources: the Greek and Latin Fathers; the Anglican
moderates; Roman Catholic spiritual writers of various, sometimes opposed,

---

57   Wesley, Sermon 53, "On the Death of George Whitefield," 3, 1, in Outler, ed., *Works of John
      Wesley*, Vol. 2, pp. 330–47, p. 341; Sermon 20, "The Lord our Righteousness," 2, 16, in Outler,
      ed., *Works of John Wesley*, Vol. 1, pp. 449–65, at p. 461.

58   Cell, *The Rediscovery of John Wesley*, p. 347. For Wesley's doctrine of baptism, see below
      195–96.

59   More, *Grand Mystery of Godliness*, p. 176; English, "Wesley and the Anglican Moderates,"
      p. 219; Whichcote, Aphorism 103, *Aphorisms*, p. li; Aphorism 130, *Aphorisms*, p. liv. Henry
      More (1614–1687) was one of the Cambridge Platonists; see Crocker's eponymous
      biography.

60   *Remains*, Vol. 3, p. 131.

61   Pierce, "Comprehensive Vision," p. 76.

62   *Remains*, Vol. 4, p. 147 (format slightly altered). The Latin quotation comes from Horace,
      Odes, 4, 2, 27–28: "following the method and custom of the Apulian bee" (my translation).

63   *Remains*, Vol. 4, p. 147.

traditions; Puritans; and Pietists.[64] His eclecticism was not, however, random or whimsical: "the light of Scripture" was his constant guide, together with "the semper creditum est," the rule laid down by Vincent of Lérins.[65]

Eclecticism is a trait which Knox shares with Wesley, "a born borrower," as Outler terms him, whose use of multiple sources is a commonplace among scholars.[66] Eclecticism is also a characteristic of the moderates' theology. It was their "general *intention*," in Whichcote's words, "to entertain and submit to all truth whatsoever, whensoever it shall appear." "Truth is truth, whosoever hath spoken it," he declared.[67] Among the Fathers, this principle is amply illustrated by Clement of Alexandria, whose work Osborn has summed up as a "skillful synthesis of Athens and Jerusalem," embracing Jewish, Christian and even "heterodox" sources.[68] That is not to say that Clement directly influenced Knox's eclecticism, but it does point to a feature of the Platonic tradition which was shared by the two writers.

Hughes has suggested that Knox's eclecticism was the result of his being an autodidact and Knox himself asserts that he "caught religion by the means of [no] party."[69] Whatever the truth of this, eclecticism was a hall-mark of Enlightenment thinking. "The eclectic dares to think for himself," Diderot proclaimed. "He recognizes no master." And, although Knox would certainly not have gone to the lengths advocated by the *encylopédiste*, he was equally ready to proclaim: "To think for himself is the hereditary right of every man born into the world."[70]

6   A "Philosophic" Theology

Given the influence of the Enlightenment on Knox, it comes as little surprise to learn that he described his theology as "philosophic."

---

64   See, below, p. 131.
65   *Remains*, Vol. 4, p. 147; *Correspondence*, Vol. 2, p. 297, "that which has always been believed."
66   Outler, ed., *The Works of John Wesley*, Vol. 1, p. 55. See, too, Hempton, *Methodism: Empire of the Spirit*, pp. 56–7.
67   Whichcote, Discourse 25, "That those who are truly Religious will be delivered from all dangerous errors about Religion," *Works*, Vol. 2, pp. 1–21, p. 6; "Second Letter to Dr. Tuckney," *Aphorisms*, pp. 41–65, at p. 57 (spelling modernized).
68   Osborn, *Clement of Alexandria*, pp. xii, 23.
69   Hughes, "Life and Work," p. 11; *Remains*, Vol. 1, p. 153.
70   Diderot, art., ÉCLECTICISME, pp. 52–3; Knox, *Free Thoughts*, p. 2.

> Knowledge can be communicated but in two methods, – the dogmatic and the philosophic. In the dogmatic method, propositions are authoritatively pronounced, and implicitly adopted; in the philosophic, principles are rationally developed, and received on conviction. Our Divine Religion has made use of both methods ... [b]ut the Gospel is essentially philosophical, as implying liberty (Gal. v. 1), maturity of understanding (1 Cor. xiv. 20), unreserved communication (St John xv. 15), and the giving of a reason of the hope which is in us (1 St Peter, iii. 15), which implies that the hope itself has been rationally conceived.[71]

This rational approach to religion is something that Knox shares with Wesley and the seventeenth-century Anglican moderates, who invoked it in reaction to the dogmatism of Calvinism and the bitterness of the English Civil War. Wesley admitted "no method of bringing any to the knowledge of the truth, except the methods of reason and persuasion;" for the religion which he proclaimed was "founded on reason, and every way agreeable thereto."[72] As for the moderates, one may cite Cudworth who, in his sermon to the House of Commons, exhorted his hearers to "strive with all meekness to instruct and convince one another ... This was the way, by which the gospel at first was propagated in the world ... Sweetness and ingenuity will more command men's minds than passion, sourness and severity." As Whichcote expressed it: The longest Sword, the strongest Lungs, the most Voices are false measures of *Truth* ... *God* applies to our Faculties; and deals with us by *Reason* and Argument. Let *us* learn of God, to deal with One another in Meekness, Calmness, and *Reason*; and so Represent God.[73]

Knox's "philosophic" approach was above all something which he attributed to his Anglicanism. "[T]he Church of England encourages all her competent children to make inquiry for themselves," he wrote, contrasting this liberty with what he believed to be the "mental tyranny" of the Roman Catholic Church.[74]

---

71   *Remains*, Vol. 3, pp. 138–9.
72   Wesley, Sermon 112, "On Laying of the Foundation of the New Chapel," 2, 11, in Outler, ed., *Works of John Wesley*, Vol. 3, pp. 579–92, at p. 588; *An Earnest Appeal to Men of Reason and Religion*, 28, in Cragg, ed., *Works of John Wesley*, Vol. 11, pp. 45–94, at p. 55.
73   Cudworth, "Sermon I," *Works*, Vol. 4, pp. 289–350, at pp. 335–56; Whichcote, Aphorism 500, *Aphorisms*, p. xcviii; Aphorism 572, *Aphorisms*, p. cviii.
74   *Remains*, Vol. 3, pp. 297, 317–22. Note the qualifier "competent." Knox's religion was very much one for the educated classes. See *Remains*, Vol. 1, p. 187; Vol. 4, pp. 586–7; P. R. O. N. I., D3030/1612, fol. 3, Knox to Lord Castlereagh, letter, February 19, 1801. See above p. 40.

7   **Conclusion**

In this chapter we have examined the general characteristics of Knox's theology and have found it to be coherent and consistent. We have seen, too, that its traits were shared with both Wesley and the moderates of the seventeenth century, which confirms Knox's status as a Platonist, as well as helping to clarify the lineaments of the Platonic tradition more generally, especially as it appears historically in Anglicanism. It is practical, rather than speculative; eirenic and consensual; eclectic and rational. These features reflect Knox's Enlightenment background, although Knox himself presented them not as expressions of the age in which he lived, but rather as a perpetuation of the patristic spirit, a spirit by which, he believed, the Church of England continued to be animated. In short, the characteristics of Knox's theology reveal him as a Platonist; as a child of his times; as thinker who desired to root himself in the early church and in the heritage of the English Church. The same is true of his theological methodology, to which we now turn.

CHAPTER 7

Alexander Knox's Theological Methodology

This chapter examines Knox's methodology, beginning with his understanding of theology as a science, seen in post-Enlightenment terms as a quest for truth. It then goes on to examine the elements that he employed in this quest: Scripture, tradition,[1] and experience, including, with regard to the latter, a discussion of his understanding of intuition. The chapter also underlines again points that we have already addressed in this study: the correspondences between Knox's theology and that of John Wesley and the moderates; the ways in which his ideas reflected the age in which he lived; the roots of his thought in the patristic period; and his belief that what he taught was the doctrine of the Church of England.

1   "The Science of True Piety"

In discussing the intellectual background to Knox's thought, we saw that he spoke of theology as a science, "the science of true piety," no different in its methodology from astronomy, chemistry or mathematics.[2] In the post-Enlightenment era, the presupposition of these disciplines was the existence of objective truths, which the scientific method could discover. Knox shared this presupposition with regard to the "science" of theology, which is why he saw theology as a quest for religious truth. "[T]ruth must be sought," he wrote, "for it is confessedly not instinctive: and religious truth (being the same nature as truth in general), must be inquired after, as the truths which belong to any other art or science are sought."[3] That is to say, they must be sought through an exercise of the intellect: "a wise application of the mind to religion."[4] "Whatever views I entertain," he wrote, "are the result of the deepest and most dispassionate thought of which I am capable;" and he provides a charming vignette of himself, wandering around the streets of Dublin, lost in cogitation.[5]

---

1   On the term "tradition," see below, pp. 132–33.

2   See above, p. 94.

3   *Remains*, Vol. 1, p. 243.

4   Ibid., p. 240.

5   Ibid., p. 392; *Correspondence*, Vol. 1, p. 104.

As noted above, however, he never engaged in speculation for speculation's sake; his concern was always practical.

Knox's quest for religious truth was carried out on two levels. At times he was concerned with the more restricted question of what constituted "the true doctrine of the Church of England."[6] What, for example, was the true doctrine of the Church of England concerning baptism? What was the true doctrine of the Church of England concerning the Eucharist?[7] To answer these questions, Knox examined the Anglican formularies, especially the Prayer Book, seeking to discover from them the official position of the Church. But he also went beyond the formularies to examine the authorities to which they appealed, namely Scripture and the teaching of the Fathers. And these, too, were his sources for the other level on which he worked, asking general questions of universal significance, such as: What is the nature of Christ's salvific work? How are we justified? What is the nature of providence? Knox thus employed what is so often seen as the "classical Anglican" approach to theology, the combination of Scripture, tradition and reason, or, as he put it: "the sacred word and the writings of holy men, and his own meditations on them."[8] As this quotation shows, reason for Knox was not an authority, but an instrument, one which he used to explore the teaching of Scripture and the patristic witness, and this nuance must modify any understanding of him as a model of the "classical" approach. Moreover, as well as appealing to Scripture and tradition, Knox insisted on the importance of experience as an element in theological thinking.

2   The Bible in Knox's Thought

Charles Dickinson summed up Knox's life and work by saying that he "studied the Sacred Scriptures, with a depth and minuteness of observation," which recalls almost verbatim Knox's own description of his theological endeavors.[9] References to the Bible abound throughout his writings, and even when he does not cite Scripture expressly, its redolence marks his language. He also composed an extended bibliological treatise, the undated essay "Reflections

---

6   *Remains*, Vol. 1, p. 485.
7   Ibid., Vol. 2, p. 183.
8   Ibid., Vol. 3, p. 187.
9   *Christian Examiner*, 11.73 (July 1831), p. 563. Knox speaks of "studying the New Testament with the closest application of which my mind was capable" (*Remains*, Vol. 2, p. 57). See also *Correspondence*, Vol. 1, pp. 101–2.

on 2 Timothy, III. 15."[10] Knox took for granted that "the divine word" was God's "immediate work."[11] He spoke of Scripture as being "the written word proceeding from inspiration;" the "written dictates of Omniscience;" "the sacred word"; "the written oracles of God;" "the word of inspiration." "The Apostle ... wrote," he observed of Paul's epistles, "and the Spirit ... dictated."[12] It is thus impossible to agree with Storr when he suggests that Knox held a low view of inspiration.[13] To defend his claim, Storr cites only a single passage (*Correspondence* Vol. 1, p. 41): "It is my conjecture, that the idea usually entertained, of the holy Scripture being Θεόπνευστος [*Theopneustos*, "inspired by God," 2 Timothy 3.16] ... has kept very many back, from exercising their judgments on its structure and composition." The remark, however, occurs just after a discussion of Robert Lowth's *De Sacra Poesi* (1753), one of the leading ideas of which is that, although Scripture is inspired, it should nonetheless be the subject of critical analysis, and it is no more than this that Knox is saying.[14]

Regarding Scripture as the intimations of "the unerring Spirit," Knox conceived it to be the "polar star of truth and safety," the "one supreme standard" by which all religious teaching was to be judged.[15] He held that it contained "radically and essentially"[16] all the truths of the Christian faith and that, therefore, "nothing is, or can be fundamental, which is not to be proved from the Sacred Word."[17] Accordingly, he maintained that he valued his own thoughts only insomuch as they were "subordinate to, harmonising with, and illustrative of [Scripture]." This stance led him to claim that his doctrine was, quite simply, "the New Testament view of christianity [*sic*]," drawn from the plain teaching of the original text, read without the distorting lens of preconceived party prejudice.[18] The words that he used to describe his soteriological teaching can therefore justly be applied to his theology as a whole: "I have endeavoured to

---

10   *Remains*, Vol. 3, pp. 368–408. 2 Timothy 3.15 reads "... and from infancy you have known the Holy Scriptures, which are able to make you wise for salvation through faith in Christ Jesus."

11   *Remains*, Vol. 1, p. 248.

12   Ibid., Vol. 2, pp. 410, 57, 141, 315, 420, 417. See also Vol. 2, p. 309; *Correspondence*, Vol. 1, p. 82.

13   Storr, *Development of English Theology*, p. 90. A similar suggestion is made by Reardon who cites the same "proof-text" as Storr (*From Coleridge to Gore*, p. 41).

14   For Robert Lowth (1710–87), who, thanks to Knox, was to have a profound influence on Jebb, see Smend, *From Astruc to Zimmerli*, pp. 15–29.

15   *Remains*, Vol. 2, p. 421; Vol. 4, p. 147; Vol. 1, p. 246.

16   Ibid., Vol. 1, p. 244.

17   Ibid., Vol. 3, p. 43. On "fundamentals," see above, p. 112.

18   *Remains*, Vol. 4, p. 147; *Correspondence*, Vol. 1, p. 17. See also *Remains*, Vol. 3, p. 3; Vol. 4, pp. 209, 210, 379, 454, 460, 505, 593; *Correspondence*, Vol. 1, p. 16; Vol. 2, pp. 262, 532.

admit of no human theory whatever, but to derive all my conclusions from the representations of Holy Scripture."[19]

By holy Scripture, Knox meant both the Old and New Testaments.[20] Together, he wrote, they made up "one grand connected manifestation of God to man." "[T]he Old Testament is introductive of the New, and the New, perfective of the Old ... The New Testament, therefore, always supposes the Old."[21] Despite this, it was to the New Testament above all, and especially the Gospels, that Knox looked in his theological studies.[22] If all of Scripture is "God's gracious revelation of himself,"[23] this revelation finds its plenitude in Jesus Christ and therefore in the Gospels which record his life and teaching. "[T]he mirror in which we see [Jesus Christ] as he was, and as he is," they furnish the reader with "the immediate lessons of incarnate Godhead."[24] Therefore, he exhorted, "Let us ... be ever mindful of what was written for our learning by the Apostles of our Lord and Saviour; but still, let it be our highest and holiest care to sit, as it were, with Mary, at the feet of Him who spake as never man spake ... Let us ... endeavour to learn from our Redeemer's own words."[25]

It is clear that Knox believed the Bible to be divine revelation. Richard Niebuhr has argued that at the end of the eighteenth century, due to difficulties inherent in the concept, revelation was a word "used sparingly" in theological

---

19   *Remains*, Vol. 4, p. 505.

20   Hornby has provided an analysis of the scriptural quotations in the *Remains* which shows that Knox quoted the New Testament roughly four times more than he did the Hebrew Scriptures, his favorite source being the Gospels with John predominating. Knox alluded to, or quoted from, all the books of the New Testament, except 2 Thessalonians, Philemon and 2 and 3 John (*Remains*, Vol. 2, pp. 523–5). Forster tabulated the Biblical quotations in the *Correspondence*. Here again the New Testament predominated. All the books were cited or mentioned, except Mark, Acts, 2 Thessalonians, Titus, Philemon, James, 2 Peter, 2 and 3 John and Revelation. Luke was the most quoted Gospel; John the least. The majority of texts came from Romans and 1 Corinthians, with Romans 7.14–25 being the most cited passage, seven times in all. (*Correspondence*, Vol. 2, pp. 608–9.) One may note that in both the *Remains* and the *Correspondence*, the deuterocanonical books of the Old Testament appear only four times: *Remains*, Vol. 2, p. 292; Vol. 3, p. 372; Vol. 4, p. 323; *Correspondence*, Vol. 1, p. 230.

21   *Remains*, Vol. 3, pp. 395–6. Part of the quotation recalls the celebrated dictum: *In vetere novum latet; in novo vetus patet*; "in the Old Testament, the New lies latent; in the New, the Old becomes clear." The origin of the phrase is Augustine, *Quaestiones in Heptateuchem.* 2, q. 73, *P. L.*, Vol. 34, col. 623. For other references to the unity of the two Testaments in Knox's writings see *Remains*, Vol. 3, pp. 383, 401; *Correspondence*, Vol. 1, p. 71.

22   *Remains*, Vol. 2, p. 292.

23   Ibid., Vol. 2, pp. 422, 292. See also Vol. 2, p. 292; Vol. 3, p. 377; Vol. 4, p. 593.

24   Ibid., Vol. 2, pp. 351–2, 374–5.

25   Ibid., Vol. 2, p. 375. See also Vol. 3, p. 385.

discourse.[26] This was not the case with Knox who used the term frequently.[27] More importantly, however, Knox made the idea of revelation a lynchpin of his soteriology. According to him, God self-manifests in Jesus Christ in order to attract and drawn back human beings from the lure of sin.

> [T]he records of the Gospel respecting our Saviour's life, miracles, discourses, death, resurrection, and ascension; what he did, taught, and suffered; and what his inspired followers have written concerning him, and the ends of his coming into the world in that divine volume, the New Testament, has in it a certain ineffable energy of the divine wisdom and goodness, by which the heart of every serious and humble reader will be attracted, engaged and quickened.[28]

As this quotation indicates, although for Knox the portrayal of Jesus in the Gospels was primary, he saw the whole Bible as being "God's own most divine contrivance, for effectually manifesting himself to all, in all ages, who will hear his voice; and for leading them by the sweetest and most suitable attractions to their own true happiness, here and hereafter." Therefore, if the Bible were understood properly and properly presented, the conversion of humanity would automatically follow.[29] But how was the Bible to be understood properly? "Mere reading" was not sufficient. "[T]here must be labour," he wrote, "there must be study." One must "examine [the text] with ... attention," fulfilling the dominical command to *explore* the Scriptures.[30] He believed that the Bible was a mine with countless riches yet to be discovered – a point-of-view widespread in the Enlightenment period. As Owen Chadwick notes:

> Many of the divines of the eighteenth century ... looked to find ... a fuller understanding of the once-given revelation ... Better texts, better linguistic apparatus, better knowledge of antiquity – the possibility of a more accurate understanding of the text or context of the New Testament could not be denied. It was an easy passage from the idea of improvement in scholarship to the idea of an improved understanding of the revelation.[31]

---

26   Niebuhr, *Meaning of Revelation*, p. 2. In making his claim, Niebuhr refers explicitly to Wesley, Whitefield, Edwards and their associates.

27   See, for example: *Remains*, Vol. 1, pp. 11, 264, 275; Vol. 2, pp. 115, 250, 327; Vol. 4, p. 548.

28   Ibid., Vol. 3, p. 390.

29   Ibid., Vol. 3, pp. 397–8. On the theme of the attraction worked by Scripture, see also *Remains*, Vol. 1, pp. 244, 275; Vol. 3, p. 388; *Correspondence*, Vol. 1, pp. 60, 81–2.

30   *Correspondence*, Vol. 1, pp. 39, 38; *Remains*, Vol. 2, p. 253; Vol. 1, p. 448.

31   Chadwick, *From Bossuet to Newman*, pp. 77, 79. See, also, above, p. 94.

Knox stated that he was particularly indebted for his idea of a progressive understanding of Scripture to Robert Boyle.[32] Although Boyle is today remembered chiefly as a scientist, "the Father of Chemistry," he was also a theologian, one whose thinking placed him in the ranks of the moderates. It was as such that Knox held him to be "among the brightest examples of Christianity, that ever the church afforded," and recommended his writings to Jebb as "part of your first studies."[33]

We may discern once again, in Knox's veneration for the Bible, the influence of Wesley, *homo unius libri*, and of the milieu of Methodist piety in which Knox was raised.[34] We may discern, too, a reflection of the Fathers' bibliocentrism. For, as Congar remarks, "Scripture is everything for the Fathers. Their writings, dogmatic, spiritual and pastoral, considered as a whole, are nothing but an extended commentary on Scripture."[35] In this connection one may mention especially John Chrysostom, whose insistence on the attentive investigation of Scripture equaled Boyle's. "It is necessary for us," Chrysostom contended, "to explore the Scripture in depth. If we are idle and indolent we will not be able to perceive its meaning. It is necessary, by continual scrutiny and assiduous prayer, to penetrate ... the sacred word."[36] Above all, however, Knox saw the centrality of the Bible as a principal tenet of the Church of England, and although he does not quote it, his teaching on the Bible's authority accords exactly with the position of the Thirty-Nine Articles, which maintain that "Holy Scripture containeth all things necessary to salvation: so that whatsoever is not read therein, nor may be proved thereby, is not to be required of any man, that it should be believed as an article of the Faith, or be thought requisite [or] necessary to salvation." And by the Scripture, the Article continues, is to be understood both the Old and New Testaments. For "[t]he Old Testament is not contrary to the New: for both in the Old and New Testament everlasting life is offered to Mankind by Christ."[37]

---

32   *Remains*, Vol. 1, p. 448. Knox cites Boyle (1627–91) several times in his writings; see *Remains*, Vol. 4, pp. 142–4, 590; *Correspondence*, Vol. 1, p. 27; "Preface to the First Dublin Edition," p. xlv. (Knox included Boyle's funeral sermon in his editions of Burnet's *Lives*.) For Boyle's theology see Hunt, *Place of Religion in the Science of Robert Boyle*, and Reijer Hooykaas, *Robert Boyle*. Knox appears particularly indebted to Boyle's treatise *Some Considerations touching the Style of the Holy Scriptures* (1661).

33   *Correspondence*, Vol. 1, p. 27.

34   "A man of one book," Wesley, "Preface" to *Sermons on Several Occasions*, 5, in Outler, ed., *Works of John Wesley*, Vol. 1, pp. 103–7, at p. 105. For Wesley's biblicism, see also ibid., pp. 57–9.

35   Congar, *Tradition and Traditions*, p. 35.

36   Chrysostom, "Homily 21 on John," 1, *P. G.*, Vol. 59, col. 127. For Chrysostom as a biblical theologian see, e.g., Tofana, "John Chrysostom's View on Scripture."

37   *Remains*, Vol. 3, p. 43; Articles 6 and 7, *B. C. P.*, pp. 397–8.

3   Universal Consent

Knox believed the Bible to be the "one supreme standard" of religious truth.[38] The Bible read on its own, however, "naked Scripture," as he called it, led to the risk of "incalculable misapprehension and error." "I ... become more and more assured," he wrote, "that the Bible is not sufficient, and was never meant to be sufficient, for the interpretation of itself." Therefore, he argued: "though all religious truth is, radically and essentially, contained in Holy Scripture, yet in order to attain a competent knowledge and distinct apprehension of that truth, other aids appear to be indispensable."[39] Among these aids Knox enumerated philology, history, and philosophy, all of which he employed.[40] For him, however, the most important aid was the study of God's activity in the lives of believers. As he put it in a letter to Wilberforce, one must "recur to God's work, for the elucidation of his word."[41] Knox held that this was the "master-key" which would unlock the meaning of the Bible.[42] As he told Daniel Parken, "To study God's continued operation in his Church [is] the truest commentary on what he has declared in his Word."[43] Unfortunately, Knox's description of this "master-key" was, to use his own phrase, "very obscure." "I fear," he confessed, "it may not be easy to convey a clear idea of the duty I wish to urge."[44] He began lucidly enough, speaking, in language indicative of his post-Enlightenment background, about the whole history of the church as a "divine laboratory" in which God's "experiments" were displayed.[45] These experiments, the theologian could not ignore.

> Would any man of good sense account himself a chemist, merely because he had studied, and could quote the best books of chemistry? No; he would hold himself but a novice, till he had either made, or attended a course of experiments, in which he saw the laws of chemistry practically

---

38   *Remains*, Vol. 1, p. 246.

39   Ibid., Vol. 3, p. 290; *Correspondence*, Vol. 2, p. 502; *Remains*, Vol. 1, p. 244. The phrase "naked Scripture" may well have inspired Jebb's neologism, "gymno-biblism" (*Correspondence*, Vol. 2, p. 545). The phrase is not, however, original to Knox, being found earlier in Hooker (*Laws of Ecclesiastical Polity*, Book 2, Chapter 7, paragraph 1).

40   *Remains*, Vol. 1, pp. 244–5.

41   Knox to William Wilberforce, letter, August 31, 1818, in Wilberforce, *Correspondence*, Vol. 2, pp. 397–410, pp. 408–9 (emphasis in the original).

42   *Remains*, Vol. 3, p. 284.

43   Ibid., Vol. 1, pp. 432–33.

44   Ibid., Vol. 3, p. 286; Vol. 1, p. 248.

45   The metaphor of the church as a laboratory is employed a number of times by Knox: *Remains*, Vol. 1, pp. 247, 409; Vol. 3, 63, 283; Vol. 4, p. 251; *Correspondence*, Vol. 2, p. 36; *Wesley*, p. 492.

exemplified ... Is this less true respecting that divine chemistry, by which
God's Holy Spirit purifies and sublimates our minds and hearts?[46]

Knox explained that these "experiments" were to be discovered in the lives
and teaching of "those who were at once the wisest and holiest men," a "cloud
of witnesses," whom, varying his scientific metaphor, he called a "multitude of
specimens."[47]

But what were these specimens designed to show? It is here that Knox becomes unclear. In some passages, he seems to suggest that the way in which
one sees scripture being applied and lived out in the history of the church will
yield an explanation of what the Bible means.[48] More often, however, Knox
suggests that from a study of the wise and holy, one can "learn, from their concurrent sentiments, what it is of vital consequence for us to prefer, retain, and
pursue." As he wrote to Hannah More: "[I]f only they are fairly questioned,
their collective answer will tell us what the truths are which we should, above
all other supposed truths, lay up in our hearts."[49] This "collective answer" constituted what Knox termed the *consensus omnium*, universal consent, so-called
because the "wise and holy", from whom it was drawn, were not limited to one
particular age or place but "were brought together from the ancient church
as well as from the modern, from the Greek church as well as from the Latin,
from the unreformed as well as the reformed church."[50] Once discovered, their
consensus provided, a rule by which the Bible could be interpreted to show
"what points of belief are to be relied upon as essential, or, at least, highly con-
ducive to Christian excellence; and what may be justly considered unessential,
or, perhaps, cumbrous."[51] Knox, concerned as always with Christian practice,
was interested in the question of which truths were most helpful to a life of
holiness. He was seeking not simply to learn what the "wise and holy" thought,
but "what were the ideas in the mind, which kept up the steadiest and deepest
warmth in the heart, and the most absolute purity and charity in conduct."[52]

46   *Remains*, Vol. 1, pp. 246–47 (format slightly altered).
47   Ibid., Vol. 1, pp. 249, 434, 435.
48   See, for example: *Remains*, Vol. 1, pp. 246–48, 432–33; Knox to William Wilberforce, letter,
     August 31, 1818, in Wilberforce, *Correspondence*, Vol. 2, pp. 397–410.
49   *Remains*, Vol. 1, p. 249; Vol. 4, p. 236.
50   Ibid, Vol. 4, p. 236. See, also, Vol. 1, p. 249. For the phrase *consensus omnium*, and what it
     means for Knox, see, for example: *Remains*, Vol. 1, p. 390; Vol. 3, pp. 65–67, 284, 297, 322.
51   Ibid., Vol. 1, pp. 435–6.
52   Ibid., Vol. 1, p. 435.

4   The *Consensus Patrum*

If Knox spoke of the *consensus omnium*, he habitually narrowed his focus to the *consensus patrum*, the agreement of the Fathers, moving his appeal from universality to antiquity. He wrote frequently of interpreting "the sacred scriptures, as interpreted by the ancient Church,"[53] and to this end he read the Fathers with diligence, aiming to acquire their spirit,[54] declaring, "I am neither Roman Catholic nor Protestant, but a Christian of the six first centuries."[55] Reardon appears to be mistaken when he says that Knox "preferred, for all his deep regard for the traditions of the Church Catholic, to think for himself." On the contrary, Knox believed himself bound to follow the *consensus* of antiquity, presenting his system as one of "revived catholicity."[56]

---

53   *Answer to Duigenan*, p. 10. See also *Remains*, Vol. 4, p. 376.
54   Knox speaks of "[Imbibing the Fathers'] views, sentiments, and divine enthusiasm; and, then, [pouring] it forth, in [his] own words" (*Correspondence*, Vol. 1, p. 298). Citations from or allusions to the Fathers and other early authors abound in Knox's writings. Examples simply from the *Remains* and *Correspondence* include: Ambrose, *Remains*, Vol. 1, pp. 282–3, 350; Vol. 2, p. 355; *Correspondence*, Vol. 2, p. 213; Athanasius, *Remains*, Vol. 3, pp. 66, 281, 292; Augustine, *Remains*, Vol. 1, pp. 102, 283, 331–2, 350, 390, 392–4, 410–12, 486, 526, note; Vol. 2, pp. 132, 322, 355; Vol. 3, pp. 49, 77–9, 127, 133, 142–5, 191–8, 281; Vol. 4, pp. 281, 368, 551–2, 585; *Correspondence*, Vol. 1, pp. 130–8, 419, 543; Vol. 2, p. 213; Basil the Great, *Remains*, Vol. 1, pp. 286–8, 402; Vol. 3, pp. 211, 282; *Correspondence*, Vol. 1, pp. 511, 543, 552; Bede, *Remains*, Vol. 2, pp. 82, 152–3; Bernard, *Remains*, Vol. 1, p. 331; Vol. 3, pp. 127, 144, 288; *Correspondence*, Vol. 1, pp. 127–8, 135, 357; Vol. 2, p. 27; Boethius, *Correspondence*, Vol. 1, p. 98; Clement of Alexandria, *Remains*, Vol. 1, pp. 350–3; Vol. 3, pp. 141–2; *Correspondence*, Vol. 1, p. 419; Clement of Rome, *Remains*, Vol. 1, pp. 284–5; Cyprian, *Remains*, Vol. 3, pp. 126, 288; *Correspondence*, Vol. 1, pp. 547–9; Cyril of Jerusalem, *Remains*, Vol. 1, p. 486; Vol. 2, p. 156; Vol. 4, p. 464; *Correspondence*, Vol. 1, p. 596; Ephrem, *Correspondence*, Vol. 1, pp. 302, 471; Gregory the Great, *Remains*, Vol. 1, pp. 65, 356–7; Vol. 2, p. 357; Vol. 3, pp. 287–8; Vol. 4, p. 551; Gregory of Nazianzus, *Remains*, Vol. 3, pp. 211, 282; Ignatius of Antioch, *Remains*, Vol. 1, p. 348; *Correspondence*, Vol. 1, p. 493; Irenaeus, *Remains*, Vol. 1, p. 288; Vol. 2, pp. 177–8; Jerome, *Correspondence*, Vol. 1, p. 134; John Chrysostom, *Remains*, Vol. 1, pp. 102, 347, 402; Vol. 2, p. 136; Vol. 3, pp. 45–6, 75–80, 109, 127, 129, 132–3, 143–4, 211, 279–82, 287; Vol. 4, pp. 333, 412, 438–9; *Correspondence*, Vol. 1, pp. 76–7, 135, 137–8, 302, 491, 493–4, 545, 596; John Climacus, *Remains*, Vol. 1, p. 351; John Damascene, *Remains*, Vol. 2, p. 156; Justin Martyr, *Remains*, Vol. 2, pp. 176–7, 355; Origen, *Remains*, Vol. 2, p. 486; Vol. 3, p. 145; *Correspondence*, Vol. 2, p. 528; Pseudo-Macarius, *Remains*, Vol. 1, pp. 350, 353; Vol. 3, pp. 109, 211, 281–2; Vol. 4, p. 333; *Correspondence*, Vol. 1, p. 543; Vol. 2, p. 12; Tertullian, *Remains*, Vol. 3, p. 126; Vol. 4, pp. 169–70, 462–3; Vincent of Lérins, *Remains*, Vol. 3, pp. 292, 322–3; Vol. 4, p. 463; *Correspondence*, Vol. 2, pp. 125, 564–5.
55   *Remains*, Vol. 4, p. 402.
56   Reardon, *From Coleridge to Gore*, p. 38; *Correspondence*, Vol. 2, p. 101. It may be pointed out that Knox's expressly stated that every man has the right to think for himself. Nonetheless, he appears to have believed that a free-thinking person would automatically accept the judgment of antiquity. See above, p. 118.

That Knox should have given pride of place to the Fathers is, on two counts, not at all surprising. First, as an Anglican he believed that antiquity held an especially authoritative place in the Church. As he noted, when he spoke of himself as neither Roman Catholic nor Protestant, "It is as true of the Church of England as of me, her humble and attached member."[57] Second, he felt a spiritual affinity with the Fathers, believing that "they thought of nothing, comparatively, but the religion of the heart." Thus, "when they treat of piety ... they rise above all, except the sacred writers."[58] This helps explain why Knox found no contradiction in moving from the *consensus omnium* to the *consensus patrum*. With their concern for "practical religion," the Fathers stood, in his estimation, pre-eminent among the "wisest and holiest men;" it was the study of their teaching above all that would, he believed, yield the knowledge of which doctrines were essential to Christianity.[59] Nor did he see any contradiction between his appeal to the Fathers and his stated desire to read the Bible free from party prejudice. Knox did not perceive of his position as partisan, in the sense of being High Church as opposed to Evangelical. For him to be "Catholic" was to "be above all such things as, 'I am of Paul, and I of Apollos.'" The "wholeness" and "universality" which the word implied, were, in his mind, the very antithesis of individualism or particularity.[60]

Knox's rejection of particularity extended to the Fathers. He felt entitled to disagree with individual authors, if he thought that they had deviated from the Catholic norm, the *consensus* of their peers, a case in point being his critical treatment of Augustine.[61] This does not mean that in appealing to the patristic *phronema*, Knox neglected the individual Fathers. On the contrary, he found in them much to aid his life of piety and to nourish his theological reflection, his predilection being for those of the Greek Church, which he lauded as the "noblest portion of ancient Christianity."[62] The chief reason for this was that the Greek Fathers were the source of the Platonic doctrine which he shared with Wesley and the moderates. But other factors may also have bolstered his preference. One was the already-noted Hellenism of the Romantic era; another was the renewed contact between the Church of England and Orthodoxy brought about by the alliance of Britain with Russia in the Napoleonic Wars.[63] Third, not only did the Greek Fathers offer an arsenal of arguments against the

57 *Remains*, Vol. 4, p. 403. See, also, above, pp. 39–42.
58 *Remains*, Vol. 1, pp. 250, 257. See also Vol. 2, pp. 355–6.
59 Ibid., Vol. 3, pp. 282–3.
60 Ibid., Vol. 4, p. 138, (references are to 1 Corinthians 3.4); *Remains*, Vol. 3, pp. 49, 172.
61 *Remains*, Vol. 1, pp. 346, 390–1; Vol. 4, p. 368; *Correspondence*, Vol. 1, pp. 132, 460.
62 *Remains*, Vol. 3, p. 210. On Knox's preference for the Greek Fathers, see Rowell, "Theological Forerunners," pp. 43–4.
63 *Remains*, Vol. 3, pp. 209–12.

tenets of Evangelicalism, but they also balanced the Latin patristic tradition, to which Roman Catholicism appealled to bolster its distinctive claims.

How did Knox know the Fathers? Some of his patristic knowledge was second-hand, derived from summaries and quotations in more modern writers. Patristic quotations would have occurred in many, if not all, of the authors that Knox read, but there were a number whose specific focus was on the Fathers. These writers form an eclectic mix, both nationally and denominationally: French, German, Italian and English authors are all cited; Huguenots, Lutherans, Roman Catholics and Anglicans. The work which Knox most frequently referenced, although he often did so critically, was Joseph Milner's *History of the Church of Christ* (1794–97).[64] Other sources which he mentioned include: Cesare Baronius's *Annales* (1588–1607); Richard Baxter's *Church History* (1681); Roberto Bellarmine's *De Scriptoribus Ecclesiasticis* (1613); Louis Ellies Dupin's *Nouvelle Biliothèque des Auteurs Ecclésiastiques* (1686–1715); Claude Fleury's *Moeurs des Chrétiens* (1682) and *Histoire Ecclésiastique* (1690–1720); Johann Lorenz von Mosheim's *Institutionum Historiae Ecclesiasticae Libri Quatuor* (1755), as well as its English translation by Archibald Maclaine (1765); and the "Short View of Church History," as Knox calls it, Charles de Villers's essay on the Reformation, probably in its English translation by James Mill (1805). Knox also cited the work of the Presbyterian Nathaniel Lardner, probably referring to his *Credibility of the Gospel History* (1727–55).[65] Jebb too listed several works which, in all likelihood, were used by Knox as well: Johann Franz Buddeus, *Isagoge Historico-Theologica* (1727); Johann Albert Fabricius, *Bibliotheca Graeca* (1705–28); Pierre Poiret, *Bibliotheca Mysticorum Selecta* (1708): and the *Ecclesiastica Historia* of the Magdeburg Centuriators (1559–74).[66] Besides such general works, Knox also mentioned three particular studies: Matthieu de l'Arroque's *Histoire de l'Eucharistie* (1669); Jean Nicolas Grou's *Morale Tirée des Confessions de Saint Augustin* (1786); and John Kaye's *Ecclesiastical History of the Second and Third Centuries, illustrated from the writings of Tertullian* (1826).[67] Knox also read the Fathers in translation. He mentions the 1539 Latin version of Chrysostom by Wolfgang Musculus,

---

64   Ibid., Vol. 1, pp. 91–3, 282–91, 296–7, 300, 306, 397, 433, 436; Vol. 2, pp. 59–60, 354–8; Vol. 3, pp. 46–50, 120–2, 126–7, 288; Vol. 4, pp. 252, 376. For Milner, see below, p. 223.
65   For the works cited see: *Correspondence*, Vol. 1, p. 596; *Remains*, Vol. 1, pp. 426, 433; Vol. 2, p. 162; Vol. 3, pp. 193, 287; *Correspondence*, Vol. 2, pp. 284–5; *Remains*, Vol. 3, pp. 323–4; Vol. 4, p. 486; *Remains*, Vol. 1, p. 384; Vol. 3, pp. 290–1; *Correspondence*, Vol. 1, pp. 575–6; Vol. 2, p. 288; *Remains*, Vol. 3, pp. 142–3; Vol. 1, p. 486; *Correspondence*, Vol. 1, p. 603.
66   *Correspondence*, Vol. 1, p. 294.
67   Grou is mentioned once, *Correspondence*, Vol. 1, p. 372, as is Kaye, *Remains*, Vol. 4, pp. 462–3. L'Arroque, by contrast, is cited frequently since Knox relied on him heavily for his understanding of the Eucharist; see below, pp. 208–9.

as well as a French translation, probably that of the Jansenists of Port-Royal, published between 1664 and 1690.[68] Port-Royal was also the provenance of *Les Oeuvres de Saint Clément d'Alexandrie*, which appeared in 1696, translated by Nicolas Fontaine, and although Knox does not mention it, he may have known this, too.[69] Certainly, he seems to have read more than merely Chrysostom in French, for we find him remarking that, to those who know neither Latin nor Greek, French is an excellent substitute because the Fathers (in the plural) are "found translated into French; when they are not to be met, and, indeed, do not exist, in English."[70] As far as English translations are concerned, extracts from Pseudo-Macarius were included by Wesley in the first volume of his *Christian Library* (1749), together with the letters of Clement of Rome, Ignatius and Polycarp, as well the *passiones* of the latter two. Wesley's extracts probably provided Knox's initial introduction to Pseudo-Macarius, though he later discovered Thomas Haywood's much fuller translation, published in 1721 under the title *Primitive Morality*, and he may have subsequently purchased a copy of this for himself.[71] Knox also read the Fathers in the original Greek and Latin. For this he used what he called "the Benedictines," the Maurist editions produced between 1679 and 1778.[72] Knox references also John Fell's edition of Cyprian (1682) and the Antwerp edition of Bernard (1616), while Hornby suggests that Knox used the 1638 Paris edition of St Basil.[73] Jebb mentions Henry Savile's eight-volume edition of Chrysostom and it is possible that Knox used this text as well. Possible too is his use of another work cited by Jebb, John Potter's 1715 edition of Clement.[74]

Despite his appeal to the Fathers, "tradition" was not a word which Knox generally employed. It is not entirely absent from his vocabulary, but virtually all the occurrences are found in just three documents which were all composed within a few years of each other: a letter written in 1814 to John Harford;

---

68   *Correspondence*, Vol. 1, pp. 493–4; *Remains*, Vol. 3, pp. 75–7; Vol. 4, p. 439.

69   For the translation-work of Port-Royal see the two articles by Pascale Thouvenin: "La Traduction de Saint Jean Chrysostome à Port-Royal," and "Nicolas Fontaine."

70   *Remains*, Vol. 1, p. 262.

71   N. L. I., Ms 8868, Brodrick Papers, (folder 7), Knox to Charles Brodrick, letter, undated; *Correspondence*, Vol. 1, p. 294.

72   *Remains*, Vol. 1, pp. 288, 347, 356, 486; *Correspondence*, Vol. 2, pp. 181, 213, 297. See also above, p. 22. For the Maurists, see Laurain, "Travaux d'Erudition."

73   *Correspondence*, Vol. 1, pp. 547, 127; *Remains*, Vol. 1, p. 287, second note.

74   *Correspondence*, Vol. 2, p. 131; Vol. 1, p. 286.

the *Appendix* of 1815; and a letter to Wilberforce, dated August 31, 1818. Apart from these instances, the word occurs once in the *Correspondence*, and twice in the *Remains*.[75] The reason for this scarcity has no doubt to do with the negative connotations which "tradition" had for reformed Christians. Knox shared this attitude, regarding "the … doctrine of tradition taught by the Church of Rome" as "extravagant." Rome made tradition, in his view, "an authority co-ordinate with Scripture;" and, even worse, it had introduced "corrupt tradition," contrary to Scripture, he alleged.[76] Nonetheless, the word remains a convenient way to describe Knox's appeal both to the *consensus patrum* and the *consensus omnium*.

Knox's attitude to tradition is a reminder that for him Scripture was always the "primary standard." In fact, where Scripture was unambiguous, it was "the exclusive standard." Only when the meaning of the Bible was unclear did tradition come into play. Then it formed "an invaluable auxiliary to the sacred word; both for the elucidation of what might otherwise remain ambiguous, and for the specification of whatever has been only generally intimated." As well as "elucidating fundamentals," tradition also served to help to determine "secondary questions, relating not to the essence of Christianity, but to the well-being and right-ordering of a church." However, in these "not essential but subsidiary" matters, tradition was not to be followed automatically. "[S]ubordinate matters [are] not only alterable, but from chance of times and circumstances, often [require] alteration."[77]

In Knox's emphasis on tradition we see again traces of his post-Enlightenment situation, with its interest in the past; we see, too, similarities with Wesley and the moderates whose appeal to the Fathers has already been noted. But once more we see him above all as an Anglican. In setting out his views on tradition, he maintains that his position is that of the Church to which he belongs. In approaching the topic, the question which guides him is: "[W]hat says the Church of England?"[78]

---

75   *Remains*, Vol. 3, pp. 277–313; Wilberforce, *Correspondence*, Vol. 2, pp. 397–410, 405–7; *Appendix*, pp. 369, 371, 372, 376, 379, 391, 396–7; *Correspondence*, Vol. 2, p. 361; *Remains*, Vol. 2, p. 169; Vol. 3, p. 67.

76   *Remains*, Vol. 4, p. 463; Vol. 3, p. 291; Vol. 4, p. 427.

77   Ibid., Vol. 2, p. 298; Vol. 3, pp. 320, 291–2, 43; Knox to William Wilberforce, letter, August 31, 1818, in Wilberforce, *Correspondence*, Vol. 2, p. 407.

78   *Remains*, Vol. 3, p. 291; see, also, p. 42.

5   Experience

To what is so often seen as the classical Anglican triad of Scripture, tradition, and reason, Knox added a fourth element, experience. Experience for Knox was something to be reflected about and thought upon, just like the Bible and the teaching of antiquity. More importantly – and this is the primary meaning that experience has in his writings – it denotes the existential apprehension of doctrine, rather than a merely theoretical understanding, "a heart-knowledge of Christianity;" "knowledge by trial."[79] Stress on what he calls the "spiritual and experimental knowledge of the Holy Scriptures," runs throughout his work. "[S]tudying the Scripture will not do," he declares, "except our hearts and affections are engaged by the truths it contains." Not only has the mind to be enlightened, but, also, he urges, "the heart must be made to feel what the understanding comprehends." Only then can "the facts of religion, as record-ed in Scripture" be "apprehended as facts;" only then, "through the teaching of the heart," can one have "the surest knowledge" of the Bible's meaning. An example that he gives is Paul's declaration in 1 Corinthians 1.30, that Christ has become our "wisdom and righteousness, and sanctification, and redemp-tion." We can know this theoretically, but this theoretical knowledge can be truly verified only when, "through [Christ's] communicated grace, we become truly wise, truly righteous, and truly holy."[80] Experience, then, served for Knox to make real the teaching of the Bible; and to the Bible it was always subor-dinate. Scripture was the standard "by which every movement of spiritual life ... is ultimately to be tried." Likewise, experience had to be subordinated to the *consensus omnium*. We must, he declared, "correct, enlarge, illustrate and confirm our own individual experience by the continued experience of many successive centuries." We must "try our lights by their concurrent lights; our feelings by their concordant feelings."[81]

   Because of the importance that Knox attached to justification, he related experience especially to the "consciousness of the Redeemer's effectual grace

---

79   *Correspondence*, Vol. 1, p. 105; *Remains*, Vol. 1, p. 141, note 1. See also *Remains*, Vol. 4, p. 544. Knox also uses the word experience to connote the feeling of religious emotion, or af-fection, as he terms it (see, for example, *Remains*, Vol. 2, p. 50), but this is by far the less common meaning of the term in his writings.

80   *Remains*, Vol. 4, p. 556; Vol. 3, pp. 388, 391; Vol. 1, p. 30; Vol. 4, pp. 458–9. The last quo-tation bears a remarkable similarity to a passage in Jeremy Taylor's 1662 sermon, "*Via Intelligentiae*," "The Way of Understanding" (Taylor, *Works*, Vol. 6, pp. 373–408, at p. 403). Knox knew this sermon well, as we will see below, and doubtless he "borrowed" the pas-sage cited.

81   *Remains*, Vol. 1, pp. 246, 441.

within," something which he highlighted as the essential and distinguishing mark of genuine Christianity. As he put it in a letter to George Schoales, it is "the very soul of our Christian religion; this real and felt influence, this transmutative and regenerative energy, is the very thing which places Christianity above all philosophy, and all mere law, even though given from Heaven; and it is this which makes it, to weak and corrupted man, what St. Paul calls it, 'the power of God unto salvation.'"[82]

What was experienced, however, was not grace itself, Knox clarified, but its "enlightening, purifying, quickening, spiritualising, and of course felicitating effects." He explained: "I do not mean that [grace] is perceivable in itself – our Saviour's illustration from the wind implies the contrary, – but I mean, that the results are so self-evidently above human nature, as to satisfy the mind respecting the agency to which they are indebted."[83] This point, that Christians experience in their lives something so extraordinary that it can only be ascribed to divine power, was repeatedly made by Knox.[84] His reason for doing so was not, as one might imagine, a desire to answer the post-Kantian problem of how God can be known; rather, his aim was purely practical. Knox argued that the experience of God's transforming grace provides "a sure evidence in the heart and conduct that we are actual objects of mercy." As we have seen, he offered this teaching as a corrective to Wesley's appeal for assurance to the interior witness of the Spirit, which Knox saw as deficient because of its subjective nature.[85] But, if Knox disagreed with Wesley on this point, he disagreed more strongly still with the Calvinist teaching that believers have full assurance of final salvation. Hence, his use of the term "*actual* mercy." Grace could be lost through sin and thus salvation forfeited.[86]

In part, Knox's emphasis on experience stemmed from his historical situation. The Enlightenment valued empiricism; Romanticism believed that axioms were not axioms until they were "proved upon our pulses."[87] As always,

---

82   Ibid., Vol. 1, p. 516; Vol. 4, p. 217. The second quotation closes with a citation from Romans 1.16, which Knox frequently invoked: *Remains*, Vol. 2, pp. 19–20, 37, 40; Vol. 3, pp. 392, 416; Vol. 4, pp. 138, 145; *Correspondence*, Vol. 1, p. 21; Vol. 2, p. 529.
83   *Remains*, Vol. 1, p. 26; Vol. 2, pp. 50–1, alluding to John 3.8.
84   *Remains*, Vol. 2, pp. 19–20, 37, 40; Vol. 3, pp. 392, 416; Vol. 4, pp. 138, 145; *Correspondence*, Vol. 1, p. 21; Vol. 2, p. 529. These are, it will be noted, the same passages in which he invokes Romans 1.16, and its teaching about "the power of God."
85   *Remains*, Vol. 2, p. 469. See, also, Vol. 4, p. 378. For Knox's disagreement with Wesley's teaching on assurance, see above, p. 66.
86   *Remains*, Vol. 2, pp. 461–2.
87   John Keats to J. H. Reynolds, letter, May 3, 1818, in Scott, *Selected Letters of John Keats*, p. 123.

however, Knox himself appealed not to contemporary thinking, but to his Anglican heritage. As he told George Schoales:

> I differ from present fashionable Divines in no point more than in this; that they think the influences of the Spirit of God wholly imperceptible ... This is not the doctrine of the Church of England. It tells us (17th Article) that godly persons 'feel in themselves the working of the Spirit of Christ, mortifying the works of the flesh and their earthly members, and drawing up their mind to high and heavenly things.'[88]

This passage, written in 1803, recalls part of a sermon preached by Charles Wesley in 1742, in which he declared: "Our own excellent Church ... speaks plainly of 'feeling the Spirit of Christ;' of being 'moved by the Holy Ghost;' of knowing and 'feeling there is no other name than that of Jesus whereby we can receive life and salvation.'"[89] It recalls also John Wesley's *Letter to the Lord Bishop of Gloucester* (1763) in which Wesley gave a litany of quotations from the Prayer Book and the *Homilies* on the subject of feeling the Holy Spirit at work in the lives of believers. Nor were the Wesley brothers the first Anglicans to highlight this somewhat neglected aspect of their Church's teaching. For the moderates too the appeal to experience was fundamental. Thus Cudworth in his sermon to the House of Commons:

> All the books and writings which we converse with, they can but represent spiritual objects to our understandings; which yet we can never see in their own true figure, colour and proportion, until we have a Divine light within to irradiate and shine upon them. Though there be never such excellent truths concerning Christ and his Gospel set down in words and letters, yet they will be but unknown characters to us, until we have a willing Spirit within us, that can decipher them; until the same Spirit, by secret whispers in our hearts, do comment upon them, which did at first indite them.[90]

---

88   *Remains*, Vol. 4, pp. 126–7.
89   Charles Wesley, Sermon 3, "Awake, Thou that Sleepest," 3, 9, in Outler, ed., *Works of John Wesley*, Vol. 1, pp. 142–58, at pp. 155–6 (punctuation slightly altered). The quotations in the passage come from Article XVII, the article cited by Knox; the service for the ordering of deacons; and the service of the visitation of the sick (see *B. C. P.*, pp. 400, 230, for the first and third quotation; Jackson, *Anglican Ordinal*, p. 47, for the second).
90   Cudworth, "Sermon I," *Works*, Vol. 4, pp. 289–350, at p. 321.

Similarly, John Smith, speaking of the "true way or method of attaining divine knowledge," taught that theology was "something rather to be understood by a spiritual sensation, than by any verbal description." The *"true method of knowing* ... is," Smith maintained, "not so much by notions as actions."[91] One of the most striking examples of this idea that "experience is the best learning" was provided by Jeremy Taylor in his sermon, *"Via Intelligentiae,"* which Knox cites several times in his writings.[92] One of Taylor's main themes in the sermon is that the teachings of Christianity can only truly be understood experimentally. Thus, in a passage which recalls Knox's words quoted above, Taylor made a contrast between the merely speculative, and the experimental, theologian. The first "goes about to speak of and to understand the mysterious Trinity, and does it by words and names of man's invention ... he only talks of essences and existences, hypostasies and personalities, distinctions without difference ... but knows not what [he is talking about]." On the other hand, the person who has a true knowledge of the Trinity is the one who "feels the 'power of the Father,' and he to whom 'the Son' is become 'wisdom, righteousness, sanctification and redemption;' he in 'whose heart the love of the Spirit of God is spread,' to whom God hath communicated the 'Holy Ghost the Comforter.'"[93] Whatever influence Wesley and the moderates may have had on Knox, the origins of his teaching on experience go back to the patristic period, where the experiential aspect of Christianity was of primary importance.[94] A perfect example is provided by Pseudo-Macarius. He is, as George Maloney writes, "the key writer in the tradition of spirituality that stresses the existential transformation of the total human person ... into the experienced indwelling of the Trinity." As Wesley commented in the introduction to his extracts from the spiritual homilies in the *Christian Library*, the knowledge which Macarius (as he called him) had of Scripture "was not merely literal or speculative but ... a true and practical knowledge," derived from his personal experience; a "description," as Wesley put it, "of his own heart and soul."[95]

---

91   Smith, Discourse 1, "A Discourse concerning the True Way or Method of Attaining Divine Knowledge," *Select Discourses*, pp. 3–25, at pp. 3–4 (emphasis in the original).

92   For the phrase "experience is the best learning," see Taylor's sermon, *"Via Intelligentiae,"* *Works*, Vol. 6, pp. 373–408, at p. 403. Knox cites the sermon in *Remains*, Vol. 1, pp. 359–60; *Wesley*, pp. 457–8; *Eclectic Review* 6 (May 1810), p. 395. For Taylor (1613–67), see Porter, *Jeremy Taylor*.

93   Taylor, *"Via Intelligentiae,"* *Works*, Vol. 6, pp. 373–408, at pp. 402–3, quoting 1 Corinthians 1.30, Romans 5.5 and the canticle *Te Deum*, sung at the Anglican service of Morning Prayer (*B. C. P.*, p. 34).

94   For a brief survey see Pontifical Council for Promoting Christian Unity, *On Becoming a Christian*, IV. C. "Patristic Perspectives on Experience in the Christian Life," paras. 147–150.

95   Maloney, *Pseudo-Macarius*, p. 2; Wesley, "Introduction" to "An Extract from the Homilies of Macarius," in *A Christian Library*, Vol. 1, pp. 81–3, at p. 81.

6   Intuition

Annexed to the issue of experience in Knox's thought is the topic of αἴσθησις [*aisthēsis*]. The term can denote in his writings an intuitive knowledge of right and wrong; "right discernment, in every practical instance," to quote his own words.[96] More often than not, however, he used it to signify a direct knowledge of God, analogous to knowledge derived from the senses, the primary meaning which it has in scriptural and patristic usage.[97]

> I own that the love of God, when genuine, includes in its very essence, an invaluable, and otherwise unattainable, knowledge of him whom we love: knowledge analogous to that which actual seeing gives of colours; actual hearing, of melody or harmony; or actual tasting, of flavours (perhaps the last is the truest analogy,) εἴπερ ἐγεύσασθε ὅτι χρηστὸς ὁ κύριος [*eiper egeusasthe hoti chrēstos ho kyrios*].[98]

One should note how in this passage Knox links the intuitive knowledge of God to love. One could, he held, "take cognisance of the Supreme Being through the medium of Love;" by it one is lifted up and united to God. "[T]he love of God ... is ... the substantial commencement of heaven on earth," or, as he put it in a letter to Parken, "an anticipation of heaven."[99] Yet, if he linked *aisthēsis* to love, Knox also spoke of it as a metaphor for faith, thus revealing how rich his understanding of that virtue was.[100] Faith for Knox was not an assent of the intellect to certain propositions, nor an act of trust in God or Christ, but a perception of the divine mysteries, an understanding which, as we shall see, coloured his approach to the issue of justification.[101]

---

96   *Remains*, Vol. 4, p. 382. See, also, Vol. 2, p. 334. Knox links this understanding of *aisthēsis* to Hebrews 5, 14, which speaks of those who have trained their senses [αἰσθητήρια, *aisthētēria*] to distinguish good from evil.

97   *Correspondence*, Vol. 1, p. 369, in conjunction with p. 363. For the use and meanings of *aisthēsis* in the New Testament and the Fathers, see Stewart, *Working the Earth of the Heart*, pp. 116–38.

98   *Remains*, Vol. 1, p. 326. Knox quotes in Greek 1 Peter 2, 3: "If so be ye have tasted that the Lord is gracious," as Hornby renders it in a note.

99   *Remains*, Vol. 1, p. 327; Vol. 2, p. 373; Vol. 1, p. 359. The idea of the present Christian life as an "anticipation of heaven" occurs a number of times in Knox's writings. See, for example: *Remains*, Vol. 2, pp. 102, 256; Vol. 3, pp. 435, 437; *Correspondence*, Vol. 2, p. 574.

100 *Remains*, Vol. 3, p. 164; Vol. 4, pp. 90–91; *Wesley*, pp. 496–97.

101 See below, pp. 171–72.

Knox's teaching on intuition is similar to Wesley's. For, as Knox notes, Wesley also spoke of "the spiritual sense, the divinely produced organ of the inner man, which holds commerce with [divine and heavenly things], and transmits the impression of them to the imagination, the affections, and the judgment, as the eye transmits the image formed on its retina to the sentient principle."[102] An example of this doctrine in Wesley is furnished by the *Earnest Appeal to Men of Reason and Learning* (1743) in which he writes:

> [S]eeing our ideas are not innate, but must all originally come from our senses, it is certainly necessary that you have senses capable of discerning [the things of God] ... *spiritual* senses, exercised to discern spiritual good and evil. It is necessary that you have the *hearing* ear and the *seeing* eye, emphatically so called; that you have a new class of senses opened in your soul, not depending on organs of flesh and blood, to be 'the *evidence* of things not seen' as your bodily senses are of visible things, to be avenues to the invisible world, to discern spiritual objects, and to furnish you with ideas of what the outward 'eye hath not seen, neither the ear heard.'

To quote Wesley's sermon "The Great Privilege of those that are Born of God" (1748), when a person comes to belief, all the spiritual senses of the soul are awakened: "'The eyes of his understanding' are now open, and he 'seeth him that is invisible' ... His ears are now opened ... [h]e hears and obeys the heavenly calling ... All his spiritual senses being now awakened, he has a clear intercourse with the invisible world. And hence he knows more and more of the things which before it 'could not enter into his heart to conceive.'"[103]

The same idea appeared in the Cambridge Platonists, for example in John Smith, whose teaching on intuition Knox also explicitly invoked.[104] God, declared Smith, was:

---

102   *Remains*, Vol. 3, p. 164. See, also, *Wesley*, pp. 496–97. For Wesley's doctrine of the spiritual senses, see Mealey, "Taste and See."

103   Wesley, *An Earnest Appeal to Men of Reason and Religion*, 32, in Cragg, ed., *Works of John Wesley*, Vol. 11, pp. 45–94, at pp. 56–57; Wesley, Sermon 19, "The Great Privilege of those that are Born of God," 1, 9–10, in Outler, ed., *Works*, Vol. 1, pp. 431–43, at p. 435 (punctuation slightly altered).

104   *Remains*, Vol. 4, p. 91.

best discerned νοερᾷ ἐπαφῇ [*noerāi epaphēi*], as Plotinus phraseth it, by an intellectual touch of him: we must "see with our eyes, and hear with our ears, and our hands must handle the word of life," that I may express it in Saint John's words. Ἔστι καὶ ψυχῆς αἴσθησίς τις [*esti kai psychēs aisthēsis tis*]. The soul itself hath its sense, as well the body: and, therefore David, when he would teach us how to know what the divine goodness is, calls us not for speculation but sensation, "Taste and see how good the Lord is."

Later in the same discourse Smith turned again to this theme, remarking that by a conversion from a carnal to a spiritual life one could:

> converse with God τῷ νῷ [*tōi nōi*, intuitively], whereas before we conversed with him only τῇ διανοίᾳ [*tēi dianoiāi*], with our discursive faculty, as the Platonists were wont to distinguish. Before we laid hold on him only λόγῳ ἀποδεικτικῷ [*logōi apodeiktikōi*], with a struggling, agonistical, and contentious reason, hotly combating with difficulties and sharp contests of diverse opinions, and labouring in itself, in its deductions of one thing from another; we shall then fasten our minds upon him λόγῳ ἀποφαντικῷ [*logōi apophantikōi*], with such a "serene understanding," γαλήνη νοερᾷ [*galēnēi noerāi*], such an intellectual calmness and serenity as will present us with a blissful, steady and invariable sight of him.[105]

Knox appeals also to Taylor, quoting directly from what he calls his "admirable sermon before the University of Dublin:" "[T]here is a sort of God's dear servants, who ... have a degree of clarity and divine knowledge, more than we can discourse of, and more certain than the demonstrations of geometry; brighter than the sun, and indeficient as the light of heaven ... But ... this is to be felt, and not to be talked of."[106]

The idea of the spiritual senses found in Taylor, Smith, Wesley and Knox had its genesis in the Fathers, and especially in Origen.[107] It was an important feature of the Pseudo-Macarian homilies, where the doctrine of the spiritual

---

105   Smith, Discourse 1, "A Discourse concerning the True Way or Method of Attaining Divine Knowledge," *Select Discourses*, 5; pp. 3–25, at p. 20.

106   *Remains*, Vol. 1, p. 359. I have altered the format slightly and substituted "clarity" for "charity." The former is doubtless the word which Knox wrote in his hard-to-read hand. It better suits his meaning and is also the reading given in the *Works* (Vol. 6, p. 395).

107   For the patristic roots of the doctrine, see Rahner, "The Spiritual Senses according to Origen."

senses often appears.[108] For instance, Pseudo-Macarius writes: "[T]he luminous world of the Godhead [cannot] be touched or seen with physical eyes. But to those who are spiritual, namely, who see with the eyes of the heart ... the world of divine light [lies] revealed." "The face of the soul is unveiled and it gazes with fixed eyes upon the heavenly Bridegroom, face to face, in a spiritual and ineffable light."[109] As always, however, Knox's ultimate appeal is to the formularies of the Church of England.[110] Citing the Prayer Book liturgy, he writes: "We ask that the thoughts of our hearts may be so cleansed, as to admit of our loving God perfectly; and that we may, in heart and mind, ascend with Christ into the heavens, and there with him continually dwell."[111]

7   Conclusion

This chapter has looked at Knox's methodology. In true post-Enlightenment fashion, he treated theology as a scientific quest for truth, an application of reason to Scripture, primarily the New Testament and, above all, the Gospels, though he was keen to stress the unity of both Testaments. He held the Bible to be divinely inspired, a transcript of God's self-revelation, a revelation which reached its culmination in Christ, and which was designed to attract and draw back sinful humanity to its creator. For all his veneration of the Bible, however, Knox was adamant that it could not stand alone. It needed to be interpreted, and this interpretation he sought in what he called the *consensus omnium*, the agreement of those whom he held to be the wisest and holiest "specimens" (his word) of Christianity. First among these were the Fathers, whom he aspired to imitate, describing himself as "a Christian of the six first centuries." Nevertheless, he avoided speaking of "tradition," which in his mind had associations with what he saw as the errors of Roman Catholicism. The term, however, is a convenient one to employ when discussing Knox's theology. Like the Fathers, Knox accorded an important role to experience, which he understood primarily as a practical and experiential knowledge of Christianity. He also spoke of *aisthēsis* or intuition, the spiritual sense of divine things, which

---

108 One may note Knox's comment that Taylor's expressions in the passage of the "*Via Intelligentiae*" just quoted "are as ardent as those of Macarius in his cloister" (*Remains*, Vol. 1, p. 360).

109 Maloney, *Pseudo-Macarius*, pp. 107, 89. See, also, p. 272, note 5.

110 *Remains*, Vol. 1, p. 359.

111 Ibid., p. 358. Knox alludes to the collect for purity, at the start of the Eucharist, and to the collect for Ascension Day, (*B. C. P.*, pp. 180, 122).

he equated with both love and faith. In all this, Knox revealed himself as a man of his times, but also as a disciple of Wesley and the moderates, as well as of the Fathers. Even so, his great appeal was consistently to the Church of England, whose formularies he made his own. Having looked in this chapter at Knox's methodology, we can now turn to examine the conclusions which he drew from his studies.

CHAPTER 8

Alexander Knox's Theology (1):
God and Humanity, Christ and the Holy Spirit

We come now to our main theme, "Mr. Knox's system," which this and the following chapters will examine in detail. I have already remarked that one can schematize Knox's thinking, and I therefore propose to treat his theology by examining the following topics in order: God and humanity; Christ and the Holy Spirit; justification and perfection; baptism and the Eucharist; the church; providence and predestination.[1] This order is dictated by Knox's concern for justification. Thus, the doctrine of God is taken first, focusing especially on Knox's teaching about the Trinity, because for Knox the source of justification is the love of the triune God, and, also, because his understanding of the justificatory process is profoundly Trinitarian. We look next at Knox's anthropology, humanity being the object of God's justifying love; then at Knox's Christology and pneumatology, since justification, for him, is accomplished by the agency of Christ and the Holy Spirit. After that, we will turn to justification itself, and its concomitant within Knox's theology, perfection. After that, we will consider baptism and the Eucharist, the first of which Knox views as initiating the process of justification, which the Eucharist then sustains. After this, comes an investigation of Knox's ecclesiology, since for him the sacraments build up the church, which is also the locus in which justification occurs. This part of the book concludes with an evaluation of Knox's doctrine of providence and predestination, related topics which he sees as separate from justification. Throughout our investigation, we will continue to explore the context and sources of Knox's thought, showing how his thinking reflects the post-Enlightenment era; how it parallels the teaching of Wesley and the moderates; how it echoes the doctrine of the Fathers; and how it corresponds to the patrimony of the Church of England. Before proceeding, however, let us remark briefly on an omission from the list of theological subjects which Knox addresses. The after-life receives remarkably little attention in his writings. The reason, one may suggest, is that he saw this life as being for the Christian an anticipated heaven; in it the believer already enjoys uninterrupted fellowship with God.[2]

---

1 See above, p. 108.
2 See below, p. 180.

© KONINKLIJKE BRILL NV, LEIDEN, 2020 | DOI:10.1163/9789004426986_010

1   God

Knox took the existence of God as a given; it was not a point which he discussed. With regard to the divine attributes, he was content to speak about the
deity, using the conventional terms employed by the Church of England, both
in its Articles and in its common prayer.[3] The only point of particular note is
the emphasis which he placed on God's "infinite philanthropy."[4] Knox believed
God's nature to be "essential love."[5] This was the very basis of Christianity,
which he defined as "the direct effluence of God's infinite and essential love
towards us."[6] Love was also the prism, so to speak, through which Knox re-
fracted God's other attributes. Thus, for example, he described omnipresence
as an attribute which could, at best, only excite reverence, until, viewing it in
the light of God's love, human beings realized that God was present *for them*,
that "the eye of God was specially upon them, and the hand of God directly
and effectively with them."[7] Or, again, Knox declared: "Omniscience and omnipotence would be ... but infinitely terrific," if human beings could not see
the love of God transforming them into "infinite wisdom, and inexhaustible
beneficence."[8] Knox's approach was thus a practical one: he wanted to present the divine attributes in a way which would help people in their spiritual
lives. It is this practical concern which, in part, explains his lack of interest
in exploring the doctrine of God more fully: to have delved more deeply into
the topic would have been for him pointless speculation. But also, in his view,
the teaching about God given in Scripture was so "direct and simple" as to be
"open to the plainest, as to the most powerful understanding."[9] In other words,
it needed no further elucidation.

God was the Holy Trinity for Knox. Although he addressed the doctrine
ex professo only in a single essay, "On the Nature of our Salvation through
Christ," the stated theme of which was "the incarnation of the second Person,
and the influential operation of the third,"[10] his entire theology, at least in

---

3   For brief mentions of the divine attributes, see: *Remains*, Vol. 1, pp. 50–51, 323; Vol. 2,
       pp. 331–32, 419, 422–23; Vol. 3, p. 377; Vol. 4, pp. 269–73; *Correspondence*, Vol. 1, pp. 57,
       82–83. Article 1 of the Thirty-Nine Articles declares: "There is but one living and true God,
       everlasting, without body, parts, or passions; of infinite power, wisdom, and goodness"
       (B. C. P., p. 397).
4   *Wesley*, p. 471. See, also, *Remains*, Vol. 2, p. 307–8.
5   *Remains*, Vol. 2, p. 291. Knox refers to 1 John, 4, 8: "God is love."
6   *Remains*, Vol. 2, p. 309. "God" here is explicitly the Trinity.
7   *Remains*, Vol. 2, pp. 240–1.
8   Ibid., pp. 331–2. "Terrific" is used in this context with the sense of "awe-inspiring."
9   *Remains*, Vol. 3, p. 376.
10   Ibid., Vol. 2, p. 318. The essay, which is undated, runs from pp. 316–436.

relation to justification, was marked by a staunch Trinitarian faith – a belief which was increasingly under attack. Denial of the doctrine was decriminalized in 1813, followed in 1825 by the foundation of the British and Foreign Unitarian Association. It was without doubt on account of this burgeoning anti-Trinitarianism that one finds Knox's castigating "obtrusive and sophistical opinions ... [and] [p]resumptuous speculations on the Divine nature."[11] These "opinions" and "speculations" he countered by an appeal to "the written oracles of God," although his defence of Trinitarianism was also firmly based on the *consensus omnium*, which showed that the Trinity was one of the "catholic verities," fundamental to Christianity, conceived as a living relationship with God.[12] As he wrote to Parken:

> [W]e find, throughout [the] whole retrospect [of Christian history], vital piety uniformly connected with, and growing out of a belief of [*sic*], and zeal for, the proper Godhead of the Son, and the inward energetic grace of the Spirit ... [W]hen we find the deepest character of piety, – that which most effectually transforms the earthly nature into the heavenly – composed of these recognitions, as its elementary and essential ingredients; living habitually upon these views as its resting-place, and rising upon them as its wings, when it soars highest above earthly things; what can be concluded but that these tenets belong to the essentials of our Christian faith, and that to depart from these would be to forsake 'the fountain of living waters?'[13]

For Knox, the source and origin of human salvation was "the love of the Father, Son, and Holy Ghost." The "whole three persons of the blessed Trinity" took, he affirmed, "a like gracious interest in the spiritual redemption of man." Thus he described salvation as a double movement, in which, first, "the Spirit of the Son of God [is] sent into our hearts," so that, second, "through God manifested in the flesh, [we might] continually have ... access by one spirit unto the Father."[14]

---

11   Ibid., Vol. 3, p. 425. For the anti-Trinitarianism of the late eighteenth and early nineteenth centuries see Ditchfield, "Anti-Trinitarianism" and Webb, "English Unitarianism in the Nineteenth Century."

12   For the "catholic verities," see above, pp. 112–13. For "the written oracles of God," see *Remains*, Vol. 2, p. 315.

13   *Remains*, Vol. 1, pp. 436–7, ending with a quotation from Jeremiah 2.13.

14   *Remains*, Vol. 2, pp. 309, 253 ("interest" here meaning, according to the usage of Knox's time, "participation" or "share"); p. 257 (presupposing the initial sending of the Son by the Father); Vol. 3, p. 425 (alluding to 1 Timothy 3.16, in the Authorized Version, and Ephesians 2.18).

In this way, Christians were drawn into the life of the triune God, he taught. United to the Son by the Holy Spirit, they participate in what he called "that unfathomable intercourse, within the sphere of Deity, by which the Divine Persons mutually exercise their adorable excellencies, and contribute each to the mysterious felicity of the whole."[15]

Knox's approach to the doctrine of the Trinity reflected that of Wesley. Eschewing what he called the "fruitless work" of speculation about the dogma of the Trinity, Wesley nonetheless insisted that the knowledge of the triune God belonged to "the very heart of Christianity." It lay, he proclaimed, "at the root of all vital religion." In fact, one may contend that, like Knox, his entire theology was founded on what one might term a "practical Trinitarianism," a vision of the Christian life as animated by the conjoint activity of the Father, Son, and Holy Spirit.[16] One finds the same thing in the Cambridge Platonists. For example, in the *Select Discourses* Smith never uses the term "Trinity," yet the whole of his teaching can be resumed in Trinitarian terms. It is all about "the grace of God, and the help of the mighty Spirit of Jesus Christ working in us."[17] And this is one of the reasons that, in the face of a rising deism, the Platonists championed Trinitarian belief. For them, as for Knox, "the doctrine of the Trinity ... had *vital* implications." It was "the gateway to a deified life."[18] It is the same with the Fathers, the practical nature of whose theology has already been noted.[19] This pragmatism is particularly well exemplified by the three Fathers to whom Knox especially appealed: John Chrysostom, Pseudo-Macarius and Clement of Alexandria. None of them engaged in abstract speculations about the Trinity, but, what Charles Raven writes of Clement and Origen is true for them all: they had "the root of the matter in their lives."[20]

---

15   *Remains*, Vol. 4, pp. 260–1.
16   Wesley, Sermon 55, "On the Trinity," 3, 17, in Outler, ed., *Works of John Wesley*, Vol. 2, pp. 374–86, 377, 384. For Wesley's "practical Trinitarianism," see, e.g., Wainwright, "Trinitarian Theology and Wesleyan Holiness."
17   Patrick, "A Sermon Preached at the Funeral of Mr. John Smith," in Smith, *Select Discourses*, pp. 523–557, at p. 544. For the Trinitarianism of the Cambridge Platonists, see Taliaferro, "Natural Reason."
18   Taliaferro, "Natural Reason," pp. 174–5 (emphasis added).
19   See above, p. 114.
20   Raven, *Good News*, p. 101, quoted Osborn, *Clement of Alexandria*, p. 152. On the other hand, it has been argued that if Clement knows the doctrine of the Trinity from the tradition he has received, he "does not think in a trinitarian way" (Hauschild, *Gottes Geist und der Mensch*, p. 83, quoted Bucur, *Angelomorphic Pneumatology*, p. 4).

Knox's Trinitarianism reflected the doctrine of the Church of England as set out in the Thirty-Nine Articles.[21] According to Jebb, however, Knox believed the greatest support of Trinitarian orthodoxy that the Church possessed was its liturgy. Subscription to the Articles, he regarded, according to Jebb, as "a single act; to which, a man might argue down, and persuade his scruples. But no Arian, who had a grain of religion or honesty, could persist, week after week, in reading the creeds."[22] This is an allusion to the Nicene Creed proclaimed in the Eucharist, and to the Apostles' Creed, recited at Morning and Evening Prayer. Knox himself also referred to the use of Apostles' Creed in the baptismal service.[23] The Church's Trinitarianism was not simply a series of creedal assertions, however, but a theme which ran constantly throughout its services. The daily offices of Morning and Evening Prayer both opened and closed with Trinitarian formulae; the Psalms and Canticles used during them all terminated with a Trinitarian doxology; Trinity Sunday was celebrated annually, its collect proclaiming that "true faith" meant "to acknowledge the glory of the eternal Trinity."[24] To all this, Knox would have been exposed from his earliest years and it, no doubt, is the fundamental reason for his Trinitarianism.

2   Humanity

From God, the author of justification, we turn next to humanity, the object of God's justifying love. Anthropology was a major theme for Knox, and anthropological concerns run throughout his writings. Of particular relevance are: "On Christianity, as the Way of Peace and True Happiness" (1805); "Remarks on Mrs. Barbauld's Essay" (undated, possibly 1806); and a letter to Jebb of January 29, 1801, on the subject of Christian preaching.[25]

Knox conceived of human beings in dualistic terms as a "combination of animal and spirit, or of body and mind," and both elements had a role to play in serving God.[26] It was, however, on the spiritual part of human nature that Knox focused the bulk of his theological attention. He viewed it as embracing

---

21   See particularly Articles 1, 2, 5, and 8; B. C. P., pp. 397–8.
22   Jebb, "Introduction" to Burnet's *Lives*, p. xxxviii.
23   *Remains*, Vol. 2, p. 51. See also on this point Knox's "Amicus" letter, *Christian Observer*, 15.6 (June 1816), pp. 358–365, at pp. 358–9.
24   B. C. P., pp. 33, 39, 42, 46, 34, 128.
25   *Remains*, Vol. 1, pp. 1–52, 468–83; *Correspondence*, Vo. 1, pp. 13–32. For the possible dating of the essay on Barbauld see *Correspondence*, Vol. 1, p. 259.
26   *Remains*, Vol. 2, p. 137. See also p. 132.

several different faculties: reason, conscience, imagination and the affections.[27] The last of these he depicted as "the noblest part of our nature,"[28] because by the affections, he meant, primarily, love. Love was "the master affection of the heart," and that fact made the heart, rather than the intellect, "the central seat of religion," because religion was, above all, love. "[T]here is no true piety but in the love of God."[29] This love was served by the intellect. We know in order to love; or, as Knox expressed it, "[intellectual] apprehensions are not ends, but means, ministering to our affections."[30] These affections were the source of human happiness, happiness which, in his vocabulary, was a "consecrated word." One might almost say that his was a theology of happiness. Postulating happiness as the "unconquerable aim" of all human beings, that which they seek above everything else, Knox contended that it could be found only in God. Twice he quoted Joseph Addison: "The supreme Author of our being has so formed the soul of man, that nothing but Himself can be its last, adequate, and proper happiness."[31] If, therefore, human beings desired to be happy, they needed to turn to Christianity. Christianity was "essentially delightful" (a theme which he repeated constantly). He taught that it brought "the human heart to the peace and happiness which it [longs] for;" and that those who embraced it necessarily found "not only … the means of everlasting safety, but … the source of the truest and most exalted pleasures which can be enjoyed on earth." He argued that Christianity was designed to satisfy all the exigencies of human nature. It had "properties respectively adapted to each of our faculties … truth for our reason, moral principle for our conscience, amiableness for our affections, and novelty, sublimity, and beauty, for our imagination." Thus it served "to attract, inform, and satisfy our minds; to operate, in the aptest way conceivable, on all our passions and affections."[32] Knox was aware

---

27   Ibid., Vol. 1, p. 474.

28   Ibid., p. 475.

29   Ibid.

30   *Remains*, Vol. 2, p. 364.

31   B. L., Add. Ms 41663, Correspondence between Alexander Knox and John Jebb 1799–1811, fol. 197, Knox to John Jebb, letter, March 17, 1809 (emphasis in the original); *Remains*, Vol. 4, p. 284; Vol. 1, pp. 17, 476. The quotation from Addison comes from *The Spectator*, 413 (June 24, 1712), p. 1. The words recall those of Augustine, "[*F*]*ecisti nos ad te, et inquietum est cor nostrum, donec requiescat in te;*" "you have made us for yourself and our hearts are restless till they rest in you," (*Confessions*, 1, 1, *P. L.*, 32, col. 661, my translation). Knox quotes this on several occasions: *Remains*, Vol. 2, pp. 132, 322; Vol. 4, pp. 281, 585. For Joseph Addison (1672–1719), essayist, and co-founder of *The Spectator* magazine; see *o. d. n. b.*

32   *Remains*, Vol. 2, p. 500; Vol. 1, p. 11; Vol. 2, pp. 500–1; Vol. 1, pp. 474, 31. See also *Remains*, Vol. 1, pp. 101, 274–5, 330–5, 346, 377; Vol. 2, pp. 146, 321, 502; Vol. 3, pp. 74, 196–97, 395; Vol. 4, pp. 45–46, 531–2, 585; *Correspondence*, Vol. 1, pp. 104–5, 283, 512–14, 544–5.

of the paradox of a man prone to depression expatiating on what he termed the "felicitating" effect of Christianity.[33]

> The thing called religious melancholy may be, for aught I know, a real disease. But I do not think that it is my disease; I rather believe that religion is my master passion; and that, of course, my bad nerves work upon that, as in a covetous man they would produce apprehensions of dying a beggar. My views of religion, when my mind is unclouded, all are cheerful and happy. I see it as a divine combination of every thing [sic] that tends to exalt and to enrich human nature; and I cannot form (I hardly think I am disposed to form) any idea of comfort, even for one moment, without it. But when I think my religion is declining, that thought is my misery.[34]

To the happiness which Christianity bestowed, Knox contrasted the misery of the Christ-less life: misery, not guilt. An early Evangelical commentator remarked that the doctrine of human sinfulness was one which Knox "laid down with a boldness and a clearness which leaves no doubt of the writer's sentiments." In this, I would contend, that commentator was mistaken.[35] Knox implacably opposed what he understood to be the Evangelical doctrine of sin, which he perceived as teaching that humanity had incurred "legal guilt," and was in a state of enmity with God, lying under the divine curse and malediction; all of which was cognate, in his estimation, with the Evangelical doctrines of substitutionary atonement and "forensic acquittal." "I admit natural frailty and natural predominance of animality," he wrote to Jebb. "But the notion of *natural enmity* with God is, in my judgment, neither countenanced by holy scripture nor by experience."[36] Instead of seeing sin in terms of a crime demanding God's punishment, Knox viewed it as a calamity, from which the divine love sought to deliver humankind.[37] It was not, therefore, on the guilt which sin allegedly incurred, but on sin itself that Knox focused his attention; this was what deprived human beings of happiness. As he observed to Jebb: "[M]an [is] by nature, (I mean in his present fallen state,) a weak, ignorant, sinful, and, of course, miserable being ... absolutely incapable of enjoying any

---

33   *Remains*, Vol. 1, pp. 21, 25, 26.
34   Ibid., Vol. 4, pp. 45–6. See also Vol. 4, pp. 561–6.
35   *Christian Examiner*, 3.35 (September 1834), p. 641. The reviewer contends here that Knox ultimately lost sight of this principle.
36   *Remains*, Vol. 2, pp. 13, 14; Vol. 1, pp. 506–7; Vol. 2, p. 345; B. L., Add. Ms 41164, Correspondence between Alexander Knox and John Jebb (1812–30), fol. 159, Knox to John Jebb, letter, April 28, 1821.
37   *Remains*, Vol. 4, p. 363; Vol. 1, pp. 507–9.

real happiness, either here or hereafter." Through sin human beings inhabited a "dark, miserable, polluting, heart-lacerating world," in which "[t]he mind ... groans under [a] degrading and lacerating bondage ... the inward hell of galled conscience, tortured pride, frantic passions, and headlong propensities."[38] The origin of this wretched plight lay in the fall of the first man. "[T]hrough Adam's transgression, a principle of moral evil was introduced into human nature." "[T]he first Adam has been to us," he wrote, "the fountain of an animal and earthly nature; and we are instructed, that ... by the fall of our earthly progenitor, sin entered into the world, and death by sin, and, thus, one man was, to all, the source of corruption and mortality."[39]

Although accepting the Fall, Knox denied the doctrine of total depravity that was held by Evangelical theologians. This was the teaching that human nature had been so ruined by Adam's sin, that it was absolutely impossible for humans to contribute anything to their salvation; they depended utterly on the grace of God. Knox believed in the necessity of grace, yet, for him, human beings were not so vitiated and corrupted that they could not desire grace or ask for it. As he told Hannah More: "The penitent, who has learned the true way of salvation, does not work, as if that were to do him any good; but pray: to ask from God what he feels he cannot himself take one effectual step toward."[40] Thus, rather than talking about "total depravity," which he judged "too crude an idea, to be made a standard expression [of theology]," Knox suggested speaking of "total captivity, or total impotency."[41] One of the reasons that Knox emphasised the weakness of human nature was his concern with practical theology. He believed that "a thorough, radical sense of depravity" was an "essential ... ingredient ... to every stage of true christianity [sic]." It was, first, a necessary prelude to conversion: "[M]en in general, need to be brought to [deep feelings of human depravity and human weakness] before they will aim at a radical change; which radical change, however, is the only substratum upon which the fabric of holiness can be erected."[42] Second, to quote the *Correspondence*: "In order that [human nature] may continually look to heaven for strength, it must be made to feel its own entire imbecility."[43] In other words, human beings had to realize their own impotence to do good, not just before their conversion

---

38   *Correspondence*, Vol. 1, pp. 19, 104; *Remains*, Vol. 2, p. 390 (punctuation slightly modified).
39   *Remains*, Vol. 2, pp. 27, 255. In the background to this thought stands Romans 5.12, to which Knox devotes a detailed exegesis, *Remains*, Vol. 3, pp. 449–51.
40   *Remains*, Vol. 3, p. 85.
41   *Correspondence*, Vol. 1, p. 382. "Depravity", without the modifier "total", was a word which Knox used to describe the fallen state of human nature.
42   *Correspondence*, Vol. 1, p. 169; *Remains*, Vol. 3, p. 79.
43   *Correspondence*, Vol. 1, p. 106.

but throughout their lives. They had to understand that only by grace could they conquer sin and grow in holiness. Third, this understanding was a help to perfection. Seeing that they looked not to their own efforts but to God's grace, Knox taught that Christians knew that it was possible to extirpate every trace of evil from their lives: "The christian [*sic*] … is solicitous to detect every, the minutest, as well the deepest, evils [*sic*]; because he knows, that the omnipotent Saviour is able to save to the uttermost, all that come unto God, by him."[44]

For Knox, therefore, religion was designed by God to be connatural with humanity. Conversely, for him anything contrary to nature could not be true. This is why, as we have seen, he rejected "modern mysticism." It was, he held, guilty of "suppressing and annihilating, our natural tastes and feelings."[45] It was also one of the reasons why he rejected Calvinism, which he castigated as, "not congenial to either taste, or understanding, or natural feeling. It adds neither grace, nor beauty, nor cheerfulness, to that cause of which it claims to be the accredited interpreter."[46]

3   Sources of Knox's Anthropology

Knox's anthropology was inevitably marked by the age in which he lived. His emphasis on happiness mirrored one of the most important concerns of the Enlightenment, while his insistence on the primacy of the affections reflected the Romantic desire to correct the Enlightenment's appeal to reason alone. At the same time, the attention he paid to the fallenness of human nature may be seen as a reaction to the denial of original sin by Enlightenment thinkers.[47] Against them, he appealed to the witness of Scripture and, as far as the misery of humanity without God was concerned, the evidence "of our own experience." If we doubt the wretchedness of human nature, he wrote, "let us judge for ourselves; let us cast our eyes over the extended mass of mankind. Let us observe the brutal ignorance … the vice and profligacy … foolish desire, unbridled passion, rankling envy, gloomy discontent …"[48] He cited, too, the authority of John Wesley, specifically referring to Wesley's equation of sin with misery,

---

44   Ibid., p. 169, alluding to Hebrews 7.25.
45   *Remains*, Vol. 1, p. 329. See above, p. 81.
46   *Remains*, Vol. 4, p. 340 (the "cause" being that of the Gospel). See, too, below, p. 234.
47   See above, p. 94.
48   For Knox's appeal to Scripture see *Correspondence*, Vol. 1, p. 19, where he invokes Romans 8.7–8; Ephesians 2.1; and 4.18, with, in the background, Romans 5.12. For his appeal to experience see *Correspondence*, Vol. 1, p. 20; *Remains*, Vol. 3, p. 371 (punctuation slightly modified).

and happiness with holiness. "No man," claimed Knox of Wesley, "ever gave deeper shaded pictures of human misery ... the actually begun hell of every heart which is at enmity with God." This was, however, Knox continued, but a prelude to Wesley's proclamation of holiness as the key to happiness. This proclamation was a "central characteristic of John Wesley's teaching." As Knox told Southey, Wesley's addresses were "directed ... prevalently to the natural desire of happiness. Regarding this inextinguishable appetite of the inner man as no other than an instinctive propension toward the supreme good, he made it his object to urge vital Christianity as that Divine provision in which alone this ceaseless craving of the heart could find satisfaction and repose."[49]

Modern scholars underline Knox's point. For instance, Isabel Rivers terms the conjunction of holiness and happiness an "essential element" in Wesley's preaching. Outler, in similar vein, speaks of it as one of Wesley's "most consistent themes, early, middle, and late."[50]

Linked to the theme of happiness, was Wesley's teaching that Christianity was "[in] every way suited to the nature of man." "[I]t begins," he asserted, "in man's knowing himself: knowing himself to be what he really is – foolish, vicious, miserable. It goes on to point out the remedy for this, to make him truly wise, virtuous, and happy, as every thinking mind (perhaps from some implicit remembrance of what it originally was) longs to be." This teaching, too, was explicitly invoked by Knox. One of the most admirable features "in my old friend's *most matured* theology," Knox insisted, was the way in which Wesley described "the strict proportion ... of the provisions of Christianity to men's exigencies and capacities."[51] Knox maintained, too, that Wesley "delighted to contemplate practical Christianity as consisting ... of ... purified affections." In this, Knox was also correct, for, although he consistently stressed the importance of reason, Wesley also made the affections central to his understanding of religion. His was a religion of the heart, its defining goal was a change of the affections from love of sin, to love of God, "the renewal of our heart after the image of [God who] created us."[52] One point on which Knox did not appeal to Wesley, but where they share a common point of view, concerns the idea of guilt in relation to original sin. Worried about its compatibility with the doctrine of the divine justice, and doubtless because he found little support

49   *Remains*, 3, p. 170; *Wesley*, pp. 469–70.

50   Rivers, *Reason, Grace and Sentiment*, 1, p. 250; Outler, ed., *Works of John Wesley*, 1, p. 185, note 18. For a useful summary of this topic, see Miles, "Happiness, Holiness and the Moral Life in John Wesley."

51   Wesley, *An Earnest Appeal to Men of Reason and Religion*, 29, in Cragg, ed., *Works of John Wesley*, 11, pp. 45–94, at p. 55; *Wesley*, p. 475 (emphasis in the original).

52   *Wesley*, pp. 474–75; Wesley, *Journal*, Vol. 2, p. 275, September 13, 1739. On this point, see Maddox, "A Change of Affections;" Clapper, *John Wesley on Religious Affections*.

for it in the Greek Fathers, Wesley came to downplay the idea that original sin involved culpability, something exemplified in his 1784 adaptation of the Thirty-Nine Articles, where he changed the description of original sin as "fault and corruption" simply to "corruption."[53]

Alongside the theological similarities between Wesley and Knox one may mention two points of difference. One concerns the doctrine of prevenient grace. Wesley taught that, as a result of Christ's saving work, grace had been bestowed on all humanity, bringing a partial healing from the effects of the fall, with the result that human beings have sufficient free will to cooperate with God's actual grace. The doctrine was, to use Maddox's word, "distinctive" of Wesley's teaching, yet Knox ignored it completely. One reason for this was, perhaps, that Knox could find no support for the doctrine in Scripture or patristic tradition. But also Knox, unlike Wesley, did not need the doctrine, on account of the second main difference in their anthropologies, the extent to which human nature had been affected by original sin. Wesley believed in the total depravity of human nature, including the will. Therefore, for Wesley, if human beings were to respond to the gospel message, their wills needed first ("preveniently") to be freed by grace. Knox did not have this problem; as noted above, he held that the corruption of humanity was not total, and that human beings are free to choose God and to ask for grace in order to be saved.[54]

With regard to the moderates, we have already seen that Knox's disagreed with them on the fallenness of human nature.[55] By contrast, on the point of Christianity being "congenial to all [our] radical tastes and faculties," Knox appealed directly to "the Church-of-England divines."[56] The idea was a prominent feature of their theology; it is what they meant when they described Christianity as "rational;" reason being, in Whichcote's words, that which is "proper and peculiar to Man." "RELIGION," Whichcote taught, "is that wherein our Happiness doth consist," because "man [is] *made* to know God," and this knowledge comes to us through reason. "[R]eason," he affirmed, "is the *recipient* of whatsoever God declares." In fact, according to Whichcote, the reason is made for God, and thus to be a rational being is to be a religious being, one whom only the knowledge of God can satisfy.

---

53   Maddox, *Responsible Grace*, p. 292, note 77. For the question as a whole, see Maddox, *Responsible Grace*, pp. 74–75. For the alternative argument that Wesley's overall position on original sin stands in the Reformed tradition of Calvin, and portrays humanity as made guilty by the fall, see, for example, Lindström, *Wesley and Sanctification*.
54   For a summary of Wesley's doctrine of prevenient grace see Maddox, *Responsible Grace*, pp. 87–93.
55   See above, p. 85.
56   *Remains*, Vol. 1, p. 101.

Intellectual nature hath a secret desire and thirst after God; and therefore
it cannot be accomplished, neither can it be satisfied, unless it find out
and pitch upon that object which is most proper and peculiar [to it] ...
[*I*]*ntellectus quaerit Deum*; it is the nature of our mind and understanding to seek after God: therefore, though a man be never so well accomplished, if he be devoid of sense and apprehension of God, he must
be unfurnished; for he is unsatisfied, he hath not enough to satisfy the
connatural desires of his immortal soul.[57]

A similar example of the same doctrine is given by Smith in his undated discourse on "The Excellency and Nobleness of True Religion." In this discourse,
Smith cited with approval Cicero's definition of reason as the *"vinculum Dei
et hominis,"* the chain which binds together God and human beings. Reason
enables "man to converse with God by knowing him and loving him."[58] The
quotation helps elucidate a point on which Knox and the moderates might
initially be thought to disagree, namely the relationship of affection to reason.
Knox seems to prioritize affection, the moderates reason. In fact, however, in
both Knox and the moderates, reason and affection go together. For the moderates, to quote Sarah Hutton, "Right reason is affective reason, directed by love
towards God." For Knox, reason fuels the affections: we love God in proportion
to the knowledge and understanding which we have of him.[59]

Like Knox and Wesley, the moderates were concerned for happiness. For
them, religion was something joyful, not something "doleful, troublesome,
[and] melancholy." "Happiness," stated Cudworth, "is the same thing, that we
call holiness," a sentiment echoed by Smith's contention that "true holiness or
religion, and true happiness are but two several notions of one thing, rather
than distinct in themselves." For Smith, "true religion ... *begets the greatest serenity, constancy, and composedness of mind, and brings the truest contentment,
the most satisfying joy and pleasure, the purest and most divine sweetness and*

57   Whichcote, Aphorism 71, *Aphorisms*, p. xlvii; sermon, "The Manifestation of Christ and
      the Deification of Man," in Patrides, *The Cambridge Platonists*, pp. 62–76, at pp. 72, 74;
      Discourse 58, "The illustrious Manifestations of God and the inexcusable Ignorance of
      Men," [part 2], *Works*, Vol. 3, pp. 175–95, at p. 182; Discourse 86, "Men have nothing to glory
      of, but Religion," [part 2], *Works*, Vol. 4, pp. 279–95, at p. 286 (emphases in the original).
58   Smith, Discourse 9, "The Excellency and Nobleness of True Religion," *Select Discourses*,
      pp. 403–87, at p. 417.
59   Hutton, "Lord Herbert Of Cherbury and the Cambridge Platonists," p. 24 (speaking specifi-
      cally of the Cambridge Platonists); *Remains*, Vol. 1, p. 326.

pleasure to the spirits of good men."[60] This sentiment was shared by the Fathers, particularly Clement of Alexandria. As Neil Anderson comments, Clement saw "an inexorable link between happiness and holiness," equating the former to God-likeness.[61] Pseudo-Macarius also stressed that God's work in the soul "brings about … unspeakable joy," bestowing on the Christian "inexpressible pleasure." This was because grace restored the soul to its natural state. Created good, it has been invaded by sin: at one point Pseudo-Macarius uses the striking image of a householder confronted by an intruder breaking into his home. The aim of Christianity, he argued, is to help believers regain full possession of their souls and expel from them what is "foreign to our nature, namely, the corruption of our passions through the disobedience of the first man." This alien corruption is then, according to Pseudo-Macarius, replaced with "[t]he fruits of the Spirit, gladness and happiness," as the soul is joined and united to God.[62]

Knox was sure that his anthropology was that of the Church of England. That is why he appealed to Wesley and the moderates; they were the Church's theologians, expounding its doctrine.[63] But he also believed that what he taught was the doctrine of the Thirty-Nine Articles, one of the rare occasions on which he invoked them as an authority. He did so particularly in defence of his views on human depravity. "A deep sense of [human depravity] appears to me necessary to true Christian perfection," he wrote, "as a sufficiently deep foundation is necessary for a lofty building." "But," he continued, "I hardly think *he* can have this, who denies that that 'infection of nature' which 'doth remain in them that are regenerated' (Art. ix Church of England) hath in it the nature of sin." The specific Article to which Knox referred, Article IX, "Of Original or Birth-Sin," teaches that all human beings have derived from fallen Adam such a "fault and corruption" of nature that they are "very far gone from original righteousness, and … inclined to evil." Although this sounds like a strong expression, it stops short of the doctrine of total depravity, and corresponds with the position espoused by Knox.[64]

---

60   Whichcote, Discourse 4, "The Joy Which the Righteous have in God," *Works*, Vol. 1, pp. 56–74, at p. 59; Cudworth, "Sermon I," *Works*, Vol. 4, pp. 289–350, at p. 327; Smith, Discourse 9, "The Excellency and Nobleness of True Religion," *Select Discourses*, pp. 481–2, 443 (emphasis in the original).

61   Anderson, *John Wesley's Appropriation of the Thought of Clement of Alexandria*, p. 270; Ashwin-Siejkowski, *Clement of Alexandria*, p. 152.

62   Maloney, *Pseudo-Macarius*, pp. 106, 55, 129, 14, 171.

63   *Remains*, Vol. 1, p. 101.

64   For the article in question, see *B. C. P.*, p. 398; for Knox's use of it, see *Correspondence*, Vol. 1, p. 167 (emphasis in the original).

4   Christology

From God and humanity, we turn next to the two agents by which they are
drawn together in Knox's theology, Christ and the Holy Spirit. We begin
with Christology, which Knox deals with especially in three undated essays:
"On Redemption and Salvation by Christ, as exhibited in the epistles to the
Romans and the Hebrews;" "On the Mediatory Character of Christ, as subsist-
ing in our Lord's manhood and flesh;" and "On the Nature of our Salvation
through Christ." Of importance, too, for his Christology, are the "Reflections
on 2 Timothy, III. 15."[65] As befits one whose interest was in praxis rather than
speculation, Knox was more concerned with the work of Christ than his person. He held that "the incarnation of the Second Person [of the Trinity], very
God of very God" was one of the "essential catholic doctrines," but what mattered for him was not this teaching *in abstracto*, so much as the fact that "God
was manifested in the flesh, for us men, and for our salvation."[66] Knox never
spoke of the incarnation by itself, but always in relation to its soteriological
purpose. The one exception to this rule occurs in the essay "On the Nature of
our Salvation through Christ."

> In [our Redeemer], the Godhead, which deigned to inhabit the ancient
> temple, has united itself far more closely to us, by coming within the
> sphere of our nature. The temple, made with human hands, was thus su-
> perseded by a living sanctuary: – the human person, formed for the fit
> inhabitation of the everlasting Word, by the omnipotent Spirit, within
> the womb of the Virgin.[67]

On the one hand, this teaching is hardly remarkable. It represents the standard orthodoxy of Christ as both human and divine. On the other hand, two
comments may be made. The first is how "Antiochene" Knox's language here
sounds; indeed, describing Jesus as "the human *person*" inhabited by the
Word has a Nestorian resonance. One might perhaps suspect this to have been
a sign of Chrysostom's influence, but in fact Chrysostom's Christology is much
more of the "Alexandrian" type. Nor does Knox's "Antiochene" language come

---

65   *Remains*, Vol. 2, pp. 44–153, 303–15, 316–436; Vol. 3, pp. 368–408.

66   Hornby, "Editor's Preface to the Third and Fourth Volumes," p. lxvii; *Remains*, Vol. 2, p. 318
      where Knox conflates the Authorized Version's rendering of 1 Timothy 3.16 with a phrase
      from the Nicene Creed (B. C. P., p. 182). For Knox's belief in the divinity of Christ, as an
      essential verity see *Remains*, Vol. 2, p. 325; Vol. 4, p. 237; and above, pp. 112–13. For his em-
      phasis on Christ's work see *Remains*, Vol. 2, pp. 26, 378–9; Vol. 3, pp. 389–94, 401, 405–8.

67   *Remains*, Vol. 2, pp. 224–25.

either from Wesley or the Cambridge Platonists, whose influence on him was
so important in other areas; they too are "Alexandrian" in the formulation of
their Christological teaching.[68] This leads to the second point: rather than re-
sorting to the technical theological terms of tradition when talking about the
person of Christ, Knox preferred to use language taken directly from the Bible,
something which can be seen as a trait of his theology generally.

With regard to the work of Christ, Knox was highly critical of the substitutionary model of atonement, and much of his soteriological writing was
motivated by the desire to refute it.[69] Central to the platform of nineteenth-
century Irish Evangelicalism, the substitutionary theory held that Christ had
put himself in the place of sinners and had satisfied the wrath of God against
them, on their behalf. Such was Knox's opposition to this view that he refused
to use the word "atonement," so often employed by Evangelicals, dismissing it
as *"slang."* "I have never used the term, and I suppose, never shall," he informed
Jebb curtly, in a letter written on Good Friday, 1821.[70] The substitutionary view
was, he believed, flawed on several counts. First, it was "liable to be so understood, as to obscure and sadden our views of the divine nature," appearing to
dwell more on the divine wrath and condemnation, rather than on God's forgiveness and love. Second, the doctrine seemed to derogate from "the essential
Godhead of the Son," appearing to present him as somehow less "awful" than
the Father, and more gracious and loving. Third, the doctrine had a "tendency
to damp the ardour of Christian virtue," since reliance for salvation was placed
on the past action of Christ rather than on the believer's actual "zeal for growing in grace." Fourth, the substitutionary theory was "either not known or not
adverted to from the close of the first century until the age of the Reformation."
It was "the doctrine of human theology, and not of Holy Scripture."[71] None of
this means that Knox rejected the *doctrine* of the atonement, which was a mistake often made by his contemporaries. Even his admirer Samuel O'Sullivan
believed that "he did not make [*sic*] sufficient account of the great doctrine
of the atonement," while Zachary Macaulay went so far as to claim that Knox

---

68   For "Alexandrian" and "Antiochene" Christologies see Grillmeier, *Christ in Christian
      Tradition*, though the differences do need to be nuanced. Knox is not a Nestorian.
      Elsewhere, one finds him describing the incarnation in more orthodox terms: *Remains*,
      Vol. 1, p. 330; Vol. 2, pp. 304–5. For John Wesley's Christology see Deschner, *John Wesley's
      Christology*; for the Christology of the Cambridge Platonists see Dockrill, "The Fathers and
      the Theology of the Cambridge Platonists."
69   *Remains*, Vol. 2, pp. 44–5, 316–17.
70   B. L., Add. Ms 41164, Correspondence between Alexander Knox and John Jebb (1811–30),
      fol. 158, Knox to John Jebb, letter, April 25, 1821 (emphasis in the original).
71   *Correspondence*, Vol. 2, p. 71; *Remains*, Vol. 2, pp. 308–9, 370, 354; Vol. 4, p. 468.

had stated: "The atonement has no place in my system."[72] In reality, however, Knox did not neglect the idea of the "sacrifice of Christ, in its expiatory aspect." What he maintained was that in Scripture the expiatory death of Christ was not "the main object of attention."[73] Rather, Scripture, according to Knox, was concerned with "the sacrifice of Christ ... neither merely, nor chiefly, in its expiation of guilt, but in its influential capacity to cleanse and sanctify the mind and heart." In defence of this thesis he repeatedly quoted Titus 2.14: "[Christ] gave himself for us, that he might redeem us from all iniquity, and purify unto himself a peculiar people, zealous of good works."[74] Basing himself on this passage, as well as on "countless others," Knox argued that "the great object of the Gospel is to bring the alienated mind of man back to God through the influential grace of the incarnate Messiah."[75] In making this claim, Knox distinguished between salvation and what he termed "salvability." "Salvability" he defined as the result of "what [Christ] did *for us*," in the past. Dying for us was, according to Knox, a "preliminary work" by which "the incarnate Word ... effected every requisite for man's salvation." In other words, through the cross Christ established the conditions necessary for human beings to be saved. These conditions were two in number: the possibility of pardon and the provision of grace. On account of Christ's death, "the gates of mercy" now stood open for the sinner to receive forgiveness of past sins; now grace was held "in constant readiness to flow into every willing heart."[76] Salvability was not, however, salvation. Salvation could be accomplished only when the individual came to Christ and received grace and mercy, here and now. "[We] must ourselves enter, and personally obtain the treasure; otherwise, what was done, once for all, on our behalf, shall, in our instance, have been done in vain."[77] Knox termed this personal participation in the work of Christ "actual salvation." It is "what [Christ] does *in us*;" "the inward life ... of effectual grace in the heart and mind," which Christ bestows, and by which human beings are changed and transformed. This is the μετάνοια [*metanoia*] of which Scripture speaks, which he defined, with reference to Acts 26.18, as the provision of grace "to enlighten [the mind] ... with a divine and saving knowledge, of what is true, and good;

---

72 *Dublin University Magazine*, 4.21 (September 1834), p. 260; *Christian Observer*, 37 (November 1837), p. 172. For Knox's statement, see also *Christian Observer*, new series, 6 (June 1838), p. 377. Zachary Macaulay (1768–1838) was a leading member of the Clapham Sect; see Hall, *Macaulay and Son*.
73 *Remains*, Vol. 2, p. 44.
74 Ibid., p. 93. For references to Titus 2.14, see: *Remains*, Vol. 2, p. 58; Vol. 3, pp. 5, 35, 163–4; Vol. 4, pp. 468, 508, 518.
75 *Remains*, Vol. 2, p. 63.
76 Ibid., p. 45 (emphasis in the original); Vol. 4, p. 468; Vol. 2, pp. 360–2 (echoing Hebrews 4, 16).
77 *Remains*, Vol. 2, p. 45.

to fill [the heart], with the love of it; and to furnish ... the power, to perform it."
In other words "that only, which [is] effected, through the omnipotent grace of
Christ, in the mind and heart, together with its everlasting results, [is] strictly
and properly *salvation*."[78] This salvation was accomplished, Knox contended,
through the power of divine attraction: "[T]he Word, which was in the beginning with God, and was God, became man, that he might act upon us with
fuller influence, and engage us by a more sympathetic attraction." "Godhead,"
Knox declared, "presents itself in human nature, in order to draw to itself ...
our predominant affection." For Knox, this was the great aim of the incarnation: the revelation of God to human beings, so that the divine nature might
be known by them. "The incarnation of the second Person is itself a provision
for dispelling all darkness of mind; 'for,' says our Lord, 'he that hath seen me,
hath seen the Father.' Duly to apprehend, therefore, the divine character of the
incarnate Word, is most truly to know him whom we worship."[79]

What we apprehend through the contemplation of the incarnate God is
"moral glory" or moral beauty, so engaging that it draws human beings to itself,
away from the lure of sin, Knox held. This beauty was manifested "through
the whole course of [Christ's] sojourning below," in "his incarnation, his birth,
his death, his resurrection." Its pre-eminent display, however, was on the cross:
there above all Christ was manifested as "the mental magnet of the world."
"[I]n that point, all the moral glories of the Incarnate Word are concentrated ...
comprehending and consummating all the perfections of his character." Drawn
to Christ by his moral beauty, the Christian is united to him and is then enabled
by this union to "not only love and obey him, but [to] become, in some sort,
as he himself was in this world;" to become, in other words, Christ's imitator.

> The affectionate apprehension of Christ crucified, cannot but conform
> us more and more to his spirit; and to be conformed to his spirit, is to
> participate in his conquest: by hating what Christ hated, and loving what
> Christ loved, we not only die with him unto sin, but rise again with him
> unto righteousness; and in the growth of this conformity, we ascend with
> him, more and more, into the heavens; and enter, with increasing depth
> and fullness, into the foretaste of that rest which remaineth for the peo-
> ple of God.[80]

---

78   Ibid., pp. 45, 47; *Correspondence*, Vol. 1, pp. 20–1; *Remains*, Vol. 2, p. 362 (emphases in the
      original).
79   *Remains*, Vol. 2 p. 318 (quoting John 1.1); Vol. 4, p. 309; Vol. 2, p. 314 (quoting John 14.9).
80   *Remains*, Vol. 2, pp. 305, 378, 381, 404–5, 379 (echoing 1 John 4.17). On p. 404 Knox echoes
      the Prayer Book service of baptism, as well as the collect for Ascension Day, B. C. P.,
      pp. 201, 122 and Hebrews 4.9.

In place of the forensic language employed by contemporary Evangelicalism, Knox frequently described the salvific process therapeutically. Rather than being a means whereby "threatened vengeance was averted," he portrayed the death of Christ as "the source of healing influence to the spirits of men," part of "a remedial and sanative plan." "[O]ur Redeemer declares himself the physician of souls … healing souls, as he healed bodies … by the exercise of his omnipotence; or, rather, by the effluence of his own essential virtue." Another image which Knox used, although much less frequently, was sustenance: Christ provided not only "medicine for the sick," but also "fit nourishment for the convalescent."[81]

Knox summed up his soteriology by saying: "[T]he grace, which reigns through righteousness, effects internal renovation … by spiritually assimilating us to Christ, in his death, and in his resurrection."[82] The word "grace" here is to be underlined, for grace is precisely what Knox meant by the transforming and assimilating influence which we have been describing. Grace was "not merely an exercise of divine favour, but, also of that divine energy, whereby God is able to subdue all things to himself."[83] This was why Knox constantly termed grace "effectual;" it worked an effect in the human heart.[84] No Pelagian, he regarded human nature as so wounded by sin that we can do nothing to save ourselves without the aid of God. "[G]race in my creed, is paramount." To quote Dickinson, "[N]o one felt more entirely [than Knox] that divine grace was the immediate and efficient cause of every permanent improvement."[85] Nonetheless, Knox was no monergist, either. "[M]an himself must be a worker together with God," he affirmed. Concomitantly, he also taught that grace can be resisted.[86]

---

81   *Remains*, Vol. 2, p. 57; *Correspondence*, Vol. 1, p. 483; *Remains*, Vol. 2, p. 320; *Correspondence*, Vol. 1, p. 121. For examples of the healing metaphor applied to salvation see *Remains*, Vol. 2, pp. 346, 382, 385, 388–9, 394, 398; *Correspondence*, Vol. 2, p. 70. For examples of the metaphor of sustenance see *Remains*, Vol. 2, pp. 58, 402.

82   *Remains*, Vol. 2, p. 70 (alluding to Romans, 5.21).

83   *Remains*, Vol. 2, p. 65 (alluding to Philippians, 3.21). See also Bodleian, Ms. Eng. lett. d. 124, "Letters to C. A. Ogilvie, K-Z," fols. 85–87, Knox to C. A. Ogilvie, letter, January 23, 1827, where Knox castigates the view that grace means only God's "favour and benefit," and not "the assistance of the Holy Spirit," an infusion of spiritual life and strength from above (fol. 87).

84   For examples of the phrase "effectual grace" see *Remains*, Vol. 1, pp. 91, 158, 516, 524; Vol. 2, pp. 47, 67, 348, 468, 478–9; Vol. 3, pp. 20, 86; Vol. 4, pp. 60, 493.

85   *Remains*, Vol. 1, p. 368. *Christian Examiner*, 11.73 (July 1831), p. 563. For examples of Knox's teaching on the necessity of grace see *Remains*, Vol. 1, p. 379; Vol. 2, pp. 320, 470–1, 482–3; Vol. 3, pp. 36, 86, 434, 449; Vol. 4, pp. 352, 457; *Correspondence*, Vol. 1, p. 381.

86   *Remains*, Vol. 2, p. 361; *Wesley*, p. 473.

In Knox's writings the experience of grace was an implicit argument for the divinity of Christ. "[T]he religion, which the grace of Christ establishes in the mind and heart, expels every wrong, and satisfies every right desire," he affirmed. In this way, by his grace Christ fills the "void in the human bosom," a lack and a longing which only God could remedy. But also, for Knox, it is through the experience of grace that one comes to know Christ, and knowing him, one discovers him to be divine. "[The] present operations of redeeming grace," he wrote, "by producing felt effects, imply experimental acquaintance, not only with the blessing communicated, but with the living source from which it is derived."[87] As well as appealing to experience, Knox invoked the witness of Scripture in support of his Christology, and with it "the language of the Catholic Church."[88] Although there were important differences between Knox's soteriological teaching and that of both Wesley and the moderates, there were also substantial similarities and we may postulate that Wesley and the moderates contributed to the formulation of Knox's thought in this area as in so many others.[89] The same can be said with regard to the teaching of the Fathers, especially Clement of Alexandria, Pseudo-Macarius, and Chrysostom, with whose soteriology Knox shares several striking parallels. Clement, for example, often employs a therapeutic metaphor for salvation, as when he speaks of Christ as "our teacher, the Word [who] cures the spiritual sickness of our souls by his admonitions ... The Word of the Father, he alone is the healer of human illness, the holy physician of the sick soul ... The good Teacher, who is the Wisdom, the Logos of the Father, the maker of humanity, cures the whole of his creation, healing both soul and body ... He is the physician of human nature, the Savior."[90]

For Clement, as for Knox, this healing is a present reality and like Knox, Clement (in the words of one nineteenth-century commentator) paid scant attention to "the mystery of the Agony and the Passion on the Cross."[91] The same is true for Pseudo-Macarius. To cite Maloney, Pseudo-Macarius was concerned "not so much [with] what Jesus has done [for us] in his lifetime ... but [with] what he is now doing for us and with us by his gloriously risen life within us." Or, in the words of Andrew Louth, Pseudo-Macarius was "more interested in what the Incarnation makes possible now than in what happened in the past." Pseudo-Macarius, too, used the image of Christ as healer. Thus, for

---

87   *Remains*, Vol. 2, pp. 323, 321, 48.
88   Ibid., p. 321.
89   See above, 66–67, 85–86.
90   Clement, *Paedagogus*, 1, 2, *P. G.*, 8, col. 256. For the image of Christ the healer in Clement, see Dörnemann, *Krankheit und Heilung*, pp. 101–120.
91   Hitchcock, *Clement of Alexandria*, p. 223.

example, pointing to the woman with the issue of blood, he wrote: "[J]ust as the woman … touched the hem of the garment of the Lord and immediately received a healing and the flow of the unclean fountain of blood dried up, so everyone afflicted by the incurable wound of sin, the fountain of unclean and evil thoughts, if he only approaches Christ and begs prayerfully and truly believes in him, receives a salvific healing." "Let us, therefore," Pseudo-Macarius concludes, "believe in him and approach him in truth, so that he may speedily bring us to full and authentic health."[92]

In Chrysostom there are numerous passages which proclaim the salutary effects of the cross.[93] But, as in Wesley and the moderates, there is in Chrysostom what Jean-Marie Leroux describes as "a tension between salvation acquired once for all in principle, and the ontological necessity for human beings to bring that salvation to completion." As Leroux explains, Chrysostom believed that "God has willed to associate human beings in the work of their own salvation."[94] Thus, as we have seen, Chrysostom's preaching focused not so much on the death of Christ as on the present work of salvation carried out with the help of his grace.[95]

5   Pneumatology

Knox's pneumatology forms a pair with his Christology, since for him the Spirit is the joint-agent with Christ in the work of salvation. What he terms the Spirit's "influence and inspiration" is a topic of fundamental importance to the Christian faith, a "catholic verity, equally insisted on by the sacred word, and equally embraced by the Christian cloud of witnesses."[96] The passages where Knox deals specifically with the topic are: the start of his "Postscript to the Treatise on the Eucharist;" part of his treatise "On the Nature of our Salvation through Christ;" and his "Letter on the Personality of the Holy Spirit," all of which are undated.[97] His treatment of the subject provides a good illustration of his theological method. He reasons from several sources: what "is so repeatedly

---

92   Maloney, *Pseudo-Macarius*, pp. 19–20; Louth, *Origins of the Christian Mystical Tradition*, p. 120; Maloney, *Pseudo-Macarius*, pp. 151, 153 (punctuation slightly modified). For the parable alluded to, see Matthew 9.20.
93   See Nowak, *Le Chrétien devant la Souffrance*, pp. 108–37, where he gives a very comprehensive summary of Chrysostom's soteriological views.
94   Leroux, *"Jean Chrysostome et Le Monarchisme,"* pp. 130–1.
95   See above, pp. 79–80.
96   *Remains*, Vol. 2, p. 325.
97   Ibid., pp. 250–62, 325–36; Vol. 3, pp. 419–26.

asserted, and so emphatically dwelt upon, in Holy Scripture;" from what is taught by "all the ... luminaries of the Catholic Church;" and from experience, "the agency of the Divine Spirit ... discerned."[98] Knox understood the "Holy Spirit" (or "Holy Ghost") in the traditional sense as not simply a divine influence, but "a Divine Person," "the third person of the Trinity," who shares "the essential Godhead" of the Father and the Son.[99] Although already at work in the world prior to the Incarnation, and active during the ministry of Christ, nonetheless, "in a certain peculiar and eminent sense, the Holy Ghost was not given until the Lord Jesus Christ was glorified."[100] This was because the manner in which the Spirit was to act "under the Gospel dispensation" was to be "more excellent and effective" than any of its "former operations:" from henceforth, the Spirit was to work with the Son in fulfilling the divine plan of salvation. The grace by which Christ drew and attracted Christians was, wrote Knox, "communicated through the influence of that other Comforter, who, according to our Redeemer's promise, was to abide with the church for ever [*sic*]." As Knox put it elsewhere, Christ "associated with himself ... the third person of the ever-blessed Trinity – the Holy Ghost, the Comforter – to be his fellow-worker, within the depth of the human spirit: creating, by his omnipotent operation, in the inner man a capacity of imbibing the rays of the Sun of Righteousness."[101]

This quotation serves to underline why Knox frequently spoke of the Holy Spirit as the "Spirit of Christ." No other title, according to him, better expressed the Spirit's "evangelical character," the way in which the Spirit was, with Christ, the conjoint agent of human salvation.[102] This accent on the Spirit's agency

---

98   Ibid., Vol. 2, p. 326; Vol. 3, p. 425; Vol. 2, p. 331. For Knox's methodology, see above, chapter 7.

99   *Remains*, Vol. 3, p. 423; Vol. 2, pp. 256, 330.

100   Ibid., Vol. 2, p. 251 (alluding to John 7.39). For the activity of the Spirit prior to Pentecost, see: *Remains*, Vol. 2, pp. 250, 260–1; *Correspondence*, Vol. 2, pp. 360–1.

101   *Remains*, Vol. 2, pp. 251, 340 (alluding to John 14.16), 361 (alluding to the *Te Deum*, part of the Prayer Book service of Morning Prayer, *B. C. P.*, p. 34, and to Malachi 4.2). Knox's use of the term "dispensation" may be noted, though in his theology it hardly has the importance which it was later to receive through the elaborations of John Nelson Darby (1800–82). See Sweetnam and Gribben, "J. N. Darby and the Irish Origins of Dispensationalism." The term is present in Wesley, and played an important part in the theology of his disciple, John Fletcher (1729–85), a point made to me by Randy Maddox in a personal communication, January 23, 2012. For Wesley's teaching, see Frazier, "John Wesley's Covenantal and Dispensational View of Salvation History;" and for Fletcher's, Frazier, "The Doctrine of Dispensations in the Thought of John William Fletcher (1792–85)."

102   *Remains*, Vol. 3, p. 325 (punctuation slightly altered); Vol. 2, p. 258. See, also Vol. 2, pp. 256–7.

served to balance Knox's "Abelardian" understanding of the cross. Taken on its own, his idea that the cross attracts and draws souls could be seen as indicating something purely subjective, a reaction which springs from the human heart alone. Knox, however, was keen to stress that this is not at all the case. The heart acts under the influence of the Holy Spirit. "[A]s the loadstone attracts and assimilates, not every metal, but that metal only which is congenial," so Christ effectually draws to himself only those whom the Holy Spirit has made susceptible to his influence.[103] And, like the loadstone, the Spirit not only attracts, but also assimilates. Uniting believers to Christ, and, dwelling in their heart, the Spirit enables Christians to imitate their Lord. "Deity itself becomes, as it were, an animating principle within us." This indwelling animation was the proper work and office of the Holy Spirit. For if "each person of the ever-blessed Trinity is ... actively concurring in our spiritual restoration ... [s]till, however, there appears to be a sense in which the Holy Spirit of God enters into the mind, and actuates the powers of cordial Christians by an allotment, as it were, peculiar to himself, among the divine persons." It is this grace of the in-dwelling Spirit, purifying Christians from sin and strengthening them in holiness, which constituted "the special and peculiar blessing of the Gospel," the agency by which "the leading object of the Christian Religion" is accomplished, namely that human beings "'might be partakers of the divine nature.'"[104]

Gladstone described Knox's teaching as nothing other than the unfolding and explication of that "little-considered and ill-comprehended clause ... 'I believe in the Holy Ghost, the Lord, and *Giver of Life.*'"[105] But also, I would maintain, it is nothing other than the Christian Platonic doctrine of deification. In the Platonic tradition, the role of the Spirit is vital, and we see this in the teaching of those whom Knox portrayed as being the tradition's standard-bearers. Wesley set out the whole Christian life as the work of inspiration, in the sense of "God's breathing into the soul." For him, it was "the power of the Holy Ghost" which alone enabled human beings "to believe and love and serve God."[106] For the moderates, too, the Spirit's role was essential: we have already

103   Ibid., Vol. 2, p. 106.
104   Ibid., Vol. 2, pp. 328, 327, 259; Vol. 3, p. 13 (quoting 2 Peter 1.4).
105   B. L., Add. Ms 44724, Gladstone Papers, DCXXXIX, fols. 73–76, "memorandum," May 24, 1835, fol. 73, (alluding to the Nicene Creed; emphasis in the original).
106   Wesley, *Instructions for Children*, p. 10; Wesley, Sermon 19, "The Great Privilege of those that are born of God," 3, 2, in Outler, ed., *Works of John Wesley*, Vol. 1, pp. 431–43, at p. 442. For a detailed introduction to Wesley's pneumatology, see Starkey, *The Work of the Holy Spirit*, and Lessmann, *Rolle und Bedeutung*. As noted above, one of the influences on Wesley's pneumatology was John Pearson, and both Wesley and Pearson doubtless helped shape Knox's understanding of the Spirit's importance. (See above, p. 63.)

seen the emphasis which they placed on its work in the Christian life. What we
may note now is that the stress which Knox placed on the title "Spirit of Christ,"
which occurs only twice in the New Testament (Romans 8.9 and 1 Peter 1.11),
may be indicative of the impact which the moderates' pneumatology had on
him, given that they employed it habitually. In the Fathers, too, the role of the
Spirit is central. Certainly, pneumatology was shaped into its orthodox expression only during the latter part of the fourth century, but nonetheless, the doctrine of the Spirit existed prior to this in an inchoate form, as Clement shows.
For, although Clement so closely associated "Word" and "Spirit," that he has
been seen as identifying the two, with the result that his theology has been described as "Binitarian," yet, as G. L. Prestige has pointed out, "from the middle
of the first century the same people were both Binitarians and Trinitarians."
As H. E. W. Turner argues, there is no reason to believe that "those who
worked normally with a Binitarian phrasing in their theology were other than
Trinitarian in their religion." "Christians lived Trinitarianly before the doctrine
of the Trinity began to be thought out conceptually," Turner argues.[107] However
Clement may have understood the nature of the Spirit, he made its activity a
vital part of his teaching, as we have already seen.[108] The same was true of
Pseudo-Macarius who gave, as Maloney says, an "eminent role ... to the action
of the Holy Spirit." For him, the Spirit was "the life of the soul." He described
the Christian as "a pure dwelling-place for the adorable and Holy Spirit from
whom he receives the immortal peace of Christ, through whom he is joined
and united with the Lord." "[O]ne who has found and possesses within himself
the heavenly treasure of the Spirit fulfils all the commands justly and practices
all the virtues without blame," Pseudo-Macarius proclaims. "Let us, therefore,"
he continues, "beg God, seeking and praying him to gift us with the treasure
of the Spirit in order that we may be empowered to walk in all his commands
without blame and purely."[109] In Chrysostom, too, the role of the Spirit was
paramount. In particular one may note how, like Knox, he highlights the way in
which the Spirit works together with Christ. "For it is impossible," Chrysostom
says, "that the Spirit being present, Christ should not be present, too. For where
one Person of the Trinity is, there is the whole Trinity. For they are altogether inseparable, and strictly united." Through the Spirit's agency, therefore, Christ is
present in believers, "not," Chrysostom clarified, "because the Spirit is Christ –
but rather, because whoever has the Spirit not only belongs to Christ, but

---

107   Prestige, *God in Patristic Thought*, p. xxiii; Turner, *Pattern of Christian Truth*, pp. 134–5, 474.
108   See above, p. 77.
109   Maloney, *Pseudo-Macarius*, pp. 12, 192, 269, 142.

possesses Christ."[110] Thus, although Knox does not appeal in his pneumatology to any specific writer, these Fathers, together with Wesley and the moderates, were no doubt among those to whom he was referring, when he invoked, in his teaching on the Spirit, "the luminaries of the Catholic Church."

As with all his theology, Knox believed that what he wrote about the Spirit was nothing other than the doctrine of the Church of England. The Church, Knox wrote, "earnestly" maintained that "from the first to the last step of our Christian course, we can accomplish nothing effectually by our own power, but must obtain both the implantation and the increase of every pure principle, of every right temper, and of every spiritual affection, from the grace of God, and of the Lord Jesus Christ, infused into us by the operation of the Holy Ghost."[111] This operation of the Holy Ghost is something which appears throughout the Prayer Book, which constantly refers, in the words of the Catechism, to the Spirit's work of "[sanctifying] ... all the elect people of God." One might cite, for example, the Collect for Purity, which describes Christians' hearts being cleansed by the inspiration of the Spirit; or, the Collect for Christmas Day, which portrays Christians as being "daily renewed by [the] Holy Spirit;" or the Collect for the First Sunday of Lent, which asks that the "flesh being subdued to the Spirit," believers may "ever obey thy godly motions in righteousness, and true holiness."[112]

6   Conclusion

In this chapter, we have looked, first, at Knox's doctrine of God. Knox does not discuss the arguments for God's existence, taking it as a given; nor does he have much to say about the divine attributes, except to stress the love of God for human beings. In an age where Trinitarianism was under attack, he upheld belief in the three divine persons as a vital catholic truth, seeing it as essential to salvation. From Knox's doctrine of God we moved, secondly, to his anthropology. Knox conceived of human beings in dualist terms, as composed of body and spirit, but it was on the latter that he focused most attention, especially concentrating on the affections, by which he meant primarily love, through which we are united to God. This union was for Knox the source of human happiness, and he laid great emphasis on the idea that in Christianity alone human beings could find fulfilment. He conceived of sin not in terms

---

110   Chrysostom, "Homily 13 on Romans," 8, *P. G.*, 60, col. 518–19.
111   *Remains*, Vol. 2, p. 272.
112   *B. C. P.*, pp. 213; 180; 63; 83.

of guilt to be punished, but of misery to be assuaged. He had a strong sense of human depravity, acknowledgment of which he deemed necessary to the spiritual life, but this depravity was not total; a person still had the ability to seek salvation. Thirdly, the chapter examined Knox's Christology. As a practical theologian, Knox gave priority to the work of Christ, rather than speculating about his person. He strenuously rejected the doctrine of substitutionary atonement, although this does not mean that the cross played no part in his thinking. Rather, he saw it as effecting what he termed "salvability," the conditions, that is, which make salvation possible. And by salvation he meant the work of Christ in human beings now, transforming their hearts by his grace. The latter, Knox defined in terms of divine attraction: the Incarnate God drew human beings to himself by his moral beauty. Knox closely joins the Spirit to Christ, and so from Knox's Christology we moved to his pneumatology. A strict Trinitarian, as we have seen, Knox taught that the Spirit was the third person of the Godhead. Working with Christ, the Spirit attracted human beings, but also became an "animating principle" within them, assimilating them to Christ, a teaching which is nothing other than the doctrine of *theosis*.

Our investigation of Knox's theology continues to confirm the portrait which we have been painting of him. He reflected the concerns and interests of the age in which he lived; he echoed, and often appealed to, the teaching of Wesley and the Anglican moderates, as well as that of Fathers, not least those whom he saw as being exemplars of the Platonic tradition, Clement, Pseudo-Macarius, and Chrysostom. Above all, however, Knox's theology reveals his Anglicanism. Often, he explicitly stated that his wish was simply to enunciate the teaching of the Church to which he belonged; always, one may discern the influence of that Church on the doctrines which he propounded. We will continue to see the same thing in the next chapter, in which we will examine Knox's teaching on justification and perfection, a teaching which shows the depth of Knox's Trinitarianism. For Knox, salvation did not simply originate in the philanthropic love of the triune God, nor was it simply accomplished through the activity of Father, Son, and Holy Spirit, but, above all, its aim and goal was the participation of human beings in their divine life.

CHAPTER 9

Alexander Knox's Theology (II): Justification and Perfection

We come now to the heart of "Mr. Knox's System," the doctrine of justification, and its concomitant, perfection. We will examine both of these topics in turn, in each case looking at the influences which helped to mould Knox's thought.

1 Justification

Knox dealt with justification in a number of treatises: "On Justification" (1810); "On the Leading Design of the Christian Dispensation" (undated); "On Redemption and Salvation by Christ" (undated); the "Letter to Major Woodward on Doctrinal Points" (1807); the "Letter to Mrs. Hannah More, shewing [*sic*] the theology of the New Testament not to be Calvinistic" (1807); and the "Letter to the Rev. James J. Hornby, on some passages in the epistle to the Romans" (1828). There is also a detailed letter on the subject in the *Correspondence*, dated February 25, 1818.[1] For Knox, justification was a matter of vital significance, "one of the most deeply practical questions that can interest the heart." In fact, it was for him *the* question; as he told Jebb in 1827, a few years before his death, his thoughts on this subject were "more important, than any others which have passed through my mind."[2] The reason for this was that by "justification" Knox understood "salvation." He shared this understanding with most western Christians, as a result of the Protestant Reformers' insistence that justification by faith alone is the *articulus stantis vel cadentis ecclesiae*, the point on which Christianity stands or falls. In response, the Roman Catholic Church, which up until then had paid scant attention to the topic, formulated its own doctrine *de iustificatione* at the sixth session of the Council of Trent in 1547. The issue thereafter continued to be a matter of dispute between Roman Catholics and Protestants, especially Protestants of evangelical convictions. It also, however, became a cause of conflict within Anglicanism, where it was one of the major

---

1 *Remains*, Vol. 1, pp. 281–317; Vol. 2, pp. 13–43, 44–153; Vol. 3, pp. 15–41, 71–102, 443–56; *Correspondence*, Vol. 2, pp. 349–55. For the topic of justification in general, see McGrath, *Iustitia Dei*.

2 *Remains*, Vol. 2, p. 90; *Correspondence*, Vol. 2, p. 532.

differences between Evangelicals and 'orthodox' (in Knox's language). All of this stands in the background to Knox's treatment of the subject and helps to explain why he used the word "justification." He was not starting his theology afresh, in which case he might have adopted a different term; he was joining an on-going debate. In so doing, however, one of the things that he was seeking to accomplish was an elucidation of what the New Testament has to say about salvation, and this involved using the language of justification, at least with regard to the Pauline corpus.

Knox regarded justification as "one of the most perplexing controversies which ever yet divided honest members of the Christian church."[3] Nonetheless, his own views were clear. He trenchantly rejected the contemporary Evangelical theory of a purely forensic, imputed justification, or, "reputative" justification, as he also termed it.[4] This was the teaching that justification meant, in the words of one of Ireland's leading early nineteenth-century Evangelicals, J. T. O'Brien, *"a judicial declaration of the innocence of the person justified."* This declaration was made by God, so the theory held, because the penalty incurred on account of sin had been paid by Jesus Christ, through his suffering and death on the cross, a payment which one could make one's own through faith. At the same time, the theory held, God accounted believing sinners righteous, attributing to them the righteousness of Christ, perfectly displayed throughout his life on earth. For Evangelicals, the doctrine was (to quote O'Brien again) a "fundamental doctrine of the Gospel of Christ," of "vital importance to true religion," "a truth, to which all truth – even all revealed truth, must be felt to be subordinate."[5] For Knox, by contrast, it was "the grand error of the present religious world;" "one of the greatest hindrances to the diffusion of true religion in the world, as well as to the growth of it in the individual."[6]

Knox rejected it, first, because he feared that it led to antinomianism, the idea that, because one is justified by faith, and not by works, the latter are irrelevant to the Christian life. It was a concern which strongly marked John Wesley, and this was no doubt where Knox first encountered it. Nonetheless, such concern was not unique to Wesley, being widespread in the early part of the nineteenth century. For example, the High Churchman Richard Mant cautioned against what he termed "the dangerous consequences, to which the doctrine of faith alone is calculated to lead carnal minds" and made this

---

3 *Remains*, Vol. 2, p. 90.
4 For examples of Knox's use of this term, see: *Remains*, Vol. 1, pp. 290–1, 298–9; Vol. 2, p. 23; *Correspondence*, Vol. 2, p. 353.
5 O'Brien, *Justification*, 1st edition, pp. 62 (emphasis in the original), 14 (format slightly altered), 61, 141–2. For O'Brien, see above, p. 4.
6 *Remains*, Vol. 1, p. 81; Vol. 3, p. 93.

warning one of the chief themes of his 1812 Bampton Lectures. One also finds this concern among moderate Evangelicals. The *Christian Observer*, for example, spoke in 1803 of "[i]ncautious positions, on the side of free grace, [which] feed the Antinomian's distemper."[7] Similarly, Henry Ryder, the first Evangelical to be raised to the English episcopate, devoted a major portion of his 1816 charge to the threat of antinomianism.[8] For Knox, however, even moderate Evangelicals, such as Ryder, were at risk, not of rejecting holiness, but of ignoring it. Insisting on what Knox termed a "doctrinal" or "dogmatic" religion, involving nothing more than an act of intellectual apprehension (belief in Christ's saving death), Evangelicals neglected to cultivate a "life of deep and habitual devotion," he argued. "[The] notion of a forensic and imputative salvation, seems to have weakened ... concern for the one thing needful," he alleged. It produced instead a "weak and struggling piety," the antithesis of "the real import of Evangelical doctrine ... the supreme design of the Gospel," which he deemed to be the zealous pursuit of sanctity.[9] Moreover, Knox contended, justification by faith alone was absent from the Bible, as well as from "the quod ubique, quod semper, quod ab omnibus creditum est," and unknown to any writer "during the fourteen centuries which preceded Luther and Calvin."[10] Nor, when the German and Swiss Reformers first enunciated their new doctrine, did the "Anglican Reformed Church" follow them. "[A]n exclusively forensic justification" could not "be regarded as the doctrine either of the Liturgy, the Articles, or the Homilies of the Church of England." In fact, he wrote to C. A. Ogilvie, there could not be an opinion "more contrary to ... our truly catholic formularies."[11]

In place of a purely forensic justification, Knox advocated a doctrine of ontological, imparted justification: "moral justification, rather than reputative justification."[12] "Moral" here means having a moral effect. As Knox explained: "[T]o be justified ... is to be made righteous in mind and heart, through the effectual grace of Our Lord Jesus Christ."[13] It is important to realize that, in asserting this, Knox did not jettison the notion of imputed justification. He wanted to be faithful to the position held by the Church of England, and it, he

---

7   Mant, *Appeal to the Gospel*, p. 105; *Christian Observer*, 2.7 (July 1803), p. 431. For Richard Mant (1776–1848), see *O. D. N. B.*
8   For Ryder (1777–1836) and his *Charge*, see Smith, "Henry Ryder."
9   *Remains*, Vol. 2, p. 364; Vol. 4, p. 587; Vol. 1, pp. 268, 353; Vol. 4, p. 518; Vol. 1, p. 361.
10   Ibid., Vol. 3, pp. 99–100; Vol. 1, p. 316; Vol. 4, p. 376; Vol. 1, p. 268.
11   Ibid., Vol. 1, pp. 289, 298; Bodleian, Ms. Eng. lett. d. 124, "Letters to C. A. Ogilvie, K-Z," fols. 85–87, Knox to C.A. Ogilvie, letter, January 23, 1827, fol. 87.
12   *Remains*, Vol. 1, p. 291.
13   Ibid, Vol. 2, p. 33.

believed, had developed the teaching of the Fathers, for whom justification was purely "moral," "by recognizing the reputative, as well as the efficient part of justification." The two went together, in Knox's estimation: "reputative" justification was, for him, the consequence of the sinner's "efficient" justification. In other words, for Knox, God made human beings righteous, and then reputed them righteous.

> [O]ur being reckoned righteous coram Deo (before God), always, and essentially, implies a substance of Δικαιοσύνη [*Dikaiosynē*] (righteousness), previously implanted in us ... [O]ur reputative justification is the strict and inseparable result of this previous efficient moral justification. I mean that the reckoning of us righteous, indispensably presupposes an inward reality of righteousness, on which this reckoning is founded.

Knox added the caveat that any notion of temporality in the divine act of justification was an accommodation to human limitations. "What God speaks, he performs," Knox remarked, and, therefore, he asked: "In Him, whose word is Omnipotence, can we form any other than the most merely figurative distinction between what he says and what he does?"[14]

Knox spoke of justification by faith. There was for him, however, no dichotomy between faith and works; they were inseparable: the one was the root, the other the fruit, an image which he perhaps derived from the Thirty-Nine Articles, which describe good works as springing out "necessarily of a true and lively faith, insomuch that by them a lively faith may be as evidently known as a tree is discerned by the fruit." Another, more striking, metaphor which Knox employed was faith being "pregnant" with good works, which he may have derived from Robert Boyle.[15] Whichever metaphor he used, however, faith for Knox was always productive of good works, because of his understanding of faith as knowledge of God; and "rightly to know [God] is to love him ... the one is the infinitely certain result of the other." One cannot help but be

---

14   *Remains*, Vol. 1, pp. 308, 299; 306; Vol. 2, p. 148; Vol. 3, p. 102.

15   For the metaphor of faith and works as root and fruit, see: *Remains*, Vol. 3, pp. 56, 85; *Correspondence*, Vol. 2, pp. 352–53. For the image in the Thirty-Nine Articles, see B. C. P., p. 399. For the metaphor of faith pregnant with good works, see *Remains*, Vol. 3, p. 34. The phrase is often attributed to Calvin, but seems to have originated with the Roman Catholic martyr-bishop John Fisher (1469–1535); see Laemmer, *Die Vortridentinisch-Katholische Theologie*, p. 145. For Boyle's use of the image, see *Some Motives and Incentives to the Love of God*, fourth edition (1665), p. 76: "[T]rue faith ... be ever the pregnant mother of good works."

drawn towards the beauty and goodness of the deity which faith reveals, Knox insisted.[16] He summed up this doctrine by saying:

> We have here ... beyond controversy, the true nature of justifying faith. It is such obedience, from the heart, to the objective faith of the Gospel, – in other words, such an affectionate reception of the divine facts and principles which the gospel propounds, – as alters the course, changes the character, and morally renovates the man: this is, self-evidently, obedience unto righteousness, or ... "believing with the heart unto righteousness."[17]

Not surprisingly, Knox's doctrine of justification proved highly controversial. The main criticism came from Evangelicals. They censured him for denying what they saw as the Bible's most basic doctrine, a doctrine which, they believed, the English Reformers had fervently championed. Thus, they argued, Knox's position, far from representing the teaching of the Church of England, was, in fact, "exactly analogous to that of the decrees of the council of Trent."[18] The charge did not perturb Knox. He wrote:

> I doubt really whether, on the point of justification, the Romish language is not much more scriptural and rational [than that of Protestants], as it involves in that term not the mere accounting, but also the making righteous; which, when ascribed solely to Divine grace, is so far from being, in my mind, an erroneous idea, that I think the scriptural meaning of justification strictly requires it.[19]

What was this "Romish language?" After much debate on the subject, the Council of Trent had decreed in 1547 that justification consisted "not only in the remission of sins, but also in sanctification and interior renovation, through the voluntary reception of graces and gifts, whence from being unrighteous a person is made righteous." "God makes us righteous," the Council declared; "we are not only reputed righteous, but are truly so called and are righteous," through "the love of God poured into [our] hearts by the Holy Spirit." Certainly, the Council admitted, Scripture speaks of justification by faith, but it also teaches that "faith without works is dead and barren," which is

---

16   *Remains*, Vol. 3, p. 165. For Knox's understanding of faith, see above, p. 138.
17   *Remains*, Vol. 2, pp. 74–5. The closing quotation comes from Romans 10.10.
18   *Christian Examiner*, 3.36 (October 1834), p. 699. See also 2.26 (Supplement 1837), pp. 821–2. G. S. Faber makes the assertion repeatedly in his *Primitive Doctrine of Justification*; see, e.g., pp. vi, xviii, 30, 47–8.
19   *Remains*, Vol. 4, p. 305.

why faith is to be understood as "the beginning of human salvation, the foundation and root of all righteousness." From this beginning, the Council continued, the justified "advancing from virtue to virtue, and renewed, as the Apostle says, day by day ... grow in the righteousness that they have received." Knox's doctrine accorded with this teaching: the only major point on which he and Trent disagreed was merit. Trent held that good works were meritorious and would therefore be rewarded by God, a concept Knox ignored.[20] It is perhaps the proximity of Knox's thought to the Tridentine decrees, rather than to the Anglican formularies, which led to his views on justification to be criticised not only by Evangelicals, but also by High Churchmen. Gladstone, for instance, taxed Knox with "what it is scarcely safe or right to characterise as anything less than a serious error: his denial of forensic justification," which Gladstone regarded as a departure both from the teaching of Scripture and of the Church of England. Similar concerns were raised in the *British Critic*, which declared Knox's views on justification to be "somewhat startling." Reviewing the first two volumes of the *Remains*, it described his position as "at least partially erroneous." A portion of his error, according to the reviewer, lay in the fact that both St. Paul and, following him, the Church of England, describe justification primarily in terms of the imputed rather than imparted righteousness, thus marking a clear distinction between justification and sanctification.[21]

2   **Sources of Knox's Doctrine of Justification**

Knox saw his teaching on justification as that "that which is maintained throughout the New Testament," not least by St. Paul. "I wish to understand this term [justification], exactly as St. Paul uses it," he told Jebb.[22] He thus turned to philology, arguing that words ending in -οσύνη [*-osynē*] "express actual and personal habits, rooted in the mind, and manifested in the conduct."[23] He also argued exegetically, maintaining that when Paul used δικαιοσύνη [*dikaiosynē*,

---

20   Council of Trent, *Decretum de Iustificatione*, chapters 7, 8, 10, 16 (D. S., paras. 1528–1532, 1535, 1545–46), translation mine. For the debate over justification at Trent, see Jedin, *History*, Vol. 2, pp. 166–96, 234–67, 283–316.

21   B. L., Add. Ms 44724, Gladstone Papers, DCXXXIX, fols. 73–76, "memorandum," May 24, 1835 (emphasis in the original), fols. 74–75; *British Critic*, 23.45 (January 1838), p. 1; *British Critic*, 17.34 (April 1835), p. 262.

22   *Remains*, Vol. 3, p. 87; *Correspondence*, Vol. 2, p. 353.

23   *Remains*, Vol. 1, p. 303. "It is not true," replied O'Brien (*Justification*, 3rd edition, p. 566). More gently, the *British Critic* remarked: "Philology was not altogether Mr. Knox's strongest point" (27.34 April 1835, p. 270).

righteousness] and its cognates, he employed them in a "moral" sense, that is, in relation to a real moral change wrought in the heart and life of the believer. For example, Knox claimed that, when Paul says in Romans 9.30–31 that the Gentiles have obtained righteousness through faith, while the Jews did not obtain it through the Law, he must have been talking about a moral righteousness. For, Knox contended, the righteousness that the Law offered was evidently a moral righteousness, therefore the righteousness that comes by faith must be moral, too.[24] Or, again, Knox held, Paul contrasts righteousness with sin; but sin is a moral condition, therefore righteousness must be moral, also.[25] Another example: Paul speaks about ὑπακοὴ πίστεως, [*hypakoē pisteōs*, the obedience of faith]. The inculcation of this obedience was, Knox claimed, "the great purpose of [Paul's] mission" as an apostle, showing "briefly, yet conclusively" that this mission "was strictly and essentially of a moral nature," for obedience, Knox reasoned, "is a moral habit of mind and heart."[26] In defence of his teaching, Knox adduced the authority of John Wesley. Knox claimed that Wesley "regarded justification neither merely nor chiefly as a forensic acquittal in the court of heaven; but as implying also a *conscious liberation from moral thraldom.*" Wesley's insistence on the necessity of holiness for salvation made it "impossible for him to endure the solifidian system," Knox contended. Rather, according to Knox, Wesley connected "faith so directly and exclusively with holiness, as to make the former nothing but the root and principle of the latter." "This," Knox wrote, "is John Wesley's central lesson ... the vital spirit of [his] true mission."[27] A number of modern scholars share the same understanding of Wesley's stance on justification and it is well supported by an examination of his writings.[28] Even during his most evangelical "middle" period, Wesley spoke of "faith, holiness and good works" being connected as "the root, the tree and the fruit." Although he denied that justification and sanctification were the same thing, he insisted that "pardon, the forgiveness of sins," which is how he defined justification, was inseparable from sanctification, or "being made actually just and righteous."[29] As he put it in a sermon preached in 1790, the year before his death, "[S]ome have supposed that when I began to declare,

---

24   *Remains*, Vol. 2, pp. 34–5.
25   Ibid., pp. 29–30.
26   Ibid., p. 18.
27   *Wesley*, pp. 420, 448; *Remains*, Vol. 1, pp. 181–82 (emphasis in the original).
28   See, for example: Cragg, ed., *Works of John Wesley*, Vol. 11, p. 16; Maddox, *Responsible Grace*, pp. 84–85, 152; Rack, *Reasonable Enthusiast*, pp. 390–93; Outler, ed., *Works of John Wesley*, Vol. 1, pp. 80–81, 181–82, 323, note 43.
29   Wesley, *Journal*, Vol. 2, p. 265, entry for August 30, 1739; Sermon 5, "Justification by Faith," 2, 5; 2, 1, in Outler, ed., *Works of John Wesley*, Vol. 1, pp. 181–99, at pp. 189, 187.

'By grace ye are saved, through faith' [Ephesians 2, 8], I retracted what I had before maintained: 'Without holiness no man shall see the Lord' [Hebrews 12, 14]. But it is an entire mistake. These scriptures well consist with each other, the meaning of the former being plainly this: by faith we are saved from sin, made holy."[30]

We may note two differences between Knox and Wesley on justification. The first is merely a question of language. Whereas Knox included in the meaning of justification both the forgiveness of sins and growth in holiness, Wesley distinguished between justification and sanctification.[31] Second, while Knox held that God first justified sinners and then declared them just, for Wesley the position was reversed. "God *implants* righteousness in everyone to whom he has *imputed* it," Wesley taught.[32]

The moderates held a position on justification which was substantially the same as Knox's. Faith and good works go inseparably together, they maintained. "Faith includes obedience," in Whichcote's words. To quote Richard Lucas, since "without holiness no man shall see God, if therefore my Faith do not produce this, it can avail me nothing."[33] Likewise, the moderates insisted that righteousness is both imputed and imparted. To quote again from Whichcote: "It is a dangerous error that some have taught that men may have their sins pardoned without anything being done in them. Here I must put in a *caution, that Christ is made by God to us righteousness*: This is so to be understood, as not to prejudice inherent righteousness, as if any could be righteous without inherent righteousness; this cannot be. You put a lie upon God for him to esteem any one righteous that is unrighteous."[34] Here we may observe that, as with Knox, imputation follows impartation. We find the same order in

---

30   Wesley, Sermon 127, "On the Wedding Garment," 18, in Outler, ed., *Works of John Wesley*, Vol. 4, pp. 139–48, at p. 148.

31   Basing himself on scriptural passages such as Romans 6, 22 and Galatians 5, 22–23, Knox distinguished between justification and sanctification, but held that they were both parts of one and the same process, signifying simply "the higher and lower stages of the Christian life" (*Remains*, Vol. 1, p. 354).

32   Wesley, Sermon 20, "The Lord our Righteousness," 2, 12, in Outler, ed., *Works of John Wesley*, Vol. 1, pp. 444–65, at p. 458 (emphasis in the original).

33   Whichcote, Discourse 52, "The Venerable NATURE and transcendent benefit of Christian Religion," [part 1], *Works*, Vol. 3, pp. 61–80, at p. 73; [Lucas], *Practical Christianity*, p. 13. For Richard Lucas (1648/9–1715), see *O. D. N. B.* One of the moderates admired by Knox, references to him occur throughout the latter's writings: *Remains*, Vol. 1, pp. 153, 154, 270; Vol. 3, pp. 75, 80, 221–2, 469; Vol. 4, pp. 145, 158, 178; *Correspondence*, Vol. 1, pp. 27, 29, 122; *Wesley*, pp. 457, 459–61.

34   Whichcote, Discourse 47, "The Arguments by which Men should be persuaded to Reconcile unto God," [part 2], *Works*, Vol. 2, pp. 365–82, at p. 380.

Cudworth. It would, he argues, make God "pronounce a false sentence," to say that someone is righteous, whereas in fact they are guilty.[35]

Knox regarded his teaching on justification as "substantially agreeing with the fathers." His position was "the prevalent and continuous view of the ancient church," he affirmed. "[F]rom the first century to the days of the schoolmen," justification was uniquely understood as "the being made, inwardly and practically, righteous, through the transmutative influences of the grace of Christ." As Hornby expressed it, with regard to the doctrine of justification, "Mr. Knox asserts himself to stand on the side of the concurrent sense of Catholicity for fourteen hundred years ... the universal and perpetual consent of the ancient Church.[36] Explicitly, Knox appealed to Clement of Rome, Irenaeus, Basil, Ambrose, Gregory the Great and, in particular, Augustine, as well as to his three great favorites, Clement, Pseudo-Macarius, and Chrysostom.[37] His appeal has some merit, although it must be underlined that the Fathers did not deal with the topic of justification in a sustained or systematic way. As McGrath remarks: "For the first three hundred and fifty years of the history of the church, its teaching on justification was inchoate and ill-defined."[38] This changed only with Augustine, and then, solely, in the West. Even then, however, there was no detailed treatment of the topic until the Reformation. Nor, when they do talk about the issue, do the Fathers address exactly the same questions as those which came to be so contentious in the sixteenth century and after. Nonetheless, the themes with which Knox dealt were not absent from their discourse, nor were their treatment of these themes substantially dissimilar to Knox's (a point that we have already seen, when looking at the doctrine of deification).[39] For Knox, "the agreement between the Church of England and the fathers" was "as strict as can be, respecting the state of justification."[40] This, he contended, might be proved, first, "from the whole tenor of the ... Book of Homilies," especially the "Homily on Salvation." Certainly, he conceded, expressions might "now and then" occur in the *Homilies* which savored "more of Lutheranism than of the ancient church," but, since the sermons' "ruling principle" was "to adhere steadily to the [teaching of] the ancient doctors of

---

35   Cudworth, "Sermon II," *Works*, Vol. 4, pp. 351–99, at p. 366.

36   *Remains*, Vol. 2, p. 60; Vol. 1, p. 288; Vol. 4, pp. 549–50; Hornby, "Editor's Preface to the Third and Fourth Volumes," pp. cix–cx.

37   For Knox's citation of the Fathers mentioned, other than Augustine, see: *Remains*, Vol. 1, pp. 284–90. For his invocation of Augustine, see: *Remains*, Vol. 1, p. 283; Vol. 2, pp. 59–60, 355; Vol. 3, pp. 49–50; Vol. 4, pp. 551–2.

38   McGrath, *Iustitia Dei*, Vol. 1, p. 23.

39   See above, pp. 75–80.

40   *Remains*, Vol. 1, p. 299. See also Vol. 3, p. 51.

the church," they ought, Knox claimed, to be interpreted in accordance with the patristic witness.[41] The Articles, too, set out the primitive position, Knox contended. Article XVI propounded the view that justification was accorded through baptism, in which the "life of grace in the soul" was begun. Articles XI and XII maintained that "good works spring out necessarily of a true and lively faith," and that by this conjunction of faith and works human beings are "accounted righteous before God."[42] As far as the liturgy was concerned, evidences of the correspondence between the Anglican and primitive doctrines of justification were, Knox declared, "innumerable." He listed the baptismal service; the litany; the confession at Morning and Evening Prayer; as well as a number of collects. The Prayer Book "cannot be adduced in support of merely forensic justification," he concluded, "because it is substantially the Liturgy of those who did not hold it," deriving as it does from the worship of the early church.[43]

Knox's interpretation of the Anglican formularies was contested by Evangelicals. His views were not, however, without precedent in the Church of England. As McGrath notes, during the Henrician reformation, the official documents of the Church defined justification non-forensically, in strongly transformational terms. "In general," McGrath writes, "the English Reformers [of this period] appear to have worked with a doctrine of justification in which man was understood to be *made* righteous *by fayth onley*, with good works being the natural consequence of justifying faith." Subsequently, a consensus in favor of forensic justification emerged, although this lasted only until the Restoration of 1660. Thereafter, a number of divines began to expound the view that justification was, in McGrath's words, "both an event and a process, subsuming regeneration or sanctification." Heirs of this tradition were not lacking in Knox's own time, although, in the main, a relative détente existed between Evangelicals and High Churchmen on the issue. This détente was ruined by Knox, albeit posthumously. In 1835 the first two volumes of the *Remains* appeared.[44] Instantly, the *British Critic* warned that the views concerning justification which Knox there enunciated were likely to "occasion something more than a mere rippling upon the surface of this comparatively stagnant question." The *Critic* was right. The publication of Knox's opinions shattered

---

41   Ibid., Vol. 1, pp. 296–8. See also above, p. 55. For the "Homily on Salvation," more properly called "A Sermon of the Salvation of Mankind, by only Christ our Saviour, from sin and death everlasting," see *Certain Sermons*, pp. 19–31.

42   *Remains*, Vol. 1, p. 310; Vol. 3, pp. 85, 84. See, also: Vol. 1, pp. 291–93; Vol. 3, pp. 55–56, 494–95; Vol. 2, pp. 462–65. For Articles in question, see *B. C. P.*, pp. 398–99.

43   *Remains*, Vol. 1, pp. 296, 516–28; Vol. 2, pp. 357–58, 462, 468–75; Vol. 1, p. 289. For Knox's appeal to the baptismal liturgy, see below, pp. 194–95.

44   McGrath, *Iustitia Dei*, Vol. 2, pp. 101, 109.

the relative calm that had previously existed; thanks to him, the subject of justification became once more a topic of theological dispute in the Church of England. Little wonder, therefore, that in 1838 the *Critic*, reviewing the second installment of the *Remains*, wrote of the "convulsion" and "commotion" that Knox had caused.[45]

Knox believed that his doctrine of justification was confirmed by experience. As he told Hannah More, after he had outlined his position to her:

> I here speak from feeling ... I knew [initially], by deep experience, that sin was misery; and I already felt enough to assure me, that the fear and love of God would be happiness. I saw, by degrees, that the change of heart I was solicitous for, could not be brought about by any merely moral or philosophical contemplation of God; but that I must obtain a lively, spiritual apprehension of God manifest in the flesh; such as would effectually bow my heart to the self-denying yoke of Christ, and make me actually partake of his unworldly, unselfish, divinely pure spirit and temper. For this faith in Christ, this vital principle of the life hid with Christ in God, I more and more sought; and, when it is sought as the one thing needful, it cannot be sought in vain ... Now, whatever may be the precise meaning of the scriptural term *justification*, I conceive its substance cannot be missed in such a course as I have ventured to describe.[46]

In other words, Knox's understanding of justification was confirmed by what he discovered, as he put it, "in the laboratory of my own heart."[47] Knox's treatment of justification is thus another good example of his theological method. The position he argued for was reasoned out from a study of the Bible, interpreted by tradition and lived by experience.

3   Perfection

"[T]he ultimate object of our redemption is, that we should live unto righteousness," Knox proclaimed.[48] This "living unto righteousness" he presented

---

45   *British Critic*, 17.34(April 1835), p. 277; McGrath, *Iustitia Dei*, Vol. 2, p. 122; Nockles, *Oxford Movement in Context*, p. 261; *British Critic*, 23,45(January 1838), pp. 1, 2. During Knox's lifetime, his views had already proved controversial, especially in Ireland. But with the publication of the *Remains*, they became the subject of far wider debate.

46   *Remains*, Vol. 3, pp. 93–4, quoting Matthew 11.29; Colossians 3.3; Luke 10.42.

47   *Remains*, Vol. 4, p. 280.

48   Ibid., Vol. 2, p. 145. Knox is alluding to 1 Peter 2.24.

as something dynamic. "The justified state," he wrote, "duly tended and cultivated, thrives and advances," eventually bringing the Christian, even in this
world, to a state of perfection.[49] This was, he avowed, his favorite doctrine,
and references to it occur throughout his writings. One should note especially:
"On Christianity, as the Way of Peace and True Happiness" (1805); the "Letter
to D. Parken, Esq., in answer to Mr. Parken's Reply to the Letter on Mysticism"
(1811); "The Doctrine Respecting Baptism Held by the Church of England" (undated); and the "Answer to a Letter on the Future State of Glory" (1825). The
issue is also addressed, more briefly, in part of Knox's first letter to Parken, "On
the Character of Mysticism" (1811), and in part of the letter to Hannah More
"On the Design of Providence respecting the Christian Church" (1806), as well
as in a number of shorter letters, including several to Jebb.[50] The doctrine is
crucial is identifying Knox as a Christian Platonist, for the perfection of which
he wrote is the equivalent of the deification spoken of by the Fathers. In both
cases, it means the Christian being sanctified and made holy through the operation of the indwelling Spirit. We should further note, by way of introduction
to this topic, that for Knox the theme of perfection was very far from being the
object of academic speculation. The quest for perfection was his life.

Although Knox spoke of "perfection," he also employed the term "maturity,"
as well as the adjectives "mature" and "full-grown."[51] In relation to the spiritual
life, such language better conveys the meaning of the Greek τέλειος [*teleios*]
and its cognates, and is less open to misinterpretation, although neither of
these considerations appears to have influenced Knox's usage. Nonetheless, to
speak of "mature Christianity" helps to underline the fact that, for Knox, the
attainment of perfection was gradual. Christians, Knox explained, were called
"to grow in grace, by an unremitted progress," until, "in due time," they passed
into "a new state," one of "habitual victory over all known and palpable sin."[52]
In this state, Knox taught, the Christian was "wholly sanctified," with "the mind
and heart so rectified, as to be consciously at peace with itself, and with its

---

49   *Remains*, Vol. 1, p. 311. If justification admits of increase, it can also, according to Knox, be
      lost through sin (ibid.).
50   *Remains*, Vol. 1, pp. 1–52, 367–426; Vol. 2, pp. 460–504; Vol. 3, pp. 427–42; Vol. 1, 346–62; Vol. 3,
      pp. 221–30; Vol. 4, pp. 365–6, 380–3, 443–55; *Correspondence*, Vol. 1, pp. 118–24, 165–71,
      173–5. For the avowal that perfection is Knox's favorite doctrine, see *Remains*, Vol. 4, p. 178.
51   See, e.g.: *Remains*, Vol. 1, pp. 74, 90, 92, 117, 195–6, 205, 349, 350, 353, 355, 361, 388; Vol. 2,
      p. 466; Vol. 3, pp. 222, 433, 441; Vol. 4, pp. 331–2, 367, 382, 449, 454, 545.
52   *Remains*, Vol. 1, p. 347; Vol. 2, p. 477. The metaphor of perfection as "victory" is constant
      in Knox's writings. See, e.g.: *Remains*, Vol. 1, pp. 1, 6–7; Vol. 2, pp. 476, 489; Vol. 3, pp. 163–4;
      Vol. 4, pp. 120, 136, 236, 292; *Correspondence*, Vol. 1, pp. 21, 105.

God."[53] In other words, what Knox meant by perfection was a state in which the Christian possessed "unclouded serenity of soul," untroubled by any consciousness of sin, an anticipated heaven.[54] Knox told Miss Ferguson, "I hold no perfection that excludes weakness;"[55] and because of weakness, Knox asserted that the Christian needed to exercise constant vigilance against temptation.[56] Nonetheless, and this for Knox was the important point, weakness was not wickedness;[57] at no stage did the perfect Christian willingly embrace sin, so as to forfeit "fixed friendship" with God.[58] This notion of "fixed friendship" was the key to Knox's doctrine of perfection. "The goal of Christian perfection is [for Knox] unbroken fellowship with God," to quote Hughes.[59] As Knox himself summed up the matter: "In a word, as St. Augustin [sic] long ago observed, the perfection of the Christian is a perfection of love. Whatever faults, therefore, are compatible with supreme, undeviating love of God, to these the most perfect Christian will still be liable; but, even under the sense of those faults, the consciousness of unimpaired and unabated love will preserve an uninterrupted consciousness of peace."[60]

"[S]uch [perfection] can be the lot of few," Gladstone commented, and Knox conceded that, in reality, one could find "comparatively few instances of Christian maturity."[61] Nonetheless, he held, mature Christianity had always

---

53   *Remarks*, p. 252 (alluding to 1 Thessalonians 5.23); *Remains*, Vol. 2, p. 100 (commenting on Hebrews 9.9). The description of perfection as a "state of perfect peace" (*Remains*, Vol. 1, p. 350) is, like the metaphor of "victory," used throughout Knox's writings. See, e.g.: *Remains*, Vol. 1, pp. 4, 7, 34, 41, 274; Vol. 2, pp. 112, 114, 265, 474, 477–8, 492; Vol. 3, pp. 164–5; *Correspondence*, Vol. 1, p. 98. In support of the idea, Knox frequently cites Isaiah 32.17. See, e.g.: *Remains*, Vol. 1, p. 436; Vol. 3, p. 38; Vol. 4, pp. 354–5; *Correspondence*, Vol. 1, pp. 23–4. Knox's concern with peace is perhaps related to the troubled mental state from which he suffered.
54   *Remains*, Vol. 1, p. 352; Vol. 2, pp. 111–12. For the idea of the Christian life as an anticipation of heaven, see above, pp. 138, 143.
55   *Remains*, Vol. 4, p. 228. This weakness arose from original sin: see *Remains*, Vol. 1, p. 517; Vol. 4, p. 366; *Correspondence*, Vol. 1, p. 167. See, also, above, pp. 138, 143.
56   *Remains*, Vol. 2, pp. 112–13; *Correspondence*, Vol. 1, pp. 105–6, 167–70.
57   *Remains*, Vol. 1, p. 517; Vol. 2, p. 113; Vol.4, p. 366. This is how Knox explains the teaching of the Thirty-Nine Articles about the continuance of "concupiscence and lust" even "in them that are regenerated" (Article IX, *B. C. P.*, p. 398). For him, it is frailty, not sin. See *Remains*, Vol. 1, p. 517; *Correspondence*, Vol.1, p. 167.
58   *Remains*, Vol. 4, p. 218.
59   Hughes, "Life and Work," p. 96.
60   *Remains*, Vol. 2, pp. 113–14. The reference to Augustine is perhaps to *Tractatus in Epistolam Ioannis*, 9, 4, where Augustine speaks of "*perfecta caritas*." Knox quotes the text, *Remains*, Vol. 1, pp. 392–3. For the original, see *P. L.*, Vol. 35, col., 2047.
61   B. L., Add. Ms 44724, Gladstone Papers, DCXXXIX, fols. 73–76, "memorandum," May 24, 1835, fol. 76; *Remains*, Vol. 3, p. 429.

existed in the church, proving the possibility of its attainment.[62] It was not an unrealizable ideal; in fact, as the essence of "true, complete Christianity," perfection was "not only placed within the reach of Christians," but was "equally the vocation of all." "[T]his is the state to which God calls us," Knox asserted; and, therefore, fired by "holy ambition," Christians should not cease to labour until they had entirely abolished within themselves "the whole body of sin."[63] This exhortation should apply to the whole Church, Knox enjoined. "The genuine Church of England teacher will continually urge, that to attain this state, and advance in it, is, essentially, that one thing which our Lord declared needful … [and that] no individual Christian should rest without effectually and consciously possessing [it]."[64] Such striving was, he held, the law of nature, which shows that all living things are called to growth, the spiritual life being analogous to the physical.[65] Nonetheless, though analogous, grace and nature were by no means equal. For him, nature alone could not reach spiritual perfection. It was an impossible goal for human effort unaided, but not, he stressed, for human effort helped by God's grace. "The true doctrine of Christian perfection," he wrote, "derives its strength never from merely moral, but supremely from evangelic sources: πάντα ἰσχύω ἐν τῷ ἐνδυναμοῦντί με Χριστῷ [*panta ischyō en tōi endynamounti me Christōi*]."[66] In other words, whatever the Christian achieved was achieved only with the help of God: "moral" in this context is the equivalent of "natural." But with the help of grace, progress was unlimited. "[T]he state of grace is never to be stationary," he declared. "[E]very possible degree of goodness here has still a higher degree above it," to which the Christian is called to aspire.[67]

As with his teaching on justification generally, Knox formulated his ideas on perfection in opposition to what he understood as the doctrine of contemporary Evangelicalism, which he perceived as espousing a "cold, low, unenergetic"

---

62   *Remains*, Vol. 3, p. 430. See also Vol. 1, p. 452, where Knox suggests that, "as the Church advances towards its last and happiest state on earth," the number of perfect Christians will increase.

63   *Remains*, Vol. 1, p. 19; Vol. 2, p. 135; Vol. 1, pp. 525, 20; Vol. 2, pp. 83, 491 (quoting the Anglican baptismal service, B. C. P., p. 200, itself referencing Romans 6.6).

64   *Remains*, Vol. 2, p. 488 (alluding to Luke 10.42). See, also, Vol. 4, pp. 330–1.

65   *Remains*, Vol. 1, p. 361; Vol. 3, p. 230; *Correspondence*, Vol. 1, pp. 119–20, 269. Knox owed this argument in part to Joseph Butler (*Remains*, Vol. 2, pp. 229–30; Vol. 4, p. 524; *Correspondence*, Vol. 2, p. 48), who uses it in his *Analogy of Religion* (1736), though it also appears in Wesley (see below, p. 184). For Butler (1692–1752), see O. D. N. B.

66   *Remains*, Vol. 1, p. 379. The quotation ends with the words of Philippians 4.13, "I can do all things, through Christ which strentheneth me," as Hornby translates (ibid., note).

67   *Remains*, Vol. 2, p. 491; Vol. 4, p. 229. For the idea of continuous advancement in perfection see also: Vol. 1, p. 400; Vol. 2, pp. 83–4, 128, 487, 490.

Christianity. Teaching that sin had inflicted an incurable wound on human nature, it held, in Knox's view, that even the regenerate were reduced to what he
called "struggling [and] staggering," rather than perfecting holiness.[68] In support of his assessment, Knox adduced John Newton's *Cardiphonia* (1781), and
if we turn to its pages, we find it speaking of Christians having to "strive and
struggle, and pant." Christians must, Newton wrote, "press through a crowd,
swim against a stream, endure hardships, run, wrestle, and fight."[69] Perhaps
no quotation could better illustrate the divergence between Knox and his
Evangelical contemporaries. This divergence can also be illustrated by Knox's
clash with John Walker, which is where, perhaps, in the heat of controversy,
Knox first forged his mature reflections on justification and perfection. As the
Christian Examiner asserted, Knox's debate with Walker "gave a controversial
turn to [Knox's] subsequent views, and to his mode of expressing himself on
religion, whether in conversation or in writing. In both he appeared the an-
tagonist of what he called Calvinism." Walker called the doctrine of perfection
a delusion. "[Our] warfare," he declared, "ceases not … but with our earthly
course." To cite his *Expostulatory Address*: "[W]hile I believe the Bible, I must
be certain that any man, who says *he has no sin* is a liar, and the truth is not in
him." Human nature is and remains, for Walker, "wholly evil" alike in the believer and the unbeliever, "as bad as in Paul the apostle … as in Saul of Tarsus."[70]

4   Sources of Knox's Doctrine of Perfection

Writing of Wesley's view of perfection, Rack says that his "tone … was coloured
by contemporary Enlightenment ideas."[71] The same can be said of Knox: his
teaching reflected the optimism of the post-Enlightenment period and what

---

68   Ibid., Vol. 1, p. 6; Vol. 3, p. 82.
69   Newton, *Cardiphonia*, p. 450. For the Evangelical John Newton (1725–1807), see *O. D. N. B.*
70   *Christian Examiner*, 3.35 (September 1834), p. 632; Walker, third letter to Alexander Knox
      (1803), in *Expostulatory Address*, pp. 121–57, at p. 153; *Expostulatory Address*, pp. 24 (allud-
      ing to 1 John 2.8; emphasis in the original), 25. For the clash between Knox and Walker,
      see above, p. 58. I must nuance the assertion that Knox's views were formed by the con-
      troversy with Walker. As we have seen, Wesley already put Knox on his guard against
      "Calvinism" in his correspondence with him (see above, pp. 62–63). Moreover, as the fol-
      lowing section will demonstrate, Knox's reading of the Fathers and the moderates would
      have inculcated perfectionism in him, even without the controversy with Walker.
71   Rack, *Reasonable Enthusiast*, p. 401. On the optimism of the Enlightenment, see above,
      pp. 94–95.

Jackson calls its "faith in human perfectibility."[72] For Knox himself, however, the doctrine that he taught was simply that of Scripture. The perfection of which he spoke was that to which the readers of Hebrews were exhorted; it was the "perfect love" described by St. John in his First Epistle; and the "mature Christianity ... placed before the Philippians by St. Paul."[73] Despite his stated desire "merely to follow the guidance of Holy Scripture," however, Knox also cited in defence of his doctrine of perfection "the ancient divines, and those in the Church of England who have followed them."[74] He believed that all three of these authorities were in agreement. As he put it, "the philosophy of our Redeemer" found in Scripture was that which "the Church of England [taught], in concurrence with the Catholic Church in all ages."[75] With respect to the Church of England and its teachers, one of those whom Knox invoked was John Wesley. Or, to be more precise, he invoked Wesley's "mature estimate" of perfection,[76] which he saw as that" countenanced by the consent of the ancient Fathers, and the most eminent anti-Calvinistic divines of the Church of England."[77] He suggested that it might become for others "a source of as deep and wide-spread [theological] utility as ever yet was derived from an uninspired instructor;" certainly it was one to which he himself was personally beholden.[78] What, then, was Wesley's "mature estimate" of perfection?[79] Wesley saw perfection as "the true goal of the Christian life," a truth which he

---

72   Jackson, "Progress and Optimism," p. 184.

73   For Knox's appeal to Scripture in general see: *Remains*, Vol. 2, p. 488; Vol. 4, p. 454. For his appeal to Hebrews (6.1), see: *Remains*, Vol. 1, pp. 96, 173, 205, 355; Vol. 2, pp. 92, 101, 107, 110, 135, 138, 497; Vol. 3, pp. 28, 110, 125, 144, 178; Vol. 4, pp. 340, 449; *Correspondence*, Vol. 1, pp. 136–67. For his appeal to John (1 John 4.18), see: *Remains*, Vol. 1, p. 353; Vol. 2, pp. 470, 492; Vol. 4, p. 367; *Correspondence*, Vol. 1, p. 24. For his appeal to Philippians see: *Remains*, Vol. 3, pp. 125, 433; Vol. 4, pp. 445–9.

74   *Remains*, Vol. 3, p. 221; *Wesley*, p. 461.

75   *Remains*, Vol. 2, pp. 488–9.

76   See above, p. 65.

77   *Wesley*, p. 455. See, also, *Remains*, Vol. 3, pp. 468–9.

78   *Remains*, Vol. 4, p. 280. For Knox's debt to Wesley's teaching on perfection, see above, p. 65.

79   For a summary of Wesley's views on perfection, see Maddox, *Responsible Grace*, pp. 180–90; cf. pp. 163–5. Rack also has a useful discussion of the topic: *Reasonable Enthusiast*, pp. 395–401. For other summaries of Wesley's perfectionism see: Bassett and Greathouse, *Exploring Christian Holiness*, pp. 203–35; Flew, *The Idea of Perfection*, pp. 313–41; and especially, Peters, *Christian Perfection and American Methodism*, chapters 1–2, "The Doctrine in Process of Formation" and "The Doctrine Stated and Qualified," pp. 15–66. With regard to Wesley's own writing, the clearest résumé of his views is *A Plain Account of Christian Perfection* (1766). Wesley's position was developed by John Fletcher. Fletcher may have been an influence on Knox, though I have found no direct evidence of this.

believed Methodism had been raised up to proclaim. Accordingly, he urged all his preachers to "make a point, of *preaching perfection* to believers constantly, strongly, and explicitly." "And all believers," he added, "should *mind this one thing*, and continually agonize for it."[80] This perfection, to be preached and striven for, Wesley understood in terms of love. "It is *perfect love*," he proclaimed, quoting 1 John 4.18. "This is the *essence* of it." Such love, Wesley taught, meant the exclusion of all sin, both outward and inward, including "evil desires and evil tempers."[81] Accordingly, as Maddox observes: "Wesley was convinced that the Christian life did not have to remain a life of continual struggle." Rather, Wesley held, for the perfect Christian "all is peace."

> After being filled with love, there is no more interruption of it, than of the beating of [the perfect Christian's] heart. And continual love bringing continual joy in the Lord, he rejoices evermore. He converses continually with the God whom he loves, unto whom in everything he gives thanks. And as he now loves God with all his heart, and with all his soul, and with all his mind, and with all his strength, so Jesus now reigns alone in his heart, the Lord of every motion there.[82]

In this emphasis on love, joy, and peace, we see clear parallels between Wesley's thought and Knox's. Wesley's distinction between sin, defined as the willing transgression of a known law, and infirmity, which included unwilling and un-witting transgressions, finds an echo in Knox's differentiation between wickedness and weakness.[83] One finds also in Wesley the argument from nature which Knox later employed. In his sermon "On the New Birth" (1760), Wesley contends that there is an "exact analogy ... between natural and spiritual things" and that just as, naturally, a child grows up to maturity, so spiritually the Christian "grows up to the measure of the full stature of Christ."[84]

---

80   Rack, *Reasonable Enthusiast*, p. 395; John Wesley to Robert Carr Brackenbury, letter, September 15, 1790, *Letters*, Vol. 8, pp. 237–8, at p. 238; Wesley, *A Plain Account of Christian Perfection*, p. 97 (emphasis in the original). "Agonize" is used here with its root-meaning of "contend."

81   Wesley, *A Plain Account of Christian Perfection*, p. 96.

82   Maddox, *Responsible Grace*, p. 188; Wesley, Sermon 83, "On Patience," 10, in Outler, ed., *Works of John Wesley*, Vol. 3, pp. 170–9, at p. 176.

83   For this distinction in Wesley, see Maddox, *Responsible Grace*, pp. 184–5.

84   Wesley, Sermon 45, "On the New Birth," 4, 3, in Outler, ed., *Works of John Wesley*, Vol. 2, pp. 187–201, at p. 198. See also on this point, *Correspondence*, Vol. 1, p. 134.

Besides Wesley, Knox cited "our best English divines," whom he named as George Herbert, Cudworth, Lucas, Smith, Taylor and Worthington.[85] As an example of their teaching, we may take the last-mentioned, John Worthington, whose *Great Duty of Self-Resignation to the Divine Will* (1675) has as its central affirmation "That a Christian is to resign his will wholly to the divine will; to make an entire oblation of himself to God." In this way, Worthington taught, the believer attains the true goal of Christianity, which is "the real bettering of man, and transforming him into the divine image." To be a Christian meant, for Worthington, "to be transformed into the divine image and likeness, to partake of the divine nature, to have one will with God."[86] Another example of the same teaching is given by Richard Lucas, for whose writings on perfection Knox had the highest regard. "Lucas," he claimed, "has made perfection a classical term, – classical, I mean, in English divinity."[87] Knox is thinking here, no doubt, of Lucas's *Enquiry After Happiness* (1685), the third part of which was specifically dedicated to the topic of *Religious Perfection* which it defined as habitual holiness. To quote from the opening chapter, words which Knox transcribed in a letter to Hannah More: "*Conversion* begins, *Perfection* consummates the habit of righteousness: in the one, religion is, as it were, in its infancy; in the other, in its strength and manhood; so that *Perfection*, in short, is nothing else, but a ripe and settled *habit* of true holiness."[88] Beyond Wesley and the moderates, Knox looked back to the primitive church for the sources of his perfectionism. "[A]ll the Fathers were on this subject essentially of the same opinion," he affirmed, at least up until "Ambrose first, and Augustin [*sic*] afterward."[89] Only with these two Fathers did the spiritual life come to be seen as "warfare and fluctuation to the last," Knox claimed, although he allowed that even Augustine "maintains [perfection] in substance."[90] Nonetheless, it was above all in the

---

85   *Remains*, Vol. 1, p. 1. For the appeal to Herbert see: *Remains*, Vol. 3, p. 469, note; for Cudworth see: *Remains*, Vol. 1, p. 44; Vol. 3, pp. 224–5, 469, note; Vol. 4, p. 330; for Lucas see: *Remains*, Vol. 3, pp. 80; 221–2, 469, note; Vol. 4, p. 178; *Correspondence*, Vol. 1, pp. 134, 145; *Wesley*, p. 459–61; for Smith see: *Remains*, Vol. 3, pp. 80, 221, 223; Vol. 4, p. 330; for Taylor see: *Remains*, Vol. 1, pp. 102–3, 359–60; Vol. 3, pp. 223–4, 469, note; *Eclectic Review*, 6 (May 1810), pp. 385–95; *Wesley*, pp. 457–59; for Worthington see: *Remains*, Vol. 1, pp. 103–5; Vol. 3, p. 469, note; Vol. 4, p. 158. For Knox's appeal to the moderates generally, see: *Remains*, Vol. 1, pp. 355, 359–60; Vol. 2, p. 492; Vol. 3, pp. 222–3, 469; *Wesley*, pp. 455, 457–61.

86   Worthington, *The Great Duty of Self Resignation to the Divine Will*, pp. 4, 1, 48.

87   *Remains*, Vol. 3, p. 80.

88   Lucas, *Religious Perfection*, p. 2. For Knox's transcription, see *Remains*, Vol. 3, p. 222.

89   *Remains*, Vol. 1, p. 350.

90   *Remains*, Vol. 1, pp. 350, 392. See also: ibid., pp. 389–90; *Correspondence*, Vol. 1, p. 134. Had he looked closer, Knox would have seen that Ambrose also maintains that by the grace

Greek Fathers that Knox found the doctrine of perfection, especially in the
writings of Clement of Alexandria, Pseudo-Macarius, and Chrysostom.[91] With
regard to Clement, Knox appealed especially to "the sixth and seventh book
of the *Stromata*."[92] In so doing he was surely right, for these books are a portrayal of the perfect Christian, the Gnostic, to use Clement's term, one who has
reached a state of ἀπάθεια [*apatheia*], conceived not as Stoic indifference, but
as a love of God so strong that no emotion can perturb it.[93] "The Gnostic," says
"Clement, " loves God constantly and is wholly united to God alone." And "it is
impossible that someone who has once been perfected through love, and who
perceives the inexpressible delight of eternal and insatiable contemplation ...
should still find pleasure in small and mean and lowly things." The Gnostic is,
in short, "assimilated to the Savior."[94] With regard to Pseudo-Macarius, Knox
wrote that "his well-known 'Fifty Homilies' abound in warm descriptions
of perfect Christianity, and in exhortations to pursue it."[95] In this analysis,
too, Knox was correct, as we have already seen.[96] For Pseudo-Macarius, the
Christian was advancing to a state of perfection, which he described as follows:

> Finally, when a person reaches the perfection of the Spirit, completely
> purified of all passions and united to and interpenetrated by the Paraclete
> Spirit in an ineffable communion, and is deemed worthy to become spirit
> in a mutual penetration with the Spirit, then it becomes all light, all eye,
> all spirit, all joy, all repose, all happiness, all love, all compassion, all good-
> ness and kindness. As in the bottom of the sea, a stone is everywhere
> surrounded by water, so such persons as these are totally penetrated by
> the Holy Spirit. They become like to Christ, putting on the virtues of the
> power of the Spirit with a constancy. They interiorly become faultless and
> spotless and pure.

To be thus "changed and transformed from [our] former state and attitude and
become a good and new person," was, for Pseudo-Macarius, the whole aim of

---

of God, it is possible to be sinless (*Expositio Evangelii secundum Lucam*, 1, 17; *P. L.*, 15,
col. 1620).

91   *Remains*, Vol. 1, p. 350; Vol. 3, p. 75.
92   Ibid., Vol. 1, p. 350.
93   "Love leaves no room for passion," is how Osborn sums up Clement's position (*Clement of
      Alexandria*, p. 235).
94   Clement, *Stromateis*, 6, 9; *P. G.*, vol. 9, cols. 293, 296–7.
95   *Remains*, Vol. 1, p. 350.
96   See above, p. 78.

the spiritual life. This change was a long and arduous process, but eventually, with the help of God, one could attain a state of what Pseudo-Macarius, like Clement, called *apatheia*. The state was described by Maloney as "the peak of all Christian perfection, which consists in the love of God with one's whole heart and soul." Its possession did not mean that the Christian was freed from temptation and spiritual assault. "Satan is never quieted, at peace and not at war," Pseudo-Macarius believed. Even so, he assured his disciples, the devil could not prevail against those who had attained perfection:

> Even if war starts externally and Satan attacks, they are still fortified interiorly by the Lord's power and are not anxious about Satan. As he tempted the Lord in the desert for forty days, what harm did he inflict on him by attacking him externally in his body? For interiorly he was God. So also Christians, granted they may be tempted exteriorly, nevertheless, interiorly they are filled with the Godhead and suffer no injury. If one has reached this degree, he has arrived at the perfect love of Christ and the fullness of the Godhead.[97]

For Knox, Chrysostom was, as we have seen, "the patriarch" of the perfectionist theologians.[98] And, as with Clement and Pseudo-Macarius, Knox was right to claim the great preacher's support. One can see the whole aim of Chrysostom's homiletics as being to help his hearers "become holy and perfect."[99] He believed that, by the grace of God, "it is possible even in this mortal body not to sin." If Christians did sin, it was only because they chose to do so. "Sin," he asserted, "reigns not by its own power, but by your laxity." On the other hand, one can choose to co-operate with the grace of God and (here Chrysostom quotes St. Paul) "mortify the body of sin." The converse of this death to sin is a new life. One becomes, according to Chrysostom, a new creature, a πνευματικὸς ἄνθρωπος [*pneumatikos anthrōpos*], literally a spiritual human being, but, more profoundly, one who is animated by the Holy Spirit.[100] To describe this state, Chrysostom used the term *apatheia*, but, unlike Clement and Pseudo-Macarius, it was a word of which he was, in Michel Spanneut's phrase, "*plutôt avare*."[101] More often, to quote Nowak: "*La vie angélique est proposée par*

---

97   Maloney, *Pseudo-Macarius*, pp. 145, 223, 20, 169.

98   See above, p. 79.

99   Young, "God's Word Proclaimed," p. 143.

100   Chrysostom, "Homily 11 on Romans," 2, *P. G.*, Vol. 60, col. 486; "Homily 13 on Romans," 7, *P. G.*, Vol. 60, col. 518.

101   Spanneut, "*L'Apatheia*," p. 45, "rather sparing" (my translation.)

Jean comme l' idéal de la perfection chrétienne," a thought which may perhaps lie behind Knox's frequent description of the Christian life as an anticipation of heaven, just as Chrysostom's description of the *pneumatikos anthropos* may have perhaps influenced Knox's use of the term "spirituality."[102]

Knox invoked the Church of England's "devotional formularies" in support of his perfectionism.[103] Scarcely a petition was offered in the Prayer Book, he contended, "which does not recognise the state of grace, guard its substance, watch its stability, pursue its advancement, aspire to its maturity; or, on the other hand, deprecate the state of sin ... and seek, above all things, its complete subjugation." This was especially the case, Knox contended, with "our more ancient and original collects," of which he cited several. As he pointed out, they ask for "a heart set to obey God's commandments; such a love of what God commands, and such a desire of what he promises, as will fix our hearts *there*, where true joys are to be found; a love of God above all, poured into the heart from above; a pardon which cleanses from all sin ... a heart so cleansed by the inspiration of the Holy Spirit, as perfectly to love God, and worthily magnify his holy name."[104]

5   Conclusion

This chapter has brought us to the heart of "Mr. Knox's system," the issue which for him was most vital: justification, which he saw as a process

---

102   Nowak, *Le Chrétien Devant la Souffrance*, p. 118, "The angelic life is set forth by John as the ideal of Christian perfection" (my translation). Nowak gives an excellent summary of the theme of the angelic life in Chrysostom's writings (ibid., note 138). In it, Nowak includes the idea, which we find so central to Knox, of friendship with God. Indeed, Nowak calls this "the essential element" of Chrysostom's understanding of the angelical life (ibid.). For Knox's teaching on friendship with God, see above, p. 180. For the idea of the Christian life as an anticipation of heaven in Knox, see above, pp. 138, 143, 180. For Knox's use of the term "spirituality," see above, pp. 111–12.

103   *Remains*, Vol. 2, p. 474. See, also, in addition to the passage cited below: *Remains*, Vol. 1, pp. 357–59, 391; Vol. 2, p. 479; Vol. 3, pp. 224–25. One might note that, if Knox's views accord with the liturgy of the Prayer Book, they sit ill with the Thirty-Nine Articles, which, inspired by James 3, 2 and 1 John 1, 10, declare that "although baptized and born again in Christ, [we] yet offend in many things, and if we say we have no sin we deceive ourselves and the truth is not in us" (Article fifteen, *B. C. P.*, p. 399).

104   *Remains*, Vol. 2, pp. 474–75. In the last passage cited, Knox quotes the Second Collect at Evening Prayer, the Collects for the Fourth Sunday after Easter, the Sixth and Twenty-First Sundays after Trinity, and the Collect for Purity, said at the start of the Communion Service. See, *B. C. P.*, pp. 45, 120, 136, 151, 180.

leading to perfection. He formulated his ideas in opposition to contemporary Evangelicalism, and its twin doctrines of imputed righteousness and justification by faith alone, which he equated with a practical antinomianism, not the explicit rejection of good works, but a reliance on Christ's merits which undermined zeal for holiness. Knox taught that justification is both imputed and imparted; we are made righteous by the grace of Christ, not merely accounted righteous. He held that if we are justified by faith, that faith must be productive of good works. It must – for all Christians are called to this and, by the grace of God, all can achieve it – lead to perfection, or spiritual maturity, in which one gains what Knox calls "fixed friendship" with God, a relationship unperturbed by deliberate sin. Although this idea of perfection reflects Knox's Enlightenment background, he sees his teaching as nothing other than that of Scripture, found, too, in Wesley, in the moderates, and, especially, in the Fathers. It is this teaching which identifies him as a Christian Platonist, for the perfection which he proclaims is nothing other than the Platonic doctrine of *theosis*. His doctrine, nonetheless, proved highly controversial, re-igniting a debate which had been dormant until the publication of the *Remains*. Evangelicals especially excoriated Knox for denying the doctrine of Scripture and the teaching of the Church of England. Even so, Knox's great desire was to set out what he believed be the authentic Anglican position which, he was convinced, was that alike of Scripture and the undivided church. From Knox's doctrines of justification and perfection, we turn next to his understanding of the chief means by which he saw these being accomplished, the sacraments of baptism and the Eucharist.

CHAPTER 10

Alexander Knox's Theology (III): Baptism and the Eucharist

During the first part of the nineteenth century the Church of England was racked by a bitter dispute over baptismal regeneration, the doctrine that in baptism one is born again as a child of God.[1] Knox entered the fray with an essay on "The Doctrine Respecting Baptism held by the Church of England," completed early in 1820.[2] It was followed in 1824 by another sacramental tract, one of his most important works, *An Inquiry on Grounds of Scripture and Reason into the Use and Import of the Eucharistic Symbols*.[3] This chapter looks at Knox's teaching on the sacraments and the sources from which he drew.

1   The Baptismal Controversy

The annual Bampton Lectures at Oxford were delivered in 1812 by the High Churchman Richard Mant, who used them to give a vigorous re-statement of the doctrine of baptismal regeneration.[4] In response, numerous Evangelicals sprang forward to insist that the administration of the baptismal rite needed to be accompanied by personal conversion. One of the major exponents of the Evangelical position was Charles Simeon, a Fellow of King's College, Cambridge, whose clash over the issue with Herbert Marsh, the High Church Lady Margaret Professor of Divinity in the same university, led in 1813, to a

---

1   "The Baptismal Controversy was the controversy of the first half of this century" (Mozley, *Review of the Baptismal Controversy*, p. iii). Matters came to a head with the Gorham controversy of 1847–50, but even after that the fires of dispute were not entirely extinguished; see Jagger, *Clouded Witnesses*.

2   *Remains*, Vol. 1, pp. 484–528; Vol. 2, pp. 460–504. Knox's views on baptism are also conveniently summarized in a section of the tract "On Justification" (1810), as well as in a letter to Jebb, dated May 20, 1814: *Remains*, Vol. 1, pp. 307–11; *Correspondence*, Vol. 2, pp. 183–85.

3   The essay appears in the *Remains*, under the title "A Treatise on the Use and Import of the Eucharistic Symbols," Vol. 2, pp. 184–249. For the history of the *Inquiry*, see the note on it in the catalogue of the British Library; also, Tracey, ed., *L. &. D.*, Vol. 6, p. 198, note. See also below, pp. 247–48.

4   For Mant, see above, p. 170. For his baptismal doctrine, see especially the sixth of lectures, "Regeneration the Spiritual Grace of Baptism" (*An Appeal to the Gospel*, pp. 327–88).

© KONINKLIJKE BRILL NV, LEIDEN, 2020 | DOI:10.1163/9789004426986_012

bitter exchange of pamphlets.[5] It was the appraisal of these pamphlets by the *British Critic* of March 1814 which caused Knox to enter the fray. Agreeing with Jebb that "both parties [were] ... lamentably in the dark," he contemplated sending the *Critic* a letter on the subject.[6] This letter was never written, or, at least, it went unpublished, but at the end of 1819 and the beginning of 1820 Knox produced his essay on baptism, of which two versions exist. It can be dated from a letter written to Jebb on January 3, 1820, in which Knox says that he is working on a text

> to prove the doctrine of baptismal regeneration (in the case of infants,) to be that of the Church of England. I show from our formularies, what this doctrine implies; and I then point out practical consequences, which flow necessarily, or, at least, naturally, from the established premises ... I state unpalatable truths, which both sides will, on different grounds, equally disrelish; but I speak as a member of the Church of England: they may attack her; but I fight behind a better shield than that of Ajax.[7]

Both versions of the essay contain the same basic material, but have different emphases. In the first, Knox addressed the specific question of the relationship between the sacramental sign and the grace signified, concluding with a discussion concerning the preservation and increase of baptismal grace. The second version began with a general statement of what Knox saw as the Anglican doctrine of baptism, but its main theme was "the state of grace and the state of sin," which Knox dealt with from a practical point of view as relating to "spiritual life and spiritual death."[8]

2   Knox's Doctrine of Baptism

The first version of Knox's essay opens with the statement: "Amongst the various subjects which have occupied the thoughts of religious men, in this age of controversy, none has excited more attention than the doctrine of Baptism, as maintained by the Church of England." Because of this, it was necessary, Knox

---

5   For both Charles Simeon (1759–1836) and Herbert Marsh (1757–1839), see *O. D. N. B.* For the clash between them, see Thompson, *Cambridge Theology in the Nineteenth Century*, p. 46.
6   *British Critic*, new (second) series, 1.3 (March 1814), pp. 263–76; *Correspondence*, Vol. 2, pp. 184; 414.
7   *Correspondence*, Vol. 2, pp. 407–8. The allusion to the shield of Ajax comes from the *Iliad*, book 7, lines 219–24.
8   *Remains*, Vol. 2, p. 487.

continued, to set out as clearly as possible "the true doctrine of the Church of England."[9] The second version of the essay stated this doctrine as follows:

> The sacrament of Baptism, through the appointment of our blessed Saviour, and by the operation of the Holy Spirit, conveys, to all susceptible receivers, not only the outward privileges of Christian communion, but the internal blessing of regenerating grace. This grace brings with it the remission of sins; it implies a radical commencement of spiritual life, and gives a title to the everlasting inheritance.[10]

This definition of baptism is striking on account of the almost scholastic precision of its language, especially when one considers Knox's habitual verbosity.[11] Baptism is a "sacrament," something which Knox elsewhere defined in standard Anglican terms as an "outward and visible sign of ... inward and spiritual blessings."[12] It confers, first, "the outward privileges of Christian communion;" those who receive it are "incorporated into the visible Church."[13] This, however, is of secondary importance. The main object of the sacrament is to convey "the internal blessing of regenerating grace." This grace includes both "remission of sins" and "a radical commencement of spiritual life." As Knox wrote in the first version: "To be dead to sin, and alive unto righteousness is ... the essence of spiritual regeneration."[14] This regeneration comes from "the appointment of our blessed Saviour," who instituted the outward rite of baptism while on earth, and who now from heaven works its interior effect "by the operation of the Holy Spirit." Through the Spirit's agency, "a heavenly influence" is united "to the [baptismal] water." This "divine concurrence" serves "to make the ablution of the body effectual ... to the purification of the soul."[15] One should note the importance which Knox accorded to the Holy Spirit in baptism, something which reflects the overall significance of pneumatology in his thinking.

---

9   Ibid., Vol. 1, pp. 484, 485.
10   Ibid., Vol. 2, p. 460.
11   "Knox's treatment of this theme is marked throughout by clarity of thought and expression," Hughes notes, one feels with some surprise ("Life and Work," p. 133).
12   *Remains*, Vol. 1, p. 484. Knox's definition echoes that of the Prayer Book Catechism, which describes a sacrament as "an outward and visible sign of an inward and spiritual grace" (B. C. P., p. 215). Somewhat confusingly, Knox at times uses the term "sacrament" to signify simply the external sign; see, for example, *Remains*, Vol. 1, pp. 486, 489, 490, 499.
13   *Remains*, Vol. 2, p. 461.
14   Ibid., Vol. 1, p. 493. Knox's definition echoes the baptismal service (B. C. P., p. 200), itself an echo of Romans 6.11.
15   *Remains*, Vol. 1, p. 502. Knox is commenting on the prayer for blessing the baptismal water in the Prayer Book service (B. C. P., p. 196).

The Spirit makes the sacrament operative; but also, crucially, "the Holy Ghost [is] given in baptism." As Knox wrote, there is "an outward sign; but with it, as the life and soul of it, an inward grace: καὶ ἀνακαινώσεως πνεύματος ἁγίου ... And [St. Paul] adds that this renewing spirit is not scantily communicated. It is poured out upon us, πλουσίως διὰ Ἰησοῦ Χριστοῦ τοῦ σωτῆρος ἡμῶν."[16] This gift is conferred on "all susceptible receivers." The rite does not work automatically: Knox categorically refused the simple equation, "baptism is regeneration," even going so far, in his private correspondence with Jebb, to deplore this view as "anti-catholic."[17] Rather, Knox asserted, baptism is only efficacious if the recipient places no bar, or *obex*, to the grace of the sacrament. Infants are incapable of ever posing such a bar, and, therefore, Knox maintained, quoting the words of the Anglican divines at the Savoy Conference of 1661, "'we may say, in faith, of every child that is baptized, that he is regenerated by God's Holy Spirit.'"[18] By contrast, "a bar might, by possibility, be opposed" by adults, he argued, which is why the Church of England explicitly required repentance and faith from those who wanted to be baptized "in riper years."[19] This detail was critical for Knox, who described the whole controversy surrounding baptism in his day as concerned with the relationship between the outward sign and the inward grace. To quote his own words: "the great point of debate has been, in what manner the external ordinance, and the inward blessing, are connected with each other."[20] In his view, the Evangelicals had erred in separating them entirely; the High Churchmen had strayed by making them identical.

The Spirit bestowed in baptism was, according to Knox, given as the "radical commencement" of a new life, "the first stage of a vital progress" in which the Christian is called to "daily [grow] in grace, and in knowledge of his Lord and Saviour."[21] The point is significant because it was another instance of Knox differing from his High Church contemporaries, while anticipating the stance

---

16 *Remains*, Vol. 2, p. 462; Vol. 1, pp. 307–8 (format slightly altered). In the second passage cited, the Greek *kai anakainōseōs pneumatos hagiou ... plousiōs dia Iēsou Christou tou sōtēros hēmōn* means "and renewing of the Holy Ghost ... abundantly through Jesus Christ, our Saviour" (Knox's translation). The words come from Titus 3.5. For the gift of the Spirit in baptism, see, also: *Remains*, Vol. 1, p. 509; Vol. 2, p. 329.

17 *Remains*, Vol. 1, p. 485; *Correspondence*, Vol. 2, p. 184. The view is one which Knox ascribed explicitly to Daniel Waterland (1683–1740), whose *Regeneration Stated and Explained* (1740) is usually reckoned to be one of the most substantial treatises on baptism written by an Anglican theologian. For Waterland, see *O. D. N. B.* See too, Sutton, "The Sacramental Theology of Daniel Waterland."

18 *Remains*, Vol. 1, p. 487. See below, p. 195.

19 *Remains*, Vol. 1, pp. 505, 499. See, also: Vol. 2, pp. 460, 463; *B. C. P.*, p. 215.

20 *Remains*, Vol. 1, p. 484.

21 Ibid., Vol. 2, pp. 466, 490.

taken by the Tractarians. For earlier High Churchmen, "baptismal regeneration was," to borrow Pusey's words, "a change of state only;" for the Tractarians, as for Knox, it was "a new principle of life in Christ."[22] This meant that for the Tractarians, as for Knox, there was an organic bond between baptismal regeneration and subsequent holiness of life, whereas earlier High Churchmen made a "*distinction ... between regeneration and renovation.*"[23] A further point on which Knox presaged the Tractarians concerned the loss and restoration of baptismal grace. For Knox, if Christians are called to advance and grow in the grace of their baptism, yet "he who has been made dead to sin, and alive unto righteousness, may again become dead to righteousness, and alive to sin; he may, through unfaithfulness, lose the blessing of 'spiritual regeneration.'"[24] Nonetheless, Knox added, "'by the grace of God, we may rise again, and amend our lives,'" for although the outward rite of baptism could not be repeated, the grace it gave could, if lost, be restored, a point which Knox used to buttress his differentiation between the rite's visible sign and its invisible effect.[25]

A noteworthy omission from Knox's treatment of baptism is the idea of federation or covenant, which Kenneth Stevenson has shown throughout his *Mystery of Baptism in the Anglican Tradition* (1998) to be a common theme of Anglican baptismal theology. The language of covenant is not, however, immediately evident in the Prayer Book, which Knox took as the primary guide for his teaching on the sacrament, and it is this which perhaps best explains the absence of the theme from his thinking.

3   Sources of Knox's Baptismal Theology

As we have seen, Knox's main aim in dealing with baptism was to expound what he saw as the doctrine of the Church of England. Nonetheless, he rejected an appeal to individual Anglican authors. "It is a well-known fact," he wrote, "that divines of the Church of England have, in this particular instance, shewn [sic] singular disagreement." As a result, he concluded, divine might

---

22   Pusey, "Preface" to *Parochial Sermons: Volume One*, pp. v–xxiii, p. vii. See, too, Pusey, *Scriptural Views of Holy Baptism* (*Tracts* 67–69), in which he speaks of baptism implanting "a principle of life, afterwards to be developed and enlarged by fuller influxes of [God's] grace" (p. 24).

23   Waterland, *Regeneration Stated and Explained*, 2, *Works*, Vol. 4, pp. 425–58, at p. 435.

24   *Remains*, Vol. 1, p. 493. See also: ibid., Vol. 1, pp. 494–96; Vol. 2, pp. 461–62.

25   Ibid., Vol. 1, p. 494, quoting the sixteenth of the Thirty-Nine Articles (*B. C. P.*, p. 399), p. 495.

"be so quoted against divine, as perfectly to neutralise this kind of evidence."[26] Instead of individuals, therefore, Knox turned to the liturgy of the 1662 Prayer Book. "In ascertaining the judgment of the Church of England on this important subject, we must attend only to her authoritative decisions," he declared. Thus, in the first place, one had to examine "the language of the form for the public baptism of infants. It was evidently intended to make this service an authentic vehicle of instruction respecting the sacred rite with which it is connected; to ascertain its import is, consequently, to learn, in the most direct and certain manner, what the Church of England believes on the subject of infant baptism."[27]

In accordance with this principle, Knox's baptismal teaching is very largely a commentary on the Prayer Book service, and, even when he did not reference it directly, liturgical allusions mark almost every page of his two treatises. He also cited other portions of the liturgy, as well as the Articles and the Catechism. For example, in defending his proposition that the grace of baptism can be lost, he furnished a catena of quotations from the Anglican standards: the Litany, the Catechism and the Thirty-Nine Articles.[28] Knox instanced, too, the authority of those who had produced the 1662 Prayer Book, the divines of the Savoy Conference.[29] As has already been noted, he adduced their argument that an *obex* could hinder the effect of the sacrament to show that baptism was not the same as regeneration. He likewise cited their introduction, in the wake of the Conference, of an office for the baptism of "those in riper years," to support his distinction between the nature of adult and infant christening.[30]

Comparing the teaching of Knox and Wesley, one is struck by the similarities between them.[31] Like Knox, Wesley held that the privileges of regeneration "are ordinarily annexed to baptism;" that "baptism, the sign" is distinct from "regeneration, the thing signified;" that "our Church supposes that all who are baptized in their infancy are at the same time born again;" and that by baptism the Spirit of adoption comes into believers' hearts, making them temples of its in-dwelling presence. Like Knox, too, Wesley held that baptism initiates its receiver into a life of holiness, a life which, again like Knox, Wesley warned was

26   *Remains*, Vol. 1, p. 500.
27   Ibid.
28   Ibid., pp. 519, 496, 494. For the passages adduced, see B. C. P., pp. 50, 212, 399.
29   *Remains*, Vol. 1, pp. 487, 502–3, 505, 511; Vol. 2, p. 235, note. As the last-mentioned passage indicates, Knox's information about the Savoy Conference was derived, at least in part, from Richard Baxter's anonymously published *Accompt of All the Proceedings of the Commissioners of Both Perswasions* (1661).
30   *Remains*, Vol. 1, pp. 405–6. For the office, see B. C. P., pp. 205–11.
31   For Wesley's teaching on baptism, see Holland, *Baptism in Early Methodism*.

able to be lost through sin.[32] These similarities between Knox and Wesley help cast some light on the nature of Wesley's baptismal theology, which can appear somewhat opaque. Wesley has been seen as seeking to articulate an innovative position on baptism, one "that would take seriously the realities of evangelical conversions and yet not repudiate his own sacramental traditions."[33] Having read Knox, one may argue that rather than being an innovation, Wesley's baptismal teaching reflected Anglican doctrine, at least as it was represented by the Savoy divines and the Prayer Book which they produced. Their distinction between infants, who are regenerated by the sacrament *ex opere operato*, and adults, for whom regeneration is dependent on faith and repentance, can be seen as anticipating Wesley's position. Likewise, Wesley's theory that the grace of regeneration received by infants in baptism could be lost by sin, but restored by repentance, something which might involve an "evangelical conversion," may be regarded, with Knox, as the doctrine of the Thirty-Nine Articles.

There is an affinity to be noted between Knox's teaching and that espoused by the two seventeenth-century moderates who wrote at length on baptism, Jeremy Taylor and Simon Patrick.[34] Like Knox, Taylor saw the Spirit as bestowed in the sacrament. To quote his *Great Exemplar* (1649): "'[B]aptism is a new birth,' ... and from this time forward we have a new principle put into us, the spirit of grace." "The Holy Spirit," Taylor wrote, "descends upon us in baptism, to become the principle of a new life, to become a holy seed, springing up to holiness." Again like Knox, Taylor insisted that the sacrament produces its effect only in the case of "such as are servants of Christ, and hinder not the work of the Spirit of grace. For the water of the font, and the Spirit of the sacrament, are indeed to wash away our sins, and to purify our souls; but not unless we have a mind to be purified." Like Knox, too, Taylor maintained that "baptism and its effect may be separated and do not always go in conjunction; the effect may be before ... [or] after its susception [*sic*]." "God," he affirmed, "does not always give [the grace of the sacrament] at the instant, in which the church gives the sacrament."[35] Simon Patrick's views on baptism appear in his

---

32   Wesley, Sermon 18, "The Marks of the New Birth," 1, in Outler, ed., *Works of John Wesley*, Vol. 1, pp. 415–30, at p. 417; Sermon 45, "The New Birth," 4, 1, 2, in Outler, ed., *Works of John Wesley*, Vol. 2, pp. 187–201, at pp. 196, 197; Wesley, Sermon 18, "The Marks of the New Birth," 4, 2, in Outler, ed., *Works*, Vol. 1, pp. 415–30, at p. 428; Maddox, *Responsible Grace*, pp. 222–3.
33   Outler, ed., *Works of John Wesley*, Vol. 1, pp. 415–16 (italicized in the original).
34   For an introduction to the baptismal theology of these two writers, see Stevenson, *The Mystery of Baptism in the Anglican Tradition*, chapter 8, pp. 96–111, and chapter 10, pp. 125–38.
35   Taylor, *Great Exemplar*, Discourse 6, part 1, sections 16, 23, 27; part 2, sections 2, 8, in Heber, ed., *Works of Jeremy Taylor*, Vol. 2, pp. 242, 252, 255, 259, 266.

Aqua Genitalis (1658). His teaching parallels that of Knox in its insistence that, while ordinarily "we are regenerated and born again" in baptism, the mere reception of the rite is not sufficient. Baptism is "an engagement to holiness," Patrick asserted, and without the pursuit of holiness, "outward baptism will not save." For Patrick, however, baptism does not only engage Christians to holiness, it also makes holiness possible. This is because in baptism candidates receive "the promise of the Spirit, the effusion of which is likened to the pouring out of water, and so is in baptism most aptly signified and represented." The Spirit's presence means that the baptized can so grow in holiness as to reach perfection. As Patrick writes: "Through the Spirit of Christ, we shall be able to do valiantly, nothing shall be too hard to overcome, but we shall tread all our enemies under our feet", which is the same doctrine as we have already encountered in Knox.[36] Despite these similarities, Knox neither quoted nor even mentioned Wesley, Taylor or Patrick in his teaching about baptism, but such is his proximity to them, that it is hard to believe that he was not influenced by their views. In contrast, Knox explicitly invoked the Fathers, believing that the Church taught their doctrine.[37] Thus, in defence of his disjuncture of the sacramental sign from the grace it signifies, Knox appealed specifically to Cyril of Jerusalem, Origen and Augustine, from whose witness he concluded that "in the judgment of the ancient Church, the outward sacrament, and the inward blessing, were by no means considered as inseparably united, much less as identical ... they were concurrent only in such cases as offered no obstruction to the entrance of the Holy Spirit."[38] To Knox's explicit citation of the Fathers, one may add a possible allusion to Tertullian. When Knox speaks of the baptismal water serving "to make the ablution of the body effectual ... to the purification of the soul," there seems to be an echo of *De Resurrectione Carnis*, 8: "*caro abluitur, ut anima emaculetur.*"[39] The clearest patristic resonance in Knox's baptismal theology is, however, the idea that baptism is the start of a new life animated by the Holy Spirit. Clement of Alexandria, for example, "emphasizes," in Everett Ferguson's phrase, "the divine life ... that results from

---

36   Patrick, *Aqua Genitalis*, in Taylor, ed., *Works of Symon Patrick*, Vol. 1, pp. 1–64, 30, 21, 40, 25, 46.

37   *Correspondence*, Vol. 2, p. 184; *Remains*, Vol. 1, pp. 487, 486, 521; Vol. 2, p. 462.

38   *Remains*, Vol. 1, pp. 486–87. Knox translates directly from Cyril's *Procatechesis*, 2 (*P. G.*, Vol. 33, col. 336); he cites Origen's "Homily 3 on Numbers," 1 (*P. G.*, Vol. 12, col. 594); and Augustine's *De Baptismo contra Donatistas*, 4, 21, (*P. L.*, Vol. 43, col. 172).

39   *P. L.*, Vol. 2, col. 852, "the flesh is washed, that the soul may be cleansed" (my translation). For Knox's statement, see *Remains*, Vol. 1, p. 502. For his knowledge of Tertullian, see above, p. 129, note 54.

[baptismal] regeneration."[40] We find the same teaching in Pseudo-Macarius, who has what Ferguson describes as a "special concern" for the doctrine of the Holy Spirit given in baptism being the means of Christians' spiritual growth.[41] Chrysostom, likewise, frequently speaks of the Spirit in relation to baptism, which he habitually described in terms of regeneration or re-birth.[42] In this connection, he depicts the Holy Spirit as coming down to sanctify the baptismal waters, an image which, as we have already seen, Knox employed, although in Knox's case it derived more immediately from the Prayer Book.[43] For Chrysostom, as for Knox, the Spirit also descends on the baptismal candidates, to make them holy. Again like Knox, Chrysostom stressed that if God has made us holy in baptism, "we must continue holy," a theme which is especially strong in his *Baptismal Instructions*, the "predominant concern" of which is, to quote again Ferguson, "the consequences from baptism for one's moral conduct."[44]

4   The Eucharistic Presence

As with baptism, Knox saw the Eucharist as a sacrament, and thus composed both of a material and a spiritual element.[45] He viewed this bi-partite structure as an act of divine condescension to human nature, made up, as it was,

---

40   Ferguson, *Baptism in the Early Church*, p. 311; For Clement's baptismal theology, see Ferguson, ibid., pp. 309–21. See also above, p. 77.

41   Ferguson, *Baptism in the Early Church*, p. 729. Fergusson discusses the baptismal views of Pseudo-Macarius on pp. 728–32.

42   Ibid., pp. 555, 589.

43   See above, note 15. For the image in Chrysostom, see Ferguson, *Baptism in the Early Church*, p. 559.

44   Ferguson, *Baptism in the Early Church*, p. 559; Chrysostom, "Homily 1 on Ephesians," 2, *P. G.*, Vol. 62, col. 12; Ferguson, *Baptism in the Early Church*, p. 562; see also, p. 537. For Chrysostom's baptismal teaching, see ibid., pp. 533–63.

45   For Knox's Eucharistic theology, see also the essays which precede and follow the "Treatise" in the *Remains*: the "Letter to John S. Harford, Esq., Prefatory to the Treatise on the Eucharist" (1826), and the "Postscript to the Treatise on the Eucharist" (undated), *Remains*, Vol. 2, pp. 154–183, 250–85. Part of Knox's tract "On the Nature of Our Salvation Through Christ" (undated) likewise deals with the topic, *Remains*, Vol. 2, pp. 398–436. His teaching on the Eucharist is also found in several letters: two to Jebb, those of September 26, 1824, and December 31, 1829, published in the *Correspondence*, Vol. 2, pp. 505–7, 579–81; one to "Mr. S.," undated, published in the *Remains*, Vol. 4, pp. 307–11; and one to Wilberforce, dated August 31, 1818, published in Wilberforce's *Correspondence*, Vol. 2, pp. 397–410. In the secondary literature, the subject of Knox's Eucharistic theology has been dealt with at some length by Peter Barrett in his 2000 article "Alexander Knox: Lay Theologian of the Church of Ireland."

of body and soul.[46] The material element was not unimportant: "bread, the prime nourishment of human life, and wine, the prime cherisher of human weakness."[47] Nonetheless, Knox's chief focus was not on the visible, material aspect of the sacrament. For him, the Eucharist was very much more than "a mere ceremony," an external rite.[48] It was, above all, a sign and a means of grace. Because he viewed this grace as that "by which alone we can live ... [and] grow up and advance as Christians," to neglect the Eucharist was, Knox argued, "to neglect both present and everlasting salvation."[49] He charged the Church of his day with such neglect, the vital significance of the sacrament being obscured by "low notions."[50] These "low notions" Knox ascribed especially to Bishop Benjamin Hoadly, although, as Nockles has pointed out, Hoadly's opinions did not "prevail generally among the clergy" at the start of the nineteenth century.[51] Their understanding of the Eucharist was predominantly the receptionism espoused by Waterland in his *Review of the Doctrine of the Eucharist* (1737), but this doctrine, too, was rejected by Knox. The theory of receptionism maintains that, at the same time as communicants physically receive the Eucharistic bread and wine, so spiritually, by faith, they receive Christ's body and blood. Knox applauded the doctrine for its support of "the general idea of grace concurring in the sacramental act," but objected to it for denying "any mysterious connexion [*sic*] of that grace with the symbols."[52] This disconnect resulted in receptionism leading, like memorialism, to Eucharistic piety becoming "deeply chilled," Knox held. It stifled the effects which the sacrament was intended by its divine author to have on "the natural feelings of man," he charged, the "spiritual sustenance and comfort" that it was supposed to convey.[53] To remedy

---

46   *Remains*, Vol. 2, pp. 228, 414.

47   Ibid., p. 206.

48   Ibid., p. 247.

49   Ibid., pp. 273, 234. For the importance which Knox attaches to the Eucharist as a means of grace see, e.g., ibid., Vol. 2, pp. 276, 279, 400–402, 411, 419–20; Vol. 4, pp. 310–11.

50   Knox to William Wilberforce, letter, August 31, 1818, in Wilberforce, *Correspondence*, Vol. 2, pp. 397–410, at p. 405.

51   Nockles, *Oxford Movement in Context*, pp. 236–7. For Benjamin Hoadly (1676-1761) – Knox spells the name "Hoadley" – see *O. D. N. B.* His memorialism is set out in his *Plain Account* (1735). More generally for understandings of the Eucharist in the Church of England at this time, see Stone, *Doctrine of the Holy Eucharist*, Vol. 2, p. 515.

52   *Remains*, Vol. 2, p. 194 (the symbols being the bread and wine).

53   Knox to William Wilberforce, letter, August 31, 1818, in Wilberforce, *Correspondence*, Vol. 2, pp. 397–410, at p. 405; *Remains*, Vol. 2, pp. 248, 246 (punctuation slightly altered).

this situation, Knox sought to present his contemporaries with what he termed "a correct, and well-defined notion of the eucharist [*sic*]."[54]

No less than memorialism or receptionism, Knox, as we have seen, rejected transubstantiation in favour of virtualism.[55] Derived from the Latin *virtus*, this theory holds that the bread and wine are, as Knox defined it, "the vehicles of [Christ's] saving and sanctifying power."[56] But, more than this, the power of Christ was, for Knox, so closely united to the elements that they acquired a new status, becoming "the permanent representatives of his incarnate person." They were "not merely the instruments of his power, but the effectual representations of himself," Knox maintained.[57] Accordingly, the elements should be paid the greatest reverence, "valued, venerated and loved ... all but adored." And yet, if the elements themselves were not to be adored, Christ in them was, Knox argued. Distinguishing between "the visible symbols of the Eucharist [and] him who makes them 'the hiding of his power,'" he insisted that "the Lord's body is to be *discerned* in the Eucharist." Christ is, Knox asserted, "as really as ever, Emmanuel, God with us ... continually [revisiting] us, in all the majesty of his divine, and in all the meekness of his human nature ... to communicate his very self to us, and receive, in return, the homage of our hearts." This being so, Christians should "joyfully and reverently approach to do homage to [their] King, who, in this his own peculiar institution, comes to diffuse benediction in his mystical Zion."[58]

How Christ's power is united to the sacramental elements remained for Knox a mystery, a subject on which "it would be presumptuous to indulge in any hypothetic speculation." He was willing to say only that it came about "through the ever-co-operative agency of the Holy Ghost." This action of the Spirit made the Eucharist an objective blessing. "[I]n the sacred Eucharist," Knox held, "we

---

54 *Correspondence*, Vol. 2, p. 506.

55 See above, pp. 33–34.

56 *Remains*, Vol. 2, p. 155. See, also, pp. 184, 277. *Virtus* means "power."

57 *Remains*, Vol. 2, pp. 155, 209. In this regard, we may note that Alf Härdelin is, as Rowell remarks, "not quite accurate" on this point ("Theological Forerunners," p. 40). Härdelin ascribed to Knox the view that "the gift [given in the Eucharist] is Christ's body and blood in power and effect, but the elements are only considered to be the signs of this gift and not the actual instruments and vehicles of its conveyance" (*Tractarian Understanding of the Eucharist*, p. 126).

58 *Remains*, Vol. 2, pp. 432 (alluding to Habakkuk 3.4, as rendered by the Authorized Version), 430 (emphasis in the original, with an allusion to 1 Corinthians 11.29), 429, 247. See, likewise, Knox's statement that we are to "look beyond the means, to the appointed Agent, who conceals himself, as it were, behind those material veils." "We see God himself, in his appointed ordinance" (*Remains*, Vol. 2, p. 407).

do not concur, as workers together with God; but expect the blessing, directly and exclusively, from his own Almighty power."[59] Knox's intention in saying this was by no means to exclude all "strict and proper co-operation of the communicant, in his reception of the eucharistic blessing," nor to "lessen the importance, or question the necessity of, due predisposition" in order to receive the sacrament.[60] Rather, he wanted to counteract the importance placed by receptionists on the subjective faith of the communicant, which they saw as necessary to make present the body and blood of Christ.

How did Knox's understanding of the Eucharist relate to his understanding of baptism? He viewed both as sacraments, visible signs of invisible grace, which transformed the Christian. There was, however, a significant difference in his thinking on the two. With respect to baptism, he taught that the sign and the grace are distinct and separate; with respect to the Eucharist, he maintained that the sign and the grace, although distinct, are inseparably united. There is an anomaly here, it seems, which he did not address.

5   Sources of Knox's Eucharistic Theology

Knox wrote that his ideas on the Lord's Supper came from Scripture, first, and then "our formularies."[61] In appealing to Scripture, Knox took two separate lines of approach. One was to invoke what he called "the general analogy of the divine proceedings." Throughout the Bible God was seen to convey spiritual blessings by physical means, the supreme instance being the incarnation, in which God "united himself to ... human flesh." From this premise, it was reasonable to suppose that God would act in a similar way with regard to the Eucharist, Knox contended.[62] His second tactic consisted of an appeal to specific passages, especially John 6.25–71, 1 Corinthians 10.16–22 and 1 Corinthians 11.17–34, all of which he believed supported his doctrine.[63]

---

59   *Remains*, Vol. 2, pp. 225, 216, 260, 276.
60   Ibid., p. 281.
61   Ibid., Vol. 4, p. 308.
62   Ibid., Vol. 2, pp. 195, 230–1.
63   For Knox's use of John 6. 25–71, see *Remains*, Vol. 2, pp. 192, 203–6, 262–63, 267, 274, 279–80, 398–403, 412–13, 430–31. For his use of 1 Corinthians 10.16–22, see *Remains*, Vol. 2, pp. 213–220, 225, 226–27, 245–47, 260, 412–14, 417, 420. For his use of 1 Corinthians 11.17–34, see *Remains*, Vol. 2, pp. 220–25, 415–18, 426–28, 430.

In his discussion of the Eucharist, Knox was chiefly concerned, as so often, with what "our Church" teaches.[64] To explore this teaching, he turned, firstly, to the Book of Common Prayer, invoking the third exhortation at Communion, which speaks of how "we spiritually eat the flesh of Christ, and drink his blood; ... we dwell in Christ, and Christ in us; we are one with Christ, and Christ with us." "It would hardly be possible to convey the notion which I have wished to express, more strictly, more fully, or more profoundly, than in those words," he commented. He also referenced the formula used in the administration of communion: "The Body of our Lord Jesus Christ, which was given for thee, preserve thy body and soul unto everlasting life."[65] He referenced, too, the rubrics introduced (or, more properly, re-introduced, as he argued) in the 1662 revision of the Prayer Book. He saw these rubrics as effecting "a kind of revolution," returning the Church of England to a more Catholic expression of its Eucharistic belief than had existed since the promulgation of the second Edwardine Prayer Book in 1552.[66] Knox did not specify which rubrics he meant; probably he envisaged the rubric preceding the Eucharistic prayer, which speaks of it as "the prayer of consecration;" and the rubric which follows the Communion, which seems to ascribe the consecration to the words of institution. No doubt, he also had in mind the prescription that Communion was to be received "meekly kneeling," and the explanation of this practice given in the so-called "black rubric." The wording of this rubric contains a subtle change, from the disavowal in 1552 of a "real and essential presence," to the repudiation in 1662 of the "Corporal Presence of Christ's natural Flesh and Blood." This change marked, in the eyes of High Churchmen "a defence of the doctrine of the real presence, rather than a denial of it," to quote the words of the orthodox commentators, Proctor and Frere. Finally, Knox may have been thinking of the rubrics regarding the treatment of the bread and wine left over after Communion. The 1662 Prayer Book directs that the "consecrated Elements" should be placed on the altar and covered with a "fair linen cloth" until after the end of the service, when they are to be "reverently" consumed, and not carried out of the church, as was permitted for the unconsecrated elements – directions which Knox could have interpreted as supporting his views.[67]

Besides the liturgy, Knox appealed to the Thirty-Nine Articles. He quoted Article Twenty-five's teaching that the sacraments are *"effectual signs of*

64   *Remains*, Vol. 2, pp. 189, 193, 195, 262–3.
65   B. C. P., p. 188; *Remains*, Vol. 2, pp. 262–3; B. C. P., p. 192; *Remains*, Vol. 2, p. 187.
66   *Remains*, Vol. 2, p. 188.
67   B. C. P., pp. 191–2, 195; Proctor and Frere, *New History of the Book of Common Prayer*, p. 197; B. C. P., pp. 192, 195.

grace ... by [which], God works invisibly in us." In these words, "the instrumentality of the visible signs is, evidently, made the very essence of a Sacrament," he contended. He likewise cited Article Twenty-eight, which talks of the body of Christ being *"given, taken,* and *eaten"* in the Lord's Supper, as if, Knox argued, "there was a solicitude ... explicitly to maintain the union between the heavenly and spiritual blessing, and the outward and visible sign." Article Twenty-nine was similarly construed by Knox as teaching that the visible symbols of bread and wine are to be regarded as the vehicles of the grace which the sacrament conveys.[68] As well as the liturgy and the Articles, Knox invoked the Catechism, which speaks of the bread and wine as the outward and visible sign of the sacrament, by means of which "'the body and blood of Christ ... are verily and indeed taken and received by the faithful.'"[69] By this invocation of the Anglican standards, Knox aimed to show that the position he maintained was nothing less than "the ... view of the Reformed Church of England."[70]

There is a close correspondence between Knox's and Wesley's Eucharistic doctrines.[71] Like Knox, Wesley re-affirmed the centrality and importance of the Eucharist in the Christian life. "[I]t is the duty of every Christian to receive the Lord's Supper as often as he can," Wesley declared; a duty which he himself scrupulously fulfilled, communicating on average every five days. The reason was that Wesley, like Knox, held the Eucharist to be the "grand channel" of God's grace to believers.[72] Like Knox, Wesley, was a virtualist. This is denied by some scholars, such as Khoo, and Stevenson, but it is clearly the position which Wesley sets out in his Eucharistic hymns.[73] They teach, first, that the Eucharist is both a sign and a means of grace:

> The sign transmits the signified,
> And grace is by the means applied.
> This grace is the power of God.

---

68   *Remains*, Vol. 2, pp. 189–91 (emphasis in the original). For the Articles concerned, see
      B. C. P., pp. 401–402.
69   *Remains*, Vol. 2, p. 192, quoting B. C. P., p. 216.
70   *Remains*, Vol. 2, p. 189.
71   Several studies of Wesley's Eucharistic teaching have been published, most notably:
      Rattenbury, *Eucharistic Hymns*; Bowmer, *Sacrament of the Lord's Supper*; Borgen, *Wesley
      on the Sacraments*; and more recently, Khoo, *Wesleyan Eucharistic Spirituality*.
72   Wesley, Sermon 101, "The Duty of Constant Communion," in Outler, ed., *Works of John
      Wesley*, Vol. 3, pp. 427–39, at p. 428; Bowmer, *Sacrament of the Lord's Supper*, p. 17; Khoo,
      Wesleyan Eucharistic Spirituality, p. xvi.
73   For Khoo's position, see *Wesleyan Eucharistic Spirituality*, p. 72; for that of Stevenson, to
      whom she appeals, see *Covenant of Grace Renewed*, p. 172.

For example, hymn 92 affirms:

The spirit and power
Of Jesus our God,
Is ... found in this life-giving food!

In a similar vein, hymn 58 asks:

Thy power into the means infuse,
And give them now their sacred use.[74]

This virtualism in John Wesley ought not to surprise us. It had a long pedigree within the High Church tradition from which Wesley came, its great champions being the Non-Jurors, with whom he had come into contact at Oxford. The Non-Jurors, for their part, derived the doctrine from John Johnson and his *Unbloody Sacrifice* (1714–18), with which Wesley was also well-acquainted.[75]

Despite the similarities between them, Knox did not appeal to Wesley as an authority for his virtualism, nor did he cite the Non-Jurors. He mentioned Johnson, but it is clear that he had read him only after he had already formulated his own position.[76] Rather, the authorities to whom Knox referred are: Thomas Jackson; John Overall; Samuel Horsley; and, above all, Nicholas Ridley. Thomas Jackson, Dean of Peterborough, and President of Corpus Christi College, Oxford, has been described as an "Oxford Platonist." His Eucharistic teaching was not without ambiguity, but it may be interpreted in a virtualist sense. Indeed, Dugmore goes so far as to say that virtualism is a "pronounced feature of [Jackson's] teaching." This, certainly, was how Knox read him; he quoted with approval Jackson's statement that Christ as God is present in the sacrament "in an extraordinary manner ... and, by the power of his Godhead, thus extraordinarily present, he diffuseth the virtue or operation of his human nature for the vivification of those who ... receive the sacramental pledges."[77]

74   Wesley, *Hymns on the Lord's Supper*, hymn 71, verse 1, p. 86; hymn 92, verse 1, p. 102; hymn 58, verse 4, p. 78.

75   For a full discussion of the contacts between Wesley and the Non-Jurors, see Hammond, "Restoring Primitive Christianity," pp. 49–54. For the High Church tradition of virtualism, see Dugmore, *Eucharistic Doctrine*, chapter 5, "John Johnson and The Non-Jurors," pp. 140–54. For Wesley's acquaintance with Johnson, see Bowmer, *Sacrament of the Lord's Supper*, pp. 30–31.

76   *Correspondence*, Vol. 2, p. 557.

77   For Jackson (1579–1640), see Hutton, "Thomas Jackson;" for his sacramental teaching, see Stone, *Doctrine of the Holy Eucharist*, Vol. 2, pp. 293–7. Knox cites Jackson, *Remains*, Vol. 2, p. 181, quoting from book four of volume 11 of Jackson's monumental *Commentaries on the Apostles' Creed*, p. 334. For the quotation from Dugmore, see *Eucharistic Doctrine*, p. 52.

The doctrine of John Overall, Regius Professor of Divinity at Cambridge, Dean of St Paul's and Bishop of Norwich, appears clearer than Jackson's, at least in the passage which Knox quoted from him. In this passage, Overall says that Christ is truly present in the sacrament, and is truly set before us, joined to the elements, so that in receiving the bread and wine the communicant receives, at the same time, the body and blood of Christ, albeit '"modo mystico, coelesti, ac spirituali."'[78] Samuel Horsley, successively Bishop of St David's, Rochester and St Asaph, is clearer still. Knox quoted one of Horsley's episcopal charges, in which the bishop told his clergy to instruct their parishioners in what he termed the true notion of a sacrament; "that the sacraments are not only signs of grace, but means of the grace signified, the *matter of the sacrament* being by Christ's appointment, and the operation of the Holy Spirit, *the vehicle of grace* to the believer's soul."[79]

In relation to the Eucharist, the Anglican theologian to whom Knox most appealed was the man he called "[o]ur justly celebrated Ridley."[80] Knox's view of Ridley is interesting. He appears to have derived it from what he termed the "very useful preliminary discourse" which William Hopkins prefaced to his *Book of Bertram or Ratramnus ... Concerning the Body and Blood of the Lord* (1686), an edition, with English translation, of Ratramnus's *De Corpore et Sanguine Domini Liber*.[81] Ratramnus, or "Bertram" as Knox, Hopkins, and Ridley all call him, was a ninth-century monk from Corbie in Picardy, who wrote his treatise in defence of the opinion that the Eucharist was not the "true" body of Christ, but only a "figure" of his body, a view which he presented as being that of the Fathers.[82] Inspired, seemingly, by Hopkins, Knox portrayed

---

78 *Remains*, Vol. 2, p. 182: "in a mystical, heavenly and spiritual manner" (my translation). For Overall's doctrine, see: Dugmore, *Eucharistic Doctrines*, pp. 39–40; Stone, *Doctrine of the Holy Eucharist*, Vol. 2, pp. 251–3. For Overall himself (1559–1619), see *O. D. N. B.* Knox cites Overall, *Remains*, Vol. 2, pp. 181–2, quoting from his *Praelectiones seu Disputationes*, pp. 212–23.

79 *Remains*, Vol. 2, p. 195. The quotation comes from the 1800 *Charge of Samuel, Lord Bishop of Rochester*, p. 28. There was no emphasis in the original; this was added by Knox to underline Horsley's agreement with his position. For Horsley (1733–1806) see Mather, *High Church Prophet*, especially pp. 204–5 for Horsley's teaching on the Eucharist.

80 *Remains*, Vol. 2, p. 185. Ridley is eulogized repeatedly by Knox. For examples, see: *Remains*, Vol. 1, pp. 379, 380–5, 390; Vol. 2, pp. 168–71, 186, 188; Vol. 3, p. 54; Vol. 4, p. 429; *Correspondence*, Vol. 1, p. 586; *Appendix*, pp. 374, 382, 387. For Ridley (c. 1500–55), see *O. D. N. B.*

81 A copy of the book was held at the Bolton Library in Cashel and was perhaps the one consulted by Knox. The Bolton collection is now held by the University of Limerick, where it is in the process of being re-catalogued.

82 For Knox's debt to Hopkins, in his view of Ridley see *Remains*, Vol. 2, p. 160. For Hopkins (1647–1700) see *O. D. N. B.* For Ratramnus (died c. 868) and his teaching see Kilmartin, *Eucharist*, pp. 82–89.

Ridley as follows. Brought up to believe in transubstantiation, Ridley discovered the patristic doctrine of the Eucharist by reading Ratramnus, and embraced it wholeheartedly. When others, with Archbishop Thomas Cranmer
at their head, allowed themselves to be led astray by what Knox derided as
"Helvetic" influences, "the frigid notions of certain continental divines," Ridley
stood firm, seeking, in Knox's words, "to preserve Catholicity in the Church of
England." Indeed, according to Knox, he even managed to infuse the Catholic
doctrine of the Eucharist into the first Edwardine Prayer Book of 1549, behind
the production of which he was the guiding hand.[83] Although short-lived, this
liturgy influenced the Prayer Book of 1662, Knox contended, enshrining in it
the patristic understanding of the Eucharist.[84]

What is one to make of this hypothesis? Knox was certainly right to say that
Ridley's thinking was influenced by Ratramnus. "Bertram," Ridley himself relates, "was the first that pulled me by the ear, and that first brought me from
the common error of the Romish church, and caused me to search more dili-
gently and exactly both the Scriptures and the writings of the old ecclesiastical
fathers in this matter." Knox was also correct in asserting that this influence
endured. Defending his views in Oxford in 1554, Ridley declared:

> [T]hink not, that because I disallow that presence [transubstantiation], ...
> that I therefore go about to take away the true presence of Christ's body
> in his supper.... [W]ith Bertram ... I confess that Christ's body is in the
> sacrament in this respect; namely, as he writeth, because there is in it the
> Spirit of Christ, the power of the word of God, which not only feedeth the
> soul, but also cleanseth it.[85]

What did Ridley mean by this? There is, in MacCulloch's words, "an awkward
ambiguity in Ridley's stance on Eucharistic presence," and it is easier to see
what he rejected (transubstantiation), rather than to grasp what he actually believed.[86] It is possible to see him as a virtualist; nonetheless, it seems

---

83 Knox speaks both of the first Edwardine Prayer Book (*Remains*, Vol. 2, pp. 172–3), and of
    the service of 1548 (ibid., p. 169), the latter being the basis of the former.
84 *Remains*, Vol. 2, pp. 185, 169, 171. For Knox's entire thesis concerning Ridley, see ibid.,
    pp. 168–172. For Knox's view on the 1549 Prayer Book, see above, p. 55.
85 Ridley, "Disputation at Oxford," in Christmas, ed., *Works of Nicholas Ridley*, pp. 187–252, at
    pp. 206, 201–2. Knox quoted this passage verbatim, calling it an "express avowal of Ridley's
    perfect concurrence with Bertram" (*Remains*, Vol. 2, pp. 170–1). Although Ridley attributes
    the evolution of his opinions on the sacrament to "Bertram," he cannot have been im-
    mune to the influence of continental thinking, as Peter Brooks points out (*Cranmer's
    Doctrine of the Eucharist*, pp. 59–60).
86 MacCulloch, *Tudor Church Militant*, p. 69. See, too, Stone, *Doctrine of the Holy Eucharist*,
    Vol. 2, p. 195.

more compelling to understand his position as "non-realist," indistinguishable from Cranmer's.[87] Where there can be no disagreement is that Knox's portrayal of Ridley as the architect of the 1549 liturgy is mistaken: to quote again MacCulloch, "the author of the [1549] Prayer Book" was Cranmer. Nor is it realistic to see this liturgy as "Catholic" in Knox's sense of the word; as MacCulloch has also demonstrated, the "clear purpose" of the 1549 book "was to attack the notion of real presence."[88]

In discussing the Eucharist, except for a brief reference to Joseph Mede, Knox made no appeal to the writings of seventeenth-century moderates.[89] This is surprising, for the Eucharist was not a topic which they ignored. Especially remarkable is the omission of any reference to Jeremy Taylor, the Eucharist being a subject to which, he repeatedly devoted his attention, and one which inspired some of his most sublime writing.[90] The reason that Knox did not cite the moderates may be, perhaps, that their teaching was somewhat "lower" than his, yet this does not apply to Taylor, the similarity of whose doctrine to Knox's was such that it led Henry McAdoo to speculate about Taylor's influence on him.[91] Surprising, too, is the lack of attention which Knox appears to have paid to the Eucharistic teaching of the Fathers. One may infer that the lacuna was noted by Knox's friend and correspondent, John S. Harford, for we find Knox telling him:

The subject to which you turn my attention, I am scarcely qualified to write upon; as I have never actually examined the volumes of the Fathers respecting it. The truth is, I was so completely satisfied with the quotations which I had met in trustworthy writers of later times, that I felt, as I thought, no necessity for going further. The impression on my mind has

87   See MacCulloch, *Thomas Cranmer*, p. 383. For Ridley as a virtualist, see Macquarrie, *Guide to the Sacraments*, p. 125.

88   MacCulloch, *Thomas Cranmer*, pp. 211, 386. Later on in the same book MacCulloch describes as "theological fools' gold" those passages in the 1549 Prayer Book seized on by Anglo-Catholics as evidence that the first Edwardine liturgy presents a conservative view of the Eucharist (p. 486). For a full discussion of the issue, see especially pp. 410–16. See too, Brooks, *Cranmer's Doctrine of the Eucharist*, chapter 5, "Pastoral Care: The Book of Common Prayer," pp. 112–62. For the view that the 1549 liturgy is conservative and "Catholic," see, for example, Dugmore, *The Mass and the English Reformers*. Dugmore's argument, which is theologically motivated, appears historically unconvincing.

89   *Correspondence*, Vol. 2, pp. 508–10. For Joseph Mede (1586–1639), see *O. D. N. B.* Knox refers to him several times; see: *Remains*, Vol. 1, pp. 153, 155, note; Vol. 3, p. 44; *Appendix*, p. 390.

90   Porter, *Jeremy Taylor*, p. 61.

91   McAdoo and Stevenson, *The Mystery of the Eucharist in the Anglican Tradition*, p. 38. For an analysis of Taylor's sacramental teaching, see also McAdoo, *Eucharistic Theology of Jeremy Taylor Today*.

been, that the ancient writers of the Church were agreed in ascribing to the consecrated elements in the Eucharist an unutterable and efficacious mystery, in virtue of our Saviour's words of institution, by which he had made those elements, when consecrated after his example, the vehicles of his saving and sanctifying power: and, in that respect, the permanent representatives of his incarnate person. But, notwithstanding this exalted estimate of the Eucharist, the notion of a literal transubstantiation, such as was subsequently introduced into the Western Church, would appear never to have entered into their mind.[92]

This statement is perplexing. Knox had a wide knowledge of patristic writings, and by 1826, when these words were written, he would surely have discovered the Fathers' Eucharistic teaching, not least that of John Chrysostom, for whom the title *doctor eucharisticus* is a common soubriquet.[93] The reason for Knox's reticence may be that, just as he perhaps found the moderates too low in their view of the sacrament, he found the Fathers too high, offering more support for a "literal transubstantiation" than for his own virtualist position.[94] As J. N. D. Kelly remarks, the Eucharistic language of the Fathers is "in general unquestioningly realist," with the vocabulary of conversion becoming predominant from the fourth century onwards, first in the East, then in the West.[95] Knox's "writers of later times" may not, therefore, have been such trustworthy guides as he led Harford to believe. But who were these writers? Knox names them as "Bertram," who needs no further comment, and "Mons[ieur] L'Arroque."[96] A seventeenth-century Huguenot, Matthieu de l'Arroque was author of the *Histoire de l'Eucharistie* (1669), which Knox described as "examining and ascertaining what the ancient Fathers thought on the subject of the eucharist [*sic*]." De l'Arroque's conclusion was that the Fathers did not believe in transubstantiation; rather, de l'Arroque maintained, "it is on account of their efficacy and virtue … that the Fathers called the Eucharist the

---

92   *Remains*, Vol. 2, p. 155 (format slightly altered).
93   For Chrysostom's Eucharistic teaching, see Di Nola, *La Dottrina Eucaristica di Giovanni Crisostomo*.
94   For the term "a literal transubstantiation," see also above, p. 34.
95   Kelly, *Early Christian Doctrines*, pp. 443, 446. Compare Lampe, "The Eucharist in the Thought of the Early Church," in Clements, et al., *Eucharistic Theology Then and Now*, pp. 34–58. Lampe argues that before the fourth century, the patristic consensus was that the sacrament is "dynamically, i.e., in grace and power, rather than in substance, that which it signifies" (p. 46), which would accord with Knox's position.
96   *Remains*, Vol. 2, p. 163.

Body and Blood of Christ." In other words, de l'Arroque portrayed the Fathers as virtualists, the position which Knox adopted.[97]

Knox held that his teaching about the reality of Christ's presence in the sacrament was verified by experience: in receiving communion, one felt the "mystical touch ... the virtuality of [Christ] Himself." This was not a theme that he developed, however, being perhaps too personal.[98] Nonetheless, it is a further reminder of the use which Knox made of experience in his methodology, as well as underlining once more the fact that for him theology was not an intellectual exercise, but a lived reality.

Lastly, we should note how Knox's view of the Eucharist exemplifies his Romanticism. First, in contradistinction to Hoadly's memorialism, a cerebral act, which one can see as reflecting the Age of Reason, Knox's doctrine was intended to promote an affective approach to Communion, in which the believer was filled with joy and "melting ardour."[99] Second, Knox's teaching echoes the Romantic notion of symbol, the idea of what Coleridge called the "translucence of the Eternal through and in the Temporal." Coleridge likewise spoke of the symbol "always [partaking] of the Reality which it renders intelligible," and this, too, finds a resonance in Knox's teaching: the sacramental bread and wine partake in the reality of Christ's body and blood.[100]

6   The Eucharistic Sacrifice and Priesthood

Knox was chiefly concerned with the Eucharist as a sacrament, but he did not altogether ignore what he termed "the commemorative sacrifice celebrated by Christ's own appointment, in his mystical Israel."[101] Nonetheless, in regard to the Eucharistic sacrifice, his main focus was on the agency by which he saw it as being offered, the ministerial priesthood. The topic is addressed especially in his "Letter to J. S. Harford, Esq., On Certain Great Truths Dwelt upon in the

---

97   For Knox's appeal to Ratramnus and de l'Arroque, see *Remains*, Vol. 2, p. 163. For Knox's description of the latter's work, see ibid., p. 164. For de l'Arroque' s conclusion, see *Histoire de l'Eucharistie*, p. 225 (my translation). For de l'Arroque, also spelled La Roque and Larroque (1619–84), see Masson, "Larroque ou La Roque." An English translation of de l'Arroque's work appeared in 1684 under the title, *The History of the Eucharist*. Knox possessed a copy (*Remains*, Vol. 2, p. 163), and if this was what he used to explore the Eucharistic theology of the Fathers, it meant that he was one step further removed from what they themselves originally wrote.

98   *Remains*, Vol. 4, p. 311.

99   *Remains*, Vol. 2, p. 242.

100   Coleridge, "The Statesman's Manual," in Lay Sermons, in White, ed., *The Collected Works of Samuel Taylor Coleridge*, 6, pp. 3–116, at p. 30.

101   Ibid., Vol. 3, p. 254. See, also, *Candid Animadversions*, p. 15.

Epistle to the Ephesians' (1814).[102] In this letter, Knox developed a theory of what he termed "analogical Judaism," a phrase which he repeated on numerous occasions.[103] His contention was that everything "permanently useful and intrinsically valuable" in Judaism continued to exist in the Christian church.[104] One of these "permanent Judaical characters" or characteristics was a "special priesthood," distinct from "the sacerdotal dignity of Christians generally."[105] The holders of this "special priesthood" were "priests of the new dispensation, as the sons of Aaron were priests of the old dispensation." The only difference was their "greater nobleness of service, and [their] more exalted dignity derived from that Head to whom they are subordinate." As this passage shows, the priest's office was "subordinately assistant to that of the great High Priest;" acting in Christ's person, the priest "officiates in the Institutor's place."[106] His role, however, in Knox's eyes, was not simply liturgical. The priest also participated in Christ's government of the church, sharing in his office as "the king ... of his mystical Israel."[107] Knox did not expand on his ideas of priesthood and sacrifice. "Protestant prejudice must be abated, before there can be a perfect development of this invaluable conception," he felt.[108] It was a strange remark for one who wrote as Knox did about the real presence, or imparted justification. Strange, too, is the fact that Knox described his views in terms of a new discovery, whereas the idea of a sacrificial priesthood was by no means unknown within the Anglican tradition, as will be demonstrated below, nor did it altogether lack proponents in his own day. Daubeny, for example, arguing from "the analogy [drawn by the Fathers] between the ministers of the law, and those of the Gospel," unambiguously declared it one of the tasks of the clergy "to offer up to GOD the sacrifice of the altar."[109]

7   Sources of Knox's Doctrine of Priesthood

In support of his theory of a "special priesthood," Knox appealed first to the Bible. "[T]he New Testament contains a great deal more, respecting a hierarchical church, than anyone *I* know of, has yet imagined," he confided to Jebb.

---

102   *Remains*, Vol. 3, pp. 231–76.
103   Ibid., pp. 247, 248, 253, 257, 259, 263. See, also: *Correspondence*, Vol. 1, pp. 492, 494, 495.
104   *Remains*, Vol. 3, p. 237.
105   Ibid., pp. 248, 250.
106   Ibid., pp. 255, 251. See, also, p. 252, where Knox speaks of Paul as being "a priest subordinately, as Jesus Christ is a priest supremely."
107   *Remains*, Vol. 3, pp. 249–50.
108   Ibid., p. 255.
109   Daubeny, *Appendix*, pp. 24–25, 310. See, also, p. 66, and, especially, pp. 310–14.

It teaches "a more express, and circumstantial transfer of hierarchical privileges, from the jewish [*sic*] nation to the gentiles ... than, at first view, could be
thought likely."[110] In particular, Knox referenced the teaching of the Epistle to
the Ephesians, that the Gentiles have been so united with the Jews, as to form
with them one body, "'co-harmonised and compacted.'" From this, Knox concluded, the church possesses certain features derived from Judaism.[111] Knox's
logic at this point seems unclear; his thesis, however, is plain enough: Israel and
its institutions continue in the church, albeit transformed; and this includes
a ministerial priesthood. This doctrine of ministerial priesthood or "special
priesthood" Knox bolstered with an appeal to three other passages of Scripture.
The first was Romans 15.16, where Paul speaks of himself as a λειτουργός
[*leitourgos*, minister] of Jesus Christ, exercising "a priestly function in relation
to the Gospel," ἱερουργοῦντα τὸ εὐαγγέλιον [*hierourgounta to euangelion*]. The
second passage was 1 Corinthians 9.13–14, which speaks about those who serve
in the temple and those who serve at the altar, and which Knox interpreted as
making a parallel between the Jewish priesthood and the Christian ministry,
something that "implies a substantial sameness of office." The third passage
was 1 Corinthians 10.15–22, where Paul relates "the cup of blessing which we
bless" and "the bread which we break" to both Jewish and pagan sacrifices.[112]

Knox's teaching on the Eucharistic sacrifice echoed Wesley's. Wesley's
Hymns on the Lord's Supper describe Communion as a "death-recording rite,"
not simply because by it Christians "call [Christ's] death to mind," but also
because it constantly reminds the Father of the sacrifice of Calvary:

> The Lamb his Father now surveys,
> As on this altar slain;
> Still bleeding and imploring grace
> For every soul of man.[113]

If there was a sacrifice, there had to be a priesthood to offer it, Wesley reasoned.
To quote Bowmer: "[H]is conception of the Ministerial office ... was dependent
upon his conception of the Lord's Supper, particularly as it implied a sacrifice."[114]
Thus, we find Wesley writing in 1745:

---

110   *Correspondence*, Vol. 1, p. 491. Emphasis in the original.
111   *Remains*, Vol. 2, pp. 240–41. Knox gives his own translation of Ephesians 3.6.
112   *Remains*, Vol. 2, pp. 251–55.
113   Wesley, *Hymns on the Lord's Supper*, hymn 1, verse 1, p. 37; hymn 25, verse 2, p. 56; hymn
       126, verse 5, p. 131.
114   Bowmer, *Sacrament of the Lord's Supper*, p. 163. One may note that in his letter to Harford,
       Knox takes the inverse route, moving from a concept of priesthood to the concept of
       sacrifice.

We believe there is, and always was, in every Christian Church (whether dependent on the Bishop of Rome or not), an outward priesthood, ordained by Jesus Christ, and an outward sacrifice offered therein, by men authorized to act as ambassadors of Christ and stewards of the mysteries of God. On what grounds do you believe that Christ has abolished that priesthood or sacrifice?[115]

Bowmer argues that Wesley's "belief in the priesthood of the Christian ministry" was "unwavering."[116] Thus, in the year before his death, 1790, in his sermon on "The Ministerial Office," also known as "Prophets and Priests," Wesley spoke repeatedly of "the office of a priest," which he defined as being "to minister in holy things, to offer up prayers and sacrifices," meaning, more specifically under the Christian dispensation, "to baptize [and] to administer the Lord's Supper;" "to administer the sacraments."[117]

    In teaching that the Eucharist was a sacrifice, Knox held a doctrine maintained not just by Wesley, but by a large number of Anglican theologians, including such moderates as Patrick, Mede and Taylor. To quote Taylor's *Clerus Domini* (1651): 'Now Christ did also establish a number of select persons to be ministers of [his] great sacrifice, finished upon the cross; that they also should exhibit and represent to God, in the manner which their Lord appointed them, this sacrifice, commemorating the action and suffering of the great priest.'[118] Knox's doctrine also parallels that of the Non-Jurors, particularly the teaching of Henry Dodwell and George Hickes. The latter's *Two Treatises* (1707) in particular shows a number of similarities with Knox, not least the use of the same three "proof-texts:" Romans 15.16; 1 Corinthians 9.13–14; and 1 Corinthians 10.15–22.[119]

---

115   Wesley to Westley Hall, letter, 27 December 27, 1745; see Wesley, *Journal*, Vol. 3, p. 230, entry for 27 December 1745 (format slightly altered).
116   Bowmer, *Sacrament of the Lord's Supper*, p. 165.
117   Wesley, Sermon 121, "Prophets and Priests," 2, 18, 12; in Outler, ed., *Works of John Wesley*, Vol. 4, pp. 75–84, at pp. 75, 82, 80.
118   Taylor, *Clerus Domini*, 5, 2, in Heber, ed., *Works of Jeremy Taylor*, Vol. 14, pp. 415–88, at p. 452. For Taylor's doctrine of Eucharistic sacrifice and priesthood, see McAdoo, *Eucharistic Theology of Jeremy Taylor Today*, pp. 80–84, 66–73, 95–103. For the teaching of Patrick see Dugmore, *Eucharistic Doctrine*, p. 112; for that of Mede see especially his *Christian Sacrifice* in *The Works of J. Mede*, Vol. 2, pp. 471–527. For the doctrines in Anglicanism more generally see McAdoo and Stevenson, *The Mystery of the Eucharist in the Anglican Tradition*, the second part of which, authored by Stevenson, is devoted to "The Mystery of Sacrifice."
119   For both Henry Dodwell (1641–1711) and George Hickes (1642–1715) see *O. D. N. B.* For Dodwell's teaching, see especially his *Discourse concerning the One Altar and the One Priesthood*.

Among the Fathers the Eucharist was regarded, in J. N. D. Kelly's words, "as the distinctively Christian sacrifice from the closing decade of the first century, if not earlier."[120] There are in particular three patristic passages which find echoes in Knox's teaching, all from authors with whom he was familiar. The first comes from Clement of Rome's *Letter to the Corinthians*, in which Clement draws an analogy between the Jewish hierarchy and the Christian ministry, similar to that propounded by Knox. "Certain functions," Clement writes, "have been entrusted to the high priest; and a proper place is assigned to the priests; and the Levites have been invested with their own service; while the lay-man is bound by the precepts concerning him."[121] The second passage is Cyprian's letter on the Eucharist to Caecilius, which speaks of "the priest who, in the place of Christ ... offers a true and perfect sacrifice in the church to God the Father," a sacrifice which Cyprian identifies with "the passion of the Lord." Cyprian also speaks in this letter of Christ as "*sacrificii hujus auctor*," a phrase which is paralleled by Knox's description of Christ as the "Institutor" of the Eucharistic sacrifice.[122] The third passage is chapter three of Chrysostom's *On the Priesthood*, in which Chrysostom draws an analogy between the Jewish and the Christian priesthood, quoting 2 Corinthians 3.10 to describe the latter as being "of a more excellent glory." For, Chrysostom demands, "when you see the Lord lying immolated, and the priest bent over the sacrifice praying, and everything red with that precious blood, can you think that you are amongst human beings on earth? Have you not rather been carried up into heaven?"[123] More generally, the idea that the church has replaced Israel is a common patristic trope, first articulated by Justin Martyr who, in his *Dialogue with Trypho*, declares: "We are the true, the spiritual Israel."[124]

All this, clearly stated in sources with which Knox was familiar, makes his claim to have made a new discovery rather perplexing, as we have already noted. Possibly, Knox meant that he had not realized how scriptural the doctrine of Eucharistic sacrifice was, before studying the Epistle to the Ephesians. Even so, it seems strange that, having made his "discovery," he should have remained so reticent about a doctrine which had such a firm grounding both in Anglicanism and in the Fathers.

---

120   Kelly, *Early Christian Doctrines*, p. 196.

121   Clement of Rome, *Letter to the Corinthians*, 40, *P. G.*, Vol. 1, col. 289.

122   Migne numbers this letter as 63; see *P. L.*, Vol. 4, cols. 383–401. For the passages cited see: section 14, col. 397; section 17, cols. 398–99; section 1, col. 384.

123   Chrysostom, *On the Priesthood*, 3, 4, *P. G.*, Vol. 48, col. 642.

124   Justin Martyr, *Dialogue with Trypho*, 11, *P. G.*, Vol. 6, col. 500; see also 135, col. 788: "We are the true Israelite people" (my translation). For an extended discussion of these passages see, Osborn, *Justin Martyr*, chapter 13, "The True Israel," pp. 171–85. For the idea of the church as the new Israel in patristic thought, see Liebster, "*Umkehr und Erneuerung im Verhältnis von Christen und Juden*."

CHAPTER 11

Alexander Knox's Theology (IV): Ecclesiology

This chapter investigates Knox's doctrine of the church. It analyses his description of it as "mystical," visible and hierarchical and discusses his distinction between the Catholic Church and what he termed "sects." It then explores his concept of the church as a mixed society; and his views on establishment, before examining the sources from which he drew his teaching. Although it is usual in systematic theology to deal with the church before the sacraments, the order here is inverted, for two reasons. First, the sacraments were, in Knox's theology, the primary instruments of justification, and therefore it seems more natural to treat of them immediately after discussing that topic. Second, in Knox's understanding, it is the sacraments which constitute the church. Baptism admits Christians into its fellowship, and this fellowship is expressed through participation in the one Eucharist.[1]

1   Knox's Description of the Church

The doctrine of the church relates to Knox's central theme of justification because the church is the setting in which justification occurs.[2] Knox nowhere gave a sustained account of his ecclesiology, akin to his tracts on salvation and the sacraments. This is by no means to say, however, that he had no doctrine of the church, and his teaching on the subject may be gleaned from a careful study of his writings. Of particular note are: *Candid Animadversions* (1794); the *Answer to Duigenan* (1810); the "Letter to J. S. Harford, Esq., On Certain Great Truths Dwelt Upon in the Epistle to the Ephesians" (1814); the *Appendix* (1815); and the undated essay "On the Parables Contained in the Thirteen Chapter of Saint Matthew."[3] Knox often described the church using the term "mystical:" "the mystical kingdom of Christ" most frequently; the "mystical body;" the "mystical Israel;" the "mystical Zion."[4] In the common usage of the time,

---

1   *Remains*, Vol. 2, p. 461; Vol. 4, pp. 260–1; *Candid Animadversions*, p. 5.
2   *Remains*, Vol. 4, p. 437.
3   For the letter to Harford, see *Remains*, Vol. 3, pp. 231–76; for the essay on the parables, see ibid., Vol. 1, pp. 447–67.
4   For examples of the usage "mystical kingdom," see: *Remains*, Vol. 1, pp. 68, 448, 463; Vol. 3, pp. 266, 274. For examples of the usage "mystical body," see: *Remains*, Vol. 3, pp. 241, 268;

"mystical" designated something "having a spiritual character," and this was what Knox meant when he employed the term. The church was not a human institution, but a society of supernatural origin, the object of God's secret plan, the μυστήριον [*mystērion*] spoken of in the letter to the Ephesians. This plan was, Knox explained, that "the christian [*sic*] church was, on a grand scale, to take the place of judaism [*sic*], so as to become the sphere, in which, as well as the organ, by which, all the magnificent prophecies of the Old Testament were to have their final fulfilment."[5] Knox stressed that the church was "an outward and visible kingdom upon earth."[6] He did not dispute the existence of an "internal and invisible [church]," which he defined as "that company of true believers which no human observer could ever enumerate, but which is ever present to the eye of God." This was not, however, the church described in the Bible. "[T]he Church recognised in the New Testament was not that supposed assembly or society of 'true believers,' but ... a visible institute, into which baptism gave admission; in which our Saviour had established a ministry of two orders; and the design of which was, to receive all, and make as many as possible what they ought to be."[7] Knox further taught that the Church was "not merely ... visible, but ... hierarchical." It was, he held, "stamped with an hierarchical character, from its commencement," Christ endowing it with a "well-regulated polity," corresponding to the "theo-political" organization of Israel. Just as in Israel, there were princes and elders, so in the church there are bishops and priests, he maintained.[8] This explains the importance that Knox accorded to episcopacy: in his view, bishops were a "divinely instituted authority." This, he believed, was what Catholic tradition taught, the Fathers unanimously affirming, in his estimation, that "[t]he constitutional power of the Church resided in its Episcopacy, whose authority was held to be derived from our Saviour himself ... through the apostles ... to whom bishops were regarded as regular successors."[9] This visible, hierarchical or episcopal church formed one body, Knox claimed, and this body he identified as "the true Church," the Catholic Church spread throughout the world. "The visible hierarchical Church is, indeed," he wrote, "as a tree dividing, first into two trunks, Eastern and Western;

Appendix, p. 386; *Considerations*, p. 74. For "mystical Israel," see *Remains*, Vol. 3, pp. 250, 254; for "mystical Zion," see ibid., Vol. 2, p. 247. See, also, on this topic, above, p. 209.

5 *Correspondence*, Vol. 1, pp. 493–4.

6 *Remains*, Vol. 1, pp. 488–9.

7 *Remains*, Vol. 1, pp. 489, 456; Vol. 4, p. 437. The mention of the ministry of "two orders" is intriguing, since Anglicanism traditionally speaks of a three-fold ministry, that of bishop, priest and deacon. Knox means, it seems, that the episcopate and presbyterate alone were established by Christ, the diaconate being instituted by the apostles. See: *Remains*, Vol. 3, p. 249; *Appendix*, pp. 362–3.

8 *Remains*, Vol. 1, p. 455 (punctuation slightly modified); Vol. 4, pp. 291–2; Vol. 3, p. 249.

9 *Answer to Duigenan*, p. 63.

then into several stems, representative of national churches; then into yet smaller stems, corresponding to ecclesiastical provinces; then into smaller still, answering to dioceses; and, finally, into the smallest of all, parochial churches."[10] Knox took this image of the "tree dividing" from Matthew 13.31–2, the parable of the mustard seed which from tiny beginnings grew so great that birds could perch in its boughs. The image calls to mind the "branch theory" of the church, which holds that the one Catholic Church is divided into several different yet essentially united parts: Anglican, Roman Catholic, and Orthodox. The theory was developed especially by William Palmer in his *Treatise on the Church of Christ* (1838). Palmer trained for ordination under Jebb, and was almost certainly influenced by Knox through him.[11] In Knox, the theory was no more than inchoate, hints of it being discernable in his description of the various "Catholic" denominations as "portions" of the one church. For instance, he called Roman Catholicism "the yet unreformed portion of the Catholic Church," while describing Anglicanism as "our portion of the Catholic Church."[12]

2   Knox's Theory of Church and Sects

Knox contrasted the Catholic Church and its constituent members with what he termed "sects" or "societies."[13] This distinction, quite independently of Knox, later became, through the work of Max Weber and Ernst Troeltsch, standard in the sociology of religion.[14] Of the two terms, "sect" and "society," Knox usually employed the first. In his writings, the expression did not have a pejorative connotation *per se*; it simply denoted those groups that had separated themselves from the various national churches which, in his estimation, composed the Catholic Church. Knox saw the existence of these sects as ordained by providence for the better fulfilment of God's purposes. To quote Charles

---

10   *Appendix*, p. 362, citing, in part, Ephesians 4. 4; *Remains*, Vol. 1, p. 455.
11   For William Palmer (1803–85), see *O. D. N. B.*, and below, pp. 256–57.
12   *Remains*, Vol. 3, pp. 326–7. For similar uses of the term "portion," which is frequent in Knox, see: *Remains*, Vol. 1, pp. 92, 391; Vol. 3, pp. 107, 119, 204, 261, 300, 318, 320; Vol. 4, pp. 292, 442.
13   "Christianity, as a collective system, exists only under the two forms, of national Churches, and sects or societies" (*Remains*, Vol. 1, p. 168).
14   For Weber (1864–1920), Troeltsch (1865–1923) and the "church-sect theory" see, e.g., Swatos, "Weber or Troeltsch?"

Dickinson's obituary of Knox for the *Christian Examiner*, Knox's ardent attachment to Anglicanism "produced no asperity towards other Christian bodies, to each of which he felt Providence had assigned its peculiar function." According to Dickinson, Knox was keen to promote this point. "It was his opinion," Dickinson wrote, "that the end which Providence designed to effect by the existence of various Christian denominations, was not sufficiently averted to, nor the good which they possessed within themselves at all times adequately estimated. He often applied himself to unfold this to the perception of others, and thus restrain controversy within the bounds of charity and prudence."[15] Knox held that "'whatever is,' providentially, 'is right.'" As he declared: "[A]ccording to my creed, things are what they are, because God has willed them to be so."[16] Sects, he claimed, were divinely-willed to have a "re-exciting function;" they came into existence to stir up religious revival. By contrast, establishments he defined as being more sober and dignified, working without "alarm or ecstasy" to fulfil their providential role of sustaining piety in society at large and transmitting religious truth from one generation to another.[17] Knox thus saw a correlation between the church/sect division, and the distinction which he made between the traditions of holiness and of grace. In general, he believed, teachers of grace belonged to sects, teachers of holiness, to established churches.[18] Remarkably for his age, Knox's vision extended beyond the confines of Christianity to embrace Islam. "Mahammedanism," as he termed it, was "a remarkable and important feature in the great scheme of providence."[19]

While justification was the main point on which Evangelicals criticized Knox, what the *British Critic* called "the very peculiar spirit of resolute Optimism which pervaded the mind of Alexander Knox" was the facet of his teaching to which High Churchmen most objected. They argued that it legitimized, in the *Critic's* words, "the wildest perversions, and the most pernicious errors," including those of what the *Critic* termed "Sectarians," seeing them as "not merely *overruled* for good," but rather as "so many appointed instruments and

15   *Christian Examiner*, 11.73 (July 1831), p. 563.

16   *Remains*, Vol. 4, p. 96 (alluding to Pope's *Essay on Man*, Epistle 1, lines 293–4); *Remains*, Vol. 1, p. 55.

17   *Remains*, Vol. 4, pp. 291–2.

18   Ibid., pp. 92, 173. For Knox's concept of two traditions in Christianity, see above, p. 68.

19   B. L., Add. Ms 41164, Correspondence between Alexander Knox and John Jebb (1812–30), fol. 214, Knox to John Jebb, letter, August 10, 1829. With regard to Islam, we may note that Knox's thesis about its providential role was picked up and developed by Charles Forster in his *Mahometanism Unveiled* (1829).

agencies, which have been expressly ordained ... in the scheme of Providence."
As we will see in chapter thirteen, the same charge was levelled against Knox
by the Tractarians.[20] In fact, however, Knox's attitude towards "sects" was not
as liberal as the *British Critic*, or indeed Dickinson, suggested, for despite their
providential origin, Knox refused to see sects as true churches, by which he
meant that they were not constitutive members of the Catholic Church. This
was because they lacked bishops; as Knox told Samuel Whitbread, in words he
underlined: "[A]n *unepiscopal church* is not *a genuine church*, that is, does not
form a *regular member* of the mystical *polity*."[21] Knox sought to balance this
"*ecclesiastical severity*," as he termed it, with "*Christian charity*." Even though
not "fully formed *together*" in harmony with the rest of the building, sectarian
Christians were nonetheless "*living stones*," he assured Whitbread.[22] In other
words, while not part of the visible church, they were still members of the invisible. Knox also touched on this point in relation to baptism, through which
all believers were united. To quote from his *Answer to Duigenan*: "[T]he *Unity*
of BAPTISM has secured, in spite of outward dissonance, the bland and
blessed feeling of a common Christianity. In virtue of this indissoluble link,
we are still by mutual acknowledgement, not only children of the same eternal
Father, but disciples (however in each other's estimation unfaithful and un-
worthy) of the same Divine Redeemer."[23]

3   Visible Unity

The already-existing unity of Christians was, Knox believed, to be more fully
realized with the progression of time; eventually all believers would be re-
united in a single, visible church. "[I]t is our persuasion that [unity] will be
attained," he informed Wilberforce, "for our Saviour's prayer cannot always
remain unanswered: sooner or later Christians will be one."[24] In the chain of
circumstances leading to this "future union of the whole [church]," the Church

20   *British Critic*, 17.34 (April 1835), pp. 288, 287, 286 (emphasis in the original). For the
     Tractarian criticism of Knox, see below, pp. 247, 253, 255.
21   Bodleian, Ms. Wilberforce c. 52, fols. 77–82, Knox to Samuel Whitbread, copy of a letter,
     December 1, 1812, fol. 81.
22   Ibid., fol. 80 (emphasis in the original). The building metaphor which Knox employs
     is based on a conflation of Ephesians 2.21–22 and 1 Peter 2.5. For Whitbread, scion of a
     well-known brewing-family, M. P. for Bedford, 1790–1815, see Fulford, *Samuel Whitbread,
     1764–1815.*
23   *Answer to Duigenan*, p. 31 (emphasis in the original).
24   Knox to William Wilberforce, letter, August 31, 1818, in Wilberforce, *Correspondence*, Vol. 2,
     pp. 397–410, p. 409. Knox alludes to John 17.21.

of England was providentially destined "to form an intermediate link." Neither Protestant nor Roman Catholic, but containing the best elements of both, it provided a perfect model for reconciliation. "[A] rallying point for safe escape from all religious errors and extravagances, on the one side and on the other," it was the "first fruits" of the unity willed by Christ.[25] Knox's vision of this unity was not limited to Protestants and Roman Catholics. As the struggle against Bonaparte brought the British into alliance with Russia, Knox looked forward to the Eastern Orthodox finding in the Church of England a conservatory of Greek patristic thought even more authentic than their own, something which would lead them, in a manner analogous to the process which he envisioned for the Roman Catholic Church, first to reformation, then to reunion.[26]

For Knox, membership of the visible church was no guarantee of salvation. Just as some outside the visible church were members of the invisible church, so, he insisted, members of the visible church could be reprobates. He taught that Christ permitted the visible church to be a mixed body in which "the good and bad were to continue together" until the end of time. Knox thus described the church as "a great house in which are vessels, not of gold and silver only, but, also, of wood and clay; and some to honour, and some to dishonour."[27]

4   Establishment

In his early work, *Free Thoughts* (1785), Knox defined the Church of England as

> [T]hat body of professing Christians who worship God according to the form laid down in the Book of Common Prayer, and who profess to believe the Creeds and hold the Doctrines therein contained. This Church is governed by a Primate, Archbishops, Bishops, and the inferior Orders of the Clergy, each in subordination to each other ... and all in subordination to his *Britannic* Majesty ... [N]o material alteration can be made either in the Government, Form, or Doctrine of this Church without his consent.[28]

---

25   *Remains*, Vol. 1, p. 403; Vol. 2, pp. 175–6; *Correspondence*, Vol. 1, p. 547.
26   *Remains*, Vol. 3, pp. 211–12. For Knox's vision for the reunion of the Church of England with the Roman Catholic Church, see above, pp. 31–32.
27   *Candid Animadversions*, p. 5; *Remains*, Vol. 4, p. 437 (alluding to 2 Timothy 2.20). See, also: *Remains*, Vol. 1, pp. 453–4; *Candid Animadversions*, p. 10; *Considerations*, pp. 10–12.
28   *Free Thoughts*, pp. 2–3.

"His Britannic Majesty" did not feature in Knox's later writings, yet the idea of establishment remained of vital importance for him.[29] As he wrote to Castlereagh, "Church and State are, in our idea, inseparable."[30] He saw their unity as being, like visibility and a hierarchical structure, a characteristic which the church inherited from Judaism, church and nation being but one in the Old Testament.[31] As such, Knox seems to suggest, establishment was part of the church's *esse*, "derived from the will and act of its adorable Founder."[32] Knox admitted that in practice establishment was not faultless; yet it was, "in spite of all its imperfections, that ... scheme, by means of which will be finally accomplished [the] general and lasting renovation of human society."[33] At the same time, establishment was not only the means leading to, but also a foretaste of, this future *apocatastasis*. Ultimately, Knox believed, in fulfilment of the prophecies made both by the Psalmist and Isaiah, "the kingdoms of this world will be the kingdoms of our Lord."[34] This eventuality he saw as nothing other than "the principle of Church establishments freed from abuse, purified from drossy mixtures, and applied exclusively to the proper object."[35] Before this time of fulfilment arrived, providence might allow periods of "[t]emporary adversity" to befall believers, such as the one he contemplated in his essay "On the Situation and Prospects of the Established Church"(1816).[36] Yet, he reflected, "a temporary depression of the English Church might exalt its moral qualities." Established, the Church was "too prosperous to call forth our finest feelings; where there was [*sic*] nothing but wealth and power, tenderness and sympathy could have no place." Shorn of its worldly attractions, however, the Church would be loved, he believed, for its own "intrinsic excellence." It would also be able to rediscover its essential nature as a Catholic body, returning to the "ancient stock, from which [it] derived [its] best being" (this point helped to make this essay particularly congenial to the Tractarians.)[37]

---

29   See, e.g., *Remains*, Vol. 1, pp. 169–72; Vol. 3, p. 107.

30   P. R. O. N. I., Castlereagh Papers, D3030/1123, Knox, "Draft Comments on the Union of the Churches" [1798].

31   *Remains*, Vol. 3, p. 248.

32   Ibid., p. 249.

33   Ibid., Vol. 1, p. 198.

34   Ibid., p. 170 (referencing Psalm 2.10–11; Psalm 72.10–11; Isaiah 52.15; 60.3, 10, 11, 12, 16), p. 169 (referencing Revelation 11.15).

35   *Remains*, Vol. 1, p. 172.

36   *Remains*, Vol. 1, pp. 53–69. This relatively early work, written against the background of Peel's plan for tithe-reform of the Irish Church does not present Knox's usual view of church-state relations. For the phrase "temporary adversity," see *Remains*, Vol. 1, p. 57.

37   *Remains*, Vol. 1, pp. 57, 56, 67. See below, p. 251.

In part, Knox's ecclesiology may be seen as a reaction to the altered position in which the Church of England found itself vis-à-vis the nation at the start of the nineteenth century.[38] Almost certainly it was shaped by his controversies both with what we might call the "Separating Methodists" and the "Separating Evangelicals," led by John Walker and Thomas Kelly. But the Pan-Protestantism championed by Evangelicals more generally, which Knox castigated as belief in a "notional church," was also doubtless a stimulus to his reflection.[39]

5   Sources of Knox's Ecclesiology

We have seen previously that "community" was one of the favoured themes of the Romantic period.[40] Knox's ecclesiology reflected this. It also reflected an underlying element of John Wesley's ecclesiology, which was essentially Catholic, derived from his High Church background.[41] One might object that Wesley's actions *vis-à-vis* the Church of England seem hard to reconcile with such an understanding of church order. As Hempton notes: "Wesley's support of the Church of England [was] always more impressive in thought than in deed." But it was precisely Wesley's "impressive thought," rather than his deeds, which influenced Knox, and, as we have seen, in combating the Methodists' separation from the Church of England, he argued that they were acting contrary to Wesley's teaching.[42]

Knox's ecclesiology also reflected the position of the moderates. According to "S. P.," the "latitude-men" had a "deep veneration" for episcopacy, which they "steadfastly" believed to be in itself the best form of ecclesiastical government, and "the same that was practised in the times of the Apostles."[43] The moderate whose ecclesiology most closely matches Knox's was not, however, one of the

---

38   See above, p. 37.

39   N. L. I., Ms 8868, Brodrick Papers, (folder 3), Knox to Charles Brodrick, September 9, 1808; *Candid Animadversions*, p. 5; *Considerations*, pp. 12, 31–32; B. L., Add. Ms 41163, Correspondence between Alexander Knox and John Jebb (1799–1811), fol. 80, Knox to John Jebb, letter, March 20, 1805. See, also, above, p. 48. For Walker, see above p. 58, and for Kelly p. 35. Both men seceded from the Church to found their own denominations.

40   See above, p. 98.

41   Oh, *John Wesley's Ecclesiology*, pp. 21, 240, 256. As in every other aspect of his theology, Wesley was an eclectic with regard to ecclesiology, and his understanding of the church is composed of numerous strands. Nonetheless, the Catholic element is of primordial importance, as Oh demonstrates, and it is this which Knox inherited from him.

42   Hempton, *Religion of the People*, p. 83. For Wesley and the Church of England, see above, p. 71.

43   S. P., *A Brief Account of the New Sect of Latitude-Men*, p. 8.

Cambridge Platonists, to whom "S. P." was referring, but rather Jeremy Taylor. Taylor's *Of the Sacred Order and Offices of Episcopacy* (1642), usually known as *Episcopacy Asserted*, declared bishops to be, according to the judgment of antiquity, "simply necessary, even to the being and constitution of a church." Without them, Taylor argued, there could be "no priest, no ordination, no consecration of the sacrament, no absolution, no rite or sacrament legitimately ... performed, in order to eternity." Like Knox, Taylor tempered severity with charity. It is not for us to condemn the members of non-episcopal bodies, Taylor cautioned; "They stand or fall to their own master." Nonetheless, objectively those who separated themselves from their bishops were guilty of schism.[44] A similar "ecclesiastical severity," but less "Christian charity," appears in the writings of the Non-Jurors, such as Henry Dodwell's *Separation of Churches* (1679) and Thomas Brett's *Divine Right of Episcopacy* (1718), which defined the visible church in terms of communion with the episcopate, separation from which meant the sin of schism.[45] Despite the similarities between them, Knox did not mention Taylor or the Non-Jurors in relation to his ecclesiology. The three figures to whom he made explicit appeal were John Pearson, Joseph Milner and "Mrs. Barbauld." Of the first, he told Jebb in a letter: "I wish you to read, attentively, what Pearson says on the article respecting the church." "It strikes me," Knox declared, "that he says more, than any other protestant [*sic*] has ventured to say, but I should think not a tittle more, than the concurrent sense of scripture justifies and requires." Pearson's position was this:

> All the churches of God are united into one by the unity of discipline and government, by virtue whereof the same Christ ruleth in them all. For they have all the same pastoral guides appointed, authorized, sanctified, and set apart by the appointment of God, by the direction of the Spirit, to direct and lead the people of God in the same way of eternal salvation: as therefore there is no church where there is no order, no ministry; so where the same order and ministry is, there is the same church.

Pearson also underlined the fact that in "the notion of the church are comprehended good and bad." "[The church] containeth in it," he wrote, "not only such as do truly believe and are obedient to the word, but those also which are hypocrites and profane;" and he defended this proposition with numerous

---

44   Taylor, *Episcopacy Asserted*, sections 45, 32, 46, in Heber, ed. *Works of Jeremy Taylor*, Vol. 7, pp. 3–276, at pp. 232, 142, 141, 235–7.

45   For Thomas Brett (1667–1744), Non-Juring bishop, see *O. D. N. B.*

scriptural and patristic quotations.[46] As for Milner, he may have influenced Knox's views on establishment generally, although Knox only appealed to him in support of his distinction between sects and establishments.[47] Knox's main source for this distinction was, however, the Non-Conformist Anna Laetitia Barbauld. Barbauld dealt with the topic in the essay "Thoughts on The Devotional Taste, and On Sects and On Establishments," which first appeared in her anonymously-published *Devotional Pieces* (1775). The essay was reproduced by Hornby in an appendix to the *Remains*, so important did he judge its influence on Knox to be. For Barbauld sects and establishments each have a role to play in society. Sects are smaller, but more zealous, she asserted; they serve to promote a devotion which can rise to the heights of passion, though it eventually dims and fades, only to be replaced by a new, but similar group. Establishments are larger, and more restrained, yet they help, Barbauld held, to "cherish … moderate devotion," making their adherents "decent, if not virtuous, and meliorating the heart, without greatly changing it."[48] From a comparison with Knox's theory, outlined above, it is clear that he replicated her ideas exactly.

The more distant origins of Knox's ecclesiology are to be found in the Church Fathers. The themes of the church's visibility, catholicity, its mixed nature, and its relation to the civil power, were all developed by Augustine in his controversy with the Donatists. The Donatists, so-called from their leader, Donatus, Bishop of Casae Nigrae, were a group which, in fourth-century North Africa, sought to establish a pure church, untainted by the stain of those who, under threat of persecution, had sacrificed to idols. "To this Donatist dream of the church of the saints," Gerald Bonner writes, "Augustine opposes another: the Universal Church, spread throughout the world, and containing within itself both good and evil until the final separation of the Last Day." The Donatist controversy also led Augustine to formulate the idea of the civil authority being at the service of the church. Believing in Christ, Augustine argued, the emperor should serve Christ in piety, by making laws against wickedness, following the

---

46   *Correspondence*, Vol. 2, p. 306. For Pearson's ecclesiology see *Exposition of the Creed*, "Article 9: The Holy Catholic Church, the Communion of Saints," pp. 476–501. For the passages cited see pp. 487, 491. For Pearson, and his influence on Knox, see above, p. 63.

47   For Milner's teaching on establishment see *History of the Church of Christ*, Vol. 2, pp. 225–46. For his distinction between sects and establishments, see ibid., Vol. 3, p. 187. For Knox's appeal to him, see *Remains*, Vol. 1, pp. 91–2. For Joseph Milner (1745-97), see *O. D. N. B.* His *History* was subsequently revised and continued by his brother Isaac (1750–1820).

48   For Knox's appeal to Barbauld see *Remains*, Vol. 1, pp. 146–7, as well as his "Remarks on Mrs. Barbauld's Essay on Devotional Taste," ibid., pp. 468–83. For the essay itself in the *Remains*, see Vol. 2, pp. 441–59. The quotations above are taken from this source (p. 456). For Barbauld (1743–1825), poet and essayist, see *O. D. N. B.*

admonition of the psalmist, "Now, kings, understand ... and serve the Lord with fear."[49] Although there can be no doubt that Augustine's anti-Donatist writings were the ultimate source for much of Knox's thinking about the church, Knox made no mention of him with regard to ecclesiology. The Father whom he does cite, albeit briefly, is Cyprian of Carthage. Writing in 1809, Knox told Jebb, "I was led to examine St. Cyprian, a few days ago, on the points between us, and the Church of Rome: and what I found there exceeds my expectation." "I have always thought, there were just two points of real difficulty," Knox commented, "the supremacy of the pope and, transubstantiation. On both, St. Cyprian gives deep satisfaction." Although in this passage, Knox adduced Cyprian as counter to the papal claims, in a more positive way Cyprian's vision of the church, taken as a whole, accords fully with that enunciated by Knox: a visible, hierarchical body, centered on the episcopate.[50]

6   Conclusion

This chapter has examined Knox's teaching on the church. The church for him was first of all "mystical," a supernatural entity, which, in the divine plan, had taken the place of Israel, while maintaining many of its characteristics, most notably visibility and a hierarchical organization. Both characteristics, Knox associated with the episcopate, which, for him, was the constitutive element of the church's unity. This unity was compared by Knox to a tree with various different branches, an adumbration of the theory later developed by William Palmer. Distinct from the church were what Knox termed "sects," which he saw as fulfilling a providential role, and therefore as good – a position for which he was censured by the orthodox and the Tractarians. Nonetheless, according to Knox, providence also ultimately willed the visible unity of all believers, an eventuality in which he saw the Church of England having a leading role to play. This eventual unity, involving the Christianization of the entire world, was foreshadowed in ecclesiastical establishment, which he listed as another characteristic which the church inherits from Israel and which he seems to have regarded as an essential feature of the church's constitution. Although rooted primarily in his reading of the Bible, Knox's ecclesiology

---

49   Bonner, *Augustine*, p. 287; Augustine, *De Correctione Donatistarum*, chapter 5, *P. L.*, 33, col. 801. Augustine quotes Psalm 2.10–11.

50   For Knox's appeal to Cyprian (died 258), see *Correspondence*, Vol. 1, p. 547. Cyprian's ecclesiology was often invoked by apologists for Anglicanism; see Chapman, "*Cyprianus Anglicus*."

reflects Romanticism's concern with community. It reflects also the influence of Wesley, at least the Catholic and High Church aspects of Wesley's teaching: his theory, rather than his practice. Knox's thought also has parallels with the ecclesiology of the moderates, not least Jeremy Taylor, and the Non-Jurors, though Knox does not appeal to them, but rather invokes, first of all, the authority of John Pearson. He also appeals, for his ideas on sects and establishments, to Joseph Milner, though his chief inspiration in this area comes from Anna-Laetitia Barbauld. More distantly, Knox's teaching about the church is anchored in the anti-Donatist writings of St Augustine, though the Father whom Knox explicitly invokes with regard to ecclesiology is St Cyprian, whose understanding of the church, so often the object of Anglican appeals, matches his own. Already in this chapter, we have had occasion to mention Knox's doctrine of providence, and it is to this that we next turn in detail.

CHAPTER 12

Alexander Knox's Theology (v):
Providence and Predestination

For much of the time that Knox was engaged in theological reflection, "awful and unprecedented events" were shaking Europe.[1] Between 1803 and 1815 the continent was engulfed by a series of wars waged by and against Napoleon. Knox remained unperturbed by these conflicts, largely owing to his understanding of providence. In the present chapter we will examine his thinking on this topic, as well as on the concomitant doctrine of predestination.

1 Providence

For Knox, providence was a doctrine of major significance. "[E]xcepting divine grace, there is no sublimer matter of inquiry," he declared. "To study the Scripture with this special view [of reflecting on providence]," he considered, was "one of the most interesting, as well as useful employments in which our minds can be engaged."[2] References to the subject appear throughout his work. There are, however, two essays which deal specifically with the issue: the "Letter to Mrs. Hannah More on the Design of Providence respecting the Christian Church" (1806) and "On Divine Providence" (1815).[3] Providence is also an important theme in his *Remarks on the Life and Character of John Wesley* (1828).

Knox rejected the doctrine of what he called "general providence," which he defined in terms of "the clockwork of nature;" in other words, "that assemblage of seemingly mechanical movements, by which *provision is made for sustaining the system of this world, and the varieties of animal life.*"[4] There can be little doubt that Knox was thinking here of his contemporary, William Paley whose work *Natural Theology* (1802) portrayed God in terms of a cosmic watchmaker who simply set the world in motion, then took no further part in its affairs.

---

1   Jebb, *Practical Theology*, Vol. 1, p. 243. For the historical background, see Lentz, *Nouvelle Histoire du Premier Empire*.
2   *Remains*, Vol. 2, pp. 286, 298.
3   Ibid., Vol. 3, pp. 103–230; Vol. 2, 286–302.
4   Ibid., Vol. 2, p. 286.

© KONINKLIJKE BRILL NV, LEIDEN, 2020 | DOI:10.1163/9789004426986_014

Knox regarded such a view as flawed, precisely because it made God remote from creation.[5] This was the very opposite of his own understanding: for him providence meant God's direct action in human affairs; "the actual superintendence of the *omnipresent* and *omnipotent* God."[6] This providence concerned, first of all, "the great commonwealth of human society."[7] It was a providence, Knox admitted, of which most people were unaware, since to the casual observer there was nothing in the events of history which could not be explained by "human agency, or ... that which is called contingency."[8] Nonetheless, to the eye of faith, the world was, as Knox told Miss Ferguson, merely "the stage on which Providence is acting." He wrote these words on the last day of 1812, the year of Napoleon's invasion of Russia, yet Knox deemed this momentous happening but "a busy part of the drama," whose author and director was "[guiding] all things, progressively, to a good and happy issue."[9] This "issue" was "the final establishment of [God's] kingdom," the church, which Knox saw as being the second arena in which providence was at work. Indeed, for him the church was the special object of God's care. In no other instance did the deity act more directly than in relation to it, guiding it towards its "golden age," its "last and happiest state on earth." For, he was adamant, rather than having its consummation "wholly reserved for eternity," the church was destined to enjoy "triumph in this present world."[10] In this connection, one should bear in mind the ardent millennialism which marked early nineteenth-century Ireland. This was the case among both Protestants and Roman Catholics, the latter being re-enforced in their apocalyptic speculations by "Signor Pastorini," whose *General History of the Christian Church* (1777) predicted that the ultimate victory of the papacy over its foes would occur in 1825.[11] In Knox's letter to Miss

---

5   *Correspondence*, Vol. 2, p. 512. For William Paley (1743–1805), Archdeacon of Carlisle, see
     O. D. N. B.

6   *Remains*, Vol. 2, pp. 286–7 (emphasis in the original).

7   Ibid., Vol. 1, 324.

8   Ibid., Vol. 2, p. 293.

9   Ibid., Vol. 4, pp. 256, 467. One may note that earlier Knox had written: "The world at large
     is *not* the stage whereon to look for the actings of Providence" (*Remains*, Vol. 2, p. 293,
     emphasis added). However, it seems to me, from reading the passage in which this statement is made, that Knox meant people should look rather for signs of God's providence
     in their own lives, than in what he terms the "chaos" of history. There, for all but "the wise
     and confirmed Christian," divine superintendence of events was difficult to discern, he
     wrote (ibid.).

10   *Remains*, Vol. 1, pp. 232, 402, 466, 452; Vol. 3, p. 276.

11   For the background, see: Gribben and Holmes, eds., *Protestant Millennialism*; Akenson,
     Discovering the End of Time; and Donnelly, "Pastorini and Captain Rock." "Pastorini" was
     the nom-de-plume adopted by Mgr. Charles Walmesley (1722–97), vicar-apostolic of the

Ferguson, written at the end of 1812, there is a hint that for a time he may have shared the excitement of his contemporaries, believing that God was about to act decisively in human affairs. "I conceive every thing [*sic*] which is now occurring to be pregnant with results," he wrote, "and I feel my solicitude grow more intense, as the movements [of history] appear more momentous."[12] This conception went hand-in-hand with a passing interest in the Book of Revelation, an interest that marked a departure from his earlier view that conjectures on the meaning of this "mysterious" work were "not the most beneficial part of biblical study."[13] The interest did not last; by 1829 he was again speaking of the obscurity of the Apocalypse, distancing himself from what he called "the present millenarian speculation" and claiming to be unable to understand on what grounds "they conclude the nearness of the advent which they suppose approaching." Who "they" were is not specified; and, amidst what Hempton and Hill call the "epidemic of prophetical speculation [in Ireland] in the 1820s and 1830s," it is impossible to say which, if any, particular group he envisaged. Possibly Knox was talking about the circle formed around his old acquaintance Robert Daly, then Rector of Powerscourt, Co. Wicklow, hardly ten miles from Bellevue. Whoever he may have had in mind, what is interesting is how relatively sober Knox's views were, when compared to those held by many of his contemporaries.[14]

Knox believed that, in the drama of divine providence, a central role had been given to England (or Britain; he used the names interchangeably).[15] The country had, he held, been set apart, quite literally "separated from the Continent," to be prepared as a special instrument for the "restoration of the nations to the destined fullness of moral health and happiness." This restoration was to be accomplished through the English Church, which, despite the obstacles that it had to face in his day, Knox was confident would "at length, [be] made more than ever 'a praise in the earth.'" As he concluded in his 1816

---

western district of England: see *O. D. N. B.* Knox tells us that he had examined Walmesley's speculations "attentively," finding them ultimately "unfounded" (*Remains*, Vol. 4, p. 580).

12   *Remains*, Vol. 4, p. 256.

13   Ibid., p. 85. For references to Revelation, see, e.g.: *Remains*, Vol. 1, pp. 162–3, 198–9; Vol. 3, p. 276; Vol. 4, pp. 517, 580–2. It is possible to discern in these passages a certain reluctance on Knox's part to deal with the Apocalypse. One gets the impression that, even if he shared the excitement of the times, he was only led to study the book because other people questioned him about its meaning.

14   *Remains*, Vol. 4, p. 536; Hempton and Hill, *Evangelical Protestantism*, p. 93; Whelan, "Bible Gentry," pp. 66–67. For Daly, see below, p. 239.

15   See, e.g.: *Remains*, Vol. 3, pp. 215, 329; Vol. 4, p. 128; *Correspondence*, Vol. 1, pp. 227–31. Knox's view of the nation's special role was by no unique at the period; see Brown, *Providence and Empire*.

essay "On the Situation and Prospects of the Established Church:" "My persuasion of the radical excellence of the Church of England does not suffer me to doubt, that she is to be an illustrious agent in bringing the mystical Kingdom of Christ to its ultimate perfection."[16]

As well as God's providence in relation to the world and to the church, Knox also believed in "the actings of Providence for individual good," "particular Providence," as he called it, and this was the main theme of his 1815 monograph. In this essay he argued that God's providential care was directed not to all people, but rather was almost exclusively limited to "those only who fear God and keep his commandments." By this providence God supplies "the minutest of our wants; directing, guarding, and assisting us, each hour and moment, with an infinitely more vigilant and exquisite care, than our utmost self-love can ever attain to." Knox thus held that Christians could have the greatest confidence in God, something that furnished them with "an inestimable support" throughout life's trials. "God knows best what is good for me, I know nothing." Conversely, belief in providence demanded "total resignation of one's self, to the will and guidance of God."[17]

2   Sources of Knox's Doctrine of Providence

In his doctrine of providence, Knox exemplifies the optimism of the post-Enlightenment epoch. At the same time, Knox's providential reading of world events can be seen as a protest against what Avihu Zakai has called "the de-Christianization of history" by many Enlightenment writers.[18] Whatever the case, Knox himself claimed to draw his teaching directly from the Bible. "[T]he fountain-head of our information on this subject must be found in the Sacred Scriptures," he declared. "We have here the principles of divine providence laid down, its purposes declared, its movements infallibly exemplified." It was therefore by reference to this standard that all thought and reflection on providence was to be assessed.[19] Despite this appeal to Scripture, there can be little doubt that Knox was influenced in his understanding of providence by Wesley. As Outler remarks, providence was one of Wesley's "favorite themes." There was, Wesley proclaimed, "'scarce any doctrine in the whole compass of

---

16   *Remains*, Vol. 3, pp. 329, 216 (alluding to Isaiah 62, 7); Vol. 1, p. 68.
17   *Remains*, Vol. 2, p. 287; Vol. 4, p. 604; Vol. 2, pp. 292–4; Vol. 4, pp. 537–8, 557; *Correspondence*, Vol. 1, p. 46.
18   Zakai, *Jonathan Edwards's Philosophy of History*, p. 7.
19   *Remains*, Vol. 2, p. 298.

revelation ... of deeper importance," and he personally sought to impress it on the mind of "young Alleck." One of his earliest letters to Knox speaks of God's "watchful care," and of "the wisdom and goodness of Divine Providence" directing Alleck's life; and this idea is repeated in almost every subsequent communication.[20] Like Knox, Wesley rejected the idea of general providence, "stark, staring nonsense," as he called it, proclaiming instead God's direct and immediate concern for creation. This care Wesley portrayed as forming three concentric circles. Of these, "the innermost circle" was composed of those whom Wesley called "real Christians;" the "outermost circle" was "the whole race of mankind;" and, in between, "all that are called Christians, all that profess to believe in Christ," in other words, the visible church.[21] It was in regard to the church that Wesley saw "the riches both of the wisdom and the knowledge of God" as being "most eminently displayed." One could see clearly God's care for it, Wesley taught, "in planting it like a grain of mustard seed, the least of all seeds; in preserving and continually increasing it till it grew into a great tree, notwithstanding the uninterrupted opposition of all the powers of darkness."[22] This care, Wesley affirmed, would continue until the time when "all [the] glorious promises made to the Christian church" would be fully realized.

> All unprejudiced persons may see with their eyes that [God] is already renewing the face of the earth. And we have strong reason to hope that the work he hath begun he will carry on unto the day of the Lord Jesus; that he will never intermit this blessed work of his Spirit until he has fulfilled all his promises; until he hath put a period to sin and misery, and infirmity, and death; and re-established universal holiness and happiness.[23]

This providential reading of history dated back to the Hebrew Scriptures. It marked, too, the theology of the New Testament, and appeared in the early church in such writers as Eusebius of Caesarea and Lactantius. Under the influence of Augustine, however, it eventually disappeared, but was revived at

---

20   Outler, ed., *Works of John Wesley*, Vol. 2, p. 534; Wesley, Sermon 67, "On Divine Providence," 7, in ibid., pp. 535–50, at p. 537; *Remains*, Vol. 4, p. 1.

21   Wesley, Sermon 67, "On Divine Providence," 23, 18, 16, 17, in Outler, ed., *Works of John Wesley*, Vol. 2, pp. 535–50, at pp. 546, 543, 542, 543.

22   Wesley, Sermon 68, "The Wisdom of God's Counsels," 5, in Outler, ed. *Works of John Wesley*, Vol. 2, pp. 552–66, at p. 553. In this passage Wesley speaks of the divine concern for the church as a manifestation of the "manifold wisdom of God" (Ephesians 3, 10), the same verse to which Knox appeals in a similar context, *Wesley*, pp. 489–95.

23   Wesley, Sermon 63, "The General Spread of the Gospel," 26; 27, in Outler, ed., *Works of John Wesley*, Vol. 2, pp. 485–99, at pp. 498, 499.

the Reformation, not least in England.[24] Milner, whose importance to Knox
has already been noted, exemplified the tradition. One of the stated aims
of his *History of the Church of Christ* was "[t]o see and trace the goodness of
God by his Providence and Grace, in every age, taking care of his church."[25]
Another example, this time from America, is furnished by Jonathan Edwards
in his *History of the Work of Redemption* (1774), a book which Knox regarded
as furnishing "the clearest outline of what I have ventured to call the Grand
Organisation of the Gospel-scheme, that has yet been given, as far as I know, to
the world." Speaking of providence "as it manages the great commonwealth of
human society," Knox quoted directly from Edwards's *History*:

> God, doubtless, is pursuing some design, and carrying on some scheme,
> in the various changes and revolutions, which, from age to age, have come
> to pass in the world ... There is some great design, to which Providence
> subordinates all successive changes in the affairs of the world. And it is
> reasonable to suppose that all revolutions, from the beginning of the
> world, are but the various parts of the same scheme, all conspiring to
> bring to pass, what the great Creator and Governor of the world has ulti-
> mately in view.

For Edwards, the whole of human history was comprised of "so many steps
and degrees of the accomplishment of ... one event." This event was the establishment of the kingdom of Christ, which was destined, eventually, to be "set
up ... throughout the whole habitable globe." "All the world shall then be as
one church," Edwards wrote. The similarities with Knox are plain. In fact, the
only major difference between the two writers is that for Edwards America,
not England, was the nation which would play the predominant role in prepar-
ing the way "for the future glorious times of the church."[26] A similar reading
of history was given by George Miller, whose lectures at Trinity College Knox
attended, taking in them, as we have seen, a "lively interest." Miller's thesis was

---

24   For the providential reading of history in scripture, see G. von Rad, *Old Testament
     Theology: Volume One*; and Cullman, *Christ and Time*. For the patristic reading of history,
     see Patterson, *God and History*. See, too, Zakai's useful summary in *Jonathan Edwards's
     Philosophy of History*, pp. 160–73.
25   Milner, *History of the Church of Christ*, Vol. 1, p. xiii. For Knox's use of Milner, see above,
     pp. 131, 223.
26   *Remains*, 1, pp. 439, 324, slightly changed; Edwards, *History of the Work of Redemption*,
     Period 3, part 10, in Dwight, ed., *Works of President Edwards*, Vol. 3, pp. 161–436, at p. 430;
     Edwards, *History of the Work of Redemption*, Period 3, parts 1; 5; 8; 5, in Dwight, ed., *Works
     of President Edwards*, Vol. 3, pp. 161–436, at pp. 327, 376, 408.

that "human history is a drama of the divine providence;" his lectures were thus, as he expressed it, "an attempt ... to trace in the events of history the arrangements of the superintending wisdom of the Deity," the same idea that we find in Edwards, Wesley, and Knox.[27]

There are also parallels to be found between Knox's thinking and that of the seventeenth-century moderates. One may cite, for instance, John Smith, who affirmed that '[T]here is an all-seeing eye, an unbounded mind and understanding, that derives itself through the whole universe, and sitting in all the wheels of motion, guides them all, and powerfully governs the most eccentrical motions of creatures, and carries them all most harmoniously in their several orbs to one last end.' Like Knox, Smith asserted, too, that "nothing can issue and flow forth from the fountain of goodness but that which is good," and that, therefore:

> a wise man that looks from the beginning to the end of things, beholds them all in their due place and method, acting that part which the supreme mind and wisdom that governs all things hath appointed them, and to carry on one and the same eternal design, while they move according to their own proper inclinations and measures, and aim at their own particular ends.

Again like Knox, Smith insisted on the benefits and obligations of a belief in providence. The consideration of providence, Smith wrote, "quiets the spirits of a good man ... [and] keeps him in a calm and sober temper in the midst of all storms and tempests ... [and] makes him most freely to engage himself in the service of providence, without any inward reluctancy or disturbance."[28]

Ultimately, the source of Knox's teaching about providence lay in the patristic period. One of the main architects of a Christian doctrine of providence was Clement of Alexandria, who dealt with the topic not least in the seventh book of the *Stromateis*. His thinking shares several common features with that of Knox, most notably the conviction that providence rules all things and ordains everything that happens for the best, making even evils, even death, into "medicines of salvation."[29] "Not only," Clement argued, "does the divine wisdom, excellence, and power create good (for to do good is God's nature ...),

---

27   Miller, *Lectures on the Philosophy of Modern History*, Vol. 1, pp. xiii, viii. For Knox's interest in Miller, see above, p. 24.

28   Smith, Discourse 9, "The Excellency and Nobleness of True Religion," 9, *Select Discourses*, pp. 403–487, at pp. 470–4.

29   Clement, *Stromateis*, 7, 11, *P. G.*, Vol. 9, col. 485.

but it also, moreover, turns evils to some good and useful purpose." Indeed, Clement maintained, "it is the greatest work of divine providence not to allow evil to remain useless and unprofitable," but to bring good even out of evil.[30] One finds, too, the germ of the three-fold division of providence. "From [God], providence [extends] to the individual, to the community, and to all things."[31] In particular, Clement stressed the trust which the individual "Gnostic" ought to have in God's watchful care. "God aids [the Gnostic], honoring him with a closer attention," Clement asserted. And thus "the Gnostic knows that his desti-ny does not lie in luck's hands." Rather, he is convinced that "divine providence manages all things well."[32] Chrysostom, too, made providence a central part of his teaching, not only in his eponymous work on the subject, but through-out his writing and preaching. As Clement's starting point was what Osborn calls God's "exuberant goodness," so Chrysostom took as his basic premise that "God loves us ardently, with an unutterable love."[33] This being so, Chrysostom argued, we must believe that whatever befalls us, however bad it appears, is, in fact, for our good, enabling us to grow in virtue, and so, eventually, to be rewarded in heaven. Thus, for Chrysostom, the only real evil is a sinful reaction to external forces: "nothing can hurt those who do not hurt themselves," as he summed it up in the title of one of his treatises.[34]

Writing about Wesley's doctrine of providence, Outler remarks that his teaching was in direct line with the classical Anglican statements on the sub-ject by various standard divines.[35] The same remark can be applied to Knox. In the case of both Knox and Wesley, however, one should note, beyond the teaching of individual authors, the influence of the Anglican liturgy and its annual proclamation that God's "never-failing providence ordereth all things in heaven and earth;" and, more especially, that it never ceases "to help and govern them whom [God brings up] in [his] steadfast fear and love."[36] It was a teaching which Knox claimed to find verified by personal experience.

---

30   Ibid., 1, 17, *P. G.*, Vol. 9, col. 801.

31   Ibid., 7, 2, *P. G.*, Vol. 9, col. 409.

32   Ibid., 7, 7; 4, 7, *P. G.*, Vol. 9, col. 469; Vol. 8, col. 1264, reading, more comprehensibly, τύχη [*tychē*, luck], instead of ψυχή [*psychē*, soul].

33   Osborn, *Clement of Alexandria*, p. 48; Chrysostom, *Ad Eos Qui Scandalizati Sunt*, 6, *P. G.*, Vol. 52, col. 488.

34   Chrysostom, *Quod Qui Seipsum Non Laedit, Nemo Laedere Possit*, *P. G.*, Vol. 52, cols. 459–80. For a useful summary of Chrysostom's teaching on providence, see Hall, *Learning Theology with the Fathers*, chapter 8, "God's Wise and Loving Providence," pp. 183–206.

35   Outler, *Works of John Wesley*, Vol. 2, p. 534.

36   Collect for the Eighth Sunday after Trinity, *b. c. p.*, p. 138; Collect for the Second Sunday after Trinity, *b. c. p.*, p. 131. See, also, the Collect for the Second Sunday after the Epiphany, *b. c. p.*, p. 72.

"Providence has … mercifully guarded, guided and sustained me through … life;" he told Jebb; while to an unnamed correspondent he testified to his belief that providence had "graciously sustained me through the vicissitudes of life, and has done more for me than once I could have conceived imaginable, in matters respecting this world; and, I humbly trust, not less with respect to that which is to come."[37]

3   Predestination

We turn next to Knox's teaching on predestination, which he understood in terms of foreknowledge, and thus as a part of providence, God's watchful care of creation. The elect, Knox held, were those whose faith and good works were foreknown to God. This made predestination dependent on the divine wisdom, as well as on the divine will, he argued. Knox also maintained a doctrine which he termed "providential predestination," by which he meant that God so ordered events that people heard the Gospel in circumstances that disposed them to accept it.[38] However, he did not devote much attention to this subject. He saw little profit in dogmatising about "such deep mysteries", truths "too mysterious for human explanation."[39] He did, nonetheless, reject the Calvinist position – as unscriptural.[40] "I think, of few things I can be more sure," he told Jebb, "than that calvinistic [*sic*] predestination is not in the Bible." In fact, not only was it not in the Bible, it was, Knox believed, contrary to the Bible, wholly at odds with what he termed "the loveliness of the Gospel." The Gospel revealed a God who is "infinitely kind to every creature that he has made," which was the antithesis of the predestinarians' portrayal of the deity as "unyieldingly vindictive … [and] inexorably severe," "an inexorable sovereign, rather than … a loving and gracious father." At an even more basic level, that of nature rather than revelation, the Calvinist doctrine was aberrant, "gloomy and repulsive" to the human spirit and its innate desire for happiness.[41] If Knox rejected Calvinism, however, he nonetheless refused to be labelled an Arminian. As he wrote to Jebb:

---

37   *Correspondence*, Vol. 2, p. 371; *Remains*, Vol. 4, p. 533.
38   *Correspondence*, Vol. 1, pp. 185, 192–93.
39   *Remarks*, p. 5; *Remains*, Vol. 2, p. 346.
40   For Calvin's teaching, see *Institutes*, Book 3, chapter 21.
41   *Correspondence*, Vol. 1, p. 185; *Remains*, Vol. 4, pp. 346, 269; "Preface to the second Dublin edition," p. lxvi; *Wesley*, p. 476.

I am ready, sometimes, to say of myself, that I am neither arminian, nor calvinist, yet, I believe, calvinists would call me an arminian. But I imagine the name does not belong to me; nor did it, I think, belong to John Wesley. He assumed it; but, I conceive, too inconsiderately. I suspect Arminius had something of the pelagian in him; and his followers were wholly so, if not worse.[42]

What Knox meant by this was that he and Wesley were Arminians only in the loose sense of being anti-Calvinist. They were not Arminians in the proper sense of the term, adherents of the theology of Jacobus Arminius, which Knox felt to be defective. Knox, however, seems to have judged Arminius not so much on his actual teachings, as on the theology of some of his later followers, who had moved to a more "rationalistic" position, what G. F. Nuttall has described as "Arminianism of the head."[43] Knox also misjudged Wesley on this point, for the latter was demonstrably "a faithful representative of Jacobus Arminius," to quote the title of a paper by W. Stephen Gunter.

4   Sources of Knox's View of Predestination

Knox's discussion of predestination must be set against the background of the dispute with Calvinism which had marked the career of John Wesley.[44] Knox had been personally initiated into the dispute by Wesley himself, whose letters to "Alleck" maintain a firmly anti-Calvinistic position.[45] Wesley's rejection of the doctrine of predestination arose directly from his doctrine of God. To quote Maddox, "Wesley's most characteristic complaint about predestination was ... that it conflicts with the universal love and goodness of God." "For the Calvinists," Maddox writes, "the defining model was a sovereign monarch ... By contrast, Wesley more commonly employed the model of a loving parent."[46] Like Knox, Wesley linked predestination to foreknowledge. So, for example, in his sermon "On Predestination," which he preached in Derry in 1773, and which Knox thus doubtless heard firsthand, Wesley demanded: "Who are justified? None but those who were first predestinated. Who are predestinated? None

---

42 *Correspondence*, Vol. 1, pp. 184–85 (lack of capitalization in the original).
43 See Nuttall's essay, "The Influence of Arminianism in England," in *The Puritan Spirit*, pp. 67–80, especially pp. 78–79. For Arminus (1560–1609) and his teaching, see Bangs, *Arminius*.
44 For the background, see Sell, *Great Debate*, especially chapter 3, "In Full Spate," pp. 59–87.
45 See above, pp. 62–63.
46 Maddox, *Responsible Grace*, p. 56.

but those whom God foreknew as believers."[47] The moderates similarly rejected Calvinism. They did so, like Knox and Wesley, on account of their belief that
it portrayed the deity as "cruel and dreadful," to borrow Cudworth's words. As
Whichcote put it, speaking of Calvinism: "[W]hosoever doth not think God
righteous and merciful, he doth not do God right ... and is wholly a stranger to
gospel-revelation." Rather, to cite Cudworth once more, the God of Scripture
has as "the sweetest flower in all the garland of his attributes ... the richest dia-
dem in his crown of glory," the fact that "he is *mighty to save.*" To quote again
from Whichcote: "When you have done all you can, the best notion you can
have of Deity is *goodness.*"[48]

The anti-Calvinism of Knox, Wesley and the moderates was rooted in their
reading of the Greek Fathers, not least Clement and Chrysostom.[49] Clement
spoke of predestination and election, but he linked them to foreknowledge.
"Those whom God predestined," he wrote, "God knew would be righteous from
before the foundation of the world." Thus, he contended, "election is secured
by the effect of discipleship, and purification, and good works."[50] For his part,
Chrysostom, as previously noted, made God's "unutterable love" for human beings the foundation of his theology. "To have mercy," Chrysostom proclaimed,
"is the peculiar and most excellent attribute of God, and the most inherent in
his nature, whence [Paul] calls him the God of mercies." Because of this love
and mercy, God "earnestly desires, earnestly wills our salvation." If Scripture
speaks of predestination, therefore, it does so in relation to God's foreknowledge, he taught.[51]

> If human beings chose what is best and most beautiful, how much more
> God? ... Predestination is not only a question of [God's] love, but also

---

47   Wesley, Sermon 58, "On Predestination," 14, in Outler, ed., *Works of John Wesley*, Vol. 2,
      pp. 415–21, at p. 420.
48   Cudworth, "Sermon I," *Works*, Vol. 4, pp. 289–350, at p. 320; Whichcote, Discourse 40, "The
      Moral Part of RELIGION Reinforced by CHRISTIANITY," [part 2], *Works of Benjamin
      Whichcote*, Vol. 2, pp. 228–43, at p. 235; Cudworth, "Sermon I," *Works*, Vol. 4, pp. 289–350, at
      p. 319; Whichcote, Discourse 59, "The unnatural Ingratitude of the Profane and Irreligious,"
      [part 1], *Works of Benjamin Whichcote*, Vol. 3, pp. 195–217, at pp. 200–1 (emphases in the
      original).
49   For a summary of the teaching of the Fathers on predestination, see, Jorgenson,
      "Predestination according to Divine Foreknowledge in Patristic Tradition;" and Wilken,
      "Free Choice and the Divine Will in Greek Christian Commentaries on Paul."
50   Clement, *Stromateis*, 7, 17; 5, 1, *P. G.*, Vol. 9, cols. 552, 13.
51   Chrysostom, "Homily 1 on 2 Corinthians," 3, *P. G.*, Vol. 61, cols. 385–6; "Homily 1 on
      Ephesians," 2, *P. G.*, Vol. 62, col. 13.

of [our] virtue. Were it just a question of love, then everyone would be saved; were it just a question of virtue, then Christ's coming, and the whole economy, would have been pointless. And, therefore, we say that predestination is a result neither of God's love alone nor of our virtue alone, but of both.[52]

Or, as he puts it elsewhere, more briefly: "Although it be mercy, it seeks the worthy," a sentiment which finds a clear echo in Knox's claim that the "grand error of calvinism [sic] is the disjointing of God's favour and preference, from moral qualifications."[53]

5   Conclusion

For Knox, then, providence was a doctrine of prime importance. Rejecting what he termed "general providence," he affirmed that God was directly involved in human affairs, guiding the events of the events of history, watching over the church, and caring for individuals, or, at least, for believers. Knox was especially concerned with God's providential care of the church, which, he believed, was being guided to a glorious future, an idea which needs to be seen in relation both to the optimism of the post-Enlightenment era, as well as the millennialism rife in early nineteenth-century Ireland. With respect to predestination, Knox rejected Calvinism, but also refused the label Arminian. He enunciated a doctrine of what he termed "providential predestination," as well as teaching that predestination was based on God's foreknowledge. In the case of both providence and predestination, he invoked the authority of scripture, while being guided by the thought of Wesley and the moderates, as well as that of the Greek Fathers. Having thus completed our examination of Knox's teaching, it remains to see what impact this teaching had. This will be the subject of the following chapter.

---

52   Chrysostom, "Homily 1 on Ephesians." 2; *P. G.*, vol. 62, col. 12.
53   Chrysostom, "Homily 1 on 2 Corinthians," 3, *P. G.*, Vol. 61, cols. 385–6; "Homily 1 on Ephesians," 2, *P. G.*, Vol. 62, cols. 13, 12, 13; "Homily 2 on 2 Corinthians," 4, *P. G.*, Vol. 61, col. 397; *Correspondence*, Vol. 1, p. 159.

CHAPTER 13

Alexander Knox's Influence and His Relationship with the Tractarians

Having looked at Knox's life and teaching, one question that remains to be asked is that of his influence. The present chapter examines this issue, with particular reference to his relationship with Tractarianism.

1   Knox's Influence

Knox's obituary remarked that "few, in reality, have exercised a more deeply-felt influence over a large circle of acquaintance."[1] This circle included those whom Samuel O'Sullivan described as being the élite of Irish society;[2] through them Knox's ideas received an even wider diffusion. In particular, a number of clergy in the archdiocese of Cashel were marked by his teaching.[3] Among them were Jebb, the Forster brothers and the Rector of Fethard, Henry Woodward.[4] The latter's sermons exemplify the theology of the group. Downplaying the significance of the cross, they insist that salvation should be understood primarily as "the assimilation of the soul to God and participation of the Divine nature," accomplished by grace.[5] Though impregnated with Knox's thought, Woodward's sermons were doubtless his own work, but Knox recorded having drafted homilies for some other Cashel clergy, and, on at least one occasion, he wrote a charge for the Ordinary, Archbishop Brodrick.[6] Among those whom Knox helped with sermon-composition was Jebb; as the *Christian Examiner*

---

1 *Christian Examiner*, 11.73 (July 1831), p. 562.
2 *Dublin University Magazine*, 4.21 (September 1834), p. 242. See also the *Christian Observer*, 34.11 (November 1834), p. 692, which speaks of Knox's influence over "clergymen, noblemen, [and] private gentlemen."
3 *Correspondence*, Vol. 1, p. 453; Woodward, *Some Passages of My Former Life*, pp. 14, 19.
4 For Henry Woodward (1775–1863), see *Some Passages of My Former Life*.
5 Woodward, *Sermons*, p. 86; cf. pp. 135, 166, 168, 355–7.
6 B. L., Add. Ms 41164, Correspondence between Alexander Knox and John Jebb (1812–30), fol. 46, Knox to John Jebb, letter, July 25/August 2, 1814; N. L. I., Ms 8868, Brodrick Papers, (folder 8), drafts of a charge, undated.

revealed: "Mr. Jebb often asked Mr. Knox to suggest to him a text and accompany it with some hints as to the mode of handling it."[7] Knox's influence was also felt in the diocese of Cork. In a letter written to Jebb in 1812, he told of a clergyman there who "preaches both *you* and *me*" to the "young clergy," with the result that "excellent dispositions seem to be silently diffusing themselves."[8] The clergyman in question was Horace Newman, Rector of Kilbrogan and subsequently Dean of St. Finbarr's Cathedral. Knox's influence on him did not, however, endure, for Newman later became a noted Evangelical.[9] Another Evangelical vaunted by Knox as "a product of *Bellevue*" was Robert Daly.[10] Daly, though, was adamant that, although he "loved [Knox] as a friend ... admired him for his talents, and ... honoured him for his deep tone of personal piety," he was ultimately "delivered" from his "erroneous doctrines."[11] Daly and Newman are only two instances of a number of figures who, while they were impressed by Knox as a person, did not share his teaching. Another example is Samuel O'Sullivan who testified that there was "no living man with whom we are acquainted, nor has there been within our memory, to whom we could compare Alexander Knox."[12] Yet, despite this encomium, O'Sullivan was, as Hornby relates, "by no means identified with Mr. Knox's theology."[13] Similarly, Adam Clarke recorded that Knox had been "the beloved and revered guide of his youth," to whom he had "ever looked up ... with affectionate respect and reverence."[14] There is, however, no indication of Knox having influenced Clarke's doctrinal thinking.

Knox's sway was not limited to Ireland. In England, too, a number of people were touched by his ideas and this increased following the posthumous publication of his writings.[15] R. B. McDowell ranks the *Correspondence* as "one of the most influential theological works produced in Ireland," an assessment which

---

7   *Christian Examiner*, 3.36 (October, 1834), p. 692.

8   *Correspondence*, Vol. 2, p. 100 (emphasis in the original).

9   For Horace Newman (1781–1864) see *The Gentleman's Magazine*, 216.2 (February 1864), p. 216.

10   Robert Daly (1783–1872), Bishop of Cashel from 1843 until his death, was a noted Evangelical. See Madden, *Memoir*. For Knox's claim on him see: B. L., Add. Ms 41164, Correspondence between Alexander Knox and John Jebb (1812–30), fol. 15, Knox to John Jebb, letter, December 3, 1812 (emphasis in the original).

11   Robert Daly to Richard Whately, letter, undated, quoted Madden, *Memoir*, p. 34.

12   *Dublin University Magazine*, 4.21 (September 1834), p. 243.

13   Hornby, "Editor's Preface to the Third and Fourth Volumes," p. xxxix.

14   *Remains*, Vol. 4, pp. 51–2. For Adam Clarke (1762–1832), theologian and Biblical commentator see *O. D. N. B.*

15   *Correspondence*, Vol. 2, pp. 336–7.

finds confirmation in a statement made in 1856 by Charles Kingsley, who spoke of Knox, together with Samuel Taylor Coleridge, as having "changed the minds, and, with them, the acts of thousands."[16] A similar testimony comes from the 1845 debates over Maynooth in the House of Lords. The Earl of Roden, Robert Jocelyn, citing Knox as an opponent of the college, described his opinion "an authority … deserving of great weight."[17] In response, Lord Monteagle, Thomas Spring Rice, invoked Knox as a friend of Maynooth and, in so doing, affirmed that a "more excellent and pious man did not exist, or one more entitled to respect for his high principles, his earnest piety, his rare literary endowments, and his love for Ireland."[18] Not everyone shared these positive sentiments. Numerous nineteenth-century anti-Tractarian Evangelicals laid much of the blame for the Oxford Movement on what the *Christian Examiner* called Knox's "marvellous influence."[19] Looking back in 1862 over "the controversies and heresies which have been agitating the Church during the last half-century," the journal traced many of them to Knox's writings, "the suggestions," as the *Examiner* put it, "of that unsound thinker."[20]

2   William Maclagan

Several significant figures explicitly acknowledged a theological debt to Knox and in whose writings this debt is clear. One is William Maclagan, Archbishop of York from 1891 to 1908. While Archbishop, Maclagan produced an edition of Knox's tracts on the sacraments, in the preface to which he wrote of how much he himself valued Knox's writings and how greatly he desired to make them better known to his contemporaries.[21] Knox's influence on Maclagan, especially in the area of sacramental theology, is of note because Maclagan was jointly

---

16   McDowell, *Ireland in the Age of Imperialism and Revolution*, p. 205; C. K., "Hours with the Mystics," p. 315. For Charles Kingsley (1819–75), clergyman and controversialist, see *O. D. N. B.*

17   *Hansard*, "House of Lords: Debates," Vol. 80, col. 1195, June 2, 1845. For Robert Jocelyn (1788–1870) see *O. D. N. B.*

18   *Hansard*, "House of Lords: Debates," Vol. 81, col. 66, June 4, 1845. For Thomas Spring Rice (1790–1866) see *O. D. N. B.*

19   *Christian Examiner*, new series, 47 (November 1862), p. 283.

20   Ibid., pp. 282–5. For a similar view, see [McIlwaine], *Ecclesiologism Exposed*, p. 33.

21   Maclagan, "Preface" to *The Grace of Sacraments*, pp. v–xxxv, at p. viii; cf. p. xv. For William Maclagan (1826–1910) see *O. D. N. B.*

responsible with the Archbishop of Canterbury, Frederick Temple, for one of the most authoritative statements of Anglican Eucharistic doctrine, *Saepius Officio* (1897), the official reply to Pope Leo XIII's condemnation of Anglican orders, *Apostolicae Curae* (1896).[22]

3   Charles Dickinson

Another leading churchman who acknowledged Knox's influence was Charles Dickinson, Bishop of Meath from 1840 to 1842. His *Remains* (1845) were edited by John West, who prefaced them with a "Biographical Sketch."[23] In it West related how Knox's "profundity of thought and ... uncommon felicity of expression" had "undoubtedly exercised a considerable influence" on Dickinson.[24] This influence is evident in three main areas, the first of which is justification. Rejecting what he termed "SOLIFIDIAN principles," Dickinson asserted that we are justified through "a *real* righteousness ... which [the] Holy Spirit *implants in the heart*."[25] Thus, Christianity for Dickinson was not, primarily, a matter of knowledge, "the *intellectual* reception of instruction, – the entertaining of notions;" it consisted, rather, in "the keeping of [the] commandments."[26] Second, Knox's influence appears in Dickinson's soteriology. For example, in a Good Friday sermon published in his *Remains*, Dickinson insisted that, while Christ's death in the past was certainly significant, he is also "a present Saviour," offering believers sanctification as well as forgiveness.[27] The whole sermon

---

22   One should note that the actual redaction of the document appears to have been primarily the work of the Bishop of Salisbury, John Wordsworth (1843–1911). For the background, see Hill and Yarnold, eds., *Anglican Orders*.

23   John West, "Biographical Sketch," in Charles Dickinson, *Remains*, pp. xvii–lxvi. For West (1805–90), Dean of St Patrick's Cathedral, Dublin, see Leslie, *Clergy of Dublin and Glendalough*, p. 1166.

24   West, "Biographical Sketch," pp. xxviii.

25   Dickinson, *Remains*, pp. 215, 96. See also p. 101, where Dickinson asserts that justification is accomplished through a "*real* righteousness, fixed and living within the soul, implanted by the Spirit of God" (emphasis, in both quotations, is in the original).

26   Dickinson, *Remains*, p. 97 (emphasis in the original). Dickinson is alluding to 1 John 2.3. Cf. p. 135, where Dickinson speaks of justifying faith as "obedience" rather than the "profession of truth, or intelligence of doctrines."

27   Dickinson, "Sermon VI: The Lamb of God," *Remains*, pp. 105–23, at pp. 116, 118. Dickinson defends his position by quoting Titus 2.14 (p. 117), a text frequently adduced by Knox in the same sense (see above, p. 158).

closed with a long quotation from Knox (described as "a valued friend") drawn from his treatise "On the Nature of our Salvation through Christ."[28] Third, Dickinson's views on churches and "sects" clearly mirror Knox's thinking. His *Observations on Ecclesiastical Legislature and Church Reform* (1833) expatiated on the benefits of an established church, while at the same time asserting the desirability of having what he termed "dissenting communions."[29] These were different but complementary ways of diffusing religion in society.[30]

4   William Jacobson

William Jacobson came to Ireland as a young Oxford graduate to act as tutor for the La Touches' nephews, Charles and Francis.[31] This brought him into contact with Knox, who formed a high opinion of him. He told Jebb:

> There is a very sensible young gentleman at present in this house. He is a Mr Jacobson, an A. B. of Lincoln [College]. In one of his first conversations with me, he asked me if I knew the 'Appendix' to your sermons, pronouncing upon it, at the same time, as intelligent a eulogium as I had perhaps heard from anyone ... [He suggested] that it were desirable the 'Appendix' should be published in a small volume by itself, in order to give it the widest possible circulation, which he conceives the present time, especially, renders expedient.[32]

From Ireland, Jacobson returned to Oxford and ordination, eventually becoming Vice-Principal of Magdalen Hall in 1832. His most famous work was an edition of the Apostolic Fathers, largely on the basis of which he was appointed Regius Professor of Divinity at Oxford in 1848, before being elevated to the episcopate in 1865. Burgon numbered him among his *Twelve Good Men*, recording that Jacobson frequently recalled his conversations with Knox, as "having been singularly productive of fruit to himself."[33] Burgon recorded,

---

28   Dickinson, "Sermon VI: The Lamb of God", *Remains*, pp. 105–23, at pp. 121–3. For the passage which Dickson quotes, see Knox's *Remains*, Vol. 2, pp. 391–2.

29   For the text, see Dickinson's *Remains*, pp. 267–342.

30   See especially, Dickinson, *Remains*, pp. 324–7.

31   For William Jacobson (1803–84) see *O. D. N. B.*

32   *Correspondence*, Vol. 2, pp. 566–7.

33   Burgon, *Lives of Twelve Good Men*, Vol. 2, pp. 248–9.

too, Jacobson's regret that on his return from Ireland he had allowed his acquaintance with Knox to lapse. Even so, the *Remains* "occupied a conspicuous place in [his] library, and were often taken down from his shelf in illustration of something in his lectures."[34] These lectures, it should be noted, were obligatory for all candidates for Holy Orders studying at Oxford, something which argues for a wide, if unacknowledged, dissemination of Knox's thought among the English clergy.[35]

5   Francis Paget

Another Oxford don who owned the influence of Knox was Francis Paget, successively Professor of Pastoral Theology, Dean of Christ Church and Bishop of Oxford.[36] Knox's influence on Paget appears on a number of occasions, as, for example, in the sermon "The Records of the Past" (1886).[37] There Paget not only quoted Knox verbatim, but also enunciated a view of Anglicanism which was strongly redolent of Knox's teaching.[38] Expanding on the providential care which had kept the Church of England in the via media, Paget described it as "untouched by the losses which have marred the heritage of the Protestant communities abroad: and ... the accretions which have defaced the doctrine and practice of Rome."[39] The Church of England, Paget proclaimed, was distinguished by its orders, its sacraments, its daily prayers, and "a tradition of doctrine which we can bring without fear or apology or reserve to the great canon of the Catholic Faith: 'Quod semper, quod ubique, quod ab omnibus.'"[40] Paget's most notable work was the essay on the sacraments which he contributed to *Lux Mundi* (1889).[41] One of the most important books in modern Anglicanism, *Lux Mundi* sought to combine Anglo-Catholic tradition with the insights of

---

34   Ibid., p. 249.

35   For the obligatory nature of Jacobson's lectures, see the entry on Jacobson in *O. D. N. B.*

36   For Francis Paget (1851–1911) see *O. D. N. B.*

37   Paget, "The Records of the Past" in *Faculties and Difficulties*, pp. 237–56.

38   For Paget's quotation of Knox see, "The Records of the Past," *Faculties and Difficulties*, pp. 237–56, at pp. 249–50. The quotation comes from Knox, *Remains*, Vol. 1, pp. 56–7, 68, and is part of the essay "On the Situation and Prospects of the Established Church."

39   Paget, "The Records of the Past," *Faculties and Difficulties*, pp. 237–56, at p. 250.

40   Ibid, pp. 250–1.

41   For Paget's essay, see Gore, ed., *Lux Mundi*, pp. 405–33.

contemporary scholarship.[42] In his essay, Paget openly acknowledged the debt he owed to Knox's "remarkable treatise" on the Eucharist.[43] This debt is evident throughout the essay, which contains a number of quotations from or allusions to Knox.[44] It begins with Knox's definition of the sacraments as "vehicles of saving and sanctifying power," before going on to argue for one of Knox's leading tenets, that the sacraments are designed by God "to deal with the entirety of man's nature, not slighting, or excluding, or despairing of any true part of his being."[45]

6   John Jebb, Junior

A priest who professed his theological indebtedness to Knox was Bishop Jebb's nephew, John Jebb, junior.[46] Writing in *Notes and Queries* in 1877, Jebb related that, while a student at Trinity, he would seek to visit Knox as often as he could, deriving "more information and benefit" from "this great man" than "from any formal theological lectures."[47] It is an influence clearly apparent in such works as *The Divine Economy of the Church* (1840) and *The Choral Service of the United Church of England and Ireland* (1843), the latter containing for the first time in print the term "Anglican Communion."[48] These writings reveal an ecclesiology and sacramental doctrine which fully accord with those of the man whom Jebb described as "one of the greatest philosophers of our age," and "the first and main promoter of the real Catholic reaction of our days."[49]

---

42   For a summary of the book and its significance see Ramsey, *From Gore to Temple*, chapter 1, "Lux Mundi," pp. 1–16.
43   Paget, "The Sacraments," in Gore, ed., *Lux Mundi*, p. 412, note.
44   Ibid., pp. 406, 411–12, 414, 432.
45   Ibid., p. 406, quoting *Remains*, Vol. 2, p. 155. For Knox's teaching on the congruence of the sacraments with human nature see above, pp. 198–99.
46   For John Jebb, junior (1805–86), a priest of strong Tractarian views, and author of numerous books, Rector of Peterstow in Hampshire, see *O. D. N. B.*
47   *Notes and Queries*, 5th Series, 8.193 (September 8, 1877), p. 191.
48   The phrase appears in the subtitle of the book, then again on p. 545.
49   Jebb, *Three Lectures*, p. 163; *Notes and Queries*, 5th Series, 8.193 (September 8, 1877), p. 191.

7   Gladstone

The most prominent figure to acknowledge Knox's influence was the British Prime Minister, William Ewart Gladstone.[50] Gladstone was raised an Evangelical, and, in fact, his parents were acquainted with Hannah More.[51] He was, however, too young for her to have introduced him to Knox's writings, to which he came later. They were, by his own avowal, an important factor in his moving from Evangelicalism to High Churchmanship.[52] A personal memorandum on the first two volumes of the *Remains* exists among his private papers and shows the points on which Knox appealed to him.[53] First, Knox had, in Gladstone's view, "vindicated, one may almost hope for ever ... the great and essential doctrine of an inward and vital religion: a process operated upon the heart, by Divine agency."[54] Second, Gladstone praised Knox's insistence on progress in religion, the need "to pass onward from lower unto higher truths; from dimness to more clear apprehensions; from the contemplation of sin with sorrow to the study of holiness with avidity and joy."[55] Third, Gladstone was impressed by Knox's stress on the practical rather than the abstract, his emphasis on the renewal of human nature, which he made the main focus of the Christian life, and which should constitute "the *bulk* of our attention and concern."[56] Fourth, Gladstone valued Knox's arguments against mysticism.[57] "[H]e has taught with convincing and salutary effect," Gladstone wrote, "that undivided contemplation of the Divine Essence is not appointed to constitute the habitual state or furnish the constant sustenance of our souls."[58] Last, Knox

---

50   For William Ewart Gladstone (1809–98), Prime Minister 1868–74, 1880–85, 1886, 1892–94 see Morley, *Life of Gladstone*, and, more recently, Matthew, *Gladstone, 1809–1898*.

51   Morley, *Life of Gladstone*, Vol. 1, p. 12.

52   For Gladstone's religious evolution see his essay, "Present Aspect of the Church," in *Gleanings of Past Years, 1843–50: Volume 5: Ecclesiastical*, pp. 1–80, at pp. 11–12. The essay first appeared in *The Foreign and Colonial Quarterly Review*, 2.2 (October 1843), pp. 552–603. For the influence of Knox, see the "fragment" in Morley, *Life of Gladstone*, Vol. 1, pp. 159–162, at p. 161. There are also several references to Knox in Gladstone's diaries: see Matthew, ed., *The Gladstone Diaries*, Vol. 14, p. 445.

53   B. L., Add. Ms 44724, Gladstone Papers, DCXXXIX, fols. 73–76, "memorandum," March 24, 1835.

54   Ibid., fol. 73.

55   Ibid.

56   Ibid. (emphasis in the original).

57   For Knox's teaching on mysticism, see above, pp. 80–82.

58   B. L., Add. Ms 44724, Gladstone Papers, DCXXXIX fols. 73–76, "memorandum," March 24, 1835, fol. 73.

had "unfolded with great ability the beautiful results" of baptismal regeneration, expounding its consequences with "great depth of wisdom and felicity of
expression."[59] Against these positive points, Gladstone set "several defects of
considerable importance."[60] Of these, the first was Knox's conception of the
church, which Gladstone described as "low and faint."[61] Although Gladstone
was writing in 1835, before the *Remains* had been fully published, this observation is difficult to understand. The tract "On the Situation and Prospects of
the Established Church," the essay on the parables in Matthew 13, and the
two versions of "The Doctrine Respecting Baptism" all present a "high" view
of the church, which underscores its visible aspect. Likewise hard to accept is
Gladstone's charge, already noted, that Knox denied the doctrine of forensic justification, as well as its concomitant, the doctrine of Christ's expiatory death.[62]

8   Knox and the Tractarians

If Knox enjoyed such great influence, the question must be asked as to how he
came to be so largely forgotten. The answer is that he suffered the fate common to all precursors, that of being eclipsed by those whom he anticipated,
in his case the men of the Oxford Movement.[63] The remainder of this chapter
examines Knox's relationship to them. It is clear that, as Geoffrey Rowell expresses it, Knox has "a special significance in the pre-history of Tractarianism,"
foreshadowing its teachings in a number of ways.[64] What is more difficult to
determine is whether or not he had a formative influence on the development
of their theological thinking. David Newsome has written that "the assumption
can easily be made that the Tractarians found in [Knox and Jebb] all the am-
munition that they needed for their campaign."[65] This assumption is, however,
less easy to make than Newsome suggests, for, as we shall see, the Tractarians'
attitude towards Knox was, at best, ambiguous.

---

59   Ibid., fol. 74. For Knox's teaching on baptism see above, pp. 191–94.
60   B. L., Add. Ms 44724, Gladstone Papers, DCXXXIX, fols. 73–76, "memorandum," March 24,
        1835, fol. 74.
61   Ibid.
62   Ibid., fol. 76. Gladstone suggested that because Knox had travelled so far from sin along
        the road of perfection, he felt no need for these doctrines. See, also, above, p. 173.
63   A point already made, or, at least, suggested by Brilioth, *Anglican Revival*, p. 47.
64   Rowell, "Theological Forerunners," p. 38. For instances, see: pp. 19, note 59, 23 note 90, 31,
        71–72, 77, 81, 89.
65   Newsome, *The Convert Cardinals*, p. 73.

9   Knox and Froude

Speaking of Knox, Newman wrote to Robert Wilberforce in June 1838: "Froude did not like him."[66] Newman was referring to his friend Richard Hurrell Froude, and the truth of his statement is evidenced by the vitriolic attack which Froude made in an essay, composed four and a half years earlier, "On Mr. Knox's views of Church Discipline."[67] Piers Brendon has called this essay "probably Froude's most brilliant piece of polemical writing," but, in reality, it was seriously flawed. "I ... found it pointless and scurrilous so could not take the trouble to write it over," Froude admitted to Newman, while Brendon himself notes that Froude had "only come across [Knox's] views at second hand."[68] Newman nonetheless published the essay in his edition of Froude's *Remains*, although he included with it what he called a "deprecatory note."[69] The note stated that the essay was not as much directed against "so remarkable a man as Mr. Knox ... as against the doctrine which he is reported to have advocated." This doctrine, to which we will return below, was described as "the amiable endeavor, so remarkable in his writings, to prove that every thing [*sic*] is best just as it is." Somewhat disparagingly, the note sought to exculpate Knox on the grounds that he "had to struggle with many disadvantages in pursuing religious truth, and ... considering these, [he] is rather to be honoured for what he attained, than to be severely treated where he failed." The note ended by asserting Froude's acknowledgement of "the excellence and value of other writings of Mr. Knox ... such as his Essay on the Eucharist."[70] This statement may seem a little at odds with Newman's admission to Wilberforce of Froude's dislike of Knox, quoted above; nonetheless, it is true that the Tractarians repeatedly referred to Knox's Eucharistic theology in a positive way. Indeed, Newman closed his letter to Wilberforce by himself praising Knox's sacramental teaching. This teaching had become known to the Tractarians early on, when a copy of Knox's 1824 *Inquiry* had circulated in Oxford.[71] The Tractarians were slow to articu-

---

66   John Henry Newman to Robert I. Wilberforce, letter, June 9, 1838, in Tracey, ed., *L. & D.*, Vol. 6, p. 256. For Froude (1803–36) see Brendon, *Richard Hurrell Froude and the Oxford Movement*.

67   For the text, see Froude, *Remains*, Part 2, Vol. 1, pp. 298–314.

68   Brendon, *Richard Hurrell Froude and the Oxford Movement*, p. 156; Richard Hurrell Froude to John Henry Newman, letter, January 25, 1834, in Ker and Gornall, eds., *L. &. D.*, Vol. 4, pp. 214–16, at p. 215; Brendon, *Richard Hurrell Froude and the Oxford Movement*, p. 156.

69   John Henry Newman to John Keble, letter, November 29, 1838, in Tracey, ed., *L. & D.*, Vol. 6, pp. 350–51, at p. 351. For the note see Froude, *Remains*, Part 2, Vol. 1, p. 298.

70   For Froude's knowledge of Knox see John Henry Newman to J. J. Hornby, letter, May 8, 1840, in Tracey, ed., *L. & D.*, Vol. 7, p. 322.

71   See above p. 190, note 3.

late their Eucharistic theology, and it may be that Knox had an impact on the development of their ideas. This hypothesis is suggested by three things, in addition to their generalized statements of appreciation for his views. First, the Tractarians were advocates of the superiority of the 1549 Prayer Book over that of 1662. Second, they regarded Ridley as championing a "Catholic" view of the sacrament. Third, they believed in Eucharistic adoration. All three positions were, to say the least, uncommon in the Anglican tradition; but all were key features of Knox's thought.[72]

10   Newman's Correspondence with Hornby

Newman's decision to include Froude's essay in the latter's *Remains* led him into a "frank and open" exchange of letters with Knox's editor, J. J. Hornby.[73] In a letter to Newman dated March 31, 1840, Hornby complained that his ideas of justice and honesty had been wounded by the language used in reference to Knox by the Oxford men. Knox, Hornby argued, had acted as a pioneer for their ideas, laying the foundations on which they were now building: "[T]here is no Catholic truth which they uphold, that he has not been fighting over, and winning solid ground for, during the whole of the present century."[74] Newman's reply of April 5[75] proved unsatisfactory to Hornby, who wrote a second letter on April 11, asking that a statement be included in the *British Critic*, of which Newman was the editor, declaring that the note in Froude's *Remains* had been "inconsiderate," that "the substance of [Froude's] strictures [were], in many parts, unjustifiable," and that in fact Knox had been "a supporter of [the] doctrines which He [*sic*] is there supposed or asserted to deny."[76] Newman answered on April 13, stating that he yet remained to be convinced of Knox's

---

72   For the Tractarian preference for the 1549 liturgy see above, p. 43, note 49. For their attitude to Ridley as "the great upholder of catholic truth" see, e.g., *Tract 71*, p. 32; *Tract 81*, pp. 22, 24. For the Tractarian position on the veneration of the sacramental presence of Christ see Keble, *On Eucharistical Adoration*. For Knox's teaching on these points see above pp. 55, 200, 205–6.

73   When Newman initially replied to Hornby, he thanked him for "being so frank and open" (John Henry Newman to J. J. Hornby, letter, April 5, 1840, in Tracey, ed., *L. &. D.*, Vol. 7, pp. 288–290, at p. 288).

74   J. J. Hornby to John Henry Newman, letter, March 31, 1840, in Tracey, ed., *L. &. D.*, Vol. 7, p. 288, note 3.

75   Tracey, ed., *L. & D.*, Vol. 7, pp. 288–290. This letter will be analysed below.

76   Tracey, ed., *L. & D.*, Vol. 7, p. 303, notes 1 and 2.

orthodoxy with regard to the doctrine of Apostolic Succession. "I deliberately formed the opinion," Newman wrote, "*from* the various works of his which I read, that [Knox] did *not* hold the Apostolical Succession in the sense in which Mr Froude held it; and that he entertained opinions less strict and definite than the Catholic Church teaches."[77] Subsequently, Hornby wrote to Newman giving copious extracts from Knox's works to illustrate his Catholicity, adding that, if the *British Critic* did not issue the notice he desired, he would publish a defence of Knox against Froude's accusations.[78] Newman remained unmoved. "I did not suddenly take up the opinion concerning Mr Knox which I have at present," he told Hornby. "[A]nd I am not likely suddenly to relinquish it."[79] With that the matter rested. Newman published no retraction, and Hornby no apologia for Knox.

11   Newman and Knox

Newman's correspondence with Hornby is of interest for several reasons. First, it confirms that Newman was familiar with a number of Knox's works, which from elsewhere we know that he had read in earnest during 1835.[80] These works included several essays on subjects about which Newman himself would write, thus raising the issue of Knox's influence on him. We have seen that Knox fore-shadowed Newman's treatment of the via media.[81] But there can also be little doubt that, in the words of Peter Nockles, Knox had "a formative influence on Newman's formulation of the *via media*." Indeed, Newman himself hinted as much when he remarked how this "distinctive character" of Anglicanism had been noted "especially by Mr. Alexander Knox."[82] One might suspect a similar influence with regard to Newman's ideas on justification. Certainly,

77   Ibid., pp. 302–3, at p. 303 (emphases in the original).
78   J. J. Hornby to John Henry Newman, letter, April 30, 1840, in Tracey, ed. *L. & D.*, Vol. 7, p. 322, note 2.
79   John Henry Newman to J. J. Hornby, letter, May 8, 1840, in Tracey, ed., *L. & D.*, Vol. 7, p. 322.
80   See Newman's letters to Samuel Rickards, February 9, 1835, and Charles Anderson, January 24, 1836: *L. & D.*, Vol. 5, pp. 26–27, and 211–13. For Samuel Rickards (1796–1865), Rector of Stowlangtoft in Suffolk, see *O. D. N. B.* For Charles Anderson (1804–91), then a gentleman-commoner at Oriel, see Newsome, *The Parting of Friends*, especially pp. 99–100.
81   See above, p. 38.
82   Nockles, "Church or Protestant Sect," p. 464; Newman, *Lectures on Certain Difficulties*, p. 307.

"as an advocate of the doctrine of a moral as opposed to a forensic view of Justification, [Knox] is commonly regarded as a precursor of Tractarian teaching" (to quote again from Nockles).[83] In his *Lectures on Justification* (1838), Newman maintained substantially the same views as Knox, "that original and instructive writer," as Newman there termed him.[84] As he told Hornby in a letter accompanying a gift-copy of the *Lectures*, "I am sanguine that you will not find fault with the general drift – At least I think I agree with Mr Knox in the main – though I think his view of the doctrine may be presented more in verbal accordance with the formularies of our Church than he has done."[85] Newman also stated that the *Lectures* were drawn up without reference to Knox.[86] Therefore, rather than Knox having influenced Newman, it would seem truer to say that both men drew from the same sources, and so came to similar conclusions.[87]

Newman's correspondence with Hornby highlights the ambiguity of his attitude vis-à-vis Knox. One finds him expressing both positive and negative comments. On the positive side, as Newman reminded Hornby, he had extolled Knox several times in print.[88] We have already noted his description of Knox in the *Lectures*, but there are several other instances of his publicly referencing Knox in a favourable way. In "Home Thoughts from Abroad," published in two parts in the *British Magazine* in the spring of 1836, he cited Knox in defense of the Anglo-Catholic position, calling him "an acute observer" of ecclesiastical matters, and giving a lengthy quotation from the essay "On the Situation and Prospects of the Established Church."[89] Two years later, in 1838, came a laudatory review of "Mr. Knox's Treatises on the Sacrament," in which, despite reservations, Newman described Knox as a "highly-gifted and religious man," and "an instrument (if it is right so to speak) in the hands of Providence, of extensive good in the Church at this moment." "He will be found," Newman added, "to impart most valuable information, and to suggest many deep, important,

---

83   Nockles, *Oxford Movement in Context*, p. 261.
84   Newman, *Lectures*, pp. 434–5.
85   John Henry Newman to J. J. Hornby, letter, April 10, 1838, in Tracey, ed., *L. & D.*, Vol. 6, pp. 227–8, at p. 228 (period added).
86   Newman, *Lectures*, p. vii.
87   See on this point, Church's remarks in the *Guardian*, September 7, 1887, pp. 1337–8.
88   John Henry Newman to J. J. Hornby, letter, April 5, 1840, in Tracey, ed., *L. & D.*, Vol. 7, pp. 288–290, at p. 289.
89   [Newman], "Home Thoughts from Abroad," *British Magazine*, 9 (March 1836), pp. 237–248; 9 (April 1836), pp. 357–69. For the reference to Knox, see pp. 360–1. The essay was reprinted by Newman in *Discussions and Arguments* under the title "How To Accomplish It."

and practical views on a variety of subjects."[90] A year later, in 1839, Newman produced an important article for the *British Critic* on the "State of Religious Parties," a title later changed to "Prospects of the Anglican Church."[91] That this recalls Knox's "On the Situation and Prospects of the Established Church" is suggestive of a certain influence of Knox on Newman, who once again quoted from Knox's "Prospects," citing the same passage as he had done in "Home Thoughts." He prefaced the extract by describing Knox as a "sagacious observer," one who had anticipated the Tractarian reaction to the abandonment of Catholic principles. But, Newman continued, Knox did more than simply anticipate: "[H]e realizes his own position and is an instance in rudiment of those great restorations which he foresaw in development ... advancing what he anticipated."[92] Speaking of the essay in the *Apologia*, Newman made the same point, leading Martin Svaglic to comment that Newman seems to have given "special importance" to Knox as "in a peculiar way the anticipator of renewed Catholic tendencies."[93] Or, as Newman himself put it, "Could we see the scheme of things as angels see it, I fancy we should find [Knox] has his place in the growth and restoration (so be it) of Church principles."[94] Lastly, in an 1840 review of Robert Anderson's *Book of Common Prayer*, Newman's included "A. Knox" in a list of authorities, together with "Bramhall ... the Collect For All Saints day, the Prayer for the Church militant, the Burial Service, Vincentius, and Mr. Manning on the Rule of Faith."[95] Newman's positive view of Knox likewise comes across in several private letters. Writing to Simeon Lloyd Pope in August 1834, Newman invited him to read the *Correspondence*. In similar vein, writing to Samuel Rickards, he spoke of his surprise at how Knox (as well as Coleridge) bore witness to certain Church principles, a surprise which, a few

---

90   [Newman] "Notices of Books," *British Critic*, 24.47 (July 1838), pp. 230–38, at pp. 234–35. Newman refers to Hornby's edition of *The Doctrine of the Sacraments*.

91   [John Henry Newman], "State of Religious Parties," *British Critic*, 25.50 (April 1839), pp. 396–426. Newman changed the title in 1871, when he included the piece in the first volume of his *Essays Critical and Historical* (pp. 263–308).

92   [Newman], "State of Religious Parties," pp. 400–401 (punctuation slightly modified).

93   Newman, *Apologia pro Vita Sua*, p. 536. See, also, Svaglic's remarks, pp. vii, 527. For Newman's own remarks on the "State of Religious Parties," see *Apologia*, p. 94.

94   John Henry Newman to Samuel Rickards, letter, February 9, 1835, in Gornall, *L. & D.*, Vol. 5, pp. 26–27, at p. 27.

95   *British Critic*, 27.53 (January 1840), p. 246. As well as these published tokens of esteem for Knox, one may note also Newman's appeal to him in an early sermon on the Eucharist ("Christ, A Quickening Spirit," in *Parochial and Plain Sermons*, Vol. 2, pp. 139–50, at p. 146).

weeks later, he shared again with James Stephen.[96] Equally, he recommended Knox both to Charles Anderson and Miss Giberne, describing Knox to the latter as "an ingenious, able writer." "I think a person would profit by his works," he told her.[97]

These letters also contain negative views of Knox. They show, first, that Newman disparaged him for being a layman. Thus, speaking of Knox and Coleridge, he told Rickards how "remarkable" it is that laics could engage in theology.[98] As he told Hornby, he felt "less tender" to Knox than Jebb, "first because he was a layman."[99] This lay-status meant that Knox had "no *authority*" in Newman's eyes.[100] It is possible, too, that Newman depreciated Knox for not being an Oxford man, indeed, not a university man of any kind. There is no direct evidence for this, but it may perhaps be deduced from the remarks already referred to in the "deprecatory note" in Froude's *Remains*, about Knox having to struggle with numerous disadvantages in his quest for truth. As Newman put it elsewhere, more bluntly, Knox was hampered by "deficient opportunities of instruction."[101] Newman also had theological objections to Knox's teaching. We have already seen his assertion to Hornby that Knox held "opinions less strict and definite than the Catholic Church teaches," specifically with regard to the apostolic priesthood, Knox's denial of which Newman maintained into old age.[102] Newman alleged, too, that Knox was a subjectivist, a claim which appears in a letter to Froude, although when Newman publicly addressed

---

96   John Henry Newman to Samuel Rickards, letter, February 9, 1835, in Gornall, ed., *L. & D.*, Vol. 5, pp. 26–27, at p. 27; John Henry Newman to James Stephen, letter, March 16, 1835, in ibid., pp. 44–48, at pp. 47–48. In the same letter, Newman betrays the probable influence of Knox, by presenting Ridley as a champion of the "primitive" doctrine of the Eucharist (p. 47). Sir James Stephen (1789–1859), was, at the time of this letter, Assistant Under-Secretary of State for the Colonies. See *O. B. N. B.*

97   John Henry Newman to Charles Anderson, letter, January 24, 1836, *L. & D.*, Vol. 5, pp. 211–213, at p. 213. John Henry Newman to Miss M. R. Giberne, September 16, 1840, in Tracey, ed., *L. & D.*, Vol. 7, pp. 391–2, at p. 392. For Maria Rosina Giberne (1802–85), see Athié, "'My Dear Miss Giberne."

98   John Henry Newman to Samuel Rickards, letter, February 9, 1835, in Gornall, ed., *L. & D.*, Vol. 5, pp. 26–27, at p. 27.

99   John Henry Newman to J. J. Hornby, letter, April 5, 1840, in Tracey, ed., *L. & D.*, Vol. 7, pp. 288–290, at p. 289.

100   John Henry Newman to Miss M. R. Giberne, September 16, 1840, in Tracey, ed., *L. & D.*, Vol. 7, pp. 391–92, at p. 392 (emphasis in the original).

101   *British Critic*, 24.47 (July 1838), p. 235.

102   John Henry Newman to R. W. Church, letter, September 1, 1887, in Dessain and Gornall, eds., *L. & D.*, Vol. 31, p. 228.

subjectivism in *Tract 73* (1836), Knox was not mentioned by name.[103] A further accusation was that of the "amiable endeavor" cited above, the attempt, as Newman put it, to justify whatever existed by an appeal to providence; the wish "*to see* what is good in everything," as he expressed it to Rickards.[104] As will be shown below, the same issue was raised by Isaac Williams in *Tract 86*, as well as by Keble.

Despite the evidence that we have reviewed, when in his later years Newman was asked about Knox's relationship to Tractarianism, the then cardinal was categoric: "Knox had so fully *nothing* to do with the movement, that I even forget what allusions we at any time have made to him in print." Newman went on to repeat what has already been noted, that in his estimation, Knox "wrote strongly about the Eucharistic *Gift*," but denied the existence of the priesthood. "We were glad to have him as far as he went, and I think used him," Newman concluded. "But he had no more to do with us than Hampden or Arnold."[105]

12   Pusey's View of Knox

Newman's reminiscences do not seem to square with the more positive attitude displayed in his earlier writings. They do, however, accord with Liddon's assertion in his *Life of Pusey* (1893–97) that the Tractarians made but "slight use" of Knox. They felt, Liddon says, that "they could not claim him as a whole; and they certainly were not indebted to him for anything that they knew of Catholic antiquity or Catholic truth." Liddon adds in a note that he had often heard this assertion made by Pusey; then he continues by saying that the

---

103   John Henry Newman to Richard Hurrell Froude, letter, September 10, 1835, in Gornall, ed., *L. & D.*, Vol. 5, pp. 140–141, at p. 140.

104   John Henry Newman to Samuel Rickards, letter, February 9, 1835, in Gornall, ed., *L. & D.*, Vol. 5, pp. 26–27, at p. 27 (emphasis in the original). For Knox's "optimism," and High Church criticism of it, see above, pp. 217–18.

105   John Henry Newman to R. W. Church, letter, September 1, 1887, in Dessain and Gornall, eds., *L. & D.*, Vol. 31, p. 228 (emphases in the original; punctuation slightly altered). The issue was raised by Church in response to G. T. Stokes' article on Knox (see above, p. 5). Church wrote to Newman: "I always imagined that Knox was not known or thought of in the early days of the movement … I can find no trace of his influence" (R. W. Church to John Henry Newman, letter, August 31, 1887, in Dessain and Gornall, eds., *L. & D.*, Vol. 31, p. 228, note 2). Renn Dickson Hampden (1793–1868) and Thomas Arnold (1795–1842) were both regarded by Newman and the Tractarians as exemplars of liberalism. See Thomas, *Newman and Heresy*.

Tractarians did occasionally use Knox "as being a witness, in dark times, to portions of the truth which they were reasserting; and in this sense he may be described as a precursor of the Oxford revival."[106] Among the occasions on which Pusey used Knox were his various treatments of the Eucharist. Most notable in this regard is *The Doctrine of the Real Presence as set forth by the divines and others of the English Church* (1855), a catena which Pusey completed after the unexpected death of its initial editor, the Trinity College Dublin educated William Wright.[107] The work contained three lengthy extracts from Knox, thirty pages in total, prefaced by a quotation from Jebb.[108] Pusey did not cite Knox in his own Eucharistic catena, *Tract 81* (1837), but this tract does maintain one of Knox's central tenets, that Ridley upheld a traditional view of the real presence in opposition to the more radical ideas of Cranmer. Elsewhere Pusey explicitly quoted Knox's views on Communion with approval: in *Scriptural Views of Holy Baptism* (1835),[109] *The Holy Eucharist A Comfort to the Penitent* (1843),[110] *On the Tendency to Romanism* (1839)[111] and *The Real Presence* (1857) where he described Knox as "a thoughtful layman."[112] Apart from quoting Knox's teaching on the Eucharist, Pusey also referred to him twice in his tracts on baptism, once simply in passing,[113] then, somewhat ironically, to reprobate his views on justification. Although Knox championed justification as the imparting of righteousness, he, according to Pusey, "became so intent thereon, as to do away with the vividness of that … truth, that we are 'juridically pronounced righteous or absolved for CHRIST's sake:' what CHRIST worketh *in* us cast a shade over what He did and suffered *for* us."[114] We

---

106 Liddon, *Life of Pusey*, Vol. 1, p. 262.
107 For William Wright (1813–55) see *The Gentleman's Magazine*, 45 (February 1856), p. 207. See also *The Churchman's Companion*, 17.99 (March 1855), pp. 238–39, which furnishes a slightly different account of Wright's early life. One wonders if Wright had encountered Knox while at Trinity. It is of note that Wright took from Knox the epigraph for his whole work: "Dread of Transubstantiation has made the Sacrament a ceremony" (*Remains*, Vol. 1, p. 48). For Pusey's views on the Eucharist, see Douglas, *Eucharistic Theology of Pusey*.
108 For these extracts, see [Pusey], *Doctrine of the Real Presence*, Vol. 2, pp. 78–108.
109 Pusey's treatise *Scriptural Views of Holy Baptism* spanned *Tracts 67–69*, with an additional series of notes. Knox is quoted on p. 237 of the "Notes."
110 Pusey, *The Holy Eucharist A Comfort for the Penitent*, p. v, note c. A second, passing, allusion to Knox can also be found on p. 43.
111 Pusey, *On the Tendency to Romanism*, p. 126.
112 Pusey, *The Real Presence*, p. 202.
113 E. B. P[usey], *Tract 67*, p. 2.
114 This passage does not appear in the original version of the tract, which Pusey revised and enlarged for the second, 1839, edition. In that edition, for the passage quoted, see pp. 19–20 (emphasis in the original).

may thus conclude that, as Benjamin Harrison remarked to Newman, "Pusey read Knox very attentively."[115] This does not mean that, to use Liddon's word, Pusey was "indebted" to Knox, but it does suggest that Pusey had a more positive attitude towards him than Liddon implies.

13   Keble and Williams

Two other Tractarian leaders must be spoken of with regard to Knox. The first is John Keble.[116] Asked about Knox by his disciple and subsequent biographer, J. T. Coleridge, Keble replied by saying, first: "I admire him very much in some respects, and think he did the world great service by his 'Treatise on the Eucharist.'" Keble then continued, however, by criticizing Knox's "admiration of Wesley," which he saw as being founded on Knox's "own private personal interpretation of Church History." By this Keble meant that where Knox "saw the good effect of a thing, the thing itself is to be approved," the same criticism as that made by Newman, as we noted above. Keble, however, went beyond Newman to argue that Knox's view made him an eclectic.[117] The charge of eclecticism was also laid by Isaac Williams.[118] In *Tract 86* (1839) Williams spoke of "that unreal eclectic system, which confounds truth, and degrades our sense of Providence, by looking on the different forms of error only as various modes of educing good under the Divine control." Knox was not named at this juncture, but, given Newman and Keble's criticisms, it is more than probable that Williams had him in mind. Certainly, when later on in the same tract Williams censured the view that "unlawful Ministries," such as those of Methodism, were "justifiable" or "to be looked upon ... as actual Divine dispensations," he did mention Knox explicitly.[119]

---

115 Benjamin Harrison to John Henry Newman, letter, September 3, 1835, in Mozley, ed., *Letters and Correspondence of John Henry Newman*, Vol. 2, p. 119. Harrison (1808–87), later Archdeacon of Maidstone, was one of the original Tract-writers, a student and colleague of Pusey's at Christ Church. See *O. D. N. B.*

116 For John Keble (1792–1866), Professor of Poetry at Oxford, 1831–41, Rector of Hursley, 1833–66, see Coleridge, *Memoir of Keble*, and, more recently Battiscombe, *John Keble*; Blair, ed., *John Keble in Context*.

117 For Keble's remarks with regard to Knox, see Coleridge, *Memoir of Keble*, Vol. 1, p. 241–2. For Sir John Taylor Coleridge (1790–1876), nephew of the poet, see *O. D. N. B.*

118 For Isaac Williams (1802–65) see *O. D. N. B.*

119 [Isaac Williams], *Tract 86*, pp. 5, 60, note (continued from p. 59).

None of the accusations levelled against Knox was dealt with in any depth, either by Williams, Keble, Pusey, or Newman, and they must either be rejected *tout court*, or, at least, nuanced substantially, as should be evident from our survey of Knox's theology.

14   The Question of Indirect Influence

Writing to Newman in 1887 and referring to Jebb, Church raised the question of Knox's indirect influence on the Tractarians.[120] It was an issue which had already been raised by Hornby in 1840 when he spoke of the pain caused him at seeing Jebb "put forward" by the Tractarians, while "his Great Master [was] depreciated."[121] However, although Jebb was cited by the Tractarians as an authority, his actual influence on them is doubtful, except with regard to their formulation of the concept of the via media.[122] Another possible conduit of influence from Knox to the Tractarians was William Palmer.[123] "It would seem," as Nockles remarks, that "Palmer had a hand in Newman's ... education in high churchmanship," aiding him in the production of *The Arians of the Fourth Century* (1833).[124] But Palmer's influence was not confined to Newman. As Nockles notes, Tractarian liturgists owed Palmer "an enormous debt" for his work on the sources of the Prayer Book, *Origines Liturgicae* (1832).[125] Similarly, Palmer's other major work, *A Treatise on the Church of Christ* (1838), provided the Tractarians with a detailed exposition of the "Branch Theory," one of the distinctive features of their ecclesiology.[126] Palmer studied at Trinity College Dublin in the 1820s under Knox's friend George Miller, before going on to

---

120   R. W. Church to John Henry Newman, letter, August 31, 1887, in Dessain and Gornall, eds., *L. & D.*, Vol. 31, p. 228, note 2.

121   J. J. Hornby to John Henry Newman, letter, March 31, 1840, in Tracey, ed., *L. & D.*, Vol. 7, p. 288, note 4.

122   On the relationship between Jebb and the Tractarians, see Acheson, *Jebb*, especially pp. xiv, xvi, 31–34, 40, 44–45, 55–57, 95, 61. See, too, a note of June 18, 1862, where, on a much earlier letter from Robert Wilberforce, telling him that he should get to know the Bishop, Newman remarks, "I believe I never saw Mr. Jebb. I have preserved one long letter of his of this year 1836. It was too systematic to extract from and too long to transcribe" (Mozley, ed., *Letters and Correspondence of John Henry Newman*, Vol. 2, p. 216).

123   For William Palmer (1803–85), see *O. D. N. B.*

124   Nockles, "Church or Protestant Sect," p. 466.

125   Nockles, *Oxford Movement in Context*, p. 220.

126   For Knox's adumbration of the "Branch Theory," see above, p. 216.

train for ordination with Jebb.[127] Despite this fact, I have not discovered any record of Knox and Palmer meeting. Nonetheless, Palmer's proximity to Jebb does make it possible to argue that Knox indirectly influenced the Tractarians through him. A further possible link between Knox and the Tractarians is Charles Atmore Ogilvie. A Fellow of Balliol, Ogilvie was one of the leading High Churchman in the university prior to the Oxford Movement, from which he nonetheless held aloof. The son of a Methodist preacher, he was on friendly terms with both Knox and the Tractarians. Even so, there is no evidence, as far as I can see, that he mediated Knox's ideas to them.[128]

15   Romanticism

Peter Nockles has said that Knox's kinship with the Tractarians "should not be pressed too far." Nonetheless, as he also notes, "[k]inship there undoubtedly was."[129] This, we have demonstrated in the preceding pages. Yet, Knox's presaging of the Oxford Movement was more than simply doctrinal. We have seen above that Knox combined High Church teaching and practice with warmth of feeling.[130] It is this fusion which, above all, made Knox a precursor of Tractarianism, "the ecclesial form of the Romantic movement in England." Gilley describes the Tractarians as speaking "to the heart and imagination, transforming the life of doctrine by the life of devotion." It was a transformation already initiated by Knox. [131]

16   Conclusion

In this chapter we have looked Knox's "marvelous influence," not least over such significant figures as Archbishop William Maclagan, Bishops Charles Dickinson, William Jacobson, and Francis Paget, the priest-writer, John Jebb junior, and the Prime Minister, William Gladstone. We also examined his

---

127   For Miller, see above, p. 24.
128   For Charles Atmore Ogilvie (1793–1873), see *O. D. N. B.*
129   Nockles, "Continuity and Change," Vol. 2, p. 377.
130   See above, p. 46.
131   Nichols, *The Panther and the Hind*, p. 118; Gilley, "John Keble and the Victorian Churching of Romaticism," p. 236. See also, Prickett, *Romanticism and Religion*, p. 170; Brilioth, *Anglican Revival*, chapter five, "The Romantic Movement and Neo-Anglicanism," pp. 56–76.

relationship to the Tractarians, Froude, Newman, Pusey, Keble, and Isaac Williams. Although critical of Knox, many of their leading ideas were foreshadowed by him, and he may, indeed, have influenced the formation of their views, not least in relation to the Eucharist. Above all, however, Knox presaged them as a Romantic, combining High Church principles with "warmth of piety."

Conclusion

This book has been a study of the theology of Alexander Knox. To introduce Knox himself and to help understand his thought, chapter one examined his life. Chapter two looked at his theory of Anglicanism, while chapter three reviewed his relationship with John Wesley and Methodism. Chapters four and five considered Knox in the context, first, of the Christian Platonic tradition, then of the great movements of his time: heart religion, the Enlightenment, and Romanticism. Having thus situated Knox, the subsequent chapters explored his theology in detail. Chapter six looked at its characteristics, while chapter seven examined his methodology. Chapters eight to twelve then gave an analysis of his teaching on particular points, while chapter thirteen assessed his influence, especially in relation to the Tractarians.

1 Alexander Knox's Theology: a Summary

Although Knox's theological writing was always of an occasional nature, his thought does form a coherent whole, a body of theology which justly merits the designation bestowed on it by his contemporaries, "Mr. Knox's system."[1] This system was intensely practical, concerned above all with justification, which Knox saw as an on-going process, leading to perfection, which he defined in terms of love, as unbroken friendship with God. It is around the doctrine of justification that almost all his other teachings coalesce. Thus, for him, the doctrine of the Trinity revealed the origin of justification: the love of the Three-Personed God for humankind, humankind which Knox saw as having been profoundly affected by the fall. Sin was, above all, misery, and its remedy – Knox often spoke in therapeutic terms – was Christianity, which he viewed as the divinely-conceived plan for the fulfilment of every human desire. This plan was put into effect by Jesus Christ, whose death on the cross enabled what Knox termed "salvability," the conditions needed to achieve salvation.[2] Minimising what he saw as the Evangelical over-emphasis on Calvary, Knox insisted that salvation was a present affair, which Christ worked in the heart of believers, drawing them away from sin by the allure of his moral beauty. This subjective aspect of Knox's understanding of salvation was balanced by the importance that he gave to the Holy Spirit, which he described as an "animating principle"

---

1   See above, p. 107.
2   See above, p. 158.

© KONINKLIJKE BRILL NV, LEIDEN, 2020 | DOI:10.1163/9789004426986_016

in the heart of believers, helping to attract them to Christ, and enabling assimilation to him.[3] Knox placed significant emphasis on the sacraments, by which he understood baptism and the Eucharist. While upholding the doctrine of baptismal regeneration, he insisted that regeneration could only be bestowed where no obstacle was placed in its way, thus demanding in adults both faith and repentance. He was insistent, too, that baptism was only the start of a lifelong process, in which Christians were called to advance and grow continually in holiness. With regard to the Eucharist, he maintained a virtualist position, while at the same time upholding the doctrine of the Eucharistic sacrifice, and of ministerial priesthood. He held a high view of the church, seeing it as a divinely-established, visible and hierarchical institution, one which also, of its nature, ought to be established. These characteristics, Knox held, the church inherited from Israel, of which, in the divine plan, it was the replacement. Knox made a clear distinction between churches and what he termed sects. What constituted the former, from Knox's perspective, was the episcopate, separation from which meant schism. It was a judgment which was mitigated both by his insistence that individuals outside the church might nonetheless still be genuine Christians, and that the sects to which they belonged served a providential purpose as part of God's plan. This plan, according to Knox, had as its ultimate goal, the unity of all Christians in a single church spread out across the whole world, the kingdom of God on earth.

This perspective points us to Knox's second major area of interest, next to justification: the doctrine of providence. The two topics were not entirely separate in his view; he saw providence as being analogous to justification, the one concerning God's activity in the world, the other God's activity in the soul. By his providence God directed all human affairs, and most especially those things which concerned the church, which was the particular object of divine care. Nonetheless, Knox maintained, God was similarly concerned for individuals, although this concern was not for all human beings, but only for Christians. As a part of the doctrine of providence Knox touched on the topic of predestination. Regarding it as too mysterious a subject for human speculation, it was not an issue on which he dwelt. Even so, he strenuously rejected the Calvinist view of election as something purely arbitrary, preferring to see it as being based on God's foreknowledge, despite which he also rejected the label Arminian.

---

3   See above, p. 164.

2   The Importance of Alexander Knox for the Study of Anglicanism

What conclusions may be drawn from our study? To put the question another way, what is the importance of Alexander Knox for Anglicanism? Knox is important, first, in relation to his native church, the Church of Ireland, ranking as one of the most substantial theologians that it has ever produced, while, at the same time, providing a reminder of its often-neglected High Church tradition. But Knox is likewise of importance for Anglicanism as a whole. On the most elementary level, this is because he was so avowedly a confessional theologian, one who loved and venerated what he called the Church of England, and who constantly sought to conform his thought to its "doctrines and genius."[4] More significantly, he was not only one of the first writers to make habitual use the term "Anglican;" he also produced a coherent theory of what this designation signified: the steering of a middle course between Roman Catholicism and Protestantism, following the guiding star of the Vincentian canon, neither deviating by omission or addition from what has been taught and held *semper, ubique, et ab omnibus*. One of the interesting features of this theory is how, despite its apparent conservatism, it represents an adaptation to the changing condition of the Church of England in the early nineteenth century. Thus, although one should without doubt see Knox as a traditionalist, one may equally view him, in a certain sense, as an innovator.

Knox is significant, too, for Anglicans, as an example of one who employed what is often regarded as Anglicanism's classical theological method, the combined use of Scripture, tradition, and reason; or, as he himself expressed it, "the sacred word and the writings of holy men and his own meditations on them."[5] Yet, here, as well, he was innovative, at least to a certain extent, through the added appeal which he made to experience, an appeal which, nonetheless, he regarded as being firmly anchored in the heritage of the English Church. This appeal points to a further reason why Knox is significant for Anglicans, and that is the witness which he bears to what Donald Allchin has termed a "forgotten strand" within their patrimony, that of Christian Platonism. This "strand," exemplified by Knox himself and by those to whom he most appealed, Wesley and the seventeenth-century moderates, has been explored both by Allchin and, earlier and more fully, by W. R. Inge, but the study of Knox helps to give it greater definition.[6] Central to the Platonic tradition in theology is the doc-

---

4   See above, p. 9.
5   See above, p. 122.
6   Allchin, *Participation in God: A Forgotten Strand in Anglican Tradition*; Inge, *Platonic Tradition in English Religious Thought*.

trine of deification, the idea that human beings are called to be God-like, a goal that is only achieved with the help of the indwelling Spirit. But there are other characteristics of the Platonic theological tradition, besides this main concern: the prioritizing of life over dogma; the reduction of the latter to a few essential truths; tolerance and openness to those of other opinions; eclecticism; the eschewing of authoritarianism in favour of rational reflection; as well as the already-noted emphasis on experience, in the sense both of an experimental knowledge of religious truths, and of an intuitive knowledge of God.

The roots of the Platonic tradition lie in the patristic period, especially in the Eastern Church, and this fact suggests a further reason why Knox is significant: he is a prime example of the Anglican use of the Fathers. "[Imbibing] their views, sentiments, and divine enthusiasm; and, then, [pouring] it forth, in [his] own words," he wished to be, and professed himself to be, "a Christian of the six first centuries."[7] This patristic *phronema* appears above all in Knox's perfectionism, which he presented as the doctrine of Clement of Alexandria, Pseudo-Macarius, and John Chrysostom. But it was manifest in every aspect of his teaching. As we have seen, on each individual point of doctrine, the source of his thinking can be traced back to the early church. The one exception is his sacramental virtualism; yet even this he defended as being the doctrine of the Fathers. In his use of antiquity, Knox foreshadowed the position of the Tractarians, making it, rather than the teaching of the Reformers, the standard by which to interpret the teaching of the Church of England. Thus he, like them, emphasized the Church of England's Catholic identity, while denying its Protestant nature. This, together with his teaching on the Eucharist, points us to Knox's influence on the Tractarians. It was an influence which they tended to down-play, and their attitude towards him can best be described as ambivalent. Yet Knox's impact on their thinking may have been greater than they themselves realised; they may have ingested some of his ideas unwittingly. The *Appendix*, published under John Jebb's name, certainly helped to shape their thinking, as did the writings, and in the case of Newman, the personal influence, of Jebb's pupil, William Palmer. Even where Knox did not influence the Tractarians, he did anticipate their teaching on a number of issues, as well as foreshadowing their synthesis of High Church doctrine with warmth of piety. Thus Knox had, in Geoffrey Rowell's words, "a special significance in the prehistory of Tractarianism."[8] But Knox's influence was by no means limited to the Tractarians. It is no exaggeration to say with Kingsley that he impacted

---

7   See above, p. 129.
8   See above, p. 2.

"thousands."[9] During his lifetime, his letters and discourses made an impression on numerous clergy and people of consequence in Britain as well as Ireland; after his death, the publication of his *Remains* and *Correspondence* saw this influence increase, again touching several figures of rank. Among them, one may list, besides Jebb: Hannah More, William Wilberforce, Archbishop Charles Brodrick, Archbishop William Maclagan, Bishops Charles Dickinson William Jacobson and Francis Paget, the priest-writer John Jebb, junior and the Prime Minister, William Ewart Gladstone.

3   Alexander Knox as a Romantic Theologian

Knox further contributes to the study of Anglicanism by his interaction with the great movements of the age in which he lived. He provides an example of Anglican heart religion, illustrating what that concept means: a form of piety in which primacy is given to the affective and the experiential. He provides, too, an Anglican example of interaction with the thought and feelings of the post-Enlightenment period. For this reason, he certainly may be designated as a Romantic theologian, although with the caveat that he was much more besides. The idea of Knox's Romanticism was first adumbrated in chapter five, which looked at the Romantic features of his thought in general terms, as well as comparing him to Coleridge and Schleiermacher, whose Romantic traits he shared. The idea was confirmed in the chapters dealing with Knox's theology. In contrast to the aridity of aspects of the Enlightenment – so Knox portrayed it[10] – with its depiction of God as a remote and distant deity, Knox's theology gave full play to all the human faculties, especially the imagination, and, above all, the affections. Consequently, Knox's image of God was of one who is intimately experienced in a shared life. This subjectivism was balanced by the prominence which Knox gave to the church and its tradition, which was itself a reflection of the Romantic concern with community. His methodology was similarly marked by several post-Enlightenment characteristics: the conception of theology as a science; the idea of a progressive understanding of Scripture; the study of the Christian past described in scientific terms; and the stress laid on experience. The same is true of his treatment of individual doctrines. For instance, his anthropology was marked by an emphasis on the great Enlightenment theme of happiness, while in his Eucharistic theology one finds

9   See above, p. 240.
10   See above, p. 93.

an appeal to symbolism and to the affections, which resonates with the concerns of the Romantic era.

4   Alexander Knox's Significance for the Study of John Wesley

Knox is likewise of significance because of the light which he sheds on John Wesley. As we have seen, despite several quite minor divergences, when it came to "the very pith and marrow of Mr. Wesley's views, and … those matters which through his life he most prized, most dwelt upon, and which lay nearest to his heart," then, as Knox declared, there was "not one of his own nominal followers who agree[d] with him more identically" than did he.[11] Knox frequently invoked Wesley in support of his teaching. This is particularly true of Knox's teaching on justification and perfection, but it appears elsewhere, as well. For instance, in relation to the doctrine of Christianity's congruence with human nature, Knox cited his "old friend's *most matured* theology;" while in defence of his soteriology, he cited Wesley's definition of it as "a present deliverance from sin."[12] Even when Knox did not explicitly appeal to Wesley's authority, the parallels between the two men are clear. This is true not least of all in regard to Knox's High Church views: his virtualism, for example, or his teaching on Eucharistic sacrifice and priesthood, or his ecclesiology. Although Knox developed it further, his teaching on the church was inspired by principles which he had learned from Wesley. Wesley's influence on Knox is not surprising. Knox was intimate with Wesley from childhood, throughout his formative years. The depth of this intimacy is revealed in the letters which Wesley addressed to Knox over a fifteen-year period, letters which contain, in germ, several doctrines which later appear in Knox's writings. Moreover, as Knox recorded, even after Wesley's death, he continued to make Wesley's teaching the subject of his "deep reflection."[13] Because of the proximity between them, the study of Knox contributes to the study of Wesley. In particular, Knox's *Remarks* provide, in Outler's words, "one of the most probing of all the theological appraisals of Wesley by any of his own contemporaries." The essay's significance lies in the portrait which it paints of Wesley as a "Church-of-England man of the highest tone," a picture which the evidence suggests to be substantially accurate, although the rider must be added that Wesley escapes neat and easy categorisation.[14]

---

11   See above, p. 67.
12   See above, pp. 152, 67.
13   See above, p. 59.
14   See above, pp. 59, 57.

5   Alexander Knox and Christian Unity

Knox's portrayal of Wesley as a High Churchman has two practical applications. An appreciation of Wesley's Anglicanism should, first of all, encourage those of the Anglican tradition to study his thinking as a part of their own inheritance; and, second, it should help Methodists and Anglicans "to grow together," in the words of the 2002 Church of Ireland and Methodist Covenant, "so that unity may be visibly realized."[15] But Knox offers more than simply an aid to Anglican-Methodist rapprochement, desirable though that may be. The appeal which Knox made to the Fathers has far broader ecumenical implications: antiquity is a common ground on which many of those Christians who are now divided may find agreement. This is particularly true of Knox's approach to justification. His thought, rooted in the patristic witness, offers an alternative view of salvation to western Christians faced with post-Reformation antinomies. It is one, as well, which forms a point of convergence between Anglicans and Orthodox. But in other areas, too, Knox's thought has the potential to contribute to contemporary ecumenical dialogue. Knox's understanding of baptism, for example, combines a "Catholic" emphasis on regeneration with an "Evangelical" stress on the necessity of faith and repentance. Likewise, Knox's virtualism presents a belief in the real presence of Christ in the Eucharist which escapes the objections commonly raised against the doctrine of what Knox termed "a literal transubstantiation."[16] Similarly, his idea that those who are not "joined" to the edifice of the visible church may yet be "living stones," could be of ecumenical benefit to those who think of ecclesiology primarily in terms of structure. His teaching that all denominations have their role to play in the divine plan, and, as such, are good and valuable, also has ecumenical implications, while his conviction that, because it is the divine plan, corporate unity is a certitude, offers inspiration to those for whom continued divisions among Christians are a source of sadness and discouragement.

This sadness and discouragement perhaps afflict Anglican Christians more than others, as they see their Communion, and its constituent churches, riven so often by internecine disputes. Here, too, Knox offers several pointers to a way forward. In the introduction to his edition of Newman's *Arians of the Fourth Century*, Archbishop Rowan Williams suggests that the meaning of theological language needs once again to be related to use, asking if one of the reasons for "some of the bitternesses and anxieties in current theology"

15   *Covenant Between the Methodist Church in Ireland and the Church of Ireland*, in Kingston, *Working Out the Covenant*, pp. 25–27, at p. 26.
16   See above, p. 34.

does not lie in "an isolation of formulae from practice?"[17] It is a disjunction to which Knox offers the perfect solution, by insisting that doctrines are not something to be known intellectually, but to be lived out existentially. But there is a more basic solution still, almost banal, yet one which seems more often than not to be forgotten: that instead of focusing on dogmatic differences, our energies should be directed primarily to growth in holiness; that more important than the profession of any particular point of view, are, in Knox's words, the virtues of "humility, meekness, purity, and love."[18] At the same time, Knox reminds us, too, by his desire "to combine ... apparently opposite truths," that different perspectives do not need to be in conflict; one can at least seek to synthesise them.[19]

6   Alexander Knox and Spirituality

Throughout his writings, Knox was concerned above all with praxis, with how best to live the Christian life. Thus, for instance, his virtualist eucharistic doctrine was aimed at promoting a "melting ardour" in opposition to memorialism and receptionism, theories by which he believed piety had been "deeply chilled." Similarly, his opposition to the Evangelical doctrines of total depravity, substitutionary atonement, and justification by faith alone, was engendered by the concern that these teachings undermined the cultivation of "life of deep and habitual devotion."[20] As, therefore, one assesses Knox's significance as a theologian, one should not forget that he is likewise important as a spiritual writer. As well as being one of the first to employ the term "Anglican," Knox was also one of the first to speak of "spirituality" in the modern sense of the word – that which relates to the interior life. For him, this life was one animated by the Holy Spirit. It is this idea that dominates Knox's entire thought. As Gladstone put it, his teaching was, in sum, nothing other than the unfolding and explication of that "little-considered and ill-comprehended clause of the Nicene Creed, I believe in the Holy Ghost, the Lord and *Giver of Life*." This, for Knox, was the "one thing needful," which is why for him theology was not something having to do with the intellect or the understanding; it was rather "the science of true piety."[21] There is no better way to conclude the study of Knox's theology than with that definition.

---

17   Williams, "Introduction," p. xliv.
18   See above, p. 96.
19   See above, p. 115.
20   See above, pp. 209, 199, 170.
21   See above, pp. 164, 112, note 31, 121.

Bibliography

1 Manuscript Sources

1.1 *Bodleian Library*

Ms. Eng. lett. c. 140, "Papers Relating to Thomas Burgess," fol. 97, letter from Alexander Knox to James Wilson, December 27, 1825, arguing that the Association, of which Wilson was secretary, should not distribute copies of the *Homilies* to children, as they encouraged anti-Catholic bigotry.

Ms. Eng. lett. d. 123, "Letters to C. A. Ogilvie, A-J," fols. 81–82, letters from John Jebb to C. A. Ogilvie.

Ms. Eng. lett. d. 124, "Letters to C. A. Ogilvie, K-Z," fol. 59, letter from John Keble to C. A. Ogilvie, March 6, 1833; fols. 85–90, several letters from Knox to C. A. Ogilvie; fols. 101–2, letter from Hannah More to C. A. Ogilvie, dated July 19, [1815].

Ms. Wilberforce c. 52, fols. 77–82, copy of a letter from Knox to Samuel Whitbread, dated December 1, 1812, on Catholic Emancipation.

Ms. Wilberforce d. 13, fols. 310–11, letter from Knox to William Wilberforce, dated February 15, 1813, concerning the political situation in Ireland.

Ms. Wilberforce d. 15, fols. 63–64, letter from Knox to William Wilberforce, dated January 9, 1801, on Catholic Emancipation.

Ms. Wilberforce d. 15, fol. 65, letter from Knox to William Wilberforce, dated January 24, 1801, relative to Knox's *Brief Confutation*.

1.2 *British Library*

Add. Ms 41163, Correspondence between Alexander Knox and John Jebb (1799–1811).

Add. Ms 41164, Correspondence between Alexander Knox and John Jebb (1812–30).

Add. Ms 41165, Correspondence between John Jebb and Alexander Knox (1800–12).

Add. Ms 41166, Correspondence between John Jebb and Alexander Knox (1813–31).

Add. Ms 44724, Gladstone Papers, DCXXXIX, fols. 73–76, "memorandum" on Knox's *Remains*, dated March 24, 1835.

1.3 *Clark Library, Los Angeles*

The Clark Library contains a number of thus far uncatalogued letters from Hannah More to Knox, mainly related to the publication of More's *Hints towards Forming the Character of a Young Princess* (1805). Almost all the letters lack full dates. Those which concern Knox will be found in "Box 2: Hannah More Letters." They include:

Letter to Knox [1802?].

Letter to Knox, dated February 21 [1805].

Letter [to Knox], dated April 19, [1805].
Letter to Knox [1806?].
Letter to Knox, dated January 6, 1806.
Letter to Knox, dated May 10, 1806.
Letter to Knox, dated September 19 [no year].

1.4   Marsh's Library, Dublin
"Letter Written by Alexander Knox," March 20, 1805.

1.5   National Library of Ireland
Ms 8895, letters to Charles Brodrick, son of Archbishop Brodrick, from various corre-
    spondents, including Alexander Knox, 1822–35.
Ms 8868, Brodrick Papers: ninety-eight letters from Knox to Charles Brodrick, dated
    between July 3, 1799 and July 22, 1820, in eight folders.
Ms 36, 154, letter from Knox to James Wilson, dated April 15, 1822, advocating modera-
    tion in theological argument.
Ms 49, 491/ 1/1411–13; 1414 L, four letters from Knox.

1.6   Oxford Centre for Methodism and Church History
B/Wes/J, transcripts of letters from John Wesley to Alexander Knox, and one to his fa-
    ther, Alexander Knox senior, dated from July 20, 1765 to July 26, 1790. The originals,
    so far uncatalogued, are at Duke University, North Carolina. Several, but not all, of
    the letters have been published in the *Remains* and in Telford's edition of Wesley's
    Letters. The letters are numbered sequentially 1–51.

1.7   Public Record Office of Northern Ireland
Hill of Brook Hall Papers, D642/A/10/1–32: thirty-two letters written by Knox while
    Lord Castlereagh's secretary to Sir George Hill, relative to the 1798 rebellion and its
    aftermath, and to preparations for the Act of Union, 1801.
Castlereagh Papers: D3030/ 396; 402; 406; 413; 534; 1123; 1595; 1612; 1688; 1690; 1764; 1791;
    1793/A; 1793/B; 3317; 3318; letters and papers written by Knox, while secretary to
    Lord Castlereagh.
T 810/8, fol. 373, certified copy of Knox's Will, July 15, 1831.

1.8   Trinity College, Dublin
Ms 1461, volume 5, Correspondence of Joseph Cooper Walker (1761–1810), fols. 3–8; 17;
    92; 93; 99–100; 103; 105; 116–17; 129; and 134–37, ten letters written by Knox to Walker,
    mainly in relation to Knox's work on the poetry of William Cowper, dated between
    February 11, 1802 and August 29, 1803.

Ms 1461, volume 6, Correspondence of Joseph Cooper Walker (1761–1810), fols. 71–72 and 182–83, two letters from Knox to Walker, on the poetry of William Cowper, dated April 10, 1806 and March 19, 1808.

Ms 1461, volume 7, Correspondence of Joseph Cooper Walker (1761–1810), fols. 143–44, letter from Knox to Walker, on the poetry of William Cowper, dated May 18–19, 1802.

Ms 6392, Charles Forster Correspondence, fols. 4–7 and 12, bulletins from Forster to Knox about Jebb's health after his strokes in 1827 and 1829; and fol. 16, letter of condolence from Forster to Knox, on the death of Knox's housekeeper, Miss Ferguson, dated March 20, 1830.

Ms 6396–6397, Jebb Papers, Correspondence 1795–1827, fol. 7, letter to Knox from Jebb, dated September 23, 1808; fol. 9, an "Itinerary" written by Miss Ferguson, which describes the journey to England she undertook with Knox and Jebb between July 14 and September 19, 1809; fol. 19, a letter from Charles Forster to Jebb, in which he mentions Knox's close escape from falling masonry brought down by a storm in Sackville Street, dated December 21, 1814; fol. 20, a letter from Charles Forster to Jebb, which mentions how Knox had bested Dr. Graves in a theological debate, dated December 23, 1814,; fol. 183, a letter from Knox to Jebb, describing daily life at Bellevue, dated March 18, [1824],; fol. 184, a letter from Charles Forster to Jebb, relative to Knox, dated September 15, 1819; fol. 207, a letter from Knox to Jebb, dated October 15, 1824.

Ms 6398, Correspondence of the Reverend John Jebb (1805–1886), 1827–1869, fol. 53, letter from John Jebb Jnr to J. J. Hornby, on the controversy surrounding Knox's death, dated October 2, 1836.

2   Published Works of Alexander Knox (in Chronological Order)

Free Thoughts Concerning a Separation of the People called Methodists, from the Church of England. Addressed to the Preachers in the Methodist Connection. By a Layman of the Methodist Society (London: no publisher, 1785; 2nd edition, 1786, no place of publication, or publisher).

Considerations on a Separation of the Methodists from the Established Church, addressed to such of them as are friendly to that measure, and particularly to those in the City of Bristol. By a Member of the Established Church (Bristol: printed by Bulgin and Rosser, 1794).

Candid Animadversions on Mr. Henry Moore's Reply, by the Author of "Considerations on a Separation of the Methodists from the Established Church" (Bristol: printed by Bulgin and Rosser, 1794; 2nd edition, 1794).

Essays on the Political Circumstances of Ireland, written during the administration of Earl Camden, with an appendix, containing thoughts on the will of the people: and a postscript now first published. By a Gentleman of the North of Ireland (Dublin: Graisberry and Campbell, 1798; 2nd edition, London: "printed for the author by J. Plymsel," 1799).

A Brief Confutation of the Rev. Mr. Daubeny's Strictures on Mr. Richard Baxter in the Appendix to his Guide to the Church: and also of his Animadversions on Mrs. Hannah More, in a letter to the Editor of Sir James Stonehouse's Letters, by a Layman of the Established Church (Shrewsbury: J. and W. Eddowes, 1801).

Remarks on an Expostulatory Address to the Members of the Methodist Society by the Rev. J. Walker, B. D., F. T. C. D., M. R. I. A., in a letter to that gentleman (Dublin: Graisberry and Campbell, 1802).

Lives, Characters, and a Sermon preached at the Funeral of the Hon. Robert Boyle by Gilbert Burnet, Lord Bishop of Sarum (Dublin: W. Watson, 1803; 2nd edition, 1815; 3rd edition, 1824).

The Doctrine of the New Testament Respecting Military Duty (Dublin: B. Dugdale, 1803).

An Answer to the Right Honourable Patrick Duigenan's Two Great Arguments against the Full Enfranchisement of the Irish Roman Catholics, by a Member of the Establishment (Dublin: C. La Grange, 1810).

An Inquiry on Grounds of Scripture and Reason into the Use and Import of the Eucharistic Symbols (Dublin: Richard Beere and Co., 1824).

Letters on a Reunion of the Churches of England and Rome from and to the Rt. Revd. Dr. Doyle, R. C. Bishop of Kildare, John O'Driscol, Alexander Knox and Thomas Newenham, Esquires (Dublin: Richard Moore Tims, 1824).

Thirty Years' Correspondence, between John Jebb D. D., F. R. S., Bishop of Limerick, Ardfert and Aghadoe, and Alexander Knox, Esq., M. R. I. A., edited by Charles Forster, two volumes, 2nd edition (London: James Duncan and John Cochran, 1836, first published 1834).

Remains of Alexander Knox, Esq., [ed. J. J. Hornby], four volumes (volumes 1–2, 2nd edition, London: James Duncan and John Cochran, 1836 [1834]; volumes 3–4, London: James Duncan, 1837).

The Doctrine of the Sacraments, As Exhibited in Several Treatises, First Published in the Remains of Alexander Knox, Esq. [ed. J. J. Hornby] (London: James Duncan, 1838).

The Grace of Sacraments. Being Treatises on Baptism and the Eucharist, by Alexander Knox (1757–1831), ed. with a preface, by William Dalrymple Maclagan (London: Longmans, Green, and Co., 1905).

3   Secondary Sources: Books and Articles

Appendix to the First Report of the Commission on Education in Ireland (London: House of Commons, 1825).

The Book of Common Prayer and administration of the sacraments, and other rites and ceremonies of the church, according to the use of the United Church of England and Ireland (Oxford: Clarendon Press, 1815 [1662]).

Certain Sermons appointed by the Queen's Majesty to be declared and read by all parsons, vicars, and curates, every Sunday and holiday in their churches; and by Her Grace's advice perused and overseen for the better understanding of the simple people. Newly imprinted in parts according as is mentioned in the Book of Common Prayers, 1574, ed. the Syndics of the University Press (London: John W. Parker, 1850 [1574]).

Eighth Report of the Commissioners of Irish Education Inquiry: Roman Catholic College of Maynooth (London: House of Commons, 1827).

Report from the Committee of Secrecy, of the House of Commons in Ireland, as reported by the Right Honourable Lord Viscount CASTLEREAGH, August 21, 1798 (London: Printed for J. Debrett ... and J. Wright, 1798).

Sancti Gregorii Primi Papae Cognomento Magni Opera Omnia, ad manuscriptos codices Romanos, Gallicanos, Anglicanos, emendate, aucta, et illustrates notis, four volumes (Paris: Claude Rigaud, 1705).

Sixth Report of the Commissioners of Irish Education Inquiry. The Hibernian Society for the Care of Soldiers Children; &c. (London: House of Commons, 1827).

Abbot, Charles, *The Diary and Correspondence of Charles Abbot, Lord Colchester, Speaker of the House of Commons, 1802–1817*, ed. Charles, Lord Colchester, three volumes (London: John Murray, 1861).

Acheson, Alan, *A History of the Church of Ireland, 1691–1996* (Dublin: Columba Press, 1997).

Acheson, Alan, "An Eirenic High Churchman: Bishop John Jebb, 1775–1833," *Search* 23.1 (Spring 2000), pp. 29–39.

Acheson, Alan, "The Evangelicals in the Church of Ireland, 1784–1859," Ph.D. thesis, Queen's University, Belfast, 1967.

Akenson, Donald, *The Church of Ireland: Ecclesiastical Reform and Revolution, 1800–1885* (New Haven, CT: Yale University Press, 1971).

Akenson, Donald, *Discovering the End of Time: Irish Evangelicals in the Age of Daniel O'Connell* (Montreal: McGill-Queen's University Press, 2016).

Akenson, Donald, *Small Differences: Irish Catholics and Irish Protestants, 1815–1922: An International Perspective*, paperback edition (Dublin: Gill and Macmillan, 1991 [1988]).

Allchin, A. M., *Participation in God: A Forgotten Strand in Anglican Tradition* (London: Darton, Longman and Todd, 1988).

Allen, Louis, ed., *John Henry Newman and the Abbé Jager: A Controversy on Scripture and Tradition (1834–1836)* (London: Oxford University Press, 1975).

Allison, C. F., *The Rise of Moralism: The Proclamation of the Gospel from Hooker to Baxter* (New York: Seabury Press, 1966).

Anderson, Neil D., *A Definitive Study of Evidence concerning John Wesley's Appropriation of the Thought of Clement of Alexandria* (Lewiston, NY: Edwin Mellen Press, 2004).

Andrews, J. H., *A Paper Landscape: The Ordnance Survey in Nineteenth-Century Ireland* (Oxford: Clarendon Press, 1975).

Anglican Consultative Council, *The Virginia Report: The Report of the Inter-Anglican Theological and Doctrinal Commission* (London: Anglican Consultative Council, 1997).

Armour, Leslie, "Trinity, Community and Love: Cudworth's Platonism and the Idea of God," in Douglas Hedley and Sarah Hutton, eds, *Platonism at the Origins of Modernity: Studies on Platonism and Early Modern Philosophy* (Dordrecht: Springer, 2008), pp. 113–29.

Ashwin-Siejowski, Piotr, *Clement of Alexandria: A Project of Christian Perfection* (London: T. and T. Clark, 2008).

Athié, Rosario, "'My Dear Miss Giberne': Newman's Correspondence with a Friend, 1826–1840," in *Newman Studies Journal* 2.1 (Spring 2005), pp. 58–78.

Aulén, Gustaf, *Christus Victor: An Historical Study of the Three Main Types of the Idea of Atonement*, trans. A. G. Herbert (London: S. P. C. K., 1931 [1930]).

Avis, Paul, *Anglicanism and the Christian Church: Theological Resources in Historical Perspective* (Edinburgh: T. and T. Clark, 1989); 2nd edition (London: T. and T. Clark, 2002).

Avis, Paul, "Keeping Faith with Anglicanism," in Robert Hannaford, ed., *The Future of Anglicanism: Essays on Faith and Order* (Leominster: Gracewing, 1996), pp. 1–17; revised version in Paul Avis, *The Identity of Anglicanism: Essentials of Anglican Ecclesiology* (London: T. and T. Clark, 2007), pp. 1–17.

Ayers, Michael, *Locke: Epistemology and Ontology*, two volumes (London: Routledge, 1991).

Baker, Frank, *John Wesley and the Church of England* (Nashville, TN: Abingdon Press, 1970).

Baker, William J., *Beyond Port and Prejudice: Charles Lloyd of Oxford, 1784–1829* (Orono, MN: University of Maine at Orono Press, 1981).

Bangs, Carl, *Arminius: A Study in the Dutch Reformation* (Nashville, TN: Abingdon Press, 1971).

[Barbauld, Anna-Laetitia], *Devotional Pieces, compiled from the Psalms and the Book of Job, to which are prefixed thoughts on the devotional taste, on sects and on establishments* (London: Printed for J. Johnson, 1775).

Barbeau, Jeffrey W., *Coleridge, the Bible, and Religion* (Basingstoke: Palgrave Macmillan, 2008).

Barclay, J. M. G., "Πνευματικός in the Social Dialect of Pauline Christianity," in Graham N. Stanton, Bruce W. Longenecker and Stephen C. Barton, eds, *The Holy Spirit and Christian Origins: Essays in Honor of James D. G. Dunn* (Grand Rapids, MN: Eerdmans, 2004), pp. 157–67.

Barnard, L. W., *Justin Martyr: His Life and Thought* (Cambridge: Cambridge University Press, 1967).

Baronius, Cesare, *Annales Ecclesiastici*, twelve volumes (Rome: Ex Typographiis Congregationis Oratorii, apud Sanctam Mariam in Vallicella, 1588–1607).

Barrett, Peter, "Alexander Knox: Lay Theologian of the Church of Ireland," *Search* 23.1 (Spring 2000), pp. 40–50.

Barrett, Peter, "The Ecclesiology of John Jebb," M.Phil dissertation, Trinity College, Dublin, 1985.

Barth, J. Robert, *Coleridge and Christian Doctrine* (Cambridge, MA: Harvard University Press, 1969).

Barth, J. Robert, *The Symbolic Imagination: Coleridge and the Romantic Tradition*, 2nd edition (New York: Fordham University Press, 2001 [1977]).

Bassett, Paul M., and Greathouse, William M., *Exploring Christian Holiness, Volume 2: The Historical Development* (Kansas City, MO: Beacon Hill, 1985).

Battiscombe, Georgina, *John Keble: A Study in Limitations* (London: Constable, 1963).

Baumer, Franklin L., *Modern European Thought: Continuity and Change in Ideas, 1600–1950* (New York: Macmillan, 1977).

[Baxter, Richard], *An Accompt of All the Proceedings of the Commissioners of Both Perswasions, appointed by His Sacred Majesty, according to letters patents, for the review of the Book of Common Prayer* (London: Printed for R. H., 1661).

Baxter, Richard *Church History of the Government of Bishops and their Councils Abbreviated* (London: Printed by B. Griffin for Thomas Simmons, 1680).

Bayerischen Akademie der Wissenschaften: Historischen Kommission, *Neue Deutsche Biographie, Zweiter Band* (Berlin: Duncker und Humblot, 1955).

Bebbington, David, *Evangelicalism in Modern Britain: A History from the 1730s to the 1980s* (London: Unwin Hyman, 1989).

Bebbington, David, *Holiness in Nineteenth Century England* (Carlisle: Paternoster Press, 2000).

Bebbington, David, *Patterns in History: A Christian Perspective on Historical Thought*, 2nd edition (Grand Rapids, MI: Baker Book House, 1990, first published, 1979).

Beckett, J. C., "Literature in English, 1691–1800," in T. W. Moody and W. E. Vaughan, eds, *A New History of Ireland: Volume 4: Eighteenth-Century Ireland, 1691–1800* (Oxford: Clarendon Press, 1986), pp. 424–70.

Beckett, J. C., *The Making of Modern Ireland, 1603–1923*, 2nd edition (London: Faber and Faber, 1981 [1966]).

Beeke, Joel R., and Pederson, Randall J., *Meet the Puritans: With a Guide to Modern Reprints* (Grand Rapids, MI: Reformation Heritage Books, 2006).

Behr, John, *Asceticism and Anthropology in Irenaeus and Clement* (Oxford: Oxford University Press, 2000).

Beilby, James K., and Eddy, Paul R., eds., *The Nature of the Atonement: Four Views* (Westmont, IL: InterVarsity Press, 2006).

Beiser, Frederick C., "Early Romanticism and the *Aufklärung*," in James Schmidt, ed., *What is Enlightenment? Eighteenth-Century Answers and Twentieth-Century Questions* (Berkeley, CA: University of California Press, 1996), pp. 317–29.

Beiser, Frederick C., *The Romantic Imperative: The Concept of Early German Romanticism* (Cambridge, MA: Harvard University Press, 2003).

Bellanger, Claude, Godechot, Jacques, Guiral, Pierre, Terrou, Fernand, eds, *Histoire Générale de la Presse Française*, five volumes (Paris: P. U. F., 1969–76).

Bellarmine, Roberto, *De Scriptoribus Ecclesiasticis Liber Unus, cum adiunctis indicibus vndecim, & breui chronologia ab orbe condito usque ad annum M. DC. XII* (Rome: B. Zannetti, 1613).

Best, Gary, *Charles Wesley: A Biography* (London: Epworth Press, 2006).

Blair, Kirstie, ed., *John Keble in Context* (London: Anthem Press, 2004).

Blake, William, *William Blake's Writings*, ed. G. E. Bentley, Jnr., two volumes (Oxford: Clarendon Press, 1978).

Boase, Frederic, *Modern English Biography*, six volumes (Truro: Netherton and Worth, 1892–1921).

Bochet, I., and Fédou, M., eds, *L'Exégèse Patristique de Romains 9–11: grâce et liberté; Israël et nations; le mystère du Christ* (Paris: MédiaSèvres, 2007).

Bodenmann, Reinhard, *Wolfgang Musculus (1497–1563): destin d'un autodidacte lorrain au siècle des Réformes* (Geneva: Librarie Droz, 2000).

Bolton, F. R., *The Caroline Tradition of the Church of Ireland: with Particular Reference to Bishop Jeremy Taylor* (London: S. P. C. K., 1958).

Bonner, Gerald, *St Augustine of Hippo: Life and Controversies*, 2nd edition (Norwich: Canterbury Press, 1986 [1963]).

Borgen, Ole E., *John Wesley on the Sacraments: A Theological Study* (Nashville, TN: Abingdon Press, 1972).

Bowen, Desmond, *History and the Shaping of Irish Protestantism* (New York: Peter Lang, 1995).

Bowen, Desmond, *The Idea of the Victorian Church: A Study of the Church of England, 1833–1889* (Montreal: McGill University Press, 1968).

Bowmer, John C., *The Sacrament of the Lord's Supper in Early Methodism* (London: Dacre Press, 1951).

Boyle, Robert, *Some Considerations touching the Style of the H. Scriptures: extracted from several parts of a discourse (concerning divers particulars belonging to the Bible) written divers years since to a friend* (London: Printed for Henry Herringman, 1661).

Boyle, Robert, *Some Motives and Incentives to the Love of God, pathetically discours'd of in a letter to a friend*, 4th edition (London: Printed for Henry Herringman, 1665 [1659]).

Brantley, Richard E., *Locke, Wesley, and the Method of English Romanticism* (Gainesville, FL: University of Florida Press, 1984).

Brendon, Piers, *Hurrell Froude and the Oxford Movement* (London: Paul Elek, 1974).

Brett, Thomas, *The Divine Right of Episcopacy, and the necessity of an episcopal commission for preaching God's word, and for the valid ministration of the Christian sacraments, proved from the holy scriptures, and the doctrine and practice of the primitive church. Together with an impartial account of the false principles of papists, Lutherans, and Calvinists, concerning the identity of bishops and presbyters. Also, the valid succession of our English bishops vindicated, against the objections of presbyterians and romanists. And the popish fable of the Nags-Head consecration of Archbishop Parker fully refuted* (London: Printed for Henry Clements, 1718).

Brilioth, Yngve, *The Anglican Revival: Studies in the Oxford Movement* (London: Longmans, Green and Co., 1933 [1925]).

Brooks, P. N., *Thomas Cranmer's Doctrine of the Eucharist: An Essay in Historical Development*, 2nd edition (Basingstoke: Macmillan, 1992 [1st edition 1965]).

Brown, Stewart, *The National Churches of England, Ireland and Scotland, 1801–1846* (Oxford: Oxford University Press, 2001).

Brown, Stewart, *Providence and Empire: Religion, Politics and Society in the United Kingdom, 1815–1914* (Harlow: Pearson Longman, 2008).

Brown, William Adams, *The Essence of Christianity: A Study in the History of Definition* (New York: Charles Scribner's Sons, 1902).

Broxap, Henry, *The Later Non-Jurors* (Cambridge: Cambridge University Press, 1924).

Bucur, Bogdan G., *Angelomorphic Pneumatology: Clement of Alexandria and Other Early Christian Witnesses* (Leiden: Brill, 2009).

Buddeus, Johann Franz, *Isagoge Historico-Theologica ad Theologiam Universam, Singulasque ejus Partes*, two volumes (Leipzig: Thomas Fritsch, 1727).

Burgon, John William, *Lives of Twelve Good Men*, two volumes (London: John Murray, 1888).

Burnyeat, Myles, *The Theaetetus of Plato*, with trans. by M. J. Levett, rev. Myles Burnyeat (Indianapolis, IN: Hackett, 1990).

Burwick, Frederick, ed., *The Oxford Handbook of Samuel Taylor Coleridge* (Oxford: Oxford University Press, 2009).

Butler, Charles, *Life of Fenelon, Archbishop of Cambray* (London: Printed for Longman, Hurst, Rees and Orme, 1810).

Butler, Joseph, *The Analogy of Religion, Natural and Revealed, to the Constitution and Course of Nature. To which are added two brief dissertations: i. of personal identity. ii. of the nature of virtue* (London: Printed for James, John and Paul Knapton, 1736).

Butler, Perry, ed., *Pusey Rediscovered* (London: s. p. c. k., 1983).

Butler, Weeden, *Memoirs of Mark Hildesley, D. D., Lord Bishop of Sodor and Mann, and Master of Sherburn Hospital; under whose Auspices the Holy Scriptures were translated into the Manks Language* (London: Printed by J. Nichols, 1799).

Byrne, James, *Religion and the Enlightenment: From Descartes to Kant* (Louisville, KY: Westminster John Knox Press, 1997 [1996]).

Calvin, John, *Institutes of the Christian Religion*, trans. Henry Beveridge (Grand Rapids, MI: Eerdmans, 1989 [1st edition 1536]).

Campbell, Lewis, *The Theaetetus of Plato, with a revised text and English notes*, 2nd edition (Oxford: Clarendon Press, 1883 [1861]).

Campbell, Ted A., *John Wesley and Christian Antiquity: Religious Vision and Cultural Change* (Nashville, TN: Kingswood Books, 1991).

Campbell, Ted A., *The Religion of the Heart: A Study of European Religious Life in the Seventeenth and Eighteenth Centuries* (Columbia, SC: University of South Carolina Press, 1991).

Canton, William, *A History of the British and Foreign Bible Society*, five volumes (London: John Murray, 1904–10).

Carter, C. Sydney, *The Anglican* Via Media*: Being Studies in the Elizabethan Religious Settlement and in the teaching of the Caroline Divines* (London: C. J. Thynne and Jarvis, 1927).

Carter, Grayson, *Anglican Evangelicals: Protestant Secessions from the Via Media, c. 1800–1850* (Oxford: Oxford University Press, 2001).

Cell, George Croft, *The Rediscovery of John Wesley* (New York: Henry Holt, 1935).

Chadwick, Owen, *From Bossuet to Newman: The Idea of Doctrinal Development* (Cambridge: Cambridge University Press, 1957).

Chadwick, Owen, ed., *The Mind of the Oxford Movement* (London: Adam and Charles Black, 1960).

Chadwick, Owen, *The Secularisation of the European Mind in the Nineteenth Century* (Cambridge: Cambridge University Press, 1975).

Chapman, Mark D., "*Cyprianus Anglicus*: St Cyprian and the Future of Anglicanism," in Robert Hannaford, ed., *The Future of Anglicanism: Essays on Faith and Order* (Leominister: Gracewing, 1996), pp. 104–117.

Christensen, Michael J., "John Wesley: Christian Perfection as Faith Filled with the Energy of Love," in Michael J. Christiansen and Jeffrey A. Wittung, *Partakers of the Divine Nature: The History and Development of Deification in the Christian Traditions* (Madison, NJ: Fairleigh Dickinson University Press, 2007), pp. 219–30.

Christensen, Michael J., and Wittung, Jeffery A., eds., *Partakers of the Divine Nature: The History and Development of Deification in the Christian Traditions* (Madison, NJ: Fairleigh Dickinson University Press, 2007).

Christo, Gus George, "Introduction" to *St. John Chrysostom: On Repentance and Almsgiving*, trans. Gus George Christo (Washington: Catholic University of America Press, 1998), pp. xi–xviii.

Church of England Doctrine Commission, *Christian Believing: The nature of the Christian faith and its expression in Holy Scripture and creeds: a report* (London: S. P. C. K., 1976).

Church, R. W., *The Oxford Movement: Twelve Years: 1833–1845* (London: Macmillan, 1891).

Clapper, Gregory S., *John Wesley on Religious Affections: His Views on Experience and Emotion and their Role in the Christian Life and Theology* (Metuchen, NJ: Scarecrow Press, 1989).

Clapper, Gregory S., *The Renewal of the Heart is the Mission of the Church: Wesley's Heart Religion in the Twenty-First Century* (Eugene, OR: Cascade Books, 2010).

Clark, Samuel, and Donnelly, James S., Jr., eds, *Irish Peasants: Violence and Political Unrest: 1780–1914* (Madison, WI: University of Wisconsin Press, 1983).

Claydon, Tony and McBride, Ian, eds, *Protestantism and National Identity: Britain and Ireland, c.1650–c.1850* (Cambridge: Cambridge University Press, 1998).

Clements, R. E., Farrer, Austin, Lampe, G. W. H., *et al.*, *Eucharistic Theology Then and Now* (London: S. P. C. K., 1968).

Clifford, Alan C., *Atonement and Justification: English Evangelical Theology, 1640–1790: An Evaluation* (Oxford: Clarendon Press, 1990).

Cocksworth, Christopher J., *Evangelical Eucharistic Thought in the Church of England* (Cambridge: Cambridge University Press, 1993).

Coke, Thomas, and Moore, Henry, *The Life of the Rev. John Wesley, A. M., Including an Account of the Great Revival of Religion in Europe and America, of which He was the First and Chief Instrument* (London: printed by G. Paramore, 1792).

Colby, Thomas, *Ordnance Survey of the County of Londonderry: Volume 1* (Dublin: Published for Her Majesty's Government: Hodges and Smith, 1837).

Coleridge, J. T., *A Memoir of the Rev. John Keble, M. A., Late Vicar of Hursley* (Oxford and London: James Parker and Company, 1869).

Coleridge, Samuel Taylor, *Aids to Reflection*, ed. John Beer, *The Collected Works of Samuel Coleridge Taylor*, Vol. 9 (Princeton, NJ: Princeton University Press, 1993 [1st edition 1825]).

Coleridge, Samuel Taylor, *Biographia Literaria*, edited by James Engell and W. Jackson Bate, *The Collected Works of Samuel Taylor Coleridge*, Vol. 8, in 2 parts (Princeton, NJ: Princeton University Press, 1983 [1st edition 1817]).

Coleridge, Samuel Taylor, *Confessions of an Inquiring Spirit*, edited from the author's ms by Henry Nelson Coleridge (London: William Pickering, 1840).

Coleridge, Samuel Taylor, *Lay Sermons*, edited by R. J. White, *The Collected Works of Samuel Taylor Coleridge*, Vol. 6 (Princeton, NJ: Princeton University Press, 1969).

Coleridge, Samuel Taylor, *Lectures, 1795: On Politics and Religion*, edited by Lewis Patton and Peter Mann, *The Collected Works of Samuel Taylor Coleridge*, Vol. 1 (Princeton, NJ: Princeton University Press, 1971).

Coleridge, Samuel Taylor, *The Literary Remains of Samuel Taylor Coleridge*, collected and ed. Henry Nelson Coleridge, four volumes (London: William Pickering, 1836–1839).

Coleridge, Samuel Taylor, *On the Constitution of Church and State*, ed. John Colmer, *The Collected Works of Samuel Taylor Coleridge*, Vol. 10 (Princeton, NJ: Princeton University Press, 1976 [1st edition 1830]).

Colie, Rosalie L., *Light and Enlightenment: A Study of the Cambridge Platonists and the Dutch Arminians* (Cambridge: Cambridge University Press, 1957).

Colley, John, ed., *Heart Religion: Evangelical Piety in England and Ireland, 1690–1850* (Oxford: Oxford University Press, 2016).

Congar, Yves M. J., *I Believe in the Holy Spirit*, trans. David Smith, three volumes (London: Geoffrey Chapman, 1983 [1979–80]).

Congar, Yves M. J., *Tradition and Traditions: An historical and a theological essay* (New York: Macmillan, 1967 [1960–63]).

Connolly, Sean, *Religion and Society in Nineteenth-Century Ireland* (Dundalk: Dundalgan Press, 1985).

Coolahan, John, *Irish Education: History and Structure* (Dublin: Institute of Public Administration, 1981).

Cooney, Dudley Levinstone, *The Methodists in Ireland: A Short History* (Dublin: Columba Press, 2001).

Corish, Patrick J., *Maynooth College 1795–1995* (Dublin: Gill and Macmillan, 1995).

Coulson, John, *Religion and Imagination: "in aid of a grammar of assent"* (Oxford: Clarendon Press, 1981).

Coulson, John, and Allchin, A. M., eds, *The Rediscovery of Newman: An Oxford Symposium* (London: Sheed and Ward, 1967).

Cowper, William, *The Poems of William Cowper*, ed. John D. Baird and Charles Ryskamp, three volumes (Oxford: Clarendon Press, 1980–95).

Cox, Leo G., "John Wesley's Concept of Sin," *Bulletin of the Evangelical Theological Society* 5.1 (March 1962), pp. 18–24.

Cragg, Gerald R., ed., *The Cambridge Platonists* (New York: Oxford University Press, 1968).

Cragg, Gerald R., *Reason and Authority in the Eighteenth Century* (Cambridge: Cambridge University Press, 1964).

Crichton, J. D., *Saints or Sinners? Jansenism and Jansenisers in Seventeenth-Century France* (Dublin: Veritas, 1996).

Crocker, Robert, *Henry More, 1614–1687: A Biography of the Cambridge Platonist* (Dordrecht: Kluwer, 2003).

Crookshank, C. H., *History of Methodism in Ireland*, three volumes (volume 1, Belfast: R. S. Allen, 1885; volumes 2–3, London: T. Woolmer, 1886–88).

Cross, F. L., ed., *The Oxford Dictionary of the Christian Church* (London: Oxford University Press, reprinted with corrections, 1966 [1957]).

Crouter, Richard, *Friedrich Schleiermacher: Between Enlightenment and Romanticism* (Cambridge: Cambridge University Press, 2005).

Crouter, Richard, "Rhetoric and Substance in Schleiermacher's Revision of 'The Christian Faith' (1821–22)," *Religious Studies Review* 12.3–4 (July–October 1986), pp. 197–261.

Cudworth, Ralph, *The Works of Ralph Cudworth, D. D., containing The True Intellectual System of the Universe, Sermons, &c.: a new edition with references to the several quotations in the Intellectual System, and a life of the author*, ed. Thomas Birch, four volumes (Oxford: D. A. Talboys, 1829).

Cullman, Oscar, *Christ and Time: The Primitive Christian Conception of Time and History*, trans. Floyd V. Filson, revised edition (London: S. C. M. Press, 1962 [1946]).

Curtin, Nancy J., *The United Irishmen: Popular Politics in Ulster and Dublin, 1791–1798* (Oxford: Clarendon Press, 1994).

Damrau, Peter, *The Reception of English Puritan Literature in Germany* (London: Maney Publishing for the Modern Humanities Research Association and the Institute of Germanic and Romance Studies, University of London, 2006).

Daubeny, Charles, *An Appendix to the Guide to the Church; in several letters; in which the principles advanced in that work are more fully maintained, in answer to objections*, 2nd edition (London: Printed for F. C. and J. Rivington … by R. Crutwell, Bath, 1804 [1799]).

Daubeny, Charles, *A Letter to Mrs. Hannah More, on some part of her late publication entitled "Strictures on Female Education", to which is subjoined a discourse on Genesis xv .6., preached at Christ's Church in Bath* (London: J. Hatchard, and F. and C. Rivington, 1799).

Daubeny, Charles, *The Protestant's Companion, or, A Seasonable Preservative, against the errors, corruptions, and unfounded claims of a superstitious and idolatrous church; with a chapter respectfully addressed to our governors, and another to the clergy* (London: C. and J. Rivington, 1824).

Daubeny, Charles, *A Vindication of the Character of the Pious and Learned Bishop Bull, from the Unqualified Accusations brought against it by the Archdeacon of Ely, in his Charge delivered in the year 1826* (London: C. and J. Rivington, 1827).

Davies, Rupert E., and Rupp, E. Gordon, eds, *A History of the Methodist Church in Great Britain, Volume One* (London: Epworth Press, 1965).

[Delfau, F., Blampin, J., Coustant, P., and Guesnie, C.], *Sancti Aurelii Augustini Hipponensis Episcopi Opera Omnia*, eleven volumes (Paris: François Muguet, 1679–1700).

Denzinger, Heinrich, and Schönmetzer, Adolf, eds, *Enchiridion Symbolorum, Definitionum et Declarationum de Rebus Fidei et Morum*, 33rd edition (Barcelona: Herder, 1965 [1854]).

Deschner, John, *Wesley's Christology: An Interpretation* (Dallas, TX: Southern Methodist University Press, 1960).

Dessain, C. S., "Cardinal Newman and the Eastern Tradition," *Downside Review* 94.315 (April 1976), pp. 83–98.

Dever, Mark E., *Richard Sibbes: Puritanism and Calvinism in Late Elizabethan and Early Stuart England* (Macon, GA: Mercer University Press, 2000).

Dickinson, Charles, *Remains of the Most Reverend Charles Dickinson, D. D., Lord Bishop of Meath, being a selection from his sermons and tracts, with a biographical sketch*, ed. John West (London: B. Fellowes, 1845).

Diderot, Denis, *"Éclecticisme," Dictionnaire Encyclopédique*, tome 3, pp. 52–177, in *Ouevres Complètes de Diderot*, Vol. 15 (Paris: J. L. J. Brière, 1821 [1775]).

Digeser, Elizabeth de Palma, *The Making of a Christian Empire: Lactantius & Rome* (Ithaca, NY: Cornell University Press, 2000).

Dillon, John M., *The Middle Platonists: A Study of Platonism, 80 B. C.–A. D. 220* (London: Duckworth, 1977).

Ditchfield, G. M., "Anti-Trinitarianism and Toleration in Late Eighteenth Century British Politics: The Unitarian Petition of 1792," *Journal of Ecclesiastical History* 42.1 (January 1991), pp. 39–67.

Dockrill, D. W., "The Fathers and the Theology of the Cambridge Platonists," *Studia Patristica* 17 (1982), pp. 427–39.

Dodwell, Henry, *A Discourse concerning the One Altar and the One Priesthood, insisted on by the ancients in their disputes against schism: wherein the ground and solidity of that way of reasoning is explained, as also its applicableness to the case of our modern schismaticks, with particular regard to some late treatises of Mr. Richard Baxter: being a just account concerning the true nature and principles of schism according to the ancients* (London: Printed for Benj. Tooke, 1683).

Dodwell, Henry, *Separation of Churches from Episcopal Government, as practised by the present Non-Conformists, proved Schismatical from such Principles as are least controverted, and do withal most popularly explain the Sinfulness and Mischief of Schism* (London: Printed for Benj. Tooke, 1679).

Doizé, Jules, *"L'Oeuvre Érudite des Bénédictins de Saint Maur," Etudes* 114 (Janvier – Février – Mars 1908), pp. 94–117.

Donnelly, James S., Jr., "Pastorini and Captain Rock: Millenarianism and Sectarianism in the Rockite Movement of 1821–24," in Samuel Clark and James S. Donnelly, Jr., eds, *Irish Peasants: Violence and Political Unrest: 1780–1914* (Madison, WI: University of Wisconsin Press, 1983), pp. 102–39.

Dörnemann, Michael, *Krankheit und Heilung in der Theologie der frühen Kirchenväter* (Tübingen: Mohr Siebeck, 2003).

Douglas, Brian, *The Eucharistic Theology of Edward Bouverie Pusey: Sources, Context and Doctrine within the Oxford Movement and Beyond* (Leiden: Brill, 2015).

du Duc, Fronton, ed., *Sancti Patris nostri Basilii Magni Caesareae Cappadociae Archiespiscopi Opera Omnia, nunc denuo graece et latine conjunctim edita, et collatione codicum manuscriptorum, praecipue bibliothecae regis christanissimi, cum in graeco textu, tum in interpretatione correcta*, three volumes (Paris: Sébastien Cramoisy, 1638 [1618]).

Duffy, Charles Gavan, *My Life in Two Hemispheres*, two volumes (London: T. Fisher Unwin, 1898).

Dugmore, C. W., *Eucharistic Doctrine in England from Hooker to Waterland* (London: S. P. C. K., 1942).

Dugmore, C. W., *The Mass and the English Reformers* (London: Macmillan and Company, 1958).

Dumeige, G., "Le Christ Médecin dans la Litterature Chrétienne des Premiers Siècles," *Rivista di Archeologia Cristiana* 48 (1972), pp. 115–41.

Dupin, Louis Ellies, *La Nouvelle Bibliothèque des Auteurs Ecclésiastiques, contenant l'histoire de leur vie, le catalogue, la critique, et la chronologie de leurs ouverages, le somme de ce qu'il contiennent, un jugement sur leur style, et sur leur doctrine, et le dénombrement des differentes éditions de leurs oeuvres*, forty-seven volumes (Paris: André Pralard, 1686–1715).

Edwards, Jonathan, *The Works of President Edwards, with a memoir of his life*, ed. S. E. Dwight, ten volumes (New York: S. Converse, 1829–30).

Ellis, Mark A., *Simon Episcopius' Doctrine of Original Sin* (New York: Peter Lang, 2006).

Engell, James, *The Creative Imagination: Enlightenment to Romanticism* (Cambridge, MA: Harvard University Press, 1981).

English, John C., "The Cambridge Platonists in Wesley's *Christian Library*," *Proceedings of the Wesley Historical Society* 36.6 (October 1968), pp. 161–8.

English, John C., "John Wesley and the Anglican Moderates of the Seventeenth Century," *Anglican Theological Review* 51.3 (July 1969), pp. 203–20.

Ewens, J. Baird, *The Three Hermits: Short Studies in Christian Antiquity, Methodism and Tractarianism* (London: Epworth Press, 1956).

Ewing, Jon D., *Clement of Alexandria's Reinterpretation of Divine Providence: The Christianization of the Hellenistic Idea of Pronoia* (Lewiston, NY: Edwin Mellen Press, 2008).

Faber, George Stanley, *The Primitive Doctrine of Justification Investigated: relatively to the several definitions of the Church of Rome and the Church of England; and with a special reference to the opinions of the late Mr. Knox, as published in his Remains* (London: R. B. Seeley and W. Burnside, 1837).

Fabricius, Johann Albert, *Bibliotheca Graeca, sive Notitia Scriptorum Veterum Graecorum, quorumcunque monumenta integra, aut fragmenta edita exstant: tum plerorumque e mss. ac deperditis*, fourteen volumes (Hamburg: Liebezeit, 1705–28).

Fairchild, Hoxie N., "Romanticism and the Religious Revolution in England," *Journal of the History of Ideas* 2.3 (June 1941), pp. 330–8.

Farrer, William, and Brownbill, J., eds, *The Victoria History of the County of Lancaster: Volume 4* (London: Constable and Company, 1911).

[Fell], John, Bishop of Oxford, *Sancti Caecilii Cypriani Opera Recognita et Illustrata per Joannem Oxoniensem Episcopum: accedunt annals Cyprianici, sive tredecim annorum, quibus S. Cyprianus inter christianos versatus est, brevis historia chronologice delineate per Joannem Cestriensem* (Oxford: E Theatro Sheldoniano, 1682).

Fénelon, François de Salignac de la Mothe, *Explication des Maximes des Saints sur La Vie Intérieure* (Paris: Pierre Aubouin, Pierre Emery, Charles Clousier, 1697).

Ferber, Michael, ed., *A Companion to European Romanticism* (Oxford: Blackwell Publishing, 2005).

Ferguson, Adam, *An Essay on the History of Civil Society*, 2nd edition (London: A. Millar and T. Cadell, 1768 [1767]).

Ferguson, Everett, *Baptism in the Early Church: History, Theology, and Liturgy in the First Five Centuries* (Grand Rapids, MI: Eerdmans, 2009).

Ferguson, John, *Clement of Alexandria* (New York: Twayne, 1974).

Field, Richard, *Of the Church, Five Bookes* (London: Imprinted by Humfrey Lownes for Simon Waterson, 1606).

Fitzpatrick, Martin, Jones, Peter, Knellwolf, Christa, and McCalman, Iain, eds, *The Enlightenment World* (Abingdon: Routledge, 2004).

Fitzpatrick, William, *"The Sham Squire" and the Informers of 1798, with a view of their contemporaries. To which are added, in the form of an appendix, jottings about Ireland seventy years ago*, 3rd edition (Dublin: W. B. Kelly, 1866 [1865]).

Fleury, Claude, *Histoire Ecclésiastique*, twenty volumes (Paris: P. G. Le Mercier, Desaint et Saillant, Jean-Thomas Herrisant, Durand, Le Prieur, 1691–1720).

Fleury, Claude, *Les Moeurs des Chrétiens* (Paris: Clouzier, 1682).

Flew, R. Newton, *The Idea of Perfection in Christian Theology: An Historical Study of the Christian Ideal for the Present Life* (London: Oxford University Press, 1934).

[Fontaine, Nicolas], *Les Oeuvres de S. Clement d'Alexandrie, traduites du grec, avec les opuscules de plusieurs autres pères grecs* (Paris: André Pralard, 1696).

Ford, David C., "Saint Makarios of Egypt and John Wesley: Variations on the Theme of Sanctification," *Greek Orthodox Theological Review* 33.3 (1988), pp. 285–312.

Forrester, David A. R., *Young Doctor Pusey: A Study in Development* (London: Mowbray, 1989).

Forster, Charles, *The Life of John Jebb, D. D., F. R. S., Bishop of Limerick, Ardfert and Aghadoe, with a selection from his letters*, two volumes (London: James Duncan and John Cochran, 1836).

Forster, Charles, *Mahometanism Unveiled: an inquiry, in which that arch-heresy, its diffusion and continuance, are examined on a new principle, tending to confirm the evidences, and aid the propagation of the Christian faith*, two volumes (London: James Duncan and John Cochran, 1829).

Foster, Joseph, *Alumni Oxonienses: the members of the University of Oxford, 1500–1714: their parentage, birthplace, and year of birth, with a record of their degrees. Being the matriculation register of the university, alphabetically arranged, revised, and annotated*, four volumes (Oxford: James Parker, 1891–92).

Foucault, Michel, *Dits et Écrits, 1954–1988*, volume 4, *1980–1988* (Paris: Gallimard, 1994).

Franklin, R. W., *Nineteenth-Century Churches: The History of a New Catholicism in Württemberg, England, and France* (New York: Garland Publishing, 1987).

Frazier, Russell J., "John Wesley's Covenantal and Dispensational View of Salvation History," *Wesley and Methodist Studies* 1 (2009), pp. 33–54.

Frazier, Russell J., "The Doctrine of Dispensations in the Thought of John William Fletcher (1729–1785)," Ph.D. Thesis, University of Manchester, 2011.

Frend, W. H. C., *The Donatist Church: A Movement of Protest in Roman North Africa* (Oxford: Clarendon Press, 1952).

[du Frische, Jacques, and Le Nourry, Nicolas, eds.], *Sancti Ambrosii Mediolanensis Episcopi Opera, ad manuscriptos codices, Vaticanos, Gallicanos, Belgicos, etc., necnon ad editions veteras emendata, studio et labore monarchorum S. Benedicti, e congregatione S. Mauri*, two volumes (Paris: Jean-Baptiste Coignard, volume 1, 1686, volume 2, 1690).

Froude, Richard Hurrell, *The Remains of the Late Reverend Richard Hurrell Froude, M. A., Fellow of Oriel College, Oxford*, [edited by John Henry Newman and John Keble], four volumes (London: J. G. & F. Rivington, volumes 1–2, 1838, volumes 3–4, 1839).

Fulford, Roger, *Samuel Whitbread, 1764–1815: A Study in Opposition* (London: Macmillan, 1967).

Gash, Norman, *Mr. Secretary Peel: The Life of Sir Robert Peel to 1830* (London: Longmans, Green and Co., 1961).

Gay, Peter, *The Enlightenment: An Interpretation: The Rise of Modern Paganism* (New York: Alfred A. Knopf, 1966).

Gay, Peter, *The Naked Heart* (New York: W. W. Norton and Company, 1996 [1995]).

Geoghegan, Patrick M., *The Irish Act of Union: A Study in High Politics, 1798–1801* (Dublin: Gill and Macmillan, 1999).

Geoghegan, Patrick M., *Lord Castlereagh* (Dundalk: Published by the Dundalgan Press for the Historical Association of Ireland, 2002).

Gilley, Sheridan, "Introduction" to John Keble, *The Christian Year and Other Poems* (London: Published for the Society of St. Peter and St. Paul by the Church Literature Association, 1976), pp. xi–xviii.

Gilley, Sheridan, "John Keble and the Victorian Churching of Romanticism," in J. R. Watson, ed., *An Infinite Complexity: Essays in Romanticism* (Edinburgh: Edinburgh University Press, 1983), pp. 226–39.

Gladstone, W. E., *Gleanings of Past Years, 1843–78: Volume 5: Ecclesiastical, volume 1: 1843–50* (London: John Murray, 1879).

Glaire, Jean-Baptiste, *Dictionnaire Universelle des Sciences Ecclésiastiques: histoire de religion et de l'église – discipline ecclésiastique – liturgie – théologie dogmatique et morale – exégèse biblique – droit canonique – hagiographie – papes – conciles – sièges épiscopaux anciens et nouveaux, français et étrangers – abbayes – orders religieux et militaires – schismes – hérésies – biographies et bibliographies religieuses*, two volumes (Paris: Librarie Poussielgue Frères, 1868).

Golitzin, Alexander, "A Testimony to Christianity as Transfiguration: The Macarian Homilies and Orthodox Spirituality," in S. T. Kimbrough, Jnr, ed., *Orthodox and Wesleyan Spirituality* (Crestwood, NY: St. Vladimir's Seminary Press, 2002), pp. 129–56.

Goodwin, Gregory H., "Keble and Newman: Tractarian Aesthetics and the Romantic Tradition," *Victorian Studies* 30.4 (Summer 1987), pp. 475–94.

Gorday, Peter, *François Fénelon: A Biography: The Apostle of Pure Love* (Brewster, MA: Paraclete Press, 2012).

Grant, R. M., *Eusebius as Church Historian* (Oxford: Clarendon Press, 1980).

Graves, Michael, *Biblical Interpretation in the Early Church* (Minneapolis, MN: Fortress Press, 2017).

Graves, Richard, *The Whole Works of Richard Graves, D. D., Late Dean of Ardagh, and Regius Professor of Divinity in the University of Dublin, now first collected, with a memoir of his life and writings*, ed. Richard Hastings Graves, four volumes (Dublin: William Curry, 1840).

Greenfield, R. H., "The Attitude of the Tractarians to the Roman Catholic Church," D.Phil. thesis, University of Oxford, 1956.

Gribben, Crawford, and Holmes, Andrew R., eds, *Protestant Millennialism, Evangelicalism and Irish Society, 1790–2005* (Basingstoke: Palgrave Macmillan, 2006).

Grierson, H. J. C., "Classical and Romantic: A Point of View," in Robert F. Gleckner and Gerald E. Enscoe, eds, *Romanticism: Points of View*, 2nd edition (Detroit, MI: Wayne State University Press, 1975 [1962]), pp. 41–54.

Griffin, Martin, I. J., Jnr, *Latitudinarianism in the Seventeenth-Century Church of England*, ed. Richard H. Popkin and Lila Freedman (Leiden: Brill, 1992).

Grillmeier, Aloys, *Christ in Christian Tradition, Volume 1: From the Apostolic Age to Chalcedon (451)*, trans. John Bowden (London: Mowbray, 1965).

Grou, Jean Nicolas, *Morale Tirée des Confessions de Saint Augustin*, two volumes (Paris: Chez Mérigot, 1786).

Guarino, Thomas G., *Vincent of Lérins and the Development of Christian Doctrine* (Grand Rapids, MI: Baker Academic, 2013).

Gundersen, Borghild, *Cardinal Newman and Apologetics* (Oslo: Hos Jacob Dybwad, 1952).

Gunstone, J. T. A., "Alexander Knox, 1757–1831," *Church Quarterly Review* 157 (1956), pp. 463–75.

Gunter, Stephen W., "John Wesley, a faithful representative of Jacobus Arminius," *Wesleyan Theological Journal* 42.2 (Fall 2007), pp. 65–82.

Gunter, Stephen W., Jones, Scott J., Campbell, Ted A., Miles, Rebekah L., and Maddox, Randy L., *Wesley and the Quadrilateral: Renewing the Conversation* (Nashville, TN: Abingdon Press, 1997).

Hague, William, *William Wilberforce: The Life of the Great Anti-Slave Trade Campaigner* (London: Harper Press, 2007).

Hales, John, *Golden Remains of the ever Memorable Mr. John Hales of Eton College &c* (London: Printed for Timothy Garthwait, 1659).

Hall, Catherine, *Macaulay and Son: Architects of Imperial Britain* (New Haven, CT: Yale University Press, 2012).

Hall, Christopher A., *Learning Theology with the Church Fathers* (Downers Grove, IL: InterVarsity Press, 2002).

Hamilton, William, *The Exemplary Life and Character of James Bonnell, Esq., Late Accomptant General of Ireland: to which is added the sermon preach'd at his funeral by Edward, Lord Bishop of Kilmore and Ardagh* (Dublin: Jo. Ray, 1703).

Hammond, Geordan, "Restoring Primitive Christianity: John Wesley and Georgia, 1735–1737," Ph.D. thesis, University of Manchester, 2008.

Härdelin, Alf, *The Tractarian Understanding of the Eucharist* (Uppsala: Boktryckeri Aktiebolag, 1965).

Harrison, Carol, "*Delectatio Victrix*: Grace and Freedom in Saint Augustine," *Studia Patristica* 27 (1993), pp. 298–302.

Hauschild, W. D., *Gottes Geist und der Mensch: Studien zur frühchristlichen Pneumatologie*, (Munich: C. Kaiser Verlag, 1972).

Haweis, Thomas, *An Impartial and Succinct History of the Rise, Declension, and Revival of the Church of Christ; from the birth of our saviour to the present time. With faithfull characters of the principal personages, ancient and modern*, three volumes (London: Printed for J. Mawman, 1800).

Haykin, Michael A. G., and Stewart, Kenneth J., eds, *The Advent of Evangelicalism: Exploring Historical Continuities*, American edition (Nashville, TN: B. & H. Academic, 2008).

Hayley, William, *The Life and Letters of William Cowper Esq., with remarks on episto-lary writers*, 4th edition, four volumes (London: Printed for J. Johnson and Co., 1812 [1803–4]).

[Haywood, Thomas], A Presbyter of the Church of England, *Primitive Morality: or, The Spiritual Homilies of St. Macarius the Egyptian. Full of very profitable instructions concerning that Perfection which is expected from Christians, and which it is their Duty to endeavour after. Done out of Greek into English, with several considerable emen-dations, and some enlargements, from a Bodleian manuscript, never before printed* (London: Printed for W. Taylor, J. Innys, and J. Osborn, 1721).

Hazard, Paul, *La Pensée Européenne au XVIIIème Siècle: De Montesquieu à Lessing*, volume one (Paris: Boivin et Cie, 1946).

Hedley, Douglas, "Coleridge as a Theologian," in Frederick Burwick, ed., *The Oxford Handbook of Samuel Taylor Coleridge* (Oxford: Oxford University Press, 2009), pp. 473–97.

Hedley, Douglas, *Coleridge, Philosophy and Religion: Aids to Reflection and the Mirror of the Spirit* (Cambridge: Cambridge University Press, 2000).

Hedley, Douglas, "Participation in the divine life: Coleridge, the vision of God and J. H. Newman," in Paul Vaiss, ed., *From Oxford to the People: Reconsidering Newman and the Oxford Movement* (Leominster: Gracewing, 1996), pp. 238–51.

Hedley, Douglas, "Was Schleiermacher a Christian Platonist?" *Dionysius* 17 (December 1999), pp. 149–68.

Heitzenrater, Richard P., *Wesley and the People Called Methodists* (Nashville, TN: Abingdon Press, 1995).

Hempton, David, *Methodism: Empire of the Spirit* (New Haven, CT: Yale University Press, 2005).

Hempton, David, *The Religion of the People: Methodism and Popular Religion, c. 1750–1900* (London and New York: Routledge, 1996).

Hempton, David, and Hill, Myrtle, *Evangelical Protestantism in Ulster Society, 1740–1890* (London and New York: Routledge, 1992).

Hennell, Michael, *John Venn and the Clapham Sect* (London: Lutterworth Press, 1958).

Herring, George, "Tractarianism to Ritualism: A Study of Some Aspects of Tractarianism outside Oxford, from the time of Newman's Conversion in 1845 until the First Ritual Commission in 1867," D.Phil. thesis, University of Oxford, 1984.

Hickes, George, *Two Treatises, One of the Christian Priesthood, The Other of the Dignity of the Episcopal Order. Formerly Written, and now Published to obviate the Erroneous Opinions, Fallacious Reasonings, and Bold and False Assertions in a late Book, enti-tuled, The Rights of the Christian Church. With a large prefatory discourse, Wherein is contained an Answer to the said Book* (London: Printed by W. B. for Richard Sare, 1707).

Hill, Christopher, and Yarnold, Edward, eds, *Anglican Orders: The Documents in the Debate* (Norwich: Canterbury Press, 1997).

Hill, Jacqueline, *From Patriots to Unionists: Dublin Civic Politics and Irish Protestant Patriotism, 1660–1840* (Oxford: Clarendon Press, 1997).

Hiller, Mary Ruth, "*The Eclectic Review*, 1805–1868," *Victorian Periodicals Review* 27.3 (Fall 1994), pp. 179–283.

Hinchliff, Peter, *Cyprian of Carthage and the Unity of the Christian Church* (London: Geoffrey Chapman Publishers, 1974).

Hinde, Wendy, *Catholic Emancipation: A Shake to Men's Minds* (Oxford: Basil Blackwell, 1992).

Hitchcock, F. R. Montgomery, *Clement of Alexandria* (London: S. P. C. K., 1899).

[Hoadly, Benjamin], *A Plain Account of the Nature and End of the Sacrament of the Lord's-Supper. In which All the Texts in the New Testament, relating to it, are produced and explained: and the Whole Doctrine about it, drawn from Them Alone. To which are added, forms of prayer*, 3rd edition (London: Printed for James, John, and Paul Knapton, 1735).

Holland, Bernard G., *Baptism in Early Methodism* (London: Epworth Press, 1970).

Holmes, Stephen R., *God of Grace and God of Glory: An Account of the Theology of Jonathan Edwards* (Edinburgh: T. and T. Clark, 2000).

Hook, Walter Farquhar, ed., *The Church and Its Ordinances*, two volumes (London: Richard Bentley and Son, 1876).

Hooker, Richard, *The Works of that Learned and Judicious Divine Mr. Richard Hooker: with an account of his life and death by Isaac Walton*, ed. John Keble, three volumes (Oxford: Oxford University Press, 1836).

Hooykaas, Reijer, *Robert Boyle: A Study of Science and Christian Belief*, trans. H. Van Dyke, Foreword John Hedley Brooke and Michael Hunter (Lanham, MD: University Press of America, 1997 [1943]).

Hope, John Thomas, *Catalogue of a Collection of Early Newspapers and Essayists Formed by the Late John Thomas Hope and Presented to the Bodleian Library by the Late Rev. Frederick William Hope* (Oxford: Clarendon Press, 1865).

[Hopkins, William], *The Book of Bertram or Ratramnus, Priest and Monk of Corbey, Concerning the Body and Blood of the Lord, In Latine: With a New English Translation more exact than the former. Also An Historical Dissertation concerning the Author and this Work, wherein both are vindicated from the Exceptions of the Writers of the Church of Rome* (London: Printed for Ch. Shortgrave, 1686).

[Horsley, Samuel], *The Charge of Samuel, Lord Bishop of Rochester, to the Clergy of His Diocese, Delivered at His Second General Visitation in the Year 1800* (London: Printed by Nichols and Son, for James Robson, 1800).

Houghton, Esther Rhoades, and Altholz, Josef L., "The *British Critic*, 1824–1843," *Victorian Periodicals Review* 24.3 (Fall 1991), pp. 111–18.

Howsam, Leslie, *Cheap Bibles: Nineteenth-Century Publishing and the British and Foreign Bible Society* (Cambridge: Cambridge University Press, 1991).

Hughes, George Wynne, "The Life and Work of Alexander Knox (1757–1831)," Ph.D. thesis, Edinburgh University, 1937.

Hume, John, *Derry Beyond the Walls: Social and Economic Aspects of the Growth of Derry, 1825–1850* (Belfast: Ulster Historical Foundation, 2002).

Hunt, John, *Religious Thought in England in the Nineteenth Century* (London: Gibbings and Co., 1896).

Hunt, Richard McMasters, *The Place of Religion in the Science of Robert Boyle* (Pittsburgh, PA: University of Pittsburgh Press, 1955).

Hutton, Sarah, "Lord Herbert of Cherbury and the Cambridge Platonists," in Stuart Brown, ed., *British Philosophy and the Age of Enlightenment* (London: Routledge, 1996), pp. 20–42.

Hutton, Sarah, "Thomas Jackson, Oxford Platonist, and William Twisse, Aristotelean," *Journal of the History of Ideas* 39.4 (October-December 1978), pp. 635–52.

Hyde, H. M., *The Rise of Castlereagh*, Foreword The Marquess of Londonderry, K. G. (London: Macmillan and Co., 1933).

[Illyricus, Matthias Flacius, ed.], *Ecclesiastica Historia, integram ecclesiae Christi ideam, quantum ad locum, propagationem, persecutionem, tranquillitatem, doctrinam, hæreses, ceremonias, gubernationem, schismata, synodos, personas, miracula, martyria, religiones extra ecclesiam, & statum imperii politicum attinet, secundum singulas centurias, perspicuo ordine complectens: singulari diligentia & fide ex vetustissimis & optimis historicis, patribus, & aliis scriptoribus congesta, per aliquot studiosos ac pios viros in urbe Magdeburica*, thirteen volumes (Basle: Oporinus, 1559–74).

Imberg, Rune, *In Quest of Authority: The "Tracts for the Times" and the Development of the Tractarian Leaders, 1833–1841* (Lund: Lund University Press, 1987).

Inge, W. R., *The Platonic Tradition in English Religious Thought: The Hulsean Lectures at Cambridge, 1925–1926* (London: Longmans, Green and Co., 1926).

Jackson, Bloomfield, *The Anglican Ordinal, Annotated and Arranged for Use at Ordinations, Combined or Single* (London: S. P. C. K., 1897).

Jackson, Clare, "Progress and Optimism," in Martin Fitzpatrick, Peter Jones, Christa Knellwolf, and Iain McCalman, eds, *The Enlightenment World* (Abingdon: Routledge, 2004), pp. 177–93.

Jackson, Thomas, *Maran Atha or Dominus Veniet: commentaries upon the articles of the Creed, never heretofore printed. Viz., Of Christs session at the right hand of God and exaltation thereby. His being made Lord and Christ: of his coming to judge the quick and the dead. The resurrection of the body; and Life everlasting both in joy and torments. With divers sermons proper attendants upon the precedent tracts, and befitting these present times* (London: Printed by A. Maxey for Timothy Garthwait, 1657).

Jacobson, William, *S. Clementis Romani, S. Ignatii, S. Polycarpi, Patrum Apostolicorum, quae supersunt: Accedunt S. Ignatii et S. Polycarpi martyria: Ad fidem codicum recensuit, adnotationibus et suis illustravit, indicibus instruxit*, two volumes (Oxford: Clarendon Press, 1838).

Jagger, Peter J., *Clouded Witness: Initiation in the Church of England in the Mid-Victorian Period, 1850–1875* (Allison Park, PA: Pickwick Publications, 1982).

Jebb, John, ed., *Lives, Characters, and an Address to Posterity, by Gilbert Burnet, D. D., Lord Bishop of Sarum, with the two prefaces to the Dublin edition* (London: James Duncan and James Cochran, 1833).

Jebb, John, *Pastoral Instructions On The Character and Principles of the Church of England, selected from his former publications* (London: James Duncan, and Cochran and Key, 1831).

Jebb, John, *Practical Theology; comprising discourses on the liturgy and principles of the United Church of England and Ireland; critical and other tracts; and a speech delivered in the House of Peers, in the year MDCCCXXIV*, two volumes (London: James Duncan and John Cochran, 1830).

Jebb, John, *Sermons, on Subjects Chiefly Practical, with illustrative notes and an appendix, relating to the character of the Church of England, as distinguished both from other branches of the Reformation, and from the modern Church of Rome* (London: Printed for T. Cadell and W. Davies, 1815).

Jebb, John, [Jnr], *The Choral Service of England and Ireland: being an enquiry into the liturgical system of the cathedral and collegiate foundations of the Anglican Communion* (London: John W. Parker, 1843).

Jebb, John, [Jnr], *The Divine Economy of the Church* (London: Duncan and Malcolm, 1840).

Jebb, John, [Jnr], *Three Lectures on the Cathedral Service of the Church of England*, 2nd edition (Leeds: T. W. Green, 1845 [1841]).

Jedin, Hubert, *A History of the Council of Trent: Volume 2: The First Sessions at Trent, 1545–1547*, trans. Ernest Graf (Edinburgh: Thomas Nelson and Sons, 1961 [1957]).

Jenkins, Deborah, "The Correspondence of Charles Brodrick (1761–1822), Archbishop of Cashel," *Irish Archives Bulletin* (1979/80), pp. 43–49.

Jenkyns, Richard, *The Victorians and Ancient Greece* (Oxford: Basil Blackwell, 1980).

Johnson, John, *The Unbloody Sacrifice and Altar Unvail'd and Supported*, two volumes (London: Printed for Robert Knaplock, 1714–18).

Jones, M. G., *Hannah More* (Cambridge: Cambridge University Press, 1952).

Jones, Tod E., ed., *The Cambridge Platonists: A Brief Introduction: With Eight Letters of Dr. Antony Tuckney and Dr. Benjamin Whichcote*, trans. Sara E. Phang (Lanham, MD: University Press of America, 2005).

Jorgenson, James, "Predestination according to Divine Foreknowledge in Patristic Tradition," in John Meyendorff and Robert Tobias, eds, *Salvation in Christ: A Lutheran-Orthodox Dialogue* (Minneapolis, MN: Augsburg, 1992), pp. 159–69.

Kant, Immanuel, *Critik der reinen Vernunft* (Riga: Johann Friedrich Hartnoch, 1781).

Karavitis, Peter (Panayiotis), *Evil, Freedom, and the Road to Perfection in Clement of Alexandria* (Leiden: Brill, 1999).

Kärkkäinen, Veli-Matti, *One with God: Salvation as Deification and Justification* (Collegeville, MN: Liturgical Press, 2004).

Kasper, Walter, *Die Lehre von der Tradition in der römischen Schule* new edition (Freiburg: Herder, 2013 [1962]).

[Kaye], John, Bishop of Bristol, *The Ecclesiastical History of the Second and Third Centuries, illustrated from the writings of Tertullian* (Cambridge: Cambridge University Press, 1826).

Keats, John, *Selected Letters of John Keats*, ed. Grant F. Scott (Cambridge, MA: Harvard University Press, 2002).

Keble, John, *De Poeticae Vi Medica. Praelectiones Academicae Oxonii Habitae Annis MDCCCXXXII ... MDCCCXLI*, two volumes (Oxford: J. H. Parker, 1844).

Keble, John, *Keble's Lectures on Poetry: 1832–1841*, trans. Edward Kershaw Francis, two volumes (Oxford: Clarendon Press, 1912).

Keble, John, *On Eucharistical Adoration* (Oxford and London: John Henry and James Parker, 1857).

Keble, John, *Sermons, Occasional and Parochial* (Oxford and London: James Parker and Co., 1867).

Kelly, J. N. D., *Early Christian Doctrines*, 5th edition (London: Adam and Charles Black, 1977 [1958]).

Kelly, J. N. D., *Golden Mouth: The Story of John Chrysostom: Ascetic, Preacher, Bishop* (London: Duckworth, 1995).

Kelly, Thomas, *A Plea for Primitive Christianity, in answer to a pamphlet by the Rev. Peter Roe, entitled "The Evils of Separation from the Church of England"* (Dublin: Printed by Graisberry and Campbell for T. Johnston, 1815).

Keogh, Dáire, and Whelan, Kevin, eds, *Acts of Union: The Causes, Contexts, and Consequences of the Act of Union* (Dublin: Four Courts Press, 2001).

Ker, Ian, *John Henry Newman: A Biography* (Oxford: Clarendon Press, 1988).

Ker, Ian, and Merrigan, Terrence, eds, *The Cambridge Companion to John Henry Newman* (Cambridge: Cambridge University Press, 2009).

Khoo, Lorna Lock-Nah, *Wesleyan Eucharistic Spirituality: Its Nature, Sources and Future* (Hindmarsh, South Australia: A. T. F. Press, 2005).

Killian, Justin, and Timmerman, David M., "John Chrysostom," in Michelle Ballif and Michael G. Moran, eds, *Classical Rhetorics and Rhetoricians: critical studies and sources* (Westport, CT: Praeger, 2005), pp. 96–100.

Kilmartin, Edward J., *The Eucharist in the West: History and Theology*, ed. Robert J. Daly (Collegeville, MN: Liturgical Press, 1998).

Kimbrough, S. T., Jnr, ed., *Orthodox and Wesleyan Ecclesiology* (Crestwood, NY: St. Vladimir's Seminary Press, 2007).

Kimbrough, S. T., Jnr, ed., *Orthodox and Wesleyan Scriptural Understanding and Practice* (Crestwood, NY: St. Vladimir's Seminary Press, 2005).

Kimbrough, S. T., Jnr, ed., *Orthodox and Wesleyan Spirituality* (Crestwood, NY: St. Vladimir's Seminary Press, 2002).

[Kingsley, Charles], C. K., "Hours with the Mystics" [Review], *Fraser's Magazine for Town and Country* 54.321 (September 1856), pp. 315–28.

Kingston, Gillian, *Working Out The Covenant: Guidelines for the Journey* (Dublin: Church of Ireland Publishing, 2008).

Knellwolf, Christa, "The Science of Man," in Martin Fitzpatrick, Peter Jones, Christa Knellwolf, and Iain McCalman, eds, *The Enlightenment World* (Abingdon: Routledge, 2004), pp. 194–206.

Knight, Henry H., III, *The Presence of God in the Christian Life: John Wesley and the Means of Grace* (Lanham, MD: Scarecrow Press, 1992).

Kunitz, Stanley, and Haycraft, Howard, *British Authors of the Nineteenth Century* (New York: H. W. Wilson, 1936).

Laemmer, Hugo, *Die Vortridentinisch-Katholische Theologie des Reformations-Zeitalters aus den Quellen Dargestellt* (Berlin: Verlag Von Gustav Schlawitz, 1858).

Lai, Pak-Wah, "John Chrysostom and the Hermeneutics of Exemplar Portraits," Ph.D. thesis, University of Durham, 2010.

Lamm, Julia A., "Schleiermacher as Plato Scholar," *Journal of Religion* 80.2 (April 2000), pp. 206–39.

Lardner, Nathaniel, *Credibility of the Gospel History, or The Facts Occasionally Mention'd in the New Testament Confirmed by passages of ancient authors, who were contemporary with our Saviour and his apostles or lived near their time*, fourteen volumes (London: John Gray [and others], 1727–55).

de Larroque, Matthieu, *Histoire de l'Eucharistie, divisée en trois parties: dont la première traite de la forme de la célébration, la seconde de la doctrine, et la troisième du culte* (Amsterdam: Daniel Elzevier, 1669).

de Larroque, Matthieu, *The History of the Eucharist. Divided into Three Parts. The First, treating of the Form of Celebration, The Second, of the Doctrine, The Third, of Worship in the Sacrament. Written originally in French, by Monsieur L'Arroque, Minister of the Protestant Church at Quevilly, near Roan; with new additions. Done into English by J. W.* (London: Printed for George Downes, 1684).

Laurain, Madaleine, "*Les Travaux d' Érudition des Mauristes: Origine et Évolution*," *Revue de l'Histoire de l'Église de France* 43.140 (1957), pp. 231–271.

Laurence, Richard, *The Doctrine of Baptismal Regeneration Contrasted with the Tenets of Calvin, in A Sermon preached before the University of Oxford at Christ Church, on Sunday, January 29, 1815* (Oxford: Oxford University Press, 1815).

Lawrenz, Melvin E., III, *The Christology of John Chrysostom* (Lewiston, NY: Edwin Mellen Press, 1996).

Lecky, William Edward Hartpole, *A History of Ireland in the Eighteenth Century*, volume 3 (London: Longmans, Green, and Co., 1909 [1892]).

Lehmann, Hartmut, "Pietism in the World of Transatlantic Religious Revivals," in Jonathan Strom, Hartmut Lehmann, and James Van Horn Melton, eds, *Pietism in Germany and North America 1680–1820* (Farnham: Ashgate, 2009), pp. 13–21.

Leigh, Ione, *Castlereagh* (London: Collins, 1951).

Lentz, Thierry, *Nouvelle Histoire du Premier Empire*, four volumes (Paris: Éditions Fayard, volume 1, 2002; volume 2, 2004; volume 3, 2007; volume 4, 2010).

Leroux, Jean-Marie, "*Jean Chrysostome et Le Monarchisme*," in Charles Kannengiesser, ed., *Jean Chrysostome et Augustin: Actes du Colloque de Chantilly, 22–24, Septembre 1974* (Paris: Beauchesne, 1975), pp. 125–44.

Leslie, James B., *Clergy of Connor from Patrician Times to the Present Day* (Belfast: Ulster Historical Foundation, 1993).

Leslie, James B., *Clergy of Dublin and Glendalough: Biographical Succession Lists*, ed. W. J. R. Wallace (Belfast: Ulster Historical Foundation, 2001).

Lessmann, Thomas, *Rolle und Bedeutung des Heiligen Geistes in der Theologie John Wesleys* (Stuttgart: Christliches Verlaghaus, 1987).

Levin, Harry, *The Broken Column: A Study in Romantic Hellenism* (Harvard, CT: Harvard University Press, 1931).

Liddon, H. P., *Life of Edward Bouverie Pusey, D. D., Canon of Christ Church; Regius Professor of Hebrew in the University of Oxford*, four volumes, volumes 1–3 edited by J. O. Johnson and Robert J. Wilson, volume 4 edited by J. O. Johnson, Robert J. Wilson and W. C. E. Newbolt (London: Longmans, Green, and Co., 1893–97).

Liebster, W., "*Umkehr und Erneuerung im Verhältnis von Christen und Juden*," in B. Klappert and H. Starck, eds., *Umkehr und Erneurungen: Erläuterungen zum Synodalbeschluß der Rheinischen Landessynode 1980: Zur Erneuerung des Verhältnisses von Christen und Juden* (Neukirchen-Vluyn: Neukirchener Verlag, 1980), pp. 55–65.

Liechty, Joseph, "Irish Evangelicalism, Trinity College, Dublin, and the Mission of the Church of Ireland at the end of the Eighteenth Century," Ph.D. thesis, Maynooth, 1987.

Lilla, Salvatore, *Clement of Alexandria: A Study in Christian Platonism and Gnosticism* (Oxford: Oxford University Press, 1971).

Lindström, Harald, *Wesley and Sanctification: A Study in the Doctrine of Salvation* (London: Epworth Press, 1946).

Livingston, James C., *Modern Christian Thought: The Enlightenment and the Nineteenth Century*, 2nd edition (Minneapolis, MN: Fortress Press, 2006 [1971]).

Locke, John, *An Essay Concerning Human Understanding*, 27th edition (London: Printed for T. Tegg and Son, R. Griffin and Co., Tegg, Wise, and Co., 1836 [1690]).

Locke, John, *The Reasonableness of Christianity as Delivered in the Scriptures*, ed. John C. Higgins-Biddle (Oxford: Clarendon Press, 1999 [1695]).

Lossky, Nicolas, "The Oxford Movement and the Revival of Patristic Theology," in Paul Vaiss, ed., *From Oxford to the People: Reconsidering Newman and the Oxford Movement* (Leominster: Gracewing, 1996), pp. 76–82.

Lossky, Vladimir, *The Mystical Theology of the Eastern Church*, 2nd edition (Crestwood, NY: St Vladimir's Seminary Press, 1976 [1944]).

Lot-Borodine, Myrrha, *La Déification de l'Homme selon la Doctrine des Pères Grecs* (Paris: Editions du Cerf, 1970).

Louth, Andrew, *Maximus the Confessor* (London: Routledge, 1996).

Louth, Andrew, *The Origins of the Christian Mystical Tradition: From Plato to Denys* (Oxford: Clarendon Press, 1981).

Lovejoy, Arthur O., "The Meaning of Romanticism for the Historian of Ideas," *Journal of the History of Ideas* 2.3 (June 1941), pp. 257–78.

Lovejoy, Arthur O., "On the Discrimination of Romanticisms," *Publications of the Modern Language Association of America* 39.2 (June 1924), pp. 229–53.

Lowth, Robert, *De Sacra Poesi Hebraeorum: praelectiones academicae Oxonii habitae* (Oxford: E Typographeo Clarendoniano, 1753).

Löwy, Michael, and Sayre Robert, *Romanticism Against the Tide of Modernity*, translated by Catherine Porter (Durham, NC: Duke University Press, 2001 [1992]).

[Lucas, Richard], The Author of *Practical Christianity, An Enquiry after Happiness, in several parts*, two volumes (London: Printed for George Pawlett and Samuel Smith, 1685).

[Lucas, Richard], *Practical Christianity, or, An Account of the Holinesse which the Gospel Enjoyns, with the motives to it and the remedies it proposes against temptations, with a prayer concluding each distinct head* (London: R. Pawlet, 1677).

[Lucas, Richard], *Religious Perfection: or, A Third Part of the Enquiry after Happiness*, 5th edition (London: Printed for W. Innys and R. Manby, 1735 [1685]).

McAdoo, H. R., *The Eucharistic Theology of Jeremy Taylor Today* (Norwich: The Canterbury Press, 1988).

McAdoo, H. R., *The Spirit of Anglicanism: A Survey of Anglican Theological Method in the Seventeenth Century* (London: Adam and Charles Black, 1965).

McAdoo, H. R., and Stevenson, Kenneth W., *The Mystery of the Eucharist in the Anglican Tradition* (Norwich: The Canterbury Press, 1995).

McBride, Ian, "'The Common Name of Irishman': Protestantism and Patriotism in Eighteenth-Century Ireland," in Tony Claydon and Ian McBride, eds, *Protestantism and National Identity: Britain and Ireland, c.1650–c.1850* (Cambridge: Cambridge University Press, 1998), pp. 236–61.

McCormick, Kelley Steve, "John Wesley's Use of John Chrysostom on the Christian Life: Faith Filled with the Energy of Love," Ph.D. thesis, Drew University, 1983.

McDowell, R. B., *Ireland in the Age of Imperialism and Revolution, 1760–1801* (Oxford: Clarendon Press, 1979).

McDowell, R. B., *Irish Public Opinion, 1750–1800* (London: Faber and Faber, 1944).

McGinley, Michael, *The La Touche Family in Ireland* (Greystones: The La Touche Committee, 2004).

McGinn, Bernard, *The Foundations of Mysticism: Origins to the Fifth Century* (London: S. C. M. Press, 1991).

McGinn, Bernard, *The Harvest of Mysticism in Medieval Germany: 1300–1500* (New York: Crossroad Publishing, 2005).

McGinn, Bernard, "The Letter and the Spirit: Spirituality as an Academic Discipline," in Elizabeth A. Dreyer and Mark S. Burrows, eds, *Minding the Spirit: The Study of Christian Spirituality* (Baltimore, MD: The Johns Hopkins University Press, 2005), pp. 25–41.

McGrath, Alister E., *Iustitia Dei: A History of the Christian Doctrine of Justification*, two volumes (Cambridge: Cambridge University Press, 1986).

McGrath, Thomas, *Politics, Interdenominational Relations and Education in the Public Ministry of Bishop James Doyle of Kildare and Leighlin, 1786–1834* (Dublin: Four Courts Press, 1999).

McGuire, James, and Quinn, James, eds, *Dictionary of Irish Biography: from the earliest times to the year 2002*, nine volumes (Cambridge: Cambridge University Press, 2009).

[McIlwaine, William], *Ecclesiologism Exposed: being the letters of "Clericus Connorensis," as originally published in the Belfast Commercial Chronicle, with introductory remarks and an appendix* (Belfast: George Phillips, W. Curry, 1843).

McLeod, Hugh, *Religion and the People of Western Europe, 1789–1970* (Oxford: Oxford University Press, 1981).

M. McMahon, Darrin M., "Pursuing an enlightened gospel: happiness from deism to materialism to atheism," in Martin Fitzpatrick, Peter Jones, Christa Knellwolf, and Iain McCalman, eds, *The Enlightenment World* (Abingdon: Routledge, 2004), pp. 164–76.

MacCulloch, Diarmaid, *Thomas Cranmer: A Life* (New Haven, CT: Yale University Press, 1996).

MacCulloch, Diarmaid, *Tudor Church Militant: Edward VI and the Protestant Reformation* (London: Penguin, 2000 [1999]).

Mackean, W. H., *The Eucharistic Doctrine of the Oxford Movement: A Critical Survey* (London and New York: Putnam, 1933).

Macquarrie, John, *A Guide to the Sacraments* (London: S. C. M. Press, 1997).

Madden, Hamilton, Mrs., *Memoir of the Late Right Rev. Robert Daly, D. D., Lord Bishop of Cashel* (London: James Nisbet and Co., 1875).

Maddox, Randy L., ed., *Aldersgate Reconsidered* (Nashville, TN: Kingswood Books, 1990).

Maddox, Randy L., "A Change of Affections: The Development, Dynamics, and Dethronement of John Wesley's 'Heart Religion,'" in Richard B. Steele, ed., *"Heart Religion" in the Methodist Tradition and Related Movements* (Lanham, MD: Scarecrow Press, 2001), pp. 3–31.

Maddox, Randy L., "John Wesley and Eastern Orthodoxy: Influences, Convergences and Differences," *Asbury Theological Journal* 45.2 (1990), pp. 29–53.

Maddox, Randy L., *Responsible Grace: John Wesley's Practical Theology* (Nashville, TN: Kingswood Books, 1994).

Maddox, Randy L., and Vickers, Jason E., eds, *The Cambridge Companion to John Wesley* (Cambridge: Cambridge University Press, 2010).

Magee, William, *Discourses and Dissertations on the Scriptural Doctrines of Atonement and Sacrifice: and on the principal arguments advanced, and the mode of reasoning employed, by the opponents of those doctrines as held by the established church: with an appendix, containing some strictures on Mr. Belsham's account of the Unitarian scheme, in his review of Mr. Wilberforce's Treatise*, 3rd edition, two volumes (London: Printed by J. and E. Hodson for T. Cadell and W. Davies, 1812 [1801]).

Maloney, George A., *Pseudo-Macarius: The Fifty Spiritual Homilies and the Great Letter* (Mahwah, NJ: Paulist Press, 1992).

Mant, Richard, *An Appeal to the Gospel, or an inquiry into the justice of the charge, alleged by Methodists and other Objectors, that the Gospel is not Preached by the National Clergy: in a series of discourses delivered before the University of Oxford in the year 1812, at the Lecture founded by the late Rev. J. Bampton, M. A., Canon of Salisbury* (Oxford: Oxford University Press, 1812).

Mariña, Jacqueline, ed., *The Cambridge Companion to Friedrich Schleiermacher* (Cambridge: Cambridge University Press, 2005).

Mariña, Jacqueline, "Schleiermacher, Realism, and Epistemic Modesty: A Reply to My Critics," in Brent W. Sockness and Wilhelm Gräb, eds, *Schleiermacher, The Study of Religion, and the Future of Theology: A Transatlantic Dialogue* (Berlin: Walter de Gruyter, 2010), pp. 121–34.

Marsden, George M., *Jonathan Edwards: A Life* (New Haven, CT: Yale University Press, 2003).

Marsh, Herbert, *A Letter to the Rev. C. Simeon, in answer to his pretended Congratulatory Address, in Confutation of his various mis-statements, and in vindication of the efficacy ascribed by our Church to the Sacrament of Baptism. With a Postscript on the authenticity of the Abingdon letter* (Cambridge: Printed by James Hodson, 1813).

Marsh, Herbert, *A Second Letter to the Rev. Charles Simeon, M. A., in confutation of his various mis-statements, and in vindication of the efficacy ascribed by our church to the sacrament of baptism* (Cambridge: Printed by James Hodson, 1813).

Martin, Roger H., *Evangelicals United: Ecumenical Stirrings in Pre-Victorian Britain, 1795–1830* (Metuchen, NJ: Scarecrow Press, 1983).

Masson, D., "Laroque ou La Roque, Matthieu de," in M. Prévost, R. D'Amant, H. Tribout de Morembert, J.-P. Lobies, eds, *Dictionnaire de Biographie Française*, fascicule cxiii, La Rochefoucauld-Laperle (Paris: Librarie Letouzey et Ané, 2000), cols. 1097–98.

Massuet, Réné, ed., *Sancti Irenaei Episcopi Lugdunensis et Martyris, Detectionis et Eversionis Falso Cognominatae Agnitionis, seu Contra Haereses Libri Quinque* (Paris: Jean-Baptiste Coignard, 1710).

Mather, F. C., *High Church Prophet: Bishop Samuel Horsley (1733–1806) and the Caroline Tradition in the Later Georgian Church* (Oxford: Clarendon Press, 1992).

Matthew, H. C. G., *Gladstone, 1809–1898* (Oxford: Oxford University Press, 1997).

Matthew, H. C. G., ed., *The Gladstone Diaries, with Cabinet Minutes and Prime-Ministerial Correspondence: VOLUME XIV: Index* (Oxford: Clarendon Press, 1994).

Matthew, H. C. G., and Harrison, Brian, eds, *The Oxford Dictionary of National Biography*, sixty volumes (Oxford: Oxford University Press, 2004).

Mayer, Wendy, and Allen, Pauline, *John Chrysostom* (London: Routledge, 2000).

Mealey, Mark Thomas, "Taste and See that the Lord is Good: John Wesley in the Christian Tradition of Spiritual Sensation," Ph.D. thesis, Toronto School of Theology, 2006.

Mede, Joseph, *The Name Altar or Θυσιαστηριον, anciently given to the Holy Table. A common-place, or theologicall discourse, in a Colledge Chappell more than two yeares since* (London: Printed by M. F. for John Clark, 1637).

Mede, Joseph, *The Works of J. Mede: being discourses on divers texts of scripture, and four treatises revised and corrected, whereunto are added discourses never before published; also a treatise of the Christian sacrifice, etc.* (London: Printed by M. F. for John Clark, 1648).

Mede, Joseph, *The Works of the Pious and Profoundly-Learned Joseph Mede, B. D., Sometime Fellow of Christ's Colledge in Cambridge, corrected and enlarged according to the author's own manuscripts*, edited by John Worthington, two volumes (London: Printed by Roger Norton for Richard Royston, 1664).

Melton, James Van Horn, "Pietism, Print Culture, and Salzburg Protestantism on the Eve of Expulsion," in Jonathan Strom, Hartmut Lehmann, and James Van Horn Melton, eds, *Pietism in Germany and North America 1680–1820* (Farnham: Ashgate, 2009), pp. 229–49.

Merrigan, Terrence, and Ker, Ian T., eds, *Newman and the Word* (Louvain: Peeters Press, 2000).

Migne, J. P., ed., *Patrologiae Cursus Completus, Series Graeca*, 161 volumes (Paris: Migne, 1857–66).

Migne, J. P., ed., *Patrologiae Cursus Completus, Series Latina*, 217 volumes (Paris: Migne, 1844–55).

Miles, Rebekah L., "Happiness, Holiness and the Moral Life in John Wesley," in Randy L. Maddox and Jason E. Vickers, eds, *The Cambridge Companion to John Wesley* (Cambridge: Cambridge University Press, 2009), pp. 207–24.

Mill, John Stuart, "Tennyson's Poems," in J. W. M. Gibbs, ed., *Early Essays by John Stuart Mill* (London: George Bell and Sons, 1897), pp. 239–71.

Miller, George, *Lectures on the Philosophy of Modern History, delivered in the University of Dublin*, eight volumes (Dublin: Printed ... for John Murray, 1816–28).

Milner, Joseph, *The History of the Church of Christ*, three volumes (volume 1, York: Printed by George Peacock, 1794; volumes 2–3, Cambridge: Printed by John Burges, 1795–97).

Möhler, Johann Adam, *Die Einheit in der Kirche, oder das Prinzip des Katholizmus, dargestellt im Geiste der Kichenväter der drei ersten Jahrhunderte* (Tübingen: Hienrich Laupp, 1825).

Monk, Robert C., *John Wesley: His Puritan Heritage: A Study of the Christian Life* (Nashville, TN: Abingdon Press, 1966).

de Montfaucon, Bernard, ed., *Sancti Joannis Chrysostomi, Opera Omnia quae exstant vel quae ejus nomine circumferuntur* thirteen volumes (Paris: L. Guerin, C. Robustel, Jean et Jos. Barroux, G. Desprez, et Jo. Desessartz, 1718–38).

Moore, Henry, *The Life of the Rev. John Wesley, A. M., Fellow of Lincoln College, Oxford; in which are included, the life of his brother, the Rev. Charles Wesley, A. M., Student of Christ Church, and memoirs of their family: comprehending an account of the great revival of religion, in which they were the first and chief instruments*, two volumes (London: Printed for John Kershaw, 1824).

Moore, Henry, *A Reply to a Pamphlet, entitled, "Considerations on a Separation of the Methodists from the Established-Church"* (Bristol: Printed and Sold by R. Edwards, 1794).

Moorman, J. R. H., "Forerunners of the Oxford Movement," *Theology* 26.151 (January 1933), pp. 2–15.

[More, Hannah], *Coelebs in Search of a Wife. Comprehending observations on domestic habits and manners, religion and morals*, two volumes (London: Printed for T. Cadell and W. Davies, 1808).

[More, Hannah], *Hints towards Forming the Character of a Young Princess*, two volumes (London: Printed for T. Cadell and W. Davies, 1805).

[More, Hannah], Z., *The Shepherd of Salisbury Plain*, two parts (Cheap Repository Tracts, [Bath and London]: Sold by S. Hazard, J. Marshall, and R. White, [1795]).

[More, Henry], *A Brief Discourse of the Real Presence of the Body and Blood of Christ in the Celebration of the Holy Eucharist; wherein the Witty Artifices of the Bishop of Meaux and of Monsieur Maimbourg are obviated, whereby they would draw in the Protestants to imbrace the Doctrine of Transubstantiation* (London: Printed for Walter Kettilby, 1686).

More, Henry, *An Explanation of the grand Mystery of Godliness; or, A True and Faithfull Representation of the Everlasting Gospel of Our Lord and Saviour Jesus Christ, the Onely Begotten Son of God and Sovereign over men and angels* (London: Printed by J. Flesher for W. Morden, 1660).

Morley, John, *The Life of William Ewart Gladstone*, three volumes (London: Macmillan, 1903).

von Mosheim, Johann Lorenz, *Institutionum Historicae Ecclesticae Antiquae et Recentioris Libri Quatuor ex ipsis fontibus insigniter emendati, plurimis accessionbus locupletati, variis observationibus illustrati* (Helmstedt: Apud Christianum Fredericum Weygand, 1755).

von Mosheim, Johann Lorenz, *An Ecclesiastical History, ancient and modern, from the birth of Christ to the present century: in which the rise, progress, and variations of church power are considered in their connection with the state of learning and philosophy, and the political history of Europe during that period*, trans. Archibald Maclaine, two volumes (London: A. Millar, 1765).

Moxon, R. S., ed., *The Commonitorium of Vincentius of Lerins* (Cambridge: Cambridge University Press, 1915).

Mozley, Anne, ed., *Letters and Correspondence of John Henry Newman, during his life in the English Church, with a brief autobiography*, two volumes (London: Longmans, Green, and Co., 1890).

Mozley, J. B., *A Review of the Baptismal Controversy* (London: Rivington, 1862).

Mozley, Thomas, *Reminiscences Chiefly of Oriel College and the Oxford Movement*, two volumes (London: Longmans, Green, and Co., 1882).

Murphy, Francesca Aran, and Zeigler, Philip G., eds, *The Providence of God: Deus Habet Consilium* (London and New York: T. and T. Clark/Continuum, 2009).

Murphy, Martin, *Blanco White: Self-Banished Spaniard* (New Haven, CT: Yale University Press, 1989).

Musculus, Wolfgang, *Opera D. Ioannis Chrysostomi Archiepiscopi Constantinopolitani, quotquot per graecorum exemplarium facultatem in Latinam linguam hactenus traduci potuerunt ad vetutissimorum codicum fidem nativae integritate decoriq. suo reditta, per viros in utraq. Lingua insigniter exercitatos*, five volumes (Basle: Johann Herwangen, 1539).

Nafziger, George, *Napoleon's Invasion of Russia* (New York: Hippocrene Books, 1984).

"Nemo," *A Brief Record of the Female Orphan House, North Circular Road, Dublin, for over one hundred years, from 1790–1892* (Dublin: Printed by Seeley, Bryers, and Walker, 1893).

Newman, Francis W., *Contributions Chiefly to the Early History of the Late Cardinal Newman* (London: Kegan Paul, Trench, Trübner, and Co., Ltd., 1891).

Newman, John Henry, *Apologia pro Vita Sua, being a history of his religious opinions*, ed. Martin J. Svaglic (Oxford: Clarendon Press, 1967 [1864]).

Newman, John Henry, *The Arians of the Fourth Century, their doctrine, temper, and conduct, chiefly as exhibited in the councils of the church, between A. D. 325 and A. D. 381* (London: Rivington, 1833).

Newman, John Henry, *Discussions and Arguments on Various Subjects* (London: Basil Montagu Pickering, 1872).

Newman, John Henry, *An Essay in Aid of a Grammar of Assent* (London: Burns, Oates, and Co., 1870).

Newman, John Henry, *An Essay on the Development of Christian Doctrine* (London: James Toovey, 1845).

Newman, John Henry, *Essays Critical and Historical*, two volumes (London: Basil Montagu Pickering, 1871).

Newman, John Henry, *Lectures on Certain Difficulties Felt by Anglicans in Submitting to the Catholic Church* (London: Burns and Lambert, 1850).

Newman, John Henry, *Lectures on Justification* (London: Rivington and J. H. Parker, 1838).

Newman, John Henry, *Lectures on the Prophetical Office of the Church, viewed relatively to Romanism and Popular Protestantism* (London: Rivington and J. H. Parker, 1837).

[Newman, John Henry], *A Letter Addressed to the Rev. R. W. Jelf, D. D., Canon of Christ Church, in explanation of No. 90, in a series called the Tracts for the Times, by the Author* (Oxford: John Henry Parker and J. G. F and J. Rivington, 1841).

[Newman, John Henry], *The Letters and Diaries of John Henry Newman: Volume II: Tutor at Oriel: January 1827 to December 1831*, ed. Ian Ker and Thomas Gornall, S. J. (Oxford: Clarendon Press, 1979).

[Newman, John Henry], *The Letters and Diaries of John Henry Newman: VOLUME IV: The Oxford Movement: July 1833 to December 1834*, ed. Ian Ker and Thomas Gornall, S. J. (Oxford: Clarendon Press, 1980).

[Newman, John Henry], *The Letters and Diaries of John Henry Newman: Volume V: Liberalism in Oxford: January 1835 to December 1836*, ed. Thomas Gornall, S. J. (Oxford: Clarendon Press, 1981).

[Newman, John Henry], *The Letters and Diaries of John Henry Newman: Volume VI: The Via Media and Froude's* Remains: *January 1837 to December 1838*, ed. Gerald Tracey (Oxford: Clarendon Press, 1984).

[Newman, John Henry], *The Letters and Diaries of John Henry Newman: VOLUME VII: Editing the* British Critic: *January 1839 to December 1840*, ed. Gerald Tracey (Oxford: Clarendon Press, 1995).

[Newman, John Henry], *The Letters and Diaries of John Henry Newman: VOLUME XXXI: The Last Years: January 1885 to August 1890*, ed. Stephen Dessain and Thomas Gornall, S. J. (Oxford: Clarendon Press, 1976).

[Newman, John Henry], *The Letters and Diaries of John Henry Newman: VOLUME XXXII: Supplement*, ed. Francis J. McGrath, F. M. S. (Oxford: Oxford University Press, 2008).

[Newman, John Henry], *Parochial and Plain Sermons*, eight volumes (London: Longmans, Green, and Co., 1908 [1891]).

[Newman, John Henry], *Sermons, Chiefly on the Theory of Religious Belief, preached before the University of Oxford* (London: Rivington, 1843).

[Newman, John Henry], *Remarks on Certain Passages in the Thirty-Nine Articles* (London: Rivington, 1841).

[Newman, John Henry], *The Via Media of the Anglican Church, illustrated in lectures, letters, and tracts written between 1830 and 1841*, two volumes (London: Basil Montague Pickering, 1877).

[Newman, John Henry, *et al.*], Members of the University of Oxford, *Tracts for the Times*, six volumes (London: Rivington, 1833–41).

Newsome, David, *The Convert Cardinals: John Henry Newman and Henry Edward Manning* (London: John Murray, 1993).

Newsome, David, "Justification and Sanctification: Newman and the Evangelicals," *Journal of Theological Studies*, NS 15 (1964), pp. 32–53.

Newsome, David, *The Parting of Friends: A Study of the Wilberforces and Henry Manning* (London: John Murray, 1966).

Newsome, David, *Two Classes of Men: Platonism and English Romantic Thought* (London: John Murray, 1974).

Newton, John, *Cardiphonia; or, The Utterance of the Heart, in the course of a real correspondence* (London: T. Nelson and Sons, 1857 [1781]).

Nichols, Aidan, *The Panther and the Hind: A Theological History of Anglicanism* (Edinburgh: T. and T. Clark, 1993).

Niebuhr, H. Richard, *The Meaning of Revelation* (Louisville, KY: Westminster John Knox Press, 2006 [1941]).

Nockles, P. B., "Change and Continuity in Anglican High Churchmanship in Britain, 1792–1850," D.Phil. thesis, University of Oxford, 1982.

Nockles, P. B., "Church or Protestant Sect? The Church of Ireland, High Churchmanship, and the Oxford Movement, 1822–1869," *The Historical Journal* 41.2 (June 1998), pp. 457–93.

Nockles, P. B., "Church Parties in the pre-Tractarian Church of England, 1750–1833: The 'Orthodox' – Some Problems of Definition and Identity," in John Walsh, Colin Haydon, and Stephen Taylor, eds, *The Church of England, c. 1689–1833: From Toleration to Tractarianism* (Cambridge: Cambridge University Press, 1993), pp. 334–59.

Nockles, P. B., "Knox, Alexander," in H. C. G. Matthew and Brian Harrison, eds, *The Oxford Dictionary of National Biography*, sixty volumes (Oxford: Oxford University Press, 2004), vol. 32, pp. 1–5.

Nockles, P. B., *The Oxford Movement in Context: Anglican High Churchmanship, 1760–1857* (Cambridge: Cambridge University Press, 1997 [1994]).

Nockles, P. B., "Reactions to Robert Southey's *Life of Wesley* (1820) Reconsidered," *Journal of Ecclesiastical History* 63.1 (January 2012), pp. 61–80.

di Nola, Gerardo, *La Dottrina Eucaristica di Giovanni Crisostomo* (Vatican City: Libreria Editrice Vaticana, 1997).

Noll, Mark A., *The Rise of Evangelicalism: The Age of Edwards, Whitefield and the Wesleys* (Leicester: Inter-Varsity Press, 2004).

Norris, Thomas J., *Cardinal Newman for Today* (Dublin: Columba Press, 2010).

Nowak, Edward, *Le Chrétien devant la Souffrance: Étude sur la Pensée de Jean Chrysostome* (Paris: Beauchesne, 1972).

Nun, Richard, *Statutes Passed in the Parliaments held in Ireland, Volume Twelve, containing from the Thirty-Ninth Year of George III. A. D. 1799, to the Fortieth Year of George III. A. D. 1800, inclusive* (Dublin: George Grierson, 1801).

Nuttall, Geoffrey F., *The Puritan Spirit: Essays and Addresses* (London: Epworth Press, 1967).

Oakeley, Frederick, *Historical Notes on The Tractarian Movement (A. D. 1833–1845)* (London: Longman, Green, Longman, Roberts, and Green, 1865).

O'Brien, James Thomas, *An Attempt to Explain and Establish the Doctrine of Justification by Faith Only, in Ten Sermons upon the Nature and Effects of Faith, preached in the Chapel of Trinity College, Dublin* (London: Longman, Rees, Orme, Brown, Green, and Longman, 1833; 2nd edition, London: Macmillan and Co., 1862; 3rd edition, 1863).

O'Brien, James Thomas, *A Plea from "The Bible and the Bible Alone" for the Doctrine of Baptismal Regeneration* (Dublin: Hodges, Foster and Co., 1873).

Ó Ciosáin, Niall, *Print and Popular Culture in Ireland: 1758–1850* (Basingstoke: Palgrave Macmillan, 1997).

Oh, Gwang Seok, *John Wesley's Ecclesiology: A Survey in its Sources and Development* (Metcuchen, NJ: Scarecrow Press, 2007).

Ollard, S. L., *Reunion* (London: Robert Scott, 1919).

O'Raifeartaigh, T., ed., *The Royal Irish Academy: A Bicentennial History, 1785–1985* (Dublin: Royal Irish Academy, 1985).

Orbe, A., "*Teologia Bautismal de Clemente Alejandrino según Paed., 1, 26, 3–27, 2,*" *Gregorianum* 36 (1955), pp. 410–48.

Osborn, Eric, "The Bible and Christian Morality in Clement of Alexandria," in Paul M. Blowers, ed., *The Bible in Greek Christian Antiquity* (Indianapolis, IN: University of Notre Dame Press, 1997), pp. 112–130.

Osborn, Eric, *Clement of Alexandria* (Cambridge: Cambridge University Press, 2005).

Osborn, Eric, *Justin Martyr* (Tübingen: J. C. B. Mohr, 1973).

Osborn, Eric, "Reason and the Rule of Faith in the Second Century A. D.," in Rowan Williams, ed., *The Making of Orthodoxy: Essays in Honour of Henry Chadwick* (Cambridge: Cambridge University Press, 1989).

Osborn, Eric, *The Philosophy of Clement of Alexandria* (Cambridge: Cambridge University Press, 1957).

O'Sullivan, Samuel, *Remains of the Rev. Samuel O'Sullivan, D. D.*, ed. J. C. Martin and Mortimer O'Sullivan, three volumes (Dublin: James McGlashan, 1853).

Outler, Albert C., ed., *John Wesley* (Oxford: Oxford University Press, 1980 [1964]).

Outler, Albert C., "John Wesley, Folk Theologian," *Theology Today* 34.2 (July 1977), pp. 150–60.

Outler, Albert C., "The Wesleyan Quadrilateral – in John Wesley," *Wesleyan Theological Journal* 20.1 (Spring 1985), pp. 7–18.

Overall, John, *Praelectiones seu Disputationes de Patrum et Christi Anima et de Antichristo*, appendix to Campbell, Archibald, *The Doctrines of a Middle State between Death and the Resurrection, of Prayers for the Dead, and the Necessity of Purification* (London: Printed for the author and sold by W. Tayler, 1721).

Overton, J. H., *The Non-Jurors: Their Lives, Principles, and Writings* (London: Smith, Elder, and Co., 1902).

Paget, Francis, *Faculties and Difficulties for Belief and Disbelief* (London: Rivington, 1887).

Paget, Francis, "The Sacraments," in Charles Gore, ed., *Lux Mundi: A Series of Studies in the Religion of the Incarnation*, 2nd edition (London: John Murray, 1890 [1889]), pp. 405–33.

Paley, Willam, *Natural Theology: or, Evidences of the Existence and Attributes of the Deity, collected from the appearances of nature* (London: Printed for R. Faulder by Wilks and Taylor, 1802).

Palmer, William, *Origines Liturgicæ, or Antiquities of the English Ritual, and a dissertation on primitive liturgies*, two volumes (Oxford: Oxford University Press, 1832).

Palmer, William, *A Treatise on the Church of Christ: designed chiefly for the use of students in theology*, two volumes (London: Rivington, 1838).

Panichas, George A., "The Greek Spirit and the Mysticism of Henry More," *Greek Orthodox Theological Review* 1.2 (Christmas 1956), pp. 41–61.

Papageorgiou, Panayiotis, "Chrysostom and Augustine on the Sin of Adam and its Consequences: A Study of Chrysostom's 'Homily 10, on Romans,' and Augustine's Commentary on it in Contra Iulianum," *St. Vladimir's Theological Quarterly* 39.4 (1995), pp. 361–78.

Parris, John R., *John Wesley's Doctrine of the Sacraments* (London: Epworth Press, 1963).

[Patrick, Simon], "S.P. of Cambridge," *A Brief Account of the New Sect of Latitude-Men. Together with some reflections upon the new philosophy* (London: no publisher, 1662).

Patrick, Simon, *The Works of Symon Patrick, D.D., sometime Bishop of Ely, including his autobiography*, ed. Alexander Taylor, nine volumes (Oxford: Oxford University Press, 1858).

Patrides, C. A., ed., *The Cambridge Platonists* (Cambridge: Cambridge University Press, 1980 [1969]).

Patterson, L. G., *God and History in Early Christian Thought: A Study of Themes from Justin Martyr to Gregory the Great* (London: Adam and Charles Black, 1967).

de Pauley, W. C., *The Candle of the Lord: Studies in the Cambridge Platonists* (London: S. P. C. K., 1937).

Pearson, John, *An Exposition of the Creed*, ed. James Nichols (London: Ward, Lock and Co., [1854] [1659]).

Pelikan, Jaroslav, *Christian Doctrine and Modern Culture (Since 1700)* (Chicago: University of Chicago Press, 1991 [1989]).

Pereiro, James, *'Ethos' and the Oxford Movement: At the Heart of Tractarianism* (Oxford: Oxford University Press, 2008).

Peters, John L., *Christian Perfection and American Methodism* (New York: Abingdon Press, 1956).

Phelan, William, *The Bible, Not the Bible Society, being an attempt to point out that mode of disseminating the scriptures which would most effectually conduce to the security of the established church and the peace of the United Kingdom* (Dublin: Printed at the Hibernia-Press-Office for John Cumming, 1817).

Phelan, William, *The Remains of William Phelan, D. D., with a biographical memoir*, edited by John, Bishop of Limerick [Jebb], two volumes (London: James Duncan, John Duncan, R. Milliken, 1832).

Picard, Jean, ed., *Sancti Bernardi Claraevallensis Abbatis Primi, Religiossimi Doctoris Ecclesiae, Suavissimique, et quod pro eximia illius pietate non injuria dixeris, plane theodacti, Opera Omnia* (Antwerp: J. Keerbergium, 1616).

Pierce, Andrew, "Comprehensive Vision: The Ecumenical Potential of A Lost Ideal," in Gesa Elsbeth Thiessen, ed., *Ecumenical Ecclesiology: Unity, Diversity and Otherness in a Fragmented World* (London and New York: T. and T. Clark/Continuum, 2009), pp. 76–87.

Plested, Marcus, *The Macarian Legacy: The Place of Macarius-Symeon in the Eastern Christian Tradition* (Oxford: Oxford University Press, 2004).

Podmore, Colin, *Aspects of Anglican Identity* (London: Church House Publishing, 2005).

Podmore, Colin, *The Moravian Church in England, 1728–1760* (Oxford: Clarendon Press, 1998).

Poiret, Pierre, *Bibliotheca Mysticorum Selecta, tribus constans partibus: 1. theol. mysticae idea generaliori, 2. auctorum mystic. characteribus praecipuis, 3. eorumdem catalogo, ac de plerisque judicio* (Amsterdam: Wetsten, 1708).

Polet, Jean-Claude, ed., *Patrimoine Littéraire Européen: Index Général* (Brussells: De Boeck et Larcier, 2000).

Pontifical Council for Promoting Christian Unity, *On Becoming a Christian: insights from scripture and the patristic writings with some contemporary reflections* (Vatican City: Pontifical Council for Promoting Christian Unity Information Service, 2007).

Pope, Alexander, *An Essay on Man*, ed. Maynard Mack (London: Methuen, 1982 [1733–34]).

Porter, Harry Boone, *Jeremy Taylor: Liturgist (1613–1667)* (London: S. P. C. K., 1979).

Porter, Roy, *The Enlightenment*, 2nd edition (Basingstoke: Palgrave, 2001 [1990]).

Porter, Roy, "The Enlightenment in England," in Roy Porter and Mikuláš Teich, eds, *The Enlightenment in National Context* (Cambridge: Cambridge University Press, 1981), pp. 1–18.

Porter, Roy, and Teich, Mikuláš, eds, *The Enlightenment in National Context* (Cambridge: Cambridge University Press, 1981).

Potter, Christopher, *His own Vindication of Himself, by way of a letter unto Mr. V.*, in John Plaifere, *Appello Evangelium for the True Doctrine of Divine Predestination, concorded with the orthodox doctrine of Gods free- grace, and mans free-will* (London: Printed by J. G. for John Clark, 1651).

Potter, Christopher, *Want of Charity Justly Charged, on all such Romanists as dare (without truth or modesty) affirme that Protestancie destroyeth salvation in answer to a late popish pamphlet intituled Charity mistaken* (Oxford: Printed by the Printers to the University for William Webb, 1633).

Potter, John, ed., *Clementis Alexandrini Opera Omnia, Quae Extant*, two volumes (Oxford: E Theatro Sheldoniano, 1715).

Prestige, G. L., *God in Patristic Thought*, 2nd edition (London: S. P. C. K., 1952 [1936]).

Prickett, Stephen, "Literature and Religion," in Robert A. Segal, ed., *The Blackwell Companion to the Study of Religion* (Oxford: Blackwell, 2006), pp. 69–90.

Prickett, Stephen, *Romanticism and Religion: The Tradition of Coleridge and Wordsworth in the Victorian Church* (Cambridge: Cambridge University Press, 1976).

Prickett, Stephen, *Wordsworth and Coleridge: The Poetry of Growth* (Cambridge: Cambridge University Press, 1980 [1970]).

Proctor, Francis, and Frere, Walter Howard, *A New History of the Book of Common Prayer, with A Rationale of its Offices* (London: Macmillan, 1958 [1855]).

[Pusey, E. B.], *The Confessions of S. Augustine, revised from a former translation* (Oxford: John Henry Parker; London: Rivington, 1838).

Pusey, E. B., *The Doctrine of the Real Presence as set forth in the works of divines and others of the English Church since the Reformation, Part 2* (Oxford and London: John Henry and James Parker, 1855).

Pusey, E. B., *The Holy Eucharist A Comfort To The Penitent. A sermon preached before the university, in the cathedral church of Christ, in Oxford, on the fourth Sunday after Easter* (Oxford: John Henry Parker; Rivington, 1843).

Pusey, E. B., *Justification. A Sermon Preached before the University at St. Mary's, on the Twenty-Fourth Sunday after Trinity, 1853* (Oxford: John Henry Parker, 1853).

Pusey, E. B., *A Letter to the Right Hon. and Right Rev. the Lord Bishop of London, in explanation of some statements contained in a letter by the Rev. W. Dodsworth* (Oxford: John Henry Parker, 1851).

Pusey, E. B., *A Letter to the Right Rev. Father in God, Richard Lord Bishop of Oxford on the tendency to Romanism imputed to doctrines held of old, as now, in the English Church*, 2nd edition (Oxford: J. H. Parker, 1839 [1839]).

Pusey, E. B., *Nine Sermons, preached before the University of Oxford, and printed chiefly between A. D. 1843–1855. Now collected in One Volume* (Oxford: J. H. and J. Parker, and Rivington, 1859).

Pusey, E. B., *Parochial Sermons: Vol. 1: For the Season from Advent to Whitsuntide* (Oxford and London: James Parker; Rivington, 1873).

Pusey, E. B., *Patience and Confidence the Strength of the Church. A sermon preached on the fifth of November, before the University of Oxford, at St Mary's, and published at the wish of many of its Members* (Oxford: J. H. Parker; Rivington, 1837).

Pusey, E. B., *The Presence of Christ in the Holy Eucharist. A sermon, preached before the university, in the cathedral church of Christ, in Oxford, on the second Sunday after Epiphany, 1853* (Oxford: John Henry Parker, and Francis and John Rivington, 1853).

Pusey, E. B., *The Real Presence of the Body and Blood of Our Lord Jesus Christ: the doctrine of the English Church, with a vindication of the reception by the wicked and of the adoration of our Lord Jesus Christ truly present* (Oxford: John Henry Parker, 1857).

Quantin, Jean-Louis, *The Church of England and Christian Antiquity: The Construction of a Confessional Identity in the 17th Century* (Oxford: Oxford University Press, 2009).

Rack, Henry D., *Reasonable Enthusiast: John Wesley and the Rise of Methodism*, 2nd edition (Nashville, TN: Abingdon Press, 1992 [1989]).

von Rad, Gerhard, *Old Testament Theology: Volume 1: The Theology of Israel's Historical Traditions*, trans. D. M. G. Stalker, intro. Walter Brueggemann (Louisville, KY: Westminster John Knox Press, 2001 [1957]).

Rahner, Karl, "The 'Spiritual Senses' according to Origen," in *Theological Investigations: Volume 16: Experience of the Spirit: Source of Theology*, trans. David Morland (London: Darton, Longman, and Todd, 1979 [1932]), pp. 81–103.

Ramsey, [Arthur] Michael, *The Anglican Spirit*, ed. Dale Coleman, 2nd edition (New York: Church Publishing Incorporated, 2004 [1991]).

Ramsey, [Arthur] Michael, *An Era in Anglican Theology: From Gore to Temple: The Development of Anglican Theology between* Lux Mundi *and the Second World War: 1889–1939* (Eugene, OR: Wipf and Stock, 2009 [1960]).

Ratcliff, E. C., "The Savoy Conference and the Revision of the Book of Common Prayer," in Geoffrey F. Nuttall and Owen Chadwick, eds, *From Uniformity to Unity, 1662–1962* (London: S. P. C. K., 1962), pp. 89–148.

Rattenbury, J. Ernest, *The Eucharistic Hymns of John and Charles Wesley, to which is appended Wesley's Preface, extracted from Brevint's Christian Sacrament and Sacrifice, together with Hymns on the Lord's Supper* (London: Epworth Press, 1948).

Rattenbury, J. Ernest, *Wesley's Legacy to the World: Six Studies in the Permanent Value of the Evangelical Revival* (Nashville, TN: Cokesbury Press, 1928).

Raven, C. E., *Good News of God, being eight letters on present problems and based upon Romans I-VIII* (London: Hodder and Stoughton, 1943).

Raymond, Marcel, *Fénelon* (Paris: Desclée de Brouwer, 1967).

Reardon, Bernard, M. G., *From Coleridge to Gore: A Century of Religious Thought in Britain* (London: Longman, 1971).

Reardon, Bernard, M. G., *Kant as Philosophical Theologian* (London: Palgrave Macmillan, 1988).

Reardon, Bernard, M. G., *Religion in the Age of Romanticism: Studies in Early Nineteenth Century Thought* (Cambridge: Cambridge University Press, 1985).

Reid, Nicholas, *Coleridge, Form and Symbol: or The Ascertaining Vision* (Aldershot: Ashgate, 2006).

Ridley, Nicholas, *The Works of Nicholas Ridley, D. D., sometime Lord Bishop of London, Martyr, 1555*, ed. Henry Christmas (Cambridge: Cambridge University Press, 1841).

Riga, Peter, "The Ecclesiology of Johann Adam Möhler," *Theological Studies* 22 (1961), pp. 563–87.

Rivers, Isabel, *Reason, Grace, and Sentiment: A Study of the Language of Religion and Ethics*, two volumes (Cambridge: Cambridge University Press, 1991, 2000).

Roberts, William, *Memoirs of the Life and Correspondence of Mrs. Hannah More*, four volumes (London: Published by R. B. Seeley and W. Burnside, 1834).

Rogal, Samuel J., *A Biographical Dictionary of 18th Century Methodism*, ten volumes (Lewiston, NY: Edwin Mellen Press, 1997–1999).

Rogal, Samuel J., *John Wesley in Ireland, 1747–1789*, two volumes (Lewiston, NY: Edwin Mellen Press, 1993).

Rowell, Geoffrey, "'Church Principles' and 'Protestant Kempism', Some theological forerunners of the Tractarians," in Paul Vaiss, ed., *From Oxford to the People: Reconsidering Newman and the Oxford Movement* (Leominster: Gracewing, 1996), pp. 17–59.

Rowell, Geoffrey, ed., *Tradition Renewed: The Oxford Movement Conference Papers* (London: Darton, Longman and Todd, 1986).

Russell, Norman, *The Doctrine of Deification in the Greek Patristic Tradition* (Oxford: Oxford University Press, 2004).

Rylaarsdam, David, *John Chrysostom on Divine Pedagogy: The Coherence of his Theology and Preaching* (Oxford: Oxford University Press, 2014).

Savile, Henry, ed., *Του εν αγίοις Πατρός ημών Ιωάννου Αρχιεπισκόπου Κωνσταντινουπόλεως Τα Ευρισκόμενα Πάντα*, eight volumes (Eton: John Norton, 1610–13).

Schleiermacher, Friedrich, *The Christian Faith in Outline*, trans. and intro. D. M. Baillie (Edinburgh: W. F. Henderson, 1922 [German 1821–22]).

Schleiermacher, Friedrich, *A Critical Essay on the Gospel of St. Luke*, trans. and intro. [Connop Thirlwall] (London: Printed for John Taylor, 1825).

Schleiermacher, Friedrich, *On Religion: Speeches to its Cultured Despisers*, trans. and ed. Richard Crouter (Cambridge: Cambridge University Press, 1996 [German 1799]).

Scougal, Henry, *The Life of God in the Soul of Man. Or, the Nature and Excellency of the Christian Religion; with the Method of Attaining the Happiness it proposes. And an account of the beginnings and advances of a spiritual life, in two letters written to persons of honour* (London: Printed for Charles Smith and William Jacob, 1677).

Selén, Mats, *The Oxford Movement and Wesleyan Methodism, 1833–1882: A Study in Religious Conflict* (Lund: Lund University Press, 1992).

Sell, Alan, P. F., *The Great Debate: Calvinism, Arminianism and Salvation* (Worthing: H. E. Walter, Ltd., 1982).

Shedd, W. G. T., "Coleridge as a Philosopher and Theologian," in *Literary Essays* (New York: Charles Scribner's Sons, 1878 [essay first published, 1825]), pp. 271–344.

Sheridan, Thomas L., *Newman on Justification: A Theological Biography* (Staten Island, NY: Alba House, 1967).

Simeon, Charles, *Dr. Marsh's Fact; or, A Congratulatory Address to the Church-Members of the British and Foreign Bible Society. Second edition. With an appendix, answer to Dr. Marsh's Letter to the Author* (London: Printed by James Hodson, 1813).

Skinner, S. A., "Newman, the Tractarians and the *British Critic*," *Journal of Ecclesiastical History* 50 (1999), pp. 716–59.

Smart, Ninian, ed., *Nineteenth-Century Religious Thought in the West*, three volumes (Cambridge: Cambridge University Press, 1985).

Smeaton, George, *The Doctrine of the Atonement, as taught by the Apostles; or the sayings of the Apostles exegetically expounded. With historical appendix* (Edinburgh: T. and T. Clark, 1870).

Smend, Rudolf, *From Astruc to Zimmerli: Old Testament scholarship in three centuries*, trans. Margaret Kohl (Tübingen: Mohr Siebeck, 2007).

Smith, David L., *All God's People: A Theology of the Church* (Eugene, OR: Wipf and Stock, 2004 [1996]).

Smith, John, *Select Discourses, by John Smith, late Fellow of Queen's College in Cambridge. To which is added a sermon by Symon Patrick, D. D., then Fellow of the same College, afterwards Lord Bishop of Ely, containing a brief account of his life and death*, 3rd edition (London: Printed for Rivington and Cochran, 1821 [1660]).

Smith, Mark, "Henry Ryder: *A charge delivered to the clergy of the diocese of Gloucester in the year 1816*," in Mark Smith and Stephen Taylor, eds, *Evangelicalism in the Church of England, c. 1790-c. 1890* (Woodbridge: The Boydell Press/ The Church of England Record Society, 2004).

Smith, Richard, Mrs., *The Life of the Rev. Mr. Henry Moore; The Biographer and Executor of the Rev. John Wesley; including the autobiography; and the continuation, written from his own papers* (London: Simpkin, Marshall, and Co., 1844).

Snyder, Howard A., "John Wesley and Macarius the Egyptian," *Asbury Theological Review* 45.2 (Fall 1990), pp. 55–60.

Sockness, Brent W., and Gräb, Wilhelm, eds, *Schleiermacher, the Study of Religion, and the Future of Theology: A Transatlantic Dialogue* (Berlin: Walter de Gruyter, 2010).

Sorkin, David, *The Religious Enlightenment: Protestants, Jews, and Catholics from London to Vienna* (Princeton, NJ: Princeton University Press, 2008).

Spadafora, David, *The Idea of Progress in Eighteenth-Century Britain* (New Haven, CT: Yale University Press, 1990).

Spanneut, Michel, "L'Impact de l'Apatheia Stoïcienne sur la Pensée Chrétienne jusqu' à Saint Augustin," *Antigüdad y Cristianismo* 7 (1990), pp. 39–52.

Spellman, W. M., *The Latitudinarians and the Church of England, 1660–1700* (Athens, GA: University of Georgia Press, 1993).

Spener, Philip Jacob, *Pia Desideria oder herzliches Verlangen nach gottgefälliger besserung der wahren evangelischen Kirche* (Frankfurt: In Verlegung Johann David Zunners, Druckts Johann Dietrich Friedgen, 1676).

Starkey, Lycurgus M., Jnr., *The Work of the Holy Spirit: A Study in Wesleyan Theology* (New York: Abingdon Press, 1962).

Steele, Richard B., ed., *"Heart Religion" in the Methodist Tradition and Related Movements* (Lanham, MD: Scarecrow Press, 2001).

Stevens, Abel, *The History of the Religious Movement of the Eighteenth Century, called Methodism, considered in its different denominational forms and its relation to British and American Protestantism*, three volumes (New York: Carlton and Porter, 1858–61).

Stevenson, Kenneth, *Covenant of Grace Renewed: A Vision of the Eucharist in the Seventeenth Century* (London: Darton, Longman and Todd, 1994).

Stevenson, Kenneth, *The Mystery of Baptism in the Anglican Tradition* (Norwich: The Canterbury Press, 1998).

Stewart, Alexander, and Revington, George, *Memoir of the Life and Labours of the Rev. Adam Averell, for nearly thirty years president of the president of the Primitive Wesleyan Methodist Conference* (Dublin: Methodist Book Room, 1848).

Stewart, Columba, *"Working the Earth of the Heart:" The Messalian Controversy in History, Texts, and Language to A. D. 431* (Oxford: Clarendon Press, 1991).

Stewart, Dugald, *Elements of the Philosophy of the Human Mind*, volume 1 (London: A. Strachan and T. Cadell; Edinburgh: W. Creech, 1792).

Stoeffler, F. Ernest, *The Rise of Evangelical Pietism* (Leiden: Brill, 1965).

Stokes, G. T., "Alexander Knox and the Oxford Movement," *Contemporary Review* 52 (August 1887), pp. 184–205.

Stone, Darwell, *A History of the Doctrine of the Holy Eucharist*, two volumes (London: Longmans, Green, and Co., 1909).

Storr, Vernon, *The Development of English Theology in the Nineteenth Century: 1800–1860* (London: Longmans, Green and Co., 1913).

Stott, Anne, *Hannah More: The First Victorian* (Oxford: Oxford University Press, 2003).

Strom, Jonathan, Lehmann, Hartmut, and Melton, James Van Horn, eds, *Pietism in Germany and North America 1680–1820* (Farnham: Ashgate, 2009).

Sutton, Ray R., "The Sacramental Theology of Daniel Waterland," Ph.D. thesis, University of Coventry, 1998.

Swatos, William H., Jr., "Weber or Troeltsch? Methodology, Syndrome, and the Development of Church-Sect Theory," *Journal for the Scientific Study of Religion* 15.2 (June 1976), pp. 129–44.

Sweetnam, Mark, and Gribben, Crawford, "J. N. Darby and the Irish Origins of Dispensationalism," *Journal of the Evangelical Theological Society* 52.3 (September 2009), pp. 569–77.

Sykes, Norman, *Church and State in England in the XVIIIth Century* (Cambridge: Cambridge University Press, 1934).

Sykes, Norman, *William Wake: Archbishop of Canterbury, 1657–1737*, two volumes (Cambridge: Cambridge University Press, 1957).

Sykes, Stephen, "The Fundamentals of Christianity," in Stephen Sykes, John Booty, and Jonathan Knight, eds, *The Study of Anglicanism*, 2nd edition (London: S. P. C. K., 1998 [1988]), pp. 262–77.

Sykes, Stephen, *The Identity of Christianity: Theologians and the Essence of Christianity from Schleiermacher to Barth* (London: S. P. C. K., 1984).

Sykes, Stephen, *Unashamed Anglicanism* (London: Darton, Longman and Todd, 1995).

Sykes, Stephen, Booty, John, and Knight, Jonathan, eds, *The Study of Anglicanism*, 2nd edition (London: S. P. C. K., 1998 [1988]).

Taliaferro, Charles, "Natural Reason and the Trinity: Some Lessons from the Cambridge Platonists," in Melville Y. Stewart, ed., *The Trinity: East/West Dialogue* (Dordrecht: Kluwer, 2003), pp. 167–78.

Taliaferro, Charles, and Teply, Alison J., eds, *Cambridge Platonist Spirituality* (Mahwah, NJ: Paulist Press, 2004).

Taylor, G. W., *John Wesley and the Anglo-Catholic Revival* (London: S. P. C. K., 1905).

Taylor, Jeremy, *The Whole Works of the Right Rev. Jeremy Taylor, D. D., Lord Bishop of Down, Connor, and Dromore, with a life of the author and a critical examination of his writings*, ed. Reginald Heber, fifteen volumes (London: Ogle, Duncan, and Co., and Richard Priestley, J. Parker, and Deighton and Son, 1822).

Teignmouth, Lord [Charles John Shore], *Reminiscences of Many Years*, two volumes (Edinburgh: David Douglas, 1878).

[Temple, Frederick, and Maclagan, William,], *Saepius Officio: The Reply of the English Archbishops to the Bull Apostolicae Curae of Pope Leo XIII concerning Anglican Ordinations, addressed to all the Bishops of the Catholic Church* (London: Longmans, Green and Co., 1897).

Thomas, Stephen, *Newman and Heresy: The Anglican Years* (Cambridge: Cambridge University Press, 2003 [1991]).

Thompson, David M., *Cambridge Theology in the Nineteenth Century: Enquiry, Controversy and Truth* (Aldershot: Ashgate, 2008).

Thompson, Michael James, "The High Church Tradition in Ireland, 1800–1870, with particular reference to John Jebb and Alexander Knox," M.A. dissertation, University of Durham, 1993.

Thorndike, Herbert, *Of the Government of Churches; A Discourse Pointing at the Primitive Form* (Cambridge: Printed by Roger Daniel, 1641).

Thorsen, Donald A. D., "Experimental Method in the Practical Theology of John Wesley," *Wesleyan Theological Journal* 24 (1989), pp. 117–41.

Thouvenin, Pascale, "*Nicolas Fontaine et la Légende de M. de Sacy,*" in Francine Wild, ed., *Regards sur le Passé dans l'Europe des XVIᵉ et XVIIᵉ siècles* (Bern: Peter Lang, 1996), pp. 277–89.

Thouvenin, Pascale, "*La Traduction de Saint Jean Chrysostome à Port-Royal: Nicolas Fontaine et l'accusation d'hérésie nestorienne, d'après des documents inédits,*" *Chroniques de Port-Royal* 59 (2009), pp. 97–113.

Tierney, Brian, *Origins of Papal Infallibility: 1150–1350: A Study on the Concepts of Infallibility, Sovereignty and Tradition in the Middle Ages* (Leiden: Brill, 1972).

Tigerstedt, E. N., *The Decline and Fall of the Neo-Platonic Interpretation of Plato: An Outline and Some Observations* (Helsinki: Societas Scientiarum Fennica, 1974).

Todd, John M., *John Wesley and the Catholic Church* (London: Hodder and Stoughton, 1958).

Tofana, Stelian, "John Chrysostom's View on Reading and Interpreting the Scripture. A Critical Assessment," *Sacra Scriptura* 6.2 (2008), pp. 165–81.

Tristram, Henry, ed., *John Henry Newman: Centenary Essays* (London: Burns, Oates, and Washbourne, 1945).

Turner, Frank M., *John Henry Newman: The Challenge to Evangelical Religion* (New Haven, CT: Yale University Press, 2002).

Turner, H. E. W., *The Pattern of Christian Truth: A Study in the Relations Between Orthodoxy and Heresy in the Early Church* (London: Mowbray, 1954).

Tyerman, Luke, *The Life and Times of the Rev. John Wesley, M. A., Founder of the Methodists*, three volumes (London: Hodder and Stoughton, 1870–71).

Urlin, Richard Denny, *John Wesley's Place in Church History, determined with the aid of facts and documents unknown to, or unnoticed by, his biographers* (London: Rivington, 1870).

Ury, M. William, "A Wesleyan Concept of Person," *Wesleyan Theological Journal* 38.2 (Fall 2003), pp. 30–56.

Ussher, James, *A Discourse of the Religion Anciently Professed by the Irish and the British* (London: Printed by R. Y. for the Partners of the Irish Stocke, 1631).

Vacant, A., and Mangenot, E., eds, *Dictionnaire de la Théologie Catholique*, thirty volumes (Paris: Letouzey et Ainé, 1902–50).

Vane, Charles Edward, ed., *Memoirs and Correspondence of Lord Castlereagh, Second Marquess of Londonderry*, twelve volumes (London: Henry Colburn, 1848–53).

de Villers, Charles, *Essai sur l'Esprit et l'Influence de la Réformation de Luther: ouvrage qui a remporté sur cette question proposée dans la séance publique du 15 germinal an X, par l'Institut national de France: "Quelle a été l'Influence de la reformation de Luther sur la situation politique des différens Etats de l'Europe, et sur le progress des lumières* (Paris: Chez Henrichs, chez Collignon, 1804).

de Villers, Charles, *An Essay on the Spirit and Influences of the Reformation of Luther: the work which obtained the prize on the question proposed in 1802, by the National Institute of France; "What has been the Influence of the Reformation of Luther on the Political Situation of the different States of Europe, and on the Progress of Knowledge?" with a sketch of the history of the church, from its founder to the reformation; intended as an appendix to the work*, translated by James Mill (London: Printed for C. and R. Baldwin, and R. Ogle, 1805).

Voll, Dieter, *Catholic Evangelicalism: The Acceptance of Evangelical Traditions by the Oxford Movement during the Second Half of the Nineteenth Century: A Contribution to the Understanding of Recent Anglicanism*, trans. Veronica Ruffer (London: Faith Press, 1963 [1960]).

Wagenhammer, Hans, *Das Wesen des Christentums: Eine begriffsgeschichtliche Untersuchung* (Mainz: Matthias Grünewald Verlag, 1973).

Wainright, Geoffrey, "Trinitarian Theology and Wesleyan Holiness," in S. T. Kimbrough, Jnr, ed., *Orthodox and Wesleyan Spirituality* (Crestwood, NY: St. Vladimir's Seminary Press, 2002), pp. 59–80.

Walker, John, *An Address to Believers of the Gospel of Christ, on that conversation which becometh it: with an appendix, containing an account of the change in the author's sentiments, concerning the lawfulness of his former connection with the religious establishment of this country; and his letter to the provost, which occasioned his expulsion from the college of Dublin* (Dublin: Printed for the Author by Robert Napper, 1804).

Walker, John, *An Expostulatory Address to the Members of the Methodist Society in Ireland. Together with a Series of Letter to Alexander Knox, Esq., M. I. R. A. occasioned by his remarks on the author's expostulatory address to the Methodists of Ireland* (Edinburgh: Printed by J. Richie, 1806 [*Address* first published, 1802; *Letters* first published, 1803]).

Wallace-Hadrill, D. S., *Christian Antioch: A Study of Early Christian Thought in the East* (Cambridge: Cambridge University Press, 1982).

[Walmesley, Charles,], Sig. Pastorini, *The General History of the Christian Church, from her birth, to her final triumphant state in heaven, chiefly deduced from the Apocalypse of St. John the Apostle* (Dublin: Printed by J. Mehain, 1790).

Walton, Brad, *Jonathan Edwards, Religious Affections, and the Puritan Analysis of True Piety, Spiritual Sensations, and Heart Religion* (Lewiston, NY: Edwin Mellen Press, 2002).

Warburton, J., Whitelaw, J. and Walsh, Robert, *History of the City of Dublin, from the earliest accounts to the present time, containing its annals, antiquities, ecclesiastical history, and charters; its present extent, public buildings, schools, institutions, &c. To which are added, biographical notices of eminent men and copious appendices of its population, revenue, commerce, and literature*, two volumes (London: Printed for T. Cadell and W. Davies by W. Bulmer and Co., 1818).

Ward, W. R., *Early Evangelicalism: A Global History, 1670–1789* (Cambridge: Cambridge University Press, 2006).

Ward, W. R., "Power and Piety: The origins of religious revival in the early eighteenth century," *Bulletin of the John Rylands University Library of Manchester* 63.1 (Autumn 1980), pp. 231–52.

Ward, W. R., *Religion and Society in England, 1790–1850* (London: Batsford, 1972).

Ware, Kallistos, "Preface" to George A. Maloney, *Pseudo-Macarius: The Fifty Spiritual Homilies and the Great Letter* (Mahwah, NJ: Paulist Press, 1992), pp. xi–xviii.

Warnock, Mary, *Imagination* (Berkeley, CA: University of California Press, 1976).

Waterland, Daniel, *The Works of the Rev. Daniel Waterland, D. D., formerly Master of Magdalene College, Cambridge, Canon of Windsor, and Archdeacon of Middlesex; now first collected and arranged. To which is prefixed, a review of the author's life and writings*, ed. William Van Mildert, six volumes (Oxford: Oxford University Press, 1823).

Webb, R. K., "The Background: English Unitarianism in the Nineteenth Century," in Leonard Smith, ed., *Unitarian to the Core: Unitarian College, Manchester, 1854–2004* (Lancaster: Carnegie Publishing, 2004), pp. 1–29.

Welch, Claude, *Protestant Thought in the Nineteenth Century: Volume 1: 1799–1870* (New Haven, CT: Yale University Press, 1972).

Welch, Robert, ed., *The Oxford Companion to Irish Literature* (Oxford: Clarendon Press, 1996).

Wellek, René, "The Concept of 'Romanticism' in Literary History," *Comparative Literature* 1.1 (Winter 1949), pp. 1–23; 1.2 (Spring 1949), pp. 147–72.

Wenger, Antoine, ed., *Jean Chrysostome: Huits Catéchèses Baptismales Inédites* (Paris: Editions du Cerf, 1957).

Wesley, John, *A Christian Library: consisting of extracts from and abridgements of the choicest pieces of practical divinity which have been publish'd in the English Tongue*, fifty volumes (Bristol: Printed by Felix Farley, 1749–1755).

Wesley, John, *Instructions for Children* (London: Printed for M. Cooper, 1745).

Wesley, John, *The Journal of the Rev. John Wesley, A. M., sometime Fellow of Lincoln College, Oxford, enlarged from original mss., with notes from unpublished diaries, annotations, maps, and illustrations*, ed. Nehemiah Curnock, eight volumes (London: volume 1, Robert Culley; volumes 2–8, Charles H. Kelly, [1909–16]).

Wesley, John, *A Letter to a Roman Catholic* (Dublin: Printed by S. Powell, 1749).

Wesley, John, *A Letter to the Right Reverend the Lord Bishop of Gloucester: occasioned by his tract on the office and operations of the Holy Spirit* (London: Printed and sold at the Foundery [*sic*], near Moorfields, 1763).

Wesley, John, *The Letters of the Reverend John Wesley, A.M., sometime Fellow of Lincoln College, Oxford*, ed. John Telford, eight volumes (London: The Epworth Press, 1931).

Wesley, John, *A Plain Account of Christian Perfection, as believed and taught by the Rev. Mr. John Wesley, from the Year 1725, to the Year 1777*, 5th edition (London: Printed by J. Paramore, 1784 [1766]).

Wesley, John, *A Plain Account of Genuine Christianity* (Dublin: Printed by S. Powell, 1753).

Wesley, John, *A Preservative Against Unsettled Notions in Religion* (Bristol: Printed by E. Farley, 1758).

Wesley, John, *Some Remarks on Mr. Hill's Farrago Double-Distilled* (Bristol: William Pine, 1773).

Wesley, John, *The Character of a Methodist* (Bristol: Printed by Felix Farley, 1742).

Wesley, John, *The Works of John Wesley: Volume 1: Sermons I: 1–33*, edited by Albert C. Outler (Nashville, TN: Abingdon Press, 1984).

Wesley, John, *The Works of John Wesley: Volume 2: Sermons II: 34–70*, edited by Albert C. Outler (Nashville, TN: Abingdon Press, 1985).

Wesley, John, *The Works of John Wesley: Volume 3: Sermons III: 71–114*, edited by Albert C. Outler (Nashville: Abingdon Press, 1986).

Wesley, John, *The Works of John Wesley: Volume 4: Sermons IV: 115–151*, edited by Albert C. Outler (Nashville, TN: Abingdon Press, 1987).

Wesley, John, *The Works of John Wesley: Volume 11: The Appeals to Men of Reason and Religion and certain related open letters*, ed. Gerald C. Cragg (Oxford: Clarendon Press, 1975).

Wesley, John, and Wesley, Charles, *Hymns on the Lord's Supper. With A Preface concerning the Christian Sacrament and Sacrifice, extracted from Dr. Brevint*, 11th edition (London: J. Kershaw, 1825 [1745]).

Whelan, Irene, "The Bible Gentry: Evangelical Religion, Aristocracy and the New Moral Order in the Early Nineteenth Century," in Gribben, Crawford, and

Andrew R. Holmes, eds, *Protestant Millennialism, Evangelicalism and Irish Society, 1790–2005* (Basingstoke: Palgrave Macmillan, 2006), pp. 52–82.

Whelan, Irene, *The Bible War in Ireland: The 'Second Reformation' and the Polarisation of Protestant-Catholic Relations, 1800–1840* (Dublin: Lilliput Press, 2005).

Whichcote, Benjamin, *Moral and Religious Aphorisms. Collected from the Manuscript Papers of the Reverend and Learned Doctor Whichcote; and published in MDCCIII by Dr. Jeffery. Now republished with very large additions, from the transcripts of the latter*, ed. Samuel Salter (London: J. Payne, 1753).

Whichcote, Benjamin, *Select Sermons of Dr. Whichcot, in two parts* (London: Printed for Awnsham and John Churchill, 1698).

Whichcote, Benjamin, *The Works of the Learned Benjamin Whichcote, D. D., Rector of St Lawrence Jewry, London*, four volumes (Aberdeen: Printed by J. Chalmers Alexander Thompson, 1751).

Whitehead, John, *The Life of the Rev. John Wesley, M.A., some time Fellow of Lincoln College, Oxford. Collected from his private papers and printed works; and written at the request of his executors; to which is prefixed some account of his ancestors and relations; with the life of the Rev. Charles Wesley, M.A., collected from his private journal, and never before published, the whole forming a history of Methodism, in which the principles and economy of the Methodists are unfolded. To which is subjoined an appendix, containing characters of the Rev. Messrs. John and Charles Wesley, as given by several learned contemporaries*, two volumes (Dublin: John Jones, 1806 [1793–96]).

Wilberforce, William, *The Correspondence of William Wilberforce*, ed. Robert Isaac Wilberforce and Samuel Wilberforce, two volumes (London: John Murray, 1840).

Wiles, Maurice, *The Christian Fathers*, 2nd edition (Oxford: Oxford University Press, 1982 [1966]).

Wilken, Robert, "Free Choice and the Divine Will in Greek Christian Commentaries on Paul," in William S. Babcock, ed., *Paul and the Legacies of Paul* (Dallas, TX: Southern Methodist University Press, 1990), pp. 123–40.

Williams, Rowan, "Introduction" to John Henry Newman, *The Arians of the Fourth Century*, ed. and intro. Rowan Williams (Leominster: Gracewing, 2001), pp. xix–xlvii.

[Wiseman, Nicholas], "The Oxford Controversy," *Dublin Review* 1.1 (May 1836), pp. 250–265.

Wittmer, Louis, *Charles de Villers, 1765–1815, un intermédiaire entre la France et l'Allemagne et un précurseur de Mme. de Staël* (Geneva: Georg, 1908).

Wix, Samuel, *Reflections concerning the Expediency of a Council of the Church of England and the Church of Rome being holden, with a view to accommodate religious differences, and to promote the unity of religion in the bond of peace: humbly, but earnestly, recommended to the serious attention of His Royal Highness the Prince Regent; the Most Reverend the Archbishops; the Right Reverend the Bishops; the Reverend the*

Clergy; and all lay persons, who are willing and able dispassionately to consider the important subject (London: Rivington and Hatchard, 1818).

Wood, Samuel Francis, "Revival of Primitive Doctrine," in James Pereiro, *"Ethos" and the Oxford Movement: At the Heart of Tractarianism* (Oxford: Oxford University Press, 2008 [1840]), pp. 252–65.

Woodward, Henry, *Sermons* (London and Cambridge: Macmillan, 1866).

Woodward, Henry, *Some Passages of My Former Life* (Dublin: James McGlashen, 1847).

Wordsworth, Jonathan, "The Infinite I AM: Coleridge and the Ascent of Being," in Richard Gravil, Lucy Newlyn and Nicholas Roe, eds, *Coleridge's Imagination: Essays in Memory of Pete Laver* (Cambridge: Cambridge University Press, 1985), pp. 22–51.

Wordsworth, William, *Lyrical Ballads, with Other Poems*, 2nd edition, two volumes (London: Printed for T. N. Longman and O. Rees By Biggs and Co., 1800 [1798]).

Wordsworth, William, *The Prelude; or, Growth of a Poet's Mind. An Autobiographical Poem* (London: Edward Moxon, 1850).

Worthington, John, *The Great Duty of Self-Resignation to the Divine Will*, new edition (Glasgow: Printed by Andrew and John M. Duncan for C. & J. Rivington, 1826 [1675]).

[Wright, William], *The Doctrine of the Real Presence as set forth in the works of divines and others of the English church since the Reformation: Part 1* [ed. E. B. Pusey] (Oxford and London: John Henry Parker, 1855).

Yates, Arthur S., *The Doctrine of Assurance with Special Reference to John Wesley* (London: Epworth Press, 1952).

Yates, Nigel, *The Religious Condition of Ireland, 1770–1850* (Oxford: Oxford University Press, 2006).

Yoder, Timothy S., *Hume on God: Irony, Deism and Genuine Theism* (London: Continuum, 2008).

Young, B. W., *Religion and Enlightenment in Eighteenth-Century England: Theological Debate from Locke to Burke* (Oxford: Clarendon Press, 1998).

Young, Frances M., "God's Word Proclaimed: The Homiletics of Grace and Demand in John Chrysostom and John Wesley," in S. T. Kimbrough, Jnr, ed., *Orthodox and Wesleyan Ecclesiology* (Crestwood, NY: St. Vladimir's Seminary Press, 2007), pp. 137–48.

Young, Frances M., "Grace and Demand: The Heart of Preaching," *Epworth Review* 12.2 (1985), pp. 46–55.

Young, Frances M., "Inner Struggle: Some Parallels between John Wesley and John Chrysostom," in S. T. Kimbrough, Jnr, ed., *Orthodox and Wesleyan Spirituality* (Crestwood, NY: St. Vladimir's Seminary Press, 2002), pp. 157–72.

Zakai, Avihu, *Jonathan Edwards's Philosophy of History: The Re-Enchantment of the World in the Age of Enlightenment* (Princeton, NJ: Princeton University Press, 2003).

4   **Secondary Sources: Newspapers and Journals**

Arminian Magazine
British Critic
British Magazine
Christian Examiner
Christian Observer
Church of England Magazine
Churchman's Companion
Dublin Chronicle
Dublin University Magazine
Eclectic Review
Flapper
Fraser's Magazine for Town and Country
Gentleman's Magazine
Guardian
Hansard
Journal of the Association for the Preservation of the Memorials of the Dead in Ireland
Notes and Queries
Spectator
Treble Almanack

Index